CONFLICT AND HOUSING, LAND, AND PROPERTY RIGHTS

Housing, land, and property (HLP) rights, as rights, are widely recognized throughout international human rights and humanitarian law and provide a clear and consistent legal normative framework for developing better approaches to the HLP challenges faced by the United Nations and others seeking to build long-term peace. This book analyzes the ubiquitous HLP challenges present in all conflict and postconflict settings. It will bridge the worlds of the practitioner and the theorist by combining an overview of the international legal and policy frameworks on HLP rights with dozens of detailed case studies demonstrating country experiences from around the world. The book will be of particular interest to professors and students of international relations, law, human rights, and peace-and-conflict studies, but will have a wider readership among practitioners working for international institutions such as the UN and the World Bank, nongovernmental organizations, and national agencies in the developing world.

Scott Leckie is the Founder and Director of Displacement Solutions (www.displacementsolutions.org), an organization dedicated to resolving cases of forced displacement throughout the world. He also recently founded and directs the charitable organization Oneness World (www.onenessworld.org), which supports small research and other projects promoting global citizenship and peaceful and evolutionary ways of building a post-nation-state world. He is also the founder of the Centre on Housing Rights and Evictions (COHRE – www.cohre.org), an organization he headed from 1991 to 2007. Leckie has written and/or edited 9 books and more than 175 articles and reports on issues including housing rights; economic, social, and cultural rights; forced evictions; the right to housing and property restitution for refugees and internally displaced persons; and other human rights themes.

Chris Huggins is an academic and researcher specializing in the relationships between land rights, violent conflict, and postconflict development, particularly in Africa. He spent the last decade working in Eastern and Central Africa for the African Centre for Technology Studies (ACTS), an intergovernmental organization, and consulting with several major nongovernmental organizations. He is currently based in Ottawa, Canada, where he heads a consultancy firm, Land Conflict Research.

Conflict and Housing, Land, and Property Rights

A HANDBOOK ON ISSUES, FRAMEWORKS, AND SOLUTIONS

SCOTT LECKIE
Displacement Solutions, Geneva

CHRIS HUGGINS
Land Conflict Research, Ottawa

CAMBRIDGE
UNIVERSITY PRESS

CAMBRIDGE UNIVERSITY PRESS
Cambridge, New York, Melbourne, Madrid, Cape Town,
Singapore, São Paulo, Delhi, Tokyo, Mexico City

Cambridge University Press
32 Avenue of the Americas, New York, NY 10013-2473, USA

www.cambridge.org
Information on this title: www.cambridge.org/9781107005068

First published 2011

Printed in the United States of America

A catalog record for this publication is available from the British Library.

Library of Congress Cataloging in Publication data
Leckie, Scott.
Conflict and housing, land, and property rights : a handbook on issues, frameworks, and solutions / Scott Leckie, Chris Huggins.
p. cm.
Includes bibliographical references and index.
ISBN 978-1-107-00506-8 (hardback : alk. paper)
1. Postwar reconstruction. 2. Postliminy. 3. Refugees – Legal status, laws, etc. I. Huggins, Christopher. II. Title.
KZ6785.L43 2011
341.6′7–dc22 2010043980

ISBN 978-1-107-00506-8 Hardback

For those who believe in the promise of HLP rights

Contents

Opening Note and Acknowledgments

The authors of this handbook have been active in the field of housing, land, and property (HLP) rights and conflict since the Balkan wars of the 1990s. Since that time, we have worked in a range of countries enduring or emerging from conflict, including Albania, Bosnia-Herzegovina, Burma, Burundi, Cambodia, DR Congo, Georgia, Kenya, Kosovo, Nepal, Palestine/Israel, Rwanda, South Africa, Sri Lanka, Sudan, Timor Leste, and elsewhere. Based on these field experiences and work by others throughout the growing field of HLP rights, we have prepared this book to provide a wider public with the lessons learned over the past two decades about how HLP rights issues are intimately linked with conflict in a multitude of ways.

This handbook is designed to assist students, academics, field researchers and consultants, NGO advocates, UN officials, local and national government officials, and others to better grasp the wide spectrum of issues that comprise HLP rights within the context of conflict and postconflict peacebuilding.

The complexity of the issues involved and their invariably unique local manifestation and characteristics are core elements of HLP processes that have led to these issues often being placed outside the central causes, consequences, or cures of violent conflict. However, after decades of only peripheral attention by peacemakers and those engaged in acts of nation building and reconciliation following wars, in recent years, there has been a very discernible advance in the global seriousness accorded to HLP issues. This has resulted in a far greater understanding of how HLP abuses can lead to conflict, how the deprivation of HLP rights is an inevitable outcome of every violent conflict wherever it may occur, and, finally, how addressing and resolving HLP issues must form a key piece of the larger peacemaking and peacebuilding frameworks.

In putting together this book, we have reviewed hundreds of books, articles, reports, and media analyses of the vast array of HLP issues linked to conflict. Although we draw on many of these in the chapters that follow, we could only place excerpts of a small cross section of these within the book itself, though we have included a reasonably extensive bibliography at the end of each chapter for use by those seeking greater degrees of detail on the issues concerned.

We have designed the book to be user-friendly, thought provoking, and accessible. In addition to overviews of the key themes and excerpts from works on HLP rights, we have included questions for discussion and contemplation at the end of each chapter. Several practical exercises designed to promote creative, concrete, and solution-oriented thought for eventual practical application to real-life HLP challenges in the field are included as well.

We hope this book is useful to readers and that it at least partially answers the key questions concerning HLP rights and conflict. We would be very grateful to receive any comments or critiques that would make the book more readable, user-friendly, or comprehensive.

The editors are grateful to a wide range of people and institutions that helped bring this book to fruition. We would like to first thank the Swiss Federal Department of Foreign Affairs, in particular Pietro Lazzeri, for providing the funding required to complete this work. We are also thankful to our publisher, Cambridge University Press, in particular John Berger who has been a solid supporter of work on HLP issues for several years.

We are humbled and honored to have been able to work with many extraordinary colleagues throughout the world, and for the wisdom and insights provided to us by the many victims of HLP abuses in conflict zones in Africa, Asia, and Europe with whom we have been fortunate enough to exchange experiences over the years. We acknowledge all of your unique contributions to our understanding of the HLP themes addressed in this book in indescribable ways. We are also deeply appreciative to all of the authors from whose various landmark works we were able to excerpt.

Special thanks are due to Dan Lewis of UN Habitat who is not only a great human being at the forefront of UN action in support of HLP rights, but someone who was also kind enough to prepare the excellent foreword to the book. Additional thanks are owed to Ezekiel Simperingham, who assisted greatly in bringing the book to fruition.

Finally, to Sheila and Siddhartha in Ottawa and Kirsten and Pali in Rye, we hope you know we couldn't have done it without you!

Scott Leckie
Chris Huggins

Foreword

Dan Lewis
Chief, Disaster and Post Conflict Section,
UN-HABITAT

Recognizing individuals' rights to housing, land, and property (HLP) seems one of those elephants in the room that no one mentions – for good reason. However, in the relative quiet of our own homes, classrooms, and offices, where these rights are taken for granted, and even in the chaos of a camp for displaced persons off in the Darfur hinterland, the understanding that, after human life, these represent the majority of loss for every displaced person has been limited. Even less understood is the recognition that not finding the means to address these losses is a critical component undermining sustainable peace – globally.

In late 2003, following a critical review of several postwar initiatives to address restitution of lost HLP rights, a small cadre of very diverse professionals began a campaign to raise awareness and build momentum for the integration of housing, land, and property rights protection and restoration into the UN system and across the international humanitarian aid community. At the same time, several institutions, led by Sergio Paulo Pinheiro, the UN Special Rapporteur on Housing and Property Restitution from 2002 to 2005, began work on what in 2005 would be a seminal outline of principles, now referred to as the Pinheiro Principles, defining rights and obligations of states to address losses of these rights through unlawful or arbitrary means, followed by expanded work by the Internal Displacement Monitoring Centre on monitoring compliance with the 1998 Guiding Principles on Internal Displacement. Finally, by late 2008, following the UN's Humanitarian Reform Review process, the Inter-Agency Standing Committee representing all major humanitarian agencies recognized the gap in humanitarian coordination caused by displaced populations' loss of housing, land, and property rights and assets as a primary barrier to durable solutions to humanitarian crises, and established several cross-cutting fora to address these issues.

Progress? Certainly. The challenge now is to expand what remains a very small professional community with the vision and skill to correctly outline and begin to address the plight of those in particularly protracted displacement situations, whether as refugees or internally displaced persons (IDP). Focusing solely on land rights, for example – the range of professional expertise involved in addressing land tenure, land use, adjudication, dispute resolution, and administration – all elements of building secure rights of occupancy and use already spans from the lawyer to the surveyor, the politician to the farmer, and the planner to the village elder. Organizing, programming, and resourcing HLP-based interventions demand a combination of all of these and more when considering the built environment and criminal and civil justice systems.

There is new dialogue emerging looking at a finer weave of threads resulting in displacement and loss of rights that demand additional areas of expertise – the need to draw both the scientific and political communities into discussions of displacement due to sea level rise in small island states; and the plethora of intrastate secessionist agendas in former Yugoslavia, Georgia, India, Sudan, and most recently in the Catalan areas of Spain, to name only two diverse vectors of displacement, ultimately with the same consequence for displaced families.

Further, in postconflict environs, the operational terrain is highly politicized, often criminalized, and frequently driven by victors or elites at the expense of displaced and otherwise disadvantaged populations. This is not simple stuff – and worse, it is never quick.

However, failure to act – as seen in many past and recent situations (e.g., Nepal, East Timor, Colombia, Kenya, Uganda, Sudan) – inevitably leads to increased risk of renewed conflict as people, frustrated by inability of their government to address their plight, take matters into their own hands. There are cases (Myanmar, Chagos Island) where even without open conflict – for example, where forced displacement of certain populations either as a consequence of "development" projects or for other, less transparent, reasons – an early intervention could avert conflict. Of course there are others (Bosnia and Herzegovina, Kosovo) where restitution programming has produced durable solutions, and these have consequently proven a good learning platform for new approaches, dialogue, and advocacy.

According to the UN High Commissioner for Refugees, there are currently 34 million "people of concern" (refugees, IDPs, asylum seekers, and stateless persons) in seventeen different regions around the world. At the same time, there are only one or two operational interventions (e.g., DR Congo, Colombia) that recognize the need for strategic incremental engagement and the importance of building confidence of stakeholders, that a range and hierarchy of rights exists in different places and times, understand what a soft-systems approach is, and think long term while acting short term.

This book leads the reader through the issues, past the legal resources, across several case studies of best and not-so-good practices, and into the staging area for action. I encourage those studying in this important field to engage fully and to contribute to a new professionalism integrating the multiple strands of technical and social interventions that support the (re)acquisition of defendable rights to HLP for those without the capacity, the willing participation of their own governments, or the financial means to do so on their own.

1

Introduction to the Issues – HLP Rights and Sustainable Peace

Housing, land, and property (HLP) rights crises are present in all conflicts and postconflict settings, and their management by those engaged in peace efforts can often be decisive in determining the extent to which peace is sustained and the degree to which measures of remedial and restorative justice are enshrined within postconflict political and legal frameworks. Conflicts are inherently complex, fluid, and multidimensional phenomena. The causes, forms, and impacts of conflict are perceived very differently by different actors (both "insiders" and "outsiders") and change over time, so that they cannot easily be predicted or reduced to simple statements of "fact." Nevertheless, the importance of HLP issues will strike anyone who has researched or observed violent conflicts in any part of the world.

In many countries, disputes over housing, land, and property, often with ethnic or other group-identity dimensions, are one of the root causes of violent conflict. There are many different types of HLP disputes, and disputes may be perceived, described, or categorized in different ways by different actors. Some disputes involve different claims to property among actors who agree on the tenure systems in place; in other words, they agree on the rules of property ownership and use, but some stakeholders think that other actors are breaking the rules. Of course, even when actors agree on a single tenure system, their interpretations of the tenure system may be different. State legislation may be outdated, unclear, inherently contradictory, or ambiguous.

Other disputes involve actors who do not agree on the rules of use or ownership. One actor, for example, may base her claim on a particular statutory law. A second actor may base his claim on a different law, also in force, which contradicts the first – it is fairly common for countries to have contradictory and overlapping laws in force simultaneously. Another actor may argue that the traditional laws of a particular ethnic or religious group have precedence over statutory legislation. Conceptions of individual and community rights, and common or private property, may differ widely between individuals and communities in the same country. Some actors see particular forms of housing, land, and property rights as legitimate whereas others may oppose them on various grounds, including the credibility of the historical development of property rights regimes in a particular geographical area, economic and political theories, or simple self-interest.

Rapid changes to property rights regimes are now occurring around the world, due broadly to processes of globalization as well as population growth, urbanization, environmental change, and economic expansion in the global South. Much of what has customarily been viewed as public – such as common-property resources like forests and pastures – is becoming enclosed, privatized, and commodified.[1] New forms of private property are being created from common resources, so that "property is seemingly everywhere," yet resistances and dispossessions mean that property rights systems are simultaneously "coming undone."[2] In most countries in the global South, disputes over housing, land, and property represent a significant proportion of all the cases heard by any particular dispute resolution system, including the courts.

It has become common for theorists within various disciplines and of various ideological persuasions to conceive of property rights as a collection of different kinds of rights. A "bundle of rights" or entitlements may include the rights to possess; to use; to exclude others from using or to allow others to use; to sell; to give away; to dispose of by will; to recover from theft; and to receive compensation for damage.[3] Each of these rights may be held by the same, or different, persons or organizations. Rights to land also include, in some cases, rights to airspace above the land, water and minerals below the soil, and other property, though in most cases, these are limited or appropriated by the state. In most situations, rights to property are socially "embedded" and deeply entangled with other forms of community- and family-level rights and responsibilities. Different kinds of users may be able to claim some, or all, of these rights over particular pieces of property. Certain rights may be held in common by members of a group whereas others might be exclusive to an individual. Property rights tend to be particularly complex in communities that rely on the utilization of natural resources for a wide variety of subsistence purposes. Given the wide range of rights that may exist, we can envisage an extremely broad range of HLP rights instruments that could theoretically be developed. In practice, most state-backed HLP rights instruments are based on models developed in western (and

1 See e.g., Becky Mansfield (2007) "Privatization: Property and the Remaking of Nature-Society Relations. Introduction to the Special Issue." *Antipode* 39, no. 3: 393–405.

2 Bill Maurer and Gabriele Schwab (2006) *Accelerating Possession: Global Futures of Property and Personhood*, New York: Columbia University Press.

3 See e.g., Saturninas Borras (2007) *Pro-Poor Land Reform: A Critique*, Ottawa: University of Ottawa Press, 25; Theo Van Banning (2002) *The Human Right to Property*, Antwerp/Oxford/New York: Intersentia; Patricia Kameri-Mbote and Migot Aketch (2008) *Ownership and Regulation of Land Rights in Kenya: Balancing Entitlements with the Public Trust*. Paper presented at KIPPRA workshop on land issues in Kenya, KICC, 31 July.

particularly European) contexts, and do not reflect the complexities of customary tenure systems.

Generally, this volume steers clear of the complex debates around which particular forms of HLP rights are appropriate for particular situations. It certainly avoids a blanket prescriptive approach that would recommend one form of right over another. It is instructive, however, to briefly consider the ways in which different kinds of rights are perceived, in order to provide some theoretical context for the chapters that follow.

CONTESTED CONCEPTIONS OF PROPERTY RIGHTS

In most countries, the state acts as the ultimate guarantor of property rights to ensure that one rights holder does not infringe upon the rights of another to an unfair degree. However, the extent to which the state enjoys local legitimacy or has the capacity to effectively ensure that statutory laws are implemented varies widely. In many countries, customary laws, religious laws, or other systems compete with statutory laws for legitimacy. The nature and interpretation of customary and religious laws tends to vary widely within single nations, and customary law interacts in complex ways with statutory property rights systems. Ideas of tenure security vary widely among different actors, and statutory systems are not necessarily seen as preeminently legitimate or appropriate. Indeed, in many places, the state itself is the primary source of tenure insecurity through the illegal or legally dubious conversion of customary lands to private or governmental uses.

Neoliberal perspectives have emphasized the importance of formal markets in property and marginalized so-called informal markets that are regulated through customary rights systems. Formal rights, from a neoliberal perspective, are regulated by the state. However, the state's role is primarily regulatory: The state supports the functioning of the market.[4] This is in contrast to more progressive concepts of the state, which involve a redistributive function.

Tenure security is the key to market function so that property can be effectively and efficiently transacted without the possibility of limitations to property rights resulting in transaction costs. The sociopolitical complexities in property rights hinted at earlier, particularly the notion of social embeddedness, is ignored in mainstream neoliberal discourse around property rights, and "the concept of private property rights is conceptualised narrowly with a primary focus on the right to alienate through sale and inheritance as *the* defining element of private property."[5]

[4] Wendy Wolford, (2007) "Land Reform in the Time of Neoliberalism: A Many-Splendored Thing." *Antipode* 39, no. 3: 550–570.

[5] Borras, *Pro-Poor Land Reform*, 25.

Many property rights theorists argue that freehold title to land, housing, or property rights best "guarantees" property rights. A freehold title represents the combination of a number of types of rights in one single instrument, usually held by a single rights holder, through a process of privatization. The use of title to leverage credit – through a mortgage, for example – is a foundation stone of neoliberal economics that constantly seeks to invent new financial instruments. This explains the interest over the last decade in the arguments of Hernando De Soto, who claims that assigning property rights to land, housing, and property in the informal realm provides poor households with the opportunity to gain access to credit and hence use their entrepreneurial skills to get out of poverty.[6] However, a host of critics have contested these ideas.[7] De Soto and his adherents have been accused of ignoring the very mixed impacts of the many land-titling programs implemented during the last few decades. Evidence has shown that titling programs result in a loss in tenure security for many who enjoyed user rights under informal or customary systems even as they may result in increased security for others.[8] The economic benefits of titling are far from clear. Research from South and Central America suggests that land titling disproportionately benefits large-scale farmers and can reinforce existing inequalities.[9] Experts have argued that providing the majority of the population with land tenure security is a matter of long-term political determination and a pluriform set of measures, rather than of a single "silver bullet" fix such as systematic registration.[10]

Debates and disputes between academics and practitioners in the field of HLP rights are not exhaustively discussed in the present volume, but references to such debates are found in many of the readings, particularly in Chapters 8 and 9.

HOUSING, LAND, AND PROPERTY DISPUTES AS CAUSES OF CONFLICT

In some countries, lack of access to housing, land, and property is a major livelihood constraint for many people. Absolute resource scarcity is an issue in some countries, but unequal distribution of resources is a more common problem. Where major

6 Hernando De Soto (2000) *The Mystery of Capital: Why Capitalism Triumphs in the West and Fails Everywhere Else*, New York: Basic Books.

7 See e.g., Espen Sjaastad and Ben Cousins (2008) "Formalisation of Land Rights in the South: An Overview" *Land Use Policy* 26: 1–9; Nyamu-Musembi (2006) *Breathing New Life into Dead Theories of Property Rights: De Soto and Land Relations in Rural Africa*. Institute of Development Studies (IDS).

8 Van Banning (2006), 345, cites the well-known example of Kenya, where formalization of land tenure has become "an instrument for the rich to encroach on untitled land."

9 Stephen Baranyi, Carmen Deere, and Manuel Morales (2004) *Land and Development in Latin America*, Ottawa: North-South Institute/International Development Research Centre (IDRC).

10 Van Banning (2006), 346. This is not to deny the relevance of registration as part of wider measures, depending on the economic, political, and legal context.

local grievances exist, poverty can be an underlying reason for recruitment into armed groups, because militia members or members of regular forces are able to sustain themselves by looting. Land tenure may not often be mentioned as a reason for conflict, but it is linked to poverty that, in turn, is related to violence. Land scarcity, in the absence of off-farm livelihood options, is often a structural cause of conflict in parts of Africa and the developing world.

In addition to these structural aspects, HLP issues can also be proximate, or visible, causes of conflict: For example, when land disputes, tenure insecurity, or inequality in land access are recognized as major grievances that can motivate violence. Usually, grievances over land are combined with other political problems. Conflicts are, by definition, complex and have a number of causes. The nature of mediation and dispute resolution mechanisms are important factors in determining whether parties involved in a conflict will resort to violence; if they are seen as biased or ineffective, violence is always a possibility. Political and military interference in local or traditional systems, such as courts or mediation committees, can exacerbate tensions and lead to violence. In many places, local conflict reconciliation mechanisms are compromised during times of war, but can still offer a potential for addressing HLP disputes if they can regain credibility after conflict ceases.

Of course, not all land-scarce countries or areas with unequal land ownership suffer conflict. Research suggests that the key determinant of whether violence will occur is not the extent of grievance in any given society, but rather the forms of social and political organization and cleavage that enable "boundaries" to be formed and people mobilized for violent ends. Unfortunately, HLP access disputes often have ethnic dimensions because land use patterns and customary land tenure systems frequently have an ethnic basis. Hence, the frequency of disputes involving farmers and pastoralists, and the use of the "ethnic card" by conflict entrepreneurs.

In addition to the legalistic aspects of land access and control, there are other dimensions – economic, political, social, religious, and spiritual – that are equally important. For example, land may often be significant as a means of production, an area where political authority is expressed and taxes may be raised (the concept of "territory"), a means by which families and individuals maintain social status and also as a source of feelings of ancestral belonging, as ancestors are buried within traditional territories. Land and the housing and property rights often associated with it are, therefore, by definition emotional issues and linked to cultural and other values.

Control over natural resources affects land uses and commercial development of natural resources often involves individualization of communal (indigenous) rights, with loss of access resulting for some. This indicates an important aspect that is often forgotten: Land rights problems are not purely home-grown. Land issues may be embedded within other struggles – for example, over mining rights, protected areas, or hunting concessions. Where there is ethnic and regional competition over scarce resources, it is usually the result of opportunistic politicization of identity. In "wars of abundance," belligerents rely on their capacity to exploit and commercialize the resources, so such wars become self-financing, self-sustaining, and therefore not readily open to mediation.

Furthermore, the way that many of these wars are financed highlights that they develop within a globalized war economy in which the industrialized countries of the Global North and rapidly growing emerging markets such as China, India, and Brazil play a role: Most of the world's civil wars in poor countries involve a struggle for control of natural resources that are ultimately sold to wealthy and rapidly developing countries. The global economy has a huge influence in the modern climate of economic liberalization. Global forces can impinge on local land use directly, for example, when foreign investment results in the purchase of land for commercial enterprises, or indirectly, when global markets or donor conditionalities stimulate national prioritization of cash crop production and hence local land use patterns.

In all conflicts, housing becomes scarce as homes are destroyed, available housing is often occupied by persons with no legal rights to do so, ownership and tenancy disputes between competing parties often emerge and turn violent, and generally, the housing, land, and property sectors become a source of tension and instability. With habitable housing and land as two of the very few assets available to people in postconflict settings, problems of illegal occupations, squatting, and exploitative rent increases are common to all postconflict settings. Many demobilized combatants, some born in exile or long absent from their home areas, require access to housing and land in order to put food on the table, rather than resorting to banditry. Peace is often followed by a localized economic bubble associated with investment by United Nations agencies and international NGOs, and the liberalization of the economy. Rapid exposure of conflict-stunned communities to global markets and international investors can lead to disenfranchisement and conflict. HLP transactions are likely to rapidly increase in frequency, as UN and other organizations require office space and housing, and if this land rush occurs in a situation of land tenure insecurity, confusion and disputes will result. The negative effects of rapid economic change on the population may be reduced if the property rights of the poor can be secured.

And yet, despite the clear links between conflict and the HLP sectors, only recently has the international community become structurally involved in addressing these ubiquitous links. Attention to and action on housing, land, and property rights and conflict by the international community, although still in need of considerable enlargement, has expanded significantly in recent years. The issue has now been considered by numerous international agencies, institutions, and procedures, including the UN Security Council, and recently an HLP Sub-Cluster was established under the UN's Cluster Approach to humanitarian emergencies. The following extract issued by the UN Secretary General in late 2007 urges greater attention to HLP issues by States and the UN.

UN Secretary-General (28 October 2007) *Report of the Secretary-General on the Protection of Civilians in Armed Conflict* (S/2007/643).

[...] The present report provides an update on progress made in implementing... and strengthening the framework for the protection of civilians elaborated by the [Security] Council and other partners in recent years. It takes stock of positive developments and ongoing or new concerns that affect civilians in conflict situations around the world. In doing so, it highlights four challenges of particular importance to us all: the denial of life-saving access to civilians in need; the abhorrent practice of sexual violence in conflicts and its devastating impact on individuals and communities; the critical need to address more consistently the impact of conflict on housing, land and property; and the importance of eliminating the unacceptable humanitarian toll of cluster munitions. The report ends by proposing a set of key actions for the Security Council's consideration, all aimed at further strengthening the protection framework in areas that require more prompt and systematic action.

3. My visits to a number of conflict-affected countries have convinced me that for those displaced and victimized by war, our actions matter far more than our words. Their plight has left me with a deep sense of responsibility to ensure that where we cannot prevent armed conflict, the protection of civilians is, and must remain, an absolute priority: for me, as Secretary-General, for the United Nations, for the Security Council and, above all, for the Member States, with which the primary responsibility for protecting civilians lies. Enshrined in all major moral, religious, and legal codes, and not specific to any particular culture or tradition, the protection of civilians is a human, political and legal imperative that recognizes the inherent dignity and worth of every human being. It is a cause that unites us all in the responsibility to protect civilians from abuse, to mitigate the impact of warfare and to alleviate their suffering [...]

C. A more effective response to housing, land and property issues

52. Another critically important challenge is the need to more effectively address housing, land and real property issues, which are often the origins of, or result from, conflict and which are therefore inextricably linked to the achievement and consolidation of lasting peace and the prevention of future violence.

53. The majority of internal conflicts in recent memory have involved underlying disputes over housing, land or property. In places such as Côte d'Ivoire, Darfur, the Kivus of the Democratic Republic of the Congo, Liberia and Timor-Leste, conflict was driven to varying degrees by disputes over land resulting from such factors as increased demographic pressure, scarcity of resources, agricultural transformation, exploitation of natural resources, insecurity of tenure and inequalities in land distribution (in particular along ethnic, religious or other divides).

54. Housing, land and property disputes and problems are also an almost inevitable consequence of armed conflict, as people flee their homes and lands in search of safety, or are forced to flee, in particular through ethnic cleansing or sectarian violence, as currently plagues Iraq. Such situations invariably give rise to complex issues that, if not prevented in the first place, must be addressed later if any future peace is to be sustained and further violence prevented. These include forced evictions; property transactions made under duress; illegal destruction or appropriation and occupation of abandoned property; the illegal confiscation of land; discriminatory application of abandonment laws; and the loss or deliberate destruction of documentary evidence of ownership. Such problems are further compounded by the application of inheritance laws that deny women and minors the right to inherit, own or use land and property.

55. A critically important step towards resolving such issues is publicly upholding and ensuring the right to safe and unimpeded return for refugees and internally displaced persons from the very moment they become displaced. Ensuring the right to return constitutes a categorical rejection of the gains of ethnic cleansing and sectarian violence and offers some measure of justice to those displaced from their homes and land, thereby removing a source of possible future tension and conflict. After four years of conflict and continuing displacement in Darfur, reaching common agreement on land tenure and compensation for the loss of property has emerged as a key element of sustainable peace. A recent report on Southern Sudan observes that the arrival of returnees in South Kordofan exacerbated long-standing tensions between different land users, with killings and injuries related to land conflicts constituting the single largest risk to returnees and local communities.[11]

56. The Council has long recognized the importance of safe and unimpeded return for refugees and internally displaced persons, as demonstrated in resolutions on the occupied Palestinian territory, Cyprus, the former Yugoslavia, Croatia, Georgia, Kosovo, Timor-Leste and the Sudan. In some cases, such as in Bosnia and Herzegovina, it has also condemned the wrongful appropriation and destruction of homes and property. However, for the reasons cited above, such recognition of the right to return must be applied by the Council with more systematic regularity. It must, moreover, be accompanied by increased attention to its practical implementation, including the need for a more comprehensive, systematic and consistent United Nations-wide approach to housing, land and property issues in both conflict and post-conflict settings.

57. Some United Nations peace operations have been directly involved in addressing these issues. The United Nations Interim Administration Mission in Kosovo administered and managed the Housing and Property Directorate and Claims

[11] Sara Pantuliano, M. Buchanan-Smith, and P. Murphy (2007) *The Long Road Home: Opportunities and Obstacles to the Reintegration of IDPs and Refugees Returning to Southern Sudan and the Three Areas*, Overseas Development Institute. Humanitarian Policy Group.

Commission, initially established by the United Nations Human Settlements Programme, which has decided over 27,000 claims as of October 2007. The Land and Property Unit within the United Nations Transitional Authority in East Timor developed proposals for institutionally addressing property questions. Grievances that were left unaddressed are considered to have contributed to the recent political violence in Timor-Leste. By contrast, the United Nations Transitional Authority in Cambodia and UNAMA have not systematically addressed property issues. With regard to the example of South Kordofan above, the report asserts that despite the risk posed by conflict over land, the issue has not received adequate attention or analysis within United Nations reintegration efforts.

58. When peace operations do not engage in these activities, it does not necessarily mean that the issues are left unaddressed. In Afghanistan, the Office of the United Nations High Commissioner for Refugees (UNHCR) and non-governmental organizations engaged in activities to promote and assist restitution, including the provision of legal aid to returnees. In Burundi, the Peacebuilding Fund has provided, through UNHCR, initial financial support to establish a national property claims mechanism.

59. Important though these efforts are, they do not constitute an approach that ensures consistent, systematic and comprehensive treatment of housing, land and property issues. Such an approach should include:

(a) Preventive and deterrent actions, such as the strategic deployment of peacekeeping troops to prevent evictions and the illegal appropriation of land and property, and the identification and prosecution by national courts or the International Criminal Court of those criminally responsible for the illegal appropriation or destruction of land and property;
(b) Preparatory actions, such as the early identification and registration of land and property abandoned by internally displaced persons and refugees to facilitate restitution or, where necessary, compensation, and the issuance of ownership documentation where this has been lost or destroyed;
(c) Restorative actions, such as the inclusion of the right to return and restitution of housing, land or property in all future peace agreements and all relevant Council resolutions, and the inclusion of housing, land and property issues as an integral part of future peacekeeping and other relevant missions, with provisions for dedicated, expert capacity to address these issues.

International attention to HLP concerns is increasingly forming the basis for policy discussions of these within influential national governments. Detailed attention to HLP issues has also been forthcoming from a growing number of governments that recognize the central relationship between how HLP issues are addressed and longer-term peace objectives. In the following passage, David Ashley provides guidance to government officials working on foreign policy and development issues on how best to consider HLP problems.

David Ashley (2006) *Housing, Land & Property Issues in Post-Conflict Situations* (unpublished paper presented at Centre on Housing Rights and Evictions (COHRE) expert meeting, Improving Peacekeeping Operations, Chiang Mai, August 2006).

- Conflict destroys property, drives people from their homes and land (which are then often occupied by others), and invariably weakens the State. Housing, Land and Property (HLP) issues therefore arise after every conflict. Where competition over land was a major driver of conflict, or where significant destruction or population movement took place, HLP issues may also be an important and difficult subject of the peace negotiations.
- In post-conflict situations, tackling HLP issues is important to facilitate refugee/IDP return and sustainable economic recovery, as well as to respect human rights and prevent asset grabbing. Failure to do so can lead to tensions and even renewed conflict. However, their complex, long-term, multi-dimensional and politically sensitive nature mean HLP issues are often neglected.
- Frequently-used approaches to HLP issues in post-conflict situations include:
  - Restitution of property to displaced persons, which can help facilitate refugee return and reverse forced displacement including ethnic cleansing. But restitution programmes require a minimally functional State, resources, political will and a legally clear and reasonably just pre-war situation to which it is possible to return.
  - Creating dedicated mechanisms to resolve HLP disputes.
  - Supporting registration of HLP: existing property records should be protected during and after conflict. But building a comprehensive register is difficult, expensive and slow: registering property transactions may be a useful first step.
  - Some post-conflict countries have successfully implemented comprehensive HLP reform, but this requires careful preparation, wide consultation and a broad political consensus.
  - Increasing the stock of available housing and land – or providing alternative livelihood options – reduces HLP disputes and provides possibilities for those without access to housing or land even before the conflict. Encouraging returnees to go into temporary transit centres and a system to temporarily allocate available properties may help avoid future problems.
- Common dilemmas are whether to compensate for damage or destruction; how far to tackle HLP issues unrelated to the conflict; and how to combat discrimination against women on issues of inheritance or ownership.
- Options for action include encouraging recognition of HLP as an important peacebuilding topic, including inclusion in peacekeeping mandates and peace agreements; advocating for and supporting sound HLP policies; and lobbying against HLP-related human rights abuses such as forced displacement or discriminatory laws.

Housing, Land and Property as a Driver of Conflict

Competition for housing, property and, particularly, land has – when combined with political factors – played a part in many conflicts:

- Rebel movements, from Guatemala to Nepal, have often successfully tapped into popular discontent with inequitable land distribution whilst radical land reform has sometimes itself produced violent backlashes (e.g. Afghanistan in the 1970's);
- Many conflicts, such as those in the Solomon Islands and Cote d'Ivoire, have been caused by political exploitation of grievances among indigenous people about outsiders "taking their land";
- In yet other cases, such as Bougainville or parts of Sudan, conflict for land has arisen because of the natural resources which may lie beneath or on it;
- Where demographic pressures, environmental degradation or climate change increase pressure on scarce HLP resources, this can contribute to conflict and violence, as has been the case in Darfur, where competition for land is widely seen as a root cause of the current war;
- Even when not an original cause of conflict, HLP can become a tool of warfare. Since control over territory is central to almost all conflicts, warring factions often deliberately move populations to consolidate their control. This was notoriously seen in ethnic cleansing in the former Yugoslavia, with the aim of permanently expelling ethnic groups from a territory;
- HLP can also serve as an important conflict resource, competition for which can help sustain a conflict. Militia leaders in eastern DRC, for example, have recruited their troops through the promise of land and looting.

Where competition over HLP has been a major driver of conflict, or where population movement has been used as a deliberate tactic, HLP issues will often be an important subject in the peace negotiations. As the examples of Cyprus and Israel-Palestine demonstrate, tackling HLP issues can be difficult and yet critical for sustainable peace.

The diverse interests at play in postconflict situations, the political rivalries that continue into the postwar setting, the often great power differentials between victorious and "vanquished" parties, security threats (such as landmines or rogue remnants of armed groups) that may limit access to parts of the country, and the urgency with which policy decisions need to be taken combine to make postconflict governance a huge challenge. Lack of reliable information is often a major constraint.

USAID (2004) *Office of Conflict Management and Migration, Land and Conflict: A Tool Kit for Intervention*, Washington DC.

Increasing Tenure Security

Tenure security is generally addressed through tenure clarification, land titling and registration initiatives. Depending on the circumstances, initiatives that demarcate and record land tenure without going as far as granting formal titles can improve tenure security for customary or indigenous rights holders.

Nevertheless, land titling alone does not necessarily improve peoples' livelihoods, especially when other aspects of an enabling environment are weak. Social and economic impacts of titling initiatives increase significantly when credit, infrastructure, and technical assistance services are available. When institutions are weak, rights are unclear, or overlapping claims exist, land titling and registration efforts can ignite or provoke conflict. Therefore approaches that incorporate dispute mitigation and consensus-building measures and that work to clarify rights by legal reforms are needed.

Identifying and Resolving Competing Claims

Would-be interventionists must properly understand land claims before deciding among the various means of resolving disputes. A focused study can help clarify key issues such as competing claims or existing conflicts as well as potential options for resolution. It is important to keep in mind that there are nearly always multiple sides in a conflict situation, often with differing perspectives and wielding what they believe to be legitimate claims. Care must be taken to approach interventions with neutrality and not to "demonize" or "sympathize" with one party or another, risking a politicized process.

Conflicting claims commonly emerge over time as a result of contradictions, gaps, and uncertainties in a country's land law and policy regime. Appropriate legislative and policy reform is often required to prevent continued disputes. Competing claims that involve conflicting legal rights might require court proceedings to be effectively resolved, although there are exceptions.... The capacity of the courts for this task must be considered and interventions directed toward strengthening the courts might be required. In some contexts, specialized land courts have proven helpful to dispute resolution.

On the other hand, experience has also shown that many types of land disputes are best managed outside the courts. Limited court capacity to process land claims efficiently and transparently is a serious constraint in many places. Thus, alternative dispute resolution processes, especially mediation and arbitration, can be useful, while customary and community-based mechanisms for conflict resolution may be relevant in some cases. Property commissions or claims commissions may also be pertinent to certain post-conflict contexts.

Addressing Post-Conflict Land Issues

As countries emerge from armed conflict, they face multiple land-related challenges associated with post-conflict reconstruction and peace consolidation. Relevant land issues must be clearly understood and given appropriate priority because successful management of these issues can be critical to stabilization efforts. Information about land issues must be collected as early as possible through reconnaissance missions, conflict assessments, or other appropriate studies.

Various conflict-resolution techniques, as described earlier, have potential relevance to post-conflict settings. Two non-judicial dispute resolution techniques, in particular, warrant special emphasis. First, property or claims commissions can play a key role in post-conflict situations where processes of reconciliation and property reconciliation and property restitution need to be addressed in significant numbers. These commissions can facilitate dialogue and data collection while dealing with competing claims, resettlement, and compensation in the aftermath of conflicts involving large-scale population displacements. Promising cases, including Cyprus and to some extent Bosnia-Herzegovina, suggest that sustained donor intervention is a key factor for success. Efforts at facilitated repatriation, whereby the displaced are helped to return to their homes or to find new property, can be highly effective in preventing conflict and diminishing future tensions if the efforts are well coordinated and sufficiently funded. Many of these potential solutions need to be finessed and some will simply be "stop-gap" measures designed to reduce the potential for a resumption of hostilities while more lasting, long-term solutions are worked out. Second, local community-based and customary conflict-resolution mechanisms can offer effective and acceptable means of managing many kinds of land conflicts. Experience in East Timor and Kyrgyzstan showed that building on socially legitimate informal institutions was an effective way to manage a large number of post-conflict land disputes.

In post-conflict settings, investment in agricultural infrastructure, technical assistance, and the creation of market linkages can complement land policy approaches by creating and supporting new income-generating opportunities. Fostering agricultural productivity can prevent the outbreak of food crises and create employment as well as other economic opportunities.

Using Complementary Activities/Approaches

Various other activities, including non land-related interventions, can be, alone or combined with other interventions, useful in different contexts.

Public education and information campaigns

Lack of accurate information about land rights and other land issues can fuel confusion and suspicion that can lead to conflict. Early public information and education campaigns about land-related issues can help to clarify issues and correct false assumptions. When the campaigns focus on law and land rights, mechanisms may be needed to ensure access to some kind of legal assistance for those who need it.

Legal advice and orientation

Lack of knowledge or understanding about law and land rights (frequently a problem in poor communities) can also contribute to tension and conflict. Community-based legal assistance, advice and orientation initiatives that work with local people and organizations can be effective in addressing these problems. The nature of the justice system in a given country will also influence project design. For example, educating people about their rights-on-paper in a system where they have no opportunity to defend their rights-in-practice will cause frustration. Linking legal advice and orientation to processes that will protect land rights or resolve land conflicts is extremely important and is often done in conjunction with public information and education campaigns.

Justice initiatives

Activities that focus primarily on strengthening the justice system and rule of law may have relevance to land issues, such as targeted institutional strengthening or capacity building to promote more efficient handling of land disputes. Initiatives and other support could focus on the formal justice system or on non-judicial conflict-resolution mechanisms.

Local government and/or local citizen participation

A range of initiatives targeting local government and/or citizen involvement can positively influence land conflict issues. For example, strengthening local institutions to improve transparency and accountability could affect how land issues are decided locally. Building the capacity of local communities or civil society organizations can help people participate more effectively in local decision-making and planning processes relevant to land.

Creating alternative job and livelihood opportunities

Approaches that develop relevant, appropriate and, preferably, sustainable job or livelihood opportunities can significantly diminish pressures related to land inequities. For example, investing in agricultural infrastructure can foster better agricultural productivity and production that will help create new livelihood and employment opportunities. Micro-finance initiatives that target the landless and land poor may also be useful. In post-conflict settings, targeting opportunities toward members of society who are most likely to be involved in violent conflict (e.g., demobilized war veterans and young males) may help prevent continued and future violence [...]

A brief sampling of some of the more prominent HLP challenges that emerge in countries enduring or emerging from conflict reveals the extent to which these concerns are indelibly linked to conflict and postconflict recovery.

THE RETURN OF REFUGEES AND INTERNALLY DISPLACED PERSONS

Returning refugees and IDPs are increasingly recognized as possessing housing, land, and property restitution rights to recover and repossess their original homes, but these rights are routinely infringed, resulting in refugees and IDPs being unable to repossess and reinhabit their habitual homes and lands in the aftermath of conflict. The following excerpt from Arthur Helton, who was tragically killed together with Sergio Vierra d'Mello and twenty-one other UN officials when the UN Headquarters in Baghdad, Iraq were bombed in August 2003, suggests some of the complications involved.

Arthur C. Helton (2002) *The Price of Indifference: Refugees and Humanitarian Action in the New Century*, Oxford University Press.

Voluntary repatriation is enshrined in refugee policy as the international community's preferred outcome. While repatriation was played down during the ideological confrontation of the cold war, it has emerged with renewed vigour over the past decade. Initially declaring 1991 as the year of repatriation, the UNHCR then declared the 1990s to be the decade of repatriation. Refugee repatriation is associated with many positive images. Exiles return to their homes and land, take up prior positions, and resume normal lives. Contextually, conflict abates and repression ends. Functioning government institutions emerge or re-emerge, providing basic services and opportunities for redress of grievances. In optimal terms, a reliable commercial context emerges, and the environment becomes promising for the realization of individual potentialities.

But this somewhat romanticized notion of repatriation is clearly the exception to the way it usually works. Refugees are changed by their exile. Sometimes women are empowered and children grow up in internationalized settings. Refugees acquire new capabilities because of the availability of education and necessity of coping with new challenges [...]

There are many wasteful and negative outcomes as well. Refugees may have become vengeful and radicalized because of their deprivations ... they can become harbingers of conflict. In addition, the situation in a refugee's homeland is often different when the time comes to return. Homes and lands may have been lost, with no real prospect for repossession or compensation. The economy may have been devastated, eliminating livelihoods. Repatriating refugees are thus often pioneers in their own lands, sometimes swelling the ranks of the dislocated urban poor, as was the case in Cambodia. The local population that remained behind can be resentful, particularly if return assistance is given exclusively to repatriating refugees ... Refugees often return to become internally displaced. On occasion, individuals return briefly, even daily, to tend crops or visit their homes, simply to leave again to find haven across a border [...] Whether return is indeed sustainable raises a whole host of questions concerning the relationships between short-term humanitarian aid and long-term development assistance. A genuine restoration of national protection and the establishment of viable social, economic and political structures imply very significant and wide-ranging changes in societies.

United Nations and other agencies have found that an inability to access housing, land, and property can represent a disincentive for IDPs and refugees to return, and hence, a barrier to the establishment of more sustainable and inclusive society. Where large sections of the population remain unable to return home and reclaim their places of habitual residence, it may also prove difficult to organize representative political elections. The following excerpt from a UN report acknowledges the shortcomings that have characterized many repatriation programs to date.

UNHCR Inspection and Evaluation Service (May 1998) *The Problem of Access to Land and Ownership in Repatriation Operations*, UNHCR.

UNHCR has had to overcome numerous obstacles in attempting to guarantee access to agricultural land for hundreds of thousands of rural returnees in Africa, Asia and Latin America in the past few years. The UNHCR guidelines on voluntary repatriation clearly identify the Office's responsibilities: "UNHCR must attempt to protect the interests and legitimate rights of returnees with regard to access to land (which may not necessarily mean ownership) through contacts with central and local authorities as well as with traditional leaders who in many countries have a recognised land allocation function at the community level." [...]

Issues of land access can affect not only the welfare and reintegration of returnees, but indeed the whole process of national reconciliation. Among the indispensable prerequisites for any repatriation operation, therefore, a detailed analysis of the legal, cultural and traditional system(s) and procedures for the ownership or assignment of land in the country of origin, as well as its availability, will be required. This may call for rapid consultation of a wide variety of sources, and different types of expertise may be needed. In anticipation, therefore, it would be useful to build a data-bank of basic information on the land ownership systems existing in different parts of the world where major repatriation of refugees is likely to take place. In many countries, for instance, several land ownership systems may coexist, sometimes peacefully, sometimes in conflict with one another. This may have resulted from colonial domination, or revolutionary changes in legal and/or social systems.

Another prerequisite will be an in-depth study of the refugee population, providing precise data on the numbers of rural refugees and their regions of origin, as well as their wishes concerning the places to which they hope to return. Although ideally these wishes should be respected, this may not always be possible. Following an armed conflict, for example, the available arable agricultural land may be insufficient to meet the needs of all the returnees, many of whom may have been in exile for a number of years, or even generations. Large areas of agricultural land may have been rendered unfit for farming either because of war-damage or because they have been mined. UNHCR must discourage the refugees from returning there, and very probably divert the surplus rural population to other economic sectors. In anticipation, professional training programmes may be launched in refugee camps before repatriation, or later, on return. Returnees may also be provided with financial grants permitting them to establish themselves outside the agricultural sector [...]

Excessive concentration of land ownership in the hands of a few individuals or large corporations has sometimes been one of the main causes of the conflict. It will only be possible to find a solution for returnees if, in the framework of a global development policy, there is a clearly defined agricultural policy guaranteeing the rights of small landowners, coupled with adequate social security legislation protecting the rights and interests of agricultural workers. When the insufficiency of arable land is endemic, governments must choose the type of agriculture to be given priority. If, for instance, it is intended to favour intensive or industrial farming, ways of protecting the remaining small farms must be found, the absorption of surplus agricultural labourers in other economic sectors must be assured, and the rights of seasonal workers guaranteed. If they have not already done so, States confronted by such situations should be encouraged to accede to the relevant international instruments elaborated in the framework of the International Labour Organisation (ILO).

Returnees may also be excluded from access to land because of agricultural policy reforms, or because the land has been occupied by others in the absence of the refugees. Depending on the prevailing legal system of property ownership, either restitution must be made upon their return, or compensation envisaged. In order to ensure that the rights of individuals are guaranteed, such a choice should be based on the legal systems governing land ownership. The political, legal and economic imperatives, as well as ethical considerations, must also be taken into account. Likewise when women, despite their predominant role in agriculture, are excluded from access to land due to traditional attitudes and/or legal obstacles, it is imperative that their rights, including to own and inherit land, be recognised. This would require the elaboration of more equitable standards at the international level, which in turn could be incorporated by governments as mandatory provisions in national legislation. The correct balance will have to be established between the need to protect the individual, the collective rights of returnees, and the imperatives of sustainable development and national reconciliation. Many of these issues involve political choices and therefore touch upon the sovereignty of the States concerned [...]

Repatriation efforts must be integrated with longer-term planning in a process of consultation and co-operation between the different national and international economic sectors and closer co-ordination of bilateral and multilateral inputs, particularly the other main United Nations agencies concerned. There is a need to define common goals and clarify the complementary nature of actions undertaken in line with their respective mandates, as well as to pool the wealth of relevant data available in their different data-banks. In recent repatriations, practical solutions were found which permitted refugees to return in conditions of security and dignity, and enabled many returnees to become autonomous in a short time. In most cases innovative approaches were developed which now provide useful lessons and models for the future. These operations also demonstrated that repatriation should not be limited to simply ensuring that refugees have gone home. For most rural returnees, successful reintegration will depend on guaranteeing their access to land within a broader framework of reconstruction, sustainable development and national reconciliation.

SECONDARY OCCUPATION OF HOUSING, LAND, AND PROPERTY

The secondary occupation of housing, land, and property by persons without official rights to do so is common to all postconflict situations and can cause considerable tension in the aftermath of conflict. Housing may be occupied by vulnerable households who lack other alternatives, or by organized criminal gangs intent on benefiting from rent payments or extortion. In either case, the eviction of secondary occupants poses a major challenge for many governments. The police or other security services that may be called on to enforce the eviction of secondary occupants may not be adequately organized, trained, or equipped to do so in postconflict situations. The following excerpt explains the situation in postconflict Timor-Leste, which is characterized by overlapping claims to land and housing that all have some legal validity, as well as outright criminal occupation of property without any legal justification whatsoever.

Daniel Fitzpatrick (2002) *Land Claims in East Timor*, Asia Pacific Press.

Whereas most colonies only experienced one wave of dispossession, East Timor has suffered successive waves, from Portuguese colonisation to Japanese occupation to Indonesian invasion. These events have created multiple competing claims to land. Indeed, there are now four categories of potential land claimants in East Timor: underlying traditional interests; holders of titles issued in the Portuguese era; holders of titles issued in the Indonesian era; and the current occupiers.

[Addressing] land claims in a post-conflict and post-colonial environment ... proved particularly challenging for the United Nations Transitional Authority in East Timor (UNTAET). This body was established on 25 October 1999 by United Nations Security Council Resolution no. 1272 in response to East Timor's humanitarian crisis. It [had] very broad authority (including over land claims), as Article 1 vests it with full legislative and executive authority with respect to East Timor, including the administration of justice [...]

Late in 2000, the National Cabinet, a body established within UNTAET to head the East Timor administration, advised UNTAET's Transitional Administrator not to proceed with plans to establish a land claims commission. This raises a number of fundamental questions. In particular, to what extent may resolution of post-conflict issues, including re-establishing a system of land administration and providing sufficient certainty of titles for economic reconstruction, be held hostage to the politically charged question of post-colonial land claims? How can urgent measures to minimise conflict over depleted housing stock, particularly between returning refugees and internally displaced people (IDP), be taken without establishing who holds the underlying property title? In short, could East Timor afford to wait for a democratic government before it resolves the fundamental underlying issue of land claims?

[...] with large numbers of returnees, critical shortages of housing and shelter and a lack of regional economic activity, the inevitable result was large-scale migration to [the capital city] Dili. In March 2000, one senior official ... estimated that perhaps as much as one-half of all houses in Dili were occupied by people other than their pre-30 August 1999 owners (pers. Comm.) ... one ethnic group in particular, from the region around Bacau, had moved into vacant houses in Dili and allegedly resisted violently attempts at re-occupation by their original owners. Reportedly, it was social conflict caused by this group that led to the much-publicised violence in and around the Dili markets [...]

RESIDENTIAL HLP DESTRUCTION AND DAMAGE

All conflict results in massive property and asset losses, as well as the large-scale damage and destruction of housing and land resources. In some cases, damage is incidental to conflict, but in many cases, buildings, crops, and other assets belonging to civilians are targeted for destruction by armed groups as part of a deliberate strategy. Housing and other forms of property have been deliberately targeted during the Rwandan genocide, violence in Timor-Leste in 1999 and 2006, and the Kosovo conflict, to name but a few examples. The lack of housing may be exacerbated by the return of long-term IDPs or refugees who are in need of shelter and have claims to property. The following excerpt outlines some of the dimensions of the housing crisis facing most postconflict countries

Roger Zetter (2005) "Land, Housing and the Reconstruction of the Built Environment," in S. Barakat (ed.), *After the Conflict: Reconstruction and Development in the Aftermath of War*, London: I. B. Tauris.

Widespread destruction and damage to the environment – roads, bridges, urban infrastructure, public buildings and above all housing – are simultaneously an instrument and a by-product of war and conflict. Nowhere are these devastating outcomes more evident than in the complex and violent humanitarian crises of the last 15 years ... typically, most countries convulsed by violent conflict are at critical stages of economic development in which the built environment is often a leading macro-economic sector – capital formation, infrastructure investment and housing construction. Destruction of the built environment decimates these already fragile economies.... Rebuilding and rehabilitating built environments damaged by war now constitute a major operational focus of donors and NGOs operating in this post-conflict environment ... within the built environment sector as a whole, the multiple dimensions an role of housing and landed property as a fundamental component of post-conflict recovery are dominant concerns [...]

Housing:

- Is subject to widespread destruction – for example over 60% of the housing stock was damaged and 18% totally destroyed in the Bosnian conflict whilst over 50% was damaged in the Kosovan conflict. (ICMP, 1996)
- Is a basic physical need for survival, personal safety and protection which are major drivers for the reconstruction and rehabilitation of war-damaged property;
- Plays a significant macro-economic role in developing transitional economies and is a leading economic sector in post-war, post-disaster reconstruction;

- Constitutes social capital and an important social and cultural commodity which reflects the rights of people to live where they choose; this connects to the wider objectives of peacebuilding and community reconstruction after conflict, and the restoration of local economic livelihoods.
- Reconstruction and reoccupation of property provide important indicators of how previously war-torn communities, and especially returnees, perceive their security and permanency; housing is both an instrument and a metaphor for post-conflict reconstruction and trust [...]

HLP DISPUTES

As refugees and IDPs seek to reclaim their original homes, as lower-income groups seek to find places to live, and as well-connected or otherwise powerful opportunists attempt to take advantage of the breakdown in law and order, serious HLP disputes can emerge. In many postconflict situations, small arms continue to circulate, and former military personnel may make threats of violence on behalf of family members or paying clients who are involved in land disputes. Although the majority of disputes involve members of the same extended family or neighbors of the same ethnic or religious community, some disputes may put members of different identity groups into competition with each other, reflecting the same intercommunal tensions that may have been involved in the national-level conflict. HLP disputes can therefore result in greater insecurity at the societal level.

Prisca Kamungi, Johnstone Summit Oketch, and Chris Huggins (2005) "Land Access and the Return and Resettlement of IDPs and Refugees in Burundi," in C. Huggins and J. Clover (eds.), *From the Ground Up: Land Rights, Conflict and Peace in Sub-Saharan Africa*, Nairobi/Pretoria: ACTS Press/Institute for Security Studies.

The issues in recovery of property rights for refugees and the displaced differ from case to case. For example, a significant number of refugees were landless before their departure from Burundi. Research in nine provinces by Ligue ITEKA, funded by UNHCR, indicates that about 17% of returnees were in this category.[12] It is particularly important to note that there are substantial differences between those who have been living in exile or have been displaced for a relatively short period – since 1993 or more recently – and those who left their hill in 1972, for example.

With regard to the 1993 caseload, regaining access to their land may not be difficult. This is why most experts believe that some 90% of land disputes are considered to be small, local, intra-family disputes which can be resolved without significant

[12] League ITEKA (2003) *Monitoring Des Repatries*, Bujumbura, December.

external (e.g. central government) intervention.[13] Nevertheless even at this level, non-state intervention is necessary to prevent their exploitation by local politicians out to fuel ethnic conflict and hatred. Since 2001, some NGOs have initiated, in different parts of the country, mobile legal clinics in order to manage these intra-family conflicts.

People who have been away from their lands for longer will have greater difficulty in gaining access to land. This applies especially to those who fled the country in 1972.[14] This implies a regional differentiation in the nature and severity of problems, as many 1972 refugees originate from the south of the country. The situation of the long term refugees is particularly delicate because their land, especially that located in the fertile Imbo plains, was confiscated "virtually systematically" by the government. The expropriated land is now in the hands of other owners, who have a legitimate claim to it since they were issued with title deeds. In some cases, land may have changed hands several times. Other land was taken over by relatives, friends, neighbours or may have been resold. In some cases, relatives have subdivided or sold the land, and are now discouraging refugees from returning, through sending messages to the camps that security remains poor.

A 1986 land law states that if somebody occupies land for more than 30 years and there are no claims within 2–3 years of this period passing, then the government can reallocate the land.[15] A consequence of this is that many of the 1972 refugees will be unable to reclaim their lands (unless this provision is altered, and the new policy applied retroactively, which would be problematic), or the government finds a suitable alternative, such as compensation or alternative land elsewhere. Many of the refugees do not possess any documented proof of ownership, and with the total number of *sinistres* (returnees, *regroupes,* internally displaced and dispersed) representing about one sixth of the total population, the situation is fragile as people look to the government to determine policy and strategies for managing tension [...]

THE ABSENCE OF IMPARTIAL HOUSING DISPUTE RESOLUTION MECHANISMS

Postconflict peace operations generally face nonexistent, malfunctioning, or seriously overburdened judicial or dispute resolution systems, leaving victims of HLP abuse without recourse to HLP remedies. In some cases, key judicial personnel have been killed or are in exile, whereas in others, the physical infrastructure of the judicial system, including court buildings, has been destroyed. Customary dispute resolution

[13] Interviews with Francois Ngendahayo, Minister of Repatriation, Reintegration and Reconstruction; Terence Nahimana, MP; and NGO personnel, Bujumbura, April 2004.

[14] Most of the refugees who fled due to violence in 1988 returned to their hills within six months.

[15] Article 53 of the Law Code: Republique du Burundi, *Loi Portant Code Foncier Du Burundi,* Loi No 1/008, 1 September 1986.

systems tend to reassert themselves quickly after conflict because they do not rely on physical infrastructure or a centralized coordinating body, but may be tainted by a failure to remain impartial in the face of conflict.

Agnes Hurwitz, Kaysie Studdard, and Rhodri Williams (October 2005) *Housing, Land, Property and Conflict Management: Identifying Policy Options for Rule of Law Programming*, International Peace Academy.

General Principles

Housing, land and property (HLP) policies should as far as possible be addressed in conjunction to ensure that residential and land rights are dealt with more comprehensively by domestic and international actors.

HLP disputes have the potential, if not adequately handled, to aggravate or contribute to violent conflict. Unequal and discriminatory HLP policies, lack of economic opportunities and a high reliance on the agricultural sector and subsistence living may all exacerbate existing cleavages in conflict-prone or conflict-ridden countries. The linkage between HLP and conflict justifies the adoption of conflict-sensitive approaches to such policies. Furthermore, widespread HLP disputes in pre- and post-conflict settings must be granted greater attention by international development agencies, bilateral agencies and UN peace missions.

National and international actors should recognize the tensions and complexities inherent in enacting HLP programs; policies with divergent aims – such as economic growth, privatization, tenure reform, human rights protection, institutional capacity-building and pro-poor or subsistence-oriented measures – have the potential to act at cross purposes. At the very minimum, specific HLP activites should be incorporated into wider development and peacebuilding strategies.

Three fundamental objectives should underpin HLP policies: tenure security, access to HLP and restitution of HLP in cases of forced displacement. Achieving these objectives will help ensure that HLP policies contribute to social and economic development and peace and security, based on international human rights standards and the rule of law. Rule of law institutions and processes can play a crucial role in helping achieve these objectives and can support more equitable and peaceful HLP relations.

Housing, Land and Property: Conflict-Sensitive Approaches

The relevance of HLP disputes as a driver of violent conflicts should lead to the adoption of conflict-sensitive policies by UN development actors. The World Bank, USAID and the OECD are currently incorporating conflict-sensitivity into their HLP approaches. At the United Nations, The Food and Agriculture Organization (FAO) and UN-Habitat have long developed expertise on land and housing issues, respectively. Additionally, the key UN development agency, the UN Development Programme (UNDP), should incorporate HLP issues into its conflict analysis at the Bureau for Conflict Prevention and Recovery and engage with other relevant actors on the way HLP plays into conflict prevention and development practice.

In much of the developing world, customary law regulates the ownership and use of HLP. The application of customary law in fragile states should be better understood and utilized by international actors working on HLP policies. International approaches must be tailored to the strengths and weaknesses of the informal systems they are supplementing or supporting.

However, while customary tenure can demonstrably support secure and equitable property relations, it will not always adequately protect local communities from outsider interventions; it will often discriminate against specific groups, including women; local elites may manipulate customary practices for personal gain; and the presence of plural legal institutions with the authority to adjudicate upon HLP disputes may encourage "forum shopping" and lead to protracted HLP disputes.

HLP-Specific Policies

Where severe inequities in HLP distribution act as a barrier to economic growth and social development or are a potential driver of conflict, redistributive policies should be considered.

Registration and the provision of formal titles are one of the better known HLP policy tools. Yet, the impact of registration on economic and social development should be qualified. In particular, multiple titling can contribute to cyclical conflict and protracted disputes. The grant of "qualified titles" under which current occupants' rights are vested if no challenge is filed within a set time-period, can help diminish tenure insecurity. Additionally, registration systems should seek to provide legal recognition to customary or informal rights without necessarily converting these rights to imported tenure norms.

In many agrarian societies, properties that are most vulnerable to dispute are common properties, those lands like forests and pastures, which are owned jointly by members of groups or communities. These are often incorrectly treated as unowned lands. Innovative legal constructs are needed in order to allow registration of group ownership. It is also necessary to clarify distinctions between ownership and access rights; often pastoralists have customary access rights to locally owned lands. Additionally, in order to exclude elite capture or subdivision of important common properties, communities should not be encouraged to register properties owned by individuals and families until common properties have been defined and registered in a mutually agreed fashion.

In many situations the creation of a register is necessary. In order for the register to be fully accessible, accountable and useful to owners, it is important to locate registers at the lowest administrative level. Systems need to be established which enable the public to inspect the register freely and at no cost and to record ownership changes for a minimal fee. Mechanisms should also be put in place to enable and assist the resolution of HLP disputes by local actors, before submitting the matter to more remote and formal adjudication.

Placing accountability for maintaining HLP records on holders themselves rather than on the state may lower overall costs and may create incentives for consistent recording of subsequent transactions and general maintenance. Yet, where local elites are able to restrict access to records, they can become a means of consolidating political power. As such, there is a need for the creation of mechanisms at the local level for informal negotiation and mediation.

"Mainstream" Governance and Rule of Law Policies

Devolution may be particularly crucial in agrarian settings where people depend upon land for survival. Inclusive processes for policy development and dispute resolution vested at the local level can lead to the identification of principles and practices useful for building up national level policy. Local administration of HLP issues must be accountable, that is, follow clear procedures and regulations on the representation and membership of the community, as well as on decision-making and dispute resolution.

Decisions to devolve HLP policy processes should be based on participatory decision-making that goes beyond consultations in order to diminish the risk of manipulation and capture of such processes by opportunistic local elites and ensure the inclusion of local stakeholders who are traditionally disenfranchised based on ethnic, class, age or gender bias. However, a top-down approach to registration and broader HLP policy may be justified under some circumstances where local consensus is incompatible with international standards.

Informal community-based dispute settlement mechanisms are a particularly important tool to ensure effective and legitimate adjudication of HLP disputes and to promote greater equity in property relations at the community level. However, their relationship to the national judicial system should be clearly defined, in particular with regard to the existence of effective remedies.

Housing, Land and Property Policies in Post-Conflict Settings

HLP disputes are prevalent in post-conflict settings characterized by large-scale displacement, abandoned land and housing, illegal HLP occupation, overlapping claims, reduced housing stock and lack of HLP records. If not addressed, HLP disputes have a real capability of jeopardizing post-conflict peacebuilding goals of national reconciliation and sustainable economic and social development.

Where specific HLP issues were themselves among the main causes of the conflict or directly threaten the viability of the peace settlement, a peace agreement should seek to resolve these issues without delay. While it may not always be politically sound to adopt radical HLP reforms in the immediate aftermath of conflict, peace agreements should at least mention the role of HLP in the reconstruction of the country and international agencies should engage in a rigorous planning process and set clear timelines for the adoption and implementation of HLP policies. In particular, measure regulating the temporary allocation of HLP, including deeds registration systems (i.e., the basic recording of HLP transactions), should be immediately enacted in order to avoid increased tenure insecurity and social unrest in the short term.

> In accordance with international human rights and humanitarian law, restitution mechanisms are now commonly applied to redress widespread, systematic or discriminatory forced evictions and dispossessions of HLP, particularly where such acts were formally condemned by the international community. These restitution processes should, as far as possible, be integrated within a broader strategy that addresses the HLP rights of the general population with a view to improve tenure security and access to HLP.
>
> To this end, the UN should consider the adoption of rights-based HLP strategies as part of its post-conflict peacebuilding activities, and in particular have these included in the mandate of the proposed UN Peacebuilding Support Office. At the very least, HLP should be better integrated into the planning, implementation and sequencing of peacebuilding activities undertaken by UN agencies, including UNDP, UNHCR, UN-Habitat or FAO.
>
> The situation of secondary occupants of claimed HLP should be assessed at the outset of restitution programs. Acquired rights should be taken into account, at least with the provision of some form of compensation or the provision of alternative accommodation to occupants of claimed property. These should be geared to the provisional needs of the restitution program and should be better coordinated with development of long-term social assistance programs.
>
> While restitution of HLP is the most desirable solution and should be actively supported by international actors, in some cases it may not be possible. Where property and housing has been destroyed on a large scale, where land to be restituted cannot be used, and where HLP tenure was not clearly regulated and subject to dispute before the conflict, alternative forms of redress – including compensation – may be more viable. The establishment of insurance funds to cover the loss of property interests that cannot be restituted should also be considered. In settings where land and property relations were inequitable or contentious prior to the outbreak of conflict, broader HLP reform should, at a minimum, take place in a phased manner alongside restitution or compensation [...]

PRECONFLICT OWNERSHIP AND TENANCY DISPUTES

Long-standing, preconflict HLP ownership and tenancy disputes can reemerge in the postconflict period and require resolution. Worldwide, more than a quarter of the global population lives in a situation of tenure insecurity, without the required building permissions or title to land. In some instances, no clear title may have ever existed to the land or dwelling in question, whereas in others, several people may place competing claims on the same piece of land or house. Where several claimants have a valid argument, and no clear legal framework exists to guide judges or policy makers, responses to overlapping claims will by necessity have political as well as a legal dimensions. As described in the following excerpt, many long-standing struggles over land are a result of colonial processes.

Nicolas Pons-Vignon and Henri-Bernard Solignac Lecomte (2004) *Land, Violent Conflict and Development*, Working Paper No. 233, OECD Development Centre.

A major source of conflicts over access to land opposes indigenous populations and colonial or central states providing "settlers" with agricultural opportunities at the expense of the former … In Latin America, the situation of "natives" varies greatly across countries. However, although a couple of the continent's leaders are of indigenous origin, these communities typically experience difficulties in accessing political power as a group because of their lower position in society. The conflict over land is a long-lasting one, since Latin American "indigenous" people have been deprived of most of what they had (not only land) since the 16th century. However, access and security of tenure over their now small land has been an ongoing subject of political, sometimes violent struggle. Their political and economic weakness means that they have usually been unable to retain their land when it was seized for the constitution of large agricultural estates (or of mines), and have been the victims of violent retaliation when they tried to resist (Kay, 2000). Chiapas is an interesting exception, where a minority has formed a structured political movement with the support of an organised left-wing group, and managed to resist land seizure for non-agricultural exploitation. In Indonesia, the policy of Javanese colonisation involved large-scale population resettlement from the main crowded island to smaller parts of the archipelago, and involved numerous land seizures for the benefit of the settlers. The associated violence has driven several states, including Indonesian Papua, on the verge of civil war (Faure, 2002).

DISCRIMINATORY HLP LAWS

Preconflict legal frameworks may discriminate against certain ethnic groups, women, and others and will require reform to ensure equal access to HLP resources and rights. Particularly in cases where the legal and political system has been substantially undermined due to mass atrocity or protracted conflict, capacity-building interventions will be necessary to ensure that new laws that uphold international standards can be put in place quickly. The following excerpt provides guidance to those interpreting land tenure systems in order to identify potentially discriminatory elements.

UN-Habitat (2007) *Post-Conflict Land Administration and Peacebuilding Handbook*, Vol. 1, UN Habitat.

As they review the legislation, staff should assess whether the law discriminates against any groups. It is possible that at some point in the history of the country, land transactions and allocation favoured certain groups over others. This could involve subtle or blatant discriminatory procedures, such as:

- Rules demanding prior approval of transactions (or certain types thereof) by a certain authority ahead of completion. This can easily be used for discriminatory practices, such as blocking transfers from a member of one group to another group.
- Non-completion of the technical process or administrative procedure. Staff should assess land transfer activities (e.g., allocation an transactions) to establish three critical points: (1) whether transfers were completed in keeping with appropriate procedures for verification, notarisation, recording and registration; (2) whether these procedures were complemented by the updating of the registry/textual cadastre; and (3) whether these included subdivision procedures, such as surveys, preparation of plans and updating of the index/cadastral maps. These conditions may differ across various areas (urban/rural, inhabited by different groups, very mixed areas) and across different countries.
- Unrecorded transfers: Staff must identify the reasons for any unrecorded transfers of land. Has there been a tradition of recording or registering land rights? Has registration been avoided? Did people try to avoid payment because of taxes or processing fees? Did people try to avoid the lengthy and uncertain procedures required to get permission for the transfer? Were the transfers in violation of the law? Did the transfers go unrecorded because of discrimination issues?

ABANDONMENT LAWS

UN and other peace operations will also often face the consequences of arbitrarily applied or otherwise unfair housing abandonment laws that may lead to the arbitrary and illegal loss of rights over homes and lands, and that will often require formal reversal through the enforcement of restitution decisions.

Walpurga Englbrecht (2003) "Property Rights in Bosnia and Herzegovina: The Contributions of the Human Rights Ombudsperson and the Human Rights Chamber Towards Their Protection" in Scott Leckie (ed.), Returning Home: Housing and Property Restitution Rights of Refugees and Displaced Persons, Transnational Publishers, pp. 115–119.

Part II

By operation of Article 3a of the Law on Cessation of the Application of the Law on Abandoned Apartments[16] in conjunction with Article 39e of the Law on the Sale of Apartments with an Occupancy Right,[17] a number of applicants continued to be deprived of their rights and were unable to repossess their apartments.

[16] This provision came into force according to the High Representative's Decision of 1 July 1999.
[17] *Law on the Sale of Apartments with an Occupancy Right*, FBH Official Gazette, Nos. 27/97 and 11/98.

The Chamber had to assess whether these deprivations were in the public interest and subject to conditions provided for by law (rule 2).

Article 3a prevents persons who were in active military service with the JNA on 30 April 1991, who were not citizens of Bosnia and Herzegovina as of that date, and who had not been granted refugee or other equivalent protective status in a country outside of the former Socialist Federal Republic of Yugoslavia (SFRY) from repossessing apartments in Bosnia and Herzegovina. In addition, persons who remained in active military service of any armed forces outside the territory of Bosnia and Herzegovina after 14 December 1995 were also prevented from repossessing apartments in Bosnia and Herzegovina.

The respondent party argued that the laws were aimed at correcting the factual inequalities that existed between those holding occupancy rights over JNA apartments and all other occupancy right holders. It further argued that the aim was to protect the rights of others, namely active fighters and their families or, persons who were forced to leave their homes due to the war hostilities. In principle, the Chamber found them to be legitimate aims but found no evidence that the applicants were placed in an especially privileged position or that the property was necessarily being used for the housing of war veterans and their families.

It then examined, assuming that these reasons could be regarded as legitimate aims, whether there was a reasonable relationship of proportionality between the means employed and the aims sought to be realised. As established in Strasbourg case law, the requisite balance will not be found if the persons concerned have to bear 'an excessive burden'.

The Chamber noted that the effects of Article 3a of the Law on Cessation of the Application of the Law on Abandoned Apartments and Article 39 of the Law on the Sale of Apartments with an Occupancy Right was to solidify the annulment of the applicants' contractual rights. The Chamber held that this legislation had to be regarded as a very serious form of infringement of property rights and can only be justified by cogent reasons. The Chamber then examined the different conditions established by Article 3a and the compensation stipulated in Article 39e of the Law on the Sale of Apartments with an Occupancy Right.

With regard to the requirement of citizenship as of 30 April 1991, the Federation argued that the applicants, who were not registered citizens of Bosnia and Herzegovina on 30 April 1991, were not subject to an excessive burden because these persons, who fell under Article 3a, were able to seek protection in their countries of origin, such as the Federal Republic of Yugoslavia, Slovenia, the former Yugoslav Republic of Macedonia and Croatia. The Chamber remarked that it appeared that the respondent party was essentially arguing that this requirement was narrowly tailored so as to achieve its aim of providing housing to war veterans with the least possible impact on other individuals. It noted, however, that the applicants in question lived in Bosnia and Herzegovina and had not had their housing needs met elsewhere. Additionally, the Chamber stressed that many citizens who had

SFRY citizenship and were residents of the former Socialist Republic of Bosnia and Herzegovina were not registered in the citizenship books, but, in all other respects, participated fully as citizens of Bosnia and Herzegovina. Further, the Chamber argued that since citizenship in 1991 was predominantly based upon where a person was born, the citizenship requirement appeared to be targeted at persons of Serb or Croat descent, who had been born outside Bosnia and Herzegovina. The Chamber found that this requirement clearly had a disproportionate impact on persons of Croat or Serb descent. It therefore found that the requirement was discriminatory in its intent or at least in its impact and concluded that discriminatory means can never justify an otherwise legitimate aim.

As a result, the Chamber held that the distinction made under Article 3a between persons who were registered citizens of Bosnia and Herzegovina on 30 April 1991 and those who were not had no reasonable relationship of proportionality to the decision to significantly interfere with these persons' property and lacked a reasonable foundation.

As far as the requirement of active service as of 30 April 1991 is concerned, the Federation had not provided any reason for choosing this specific date in Article 3a of the Law on Cessation of the Application of the Law on Abandoned Apartments. The Chamber argued that even if one was a member of the JNA on 30 April 1991, it did not mean that person took part in the war in Bosnia and Herzegovina in armed forces opposed to the Army of the Republic of Bosnia and Herzegovina. It underlined this argument by reference that the two applicants served only very limited amounts of time in the JNA after the war broke out before they deserted or were retired.

Also in this case, the Chamber found that there was no reasonable relationship of proportionality between this date and any aim, stated or otherwise, to be achieved.

With regard to those in active military service in a foreign army after 14 December 1995, the respondent party argued that persons who fell into the category of being in active military service in a foreign army after 14 December 1995 could have their housing needs met elsewhere. The Chamber, however, did not find that excluding this category of persons from the peaceful enjoyment of their possessions in Bosnia and Herzegovina was proportional to the stated aims. It further argued that the fact that someone might possibly obtain an occupancy right elsewhere could not bar that person from exercising their rights under a valid purchase contract in Bosnia and Herzegovina.

As for the question of compensation, the Federation argued that pursuant to Article 39e of the Law on the Sale of Apartments with an Occupancy Right,[18] the applicants were entitled to compensation, therefore, the interference under Article 1 of Protocol

[18] Article 39e provides that an individual who is not entitled to repossession of the apartment in accordance with the provisions of Articles 3 and 3a of the *Law on the Cessation of the Application of the Law on Abandoned Apartments* and who entered into a legally binding contract on the purchase of an apartment with the JNA before 6 April 1992, shall have the right to submit a request to the

No. 1 was justifiable. In this respect, the Chamber found that the interference with the applicants' property rights was not justifiable in principle, because the means were not proportional to the aims. Therefore, the Chamber did not find it necessary to consider the adequacy of any potential compensation.

In conclusion, the Chamber, assuming that the reasons given by the Federation for this deprivation were 'legitimate aims', found that there was no reasonable relationship of proportionality to the differential treatment of the applicants and the accomplishment of the Federation's stated goals. The applicants were made to bear an 'individual and excessive burden' and, therefore, this interference could not be justified in the public interest. Consequently, the Chamber confirmed a violation of Article 1 of Protocol No. 1.

Judge Manfred Nowak, joined by Michèle Picard, attached a partly dissenting opinion. They disagreed with the finding that the interference with the right to property of the applicants who had remained in the active service of the JNA during the conflict and in active services of the Army of the Federal Republic of Yugoslavia subsequently was disproportionate or even discriminatory. Mr Nowak argued that such interference fell within the broad margin of discretion which governments enjoy under Article 1 of Protocol No. 1.[19]

Part III

In another case, a pensioner entered into a contract to purchase a JNA apartment over which he held an occupancy right. He was forcibly removed from the apartment in 1992, and ever since his return in 1996, had tried to regain possession and to be registered as the owner of the apartment with the relevant authorities.

The Chamber considered that the refusal to recognise the right of the applicant to be registered as the owner amounted to an interference with his right to the peaceful enjoyment of his possessions, i.e. his rights under his apartment purchase contract. Since the interference was ongoing and the applicant was still unable to register as the owner of the apartment, the Chamber examined whether the interference was justified in the public interest and subject to conditions provided for by law.

The Chamber recalled Article 39c of the Law on the Sale of Apartments with an Occupancy Right, according to which the Federation Ministry of Defence is obliged to issue an order to register as the owner of an apartment an individual who has exercised the right to repossess it pursuant to the new Law, regardless of whether that person is actually in possession of the apartment.

In the present case, the applicant exercised his right under the new Law and the condition under Article 39c had therefore been met. The Federation Ministry of Defence, however, had apparently taken the position that it would not issue the relevant order until the applicant was in possession of the apartment, contrary to

Federation Ministry of Defence for compensation for the funds paid on this basis, unless it is proved that these funds were acknowledged for purchases of an apartment outside Bosnia and Herzegovina.

19 *Miholic et al. v. Bosnia and Herzegovina and the Federation of Bosnia and Herzegovina.*

the meaning of Article 39c. Therefore, the Chamber found that the Federation Ministry of Defence was responsible for the applicant's inability to be registered as the owner. Since these actions were not in accordance with 'conditions provided for by law', the respondent party was found to have violated Article 1 of Protocol No. 1.[20] The Chamber also determined a violation of Article 8 of the Convention because the interference was not in accordance with the law (since the housing body had refused to accept the repossession claim, had not decided positively on repossession and had not decided on the case within the time limit of 30 days).

THE DESTRUCTION OF OWNERSHIP AND TENANCY RIGHTS RECORDS

The confiscation or outright destruction of housing, land, and property titles, local housing and property cadastres, property registries, and other official records giving proof of ownership, occupancy, tenancy, and other residential rights accompanies most conflicts and complicates the implementation of restitution and other remedial measures. During the conflict in East Timor in 1999, for example, the cadastral office was intentionally burned down and land ownership records were taken out of the country. Kosovo provides another example.

Margaret Cordial and Knud Rosandhaug (2009) "The Response of the United Nations Interim Administration Mission in Kosovo to Addressing Property Rights Challenges" in Scott Leckie (ed.), *Housing, Land and Property Rights and UN Peace Operations – A Comparative Survey and Proposals for Reform*, Cambridge University Press.

In 1999 the situation on the ground in Kosovo warranted urgent intervention on the part of the international community in order to give effect to the principles and ideals espoused in Security Council Resolution 1244 in relation to the property sector, which had been severely disrupted.[21] The post-conflict environment presented numerous housing and property rights challenges ranging from population displacement, refugee flows, widespread illegal occupation of properties to an incomplete property registration system. The situation was further compounded by the pre-1999 period of ethnic discrimination which had also resulted in displacement and property disputes [...]

This situation was exacerbated by legal uncertainly surrounding housing, land and property records. The cadastre and property rights register were incomplete and inaccurate as the pre-1999 system regulating it did not adequately provide for the

[20] *Anusic v. The Federation of Bosnia and Herzegovina*, Human Rights Chamber, Case No. CH/98/457, 10 October 2000, paras. 71–80.

[21] Scott Leckie (1999) *Housing and Property in Kosovo: Rights, Law & Justice: Proposals for a Comprehensive Plan of Action for the Promotion and Protection of Housing and Property Rights in Kosovo*, UNCHS.

registration of all property transfers. Further, the conclusion of unregistered and unofficial transfers which had taken place between 1991 and 1999 also rendered records unreliable. This situation was further exacerbated by the destruction of property records during the conflict, and their removal by the FRY authorities when they retreated in 1999.[22] The Yugoslav Army removed all of their archives, while the police removed approximately 50% of their records. Socially-owned enterprises were stripped of a significant amount of their documentation. Further, the majority of the cadastre records were removed to Serbia proper, and a significant number of municipalities were missing property records. All of these factors made an accurate determination of property title extremely difficult [...]

MID-CONFLICT HOUSING PRIVATIZATION

What were previously public/social housing resources are sometimes privatized during conflicts while occupied by secondary unauthorized occupants, often complicating restitution and other postconflict HLP initiatives.

Scott Leckie (July 1998) Housing and Property Restitution Issues in the Context of Return to and Within Georgia: An International Legal Perspective, UNHCR.

The housing rights problems confronting Georgia are not dissimilar to those currently confounding national efforts at reconstruction in Bosnia and Herzegovina, Rwanda and other nations where a range of related disputes have formed or continue to form serious obstacles to the return of refugees and IDPs.[23] The manner by which these countries and the international community have sought to rectify these problems can provide a useful basis for finding appropriate solutions to the complicated housing and property issues relating to the Georgian-Ossetian conflict. Before examining these, however, it is necessary to explore in more detail how the housing and property dilemmas preventing return actually transpired.

2.1 Rectifying Unjust Applications of the 'Six-month Vacancy Rule' Under the 1983 Georgian Housing Code

Although housing and property problems emerged through a variety of processes all analysts seem to agree that unjust applications of provisions under the 1983

[22] OSCE Mission in Kosovo, "Kosovo/Kosova: As Seen as Told," Part II, 28.

[23] The illegitimate occupation or adverse possession of housing lawfully owned by or registered to refugees or IDPs by persons from other ethnic groups, the establishment and application of manifestly discriminatory housing and property laws during or subsequent to armed conflicts, the creation of special laws, procedures, and enforcement bodies to enforce such laws, and a range of other housing and property-based measures represent some of the most substantial obstacles to the return of refugees and IDPs to their homes in countries that have experienced ethnic conflict in recent years. In Rwanda, for instance, the Human Rights Field Operation for Rwanda (HRFOR) frequently reported that property problems had been the biggest impediment to the rapid reintegration of the returnees (E/CN.4/1997/42). In Bosnia, up to 1.8 million people are still unable to return to their original homes, despite possessing the right to do so under annex 7 of the Dayton Agreement.

Housing Code form the basis for most of today's housing and property problems in urban areas of return. Under the Georgian Housing Code (now repealed and partially replaced by provisions of the Civil Code), the legal basis for residing in a State-owned flat was a 'Housing Order' issued by the local executive committee (raiispolkom). The Order gave rights to tenancy, but not ownership. Under article 69 such rights could be revoked in the event the right-holder did not reside in the flat in question without 'a valid cause to be absent' for a period exceeding six months. Under the law, a procedure existed to examine whether a six-month absence was valid or not, with findings being based on a report issued by the local authority, countersigned, and then presented to a Court in order to obtain an order to return the flat to the 'common housing fund'. The law stipulated eight 'valid' grounds for absence (such as military service, work obligations, compulsory medical treatment, etc).

It is the manner by which this rule was applied with respect to refugees and IDPs that has been responsible for the bulk of the housing and property dilemmas facing persons wishing to return to their original homes in urban areas. Because the six-month rule was applied so vigorously in the early 1990s, a significant number of tenants in State-owned apartments who later became (and still are) refugees or IDPs, were subsequently dispossessed of their rights to their residences.

Some returnees have recently approached local and national courts seeking to appeal these earlier decisions, but have found that the application of the six-month rule was upheld. The Courts routinely refuse to consider the Georgian-South Ossetian conflict as having been a valid reason to abandon one's home. Indeed, many original inhabitants and Government officials have claimed that there was a pattern of clear ethnic persecution in the application of this law. In a case frequently cited by refugees and IDPs reluctant to return to their original homes, the Saburtalo District Court decided that a complaint by a *Ms. Sanakoeva*, an Ossetian who fled her flat in fear for her life was baseless, leaving her without recourse to re-occupy her flat. This case is widely quoted by Ossetians fearful of facing similar decisions should they submit claims to the courts.

The *Sanakoeva* case is not entirely representative of the way all housing dispute cases are decided, however. The Supreme Court has issued some eight judgments regarding cases linked to the unjust application of the six-month rule to date; six of which resulted in the judicially sanctioned eviction of occupants of the flats concerned. In none of the cases decided thus far by the Supreme Court though, have the more complex issues of restitution, relocation, rehousing or compensation been addressed. Although a further 30 housing dispute cases are pending at the Court, the complete absence of a system of legal aid for potential claimants and the frequent retraction of complaints by refugees and IDPs once it becomes clear that they will not prevail are indicative of the unsatisfactory situation currently prevailing at present.

Most cases involving the application of the six-month rule to apartments registered to refugees and IDPs who fled their homes appear to have been based upon one or another questionable grounds.[24] Indeed, the repercussions from these decisions cause much of the lack of confidence of refugees and IDPs, who believe that they will never be able to return to their original homes on a sustained and permanent basis.[25] It is thus imperative to find some means of determining the legitimacy of these past decisions and to adequately address the current situation as a means of finding a sustainable solution to these housing and property disputes.

If the provisions of international human rights law are used as a basis for analysing the compatibility of the application of the six-month rule with the rights of the affected refugees and IDPs who are currently restricted from returning home, such actions would not be compatible with these international standards. At the most fundamental level, if the international legal principles of *reasonableness* and *proportionality* are applied to the situation prevailing at the time the six-month rule was invoked against refugees and IDPs (arguably in an arbitrary manner), any application of the rule based upon any form of racial, ethnic or national origin or other forms of discrimination would necessarily be classified as both *unreasonable and disproportionate*, and thus a violation of international law.

Under article 17 of the International Covenant on Civil and Political Rights (ICCPR), which has been ratified by the Government of Georgia, "interference with one's home" can only take place "in cases envisaged by the law". It is not enough, however, that the envisaged interference is addressed in the law, but such interference (particularly when involving the complete removal of tenancy rights without relocation, re-housing or compensation), must "be in accordance with the provisions, aims and objectives of the Covenant and should be, in any event, reasonable in the particular circumstances".[26] Once again, based upon available

[24] This is reminiscent of circumstances linked to the war in Bosnia, where all sides during the conflict adopted laws on what were questionably labelled as abandoned property. These laws have had the effect of denying hundreds of thousands of persons the ability to return to their prewar homes. Although the relevant Georgian law was not itself adopted during the period of armed conflict, it was *applied* improperly during this period. It is also worth noting the important principle established in the *Convention Governing the Specific Aspects of Refugee Problems in Africa* (1969), which provides that "refugees who voluntarily return to their country *shall in no way be penalized for having left it for any of reasons giving rise to refugee situations* ...(Art. 5[4])". Indeed, it would not be difficult to argue that what has occurred in Georgia has been a penalization of refugees and IDPs for leaving their homes in fear of persecution.

[25] Similarities exist between this situation and the law and application thereof in Croatia. *Under the Law on Renting Apartments in the Liberated Areas*, ethnic Croats who had left their flats during the armed conflict could successfully request that their tenancy rights be reinstated by invoking "justified reasons" for their prolonged absence (more than six months), including having fled enemy aggression. However, for ethnic Serbs in the same area, they would not be able to return because their flight is considered by the authorities to be voluntary. According to one paper, such distinctions are firmly enshrined in the Croatian legal system. (See Deutschlander & Roggia [January 1998] "Property and Occupancy Rights in the Republic of Croatia: An Overview," unpublished manuscript for UNHCR).

[26] General Comment No. 16 of Human Rights Committee on Article 17 of the Covenant on Civil and Political Rights (1988).

information, it is doubtful whether reasonableness was apparent in the application of the six-month rule against persons with a well-founded fear of persecution, severe enough to force them to flee their original homes despite the absolute insecurity associated with being or becoming a displaced person.

Under the *right to privacy and respect for the home* provisions of Article 8 and the right to the *peaceful enjoyment of possessions* provisions of Article 1 of Protocol One of the European Convention on Human Rights and Fundamental Freedoms (ECHR) several cases are of direct relevance in determining the legitimacy of the application of the six-month rule.[27] These cases are important as they are a reflection of the content of the ECHR; a treaty that Georgia has not yet ratified, but one it must eventually ratify if it is to become a Member State of the Council of Europe. In a very important case, the European Court on Human Rights issued the following pronouncement with respect to the legitimacy of actions by the State resulting in the deprivation of property:

In this connection, the Court recalls that not only must a measure depriving a person of his property pursue, on the facts as well as in principle, a legitimate aim "in the public interest", but there must also be a reasonable relationship of proportionality between the aim employed and the aim sought to be realized.... The requisite balance will not be found if the person concerned has had to bear an individual and excessive burden.... Clearly, compensation terms are material to the assessment whether a fair balance has been struck between the various interests at stake and, notably, whether or not a disproportionate burden has been imposed on the person who has been deprived of his possessions.[28]

[27] The case of *Gillow v. U.K.* concerned the refusal of the Guernsey authorities to allow a couple to reside in a house they owned. They were refused the requisite residence permit upon their return to Guernsey and were prosecuted and convicted for the unlawful occupation of their home under Guernsey law. "The Court considered that there was an interference with respect for the home, which was in accordance with law. The legislation restricting who could live on the island was accepted as having a legitimate aim." The Court considered that there was no violation of Article 8 as far as the contested legislation per se was concerned. But the Court went on to consider whether the manner of its application to Mr. and Mrs. Gillow violated Article 8. On the particular facts of the case, the Court concluded that the refusal of both temporary and permanent licences to occupy their home and the conviction and fine imposed were disproportionate to the legitimate aim of the legislation and constituted a violation of Article 8. (Francis G. Jacobs and Robin C. A. White (1996) *The European Convention on Human Rights*, Clarendon, 195.) In *Wiggins v. U.K.*, it was decided that a dwelling house legally acquired and occupied by the applicant for several years did not cease to be his "home" when he lived in a tent in his garden subsequent to the Guernsey authorities' refusal to let him remain in the house after his wife had left him (No. 7456/76 in Vol. 13 D. & R., p. 40 at p. 44). The requirements of a licence from the Guernsey Housing Authority was considered a legitimate aim pursued under paragraph 2, namely that of preventing the harmful overpopulation of Guernsey. This requirement was deemed necessary for the economic well-being of Guernsey and for the protection of the rights and freedoms of others.

[28] See the case of *Lithgow and Others v. U.K* (Judgment 8 July 1986, Series A, No. 102; (1986) 8 EHRR 329, para. 120).

This case mentions the now widely accepted *fair balance doctrine* which stipulates that in determining the compatibility of a certain act by a State with regard to housing and property issues, any interference in the exercise of these rights must strike a *fair balance* between the aim sought to be achieved and the nature of the act. In determining the existence of *fair balance*, the European human rights bodies have also noted in Zubani v. Italy[29], that there had been a violation of Article 1 of Protocol No. 1, as no fair balance had been struck between the interest of protecting the right to property and the demands of the general interest as a result of the length of expropriation proceedings, the difficulties encountered by the applicants to obtain full payment of the compensation awarded and the deterioration of the plots eventually returned to them. Whereas in the case of *Spadea and Scalabrino v. Italy*, the Commission opined that:

In order to establish whether a fair balance had been achieved between the general interest and the private interest of the individuals concerned in matters of rent-freezes, statutory extension of current leases and the suspension of measures enforcing evictions, the Commission considers that each case must be examined individually to assess whether the preference given to the tenant was justified with respect to the aim of the relevant law.[30]

The six-month rule under the 1983 Housing Code may have originally – in law – satisfied the criteria associated with the 'legitimate aim' doctrine by acting as a means of preventing the non-use of housing resources in an environment characterized by insufficient housing supply. However, when viewed in terms of its application by the Courts, the local authorities or housing officers, it would be difficult to find any legitimate aim in unjustly applying this rule to persons who fled their homes in fear of persecution. In the ECHR case of Loizidou v. Turkey, which involved the impossibility of return to one's property, the Court noted that:

... the complaint is not limited to access to property but is much wider and concerns a factual situation: because of the continuous denial of access the applicant had effectively lost all control, as well as all possibilities to use, to sell, to bequeath, to mortgage, to develop and to enjoy her land....The continuous denial of access

[29] European Court on Human Rights, Judgment 7 August 1996. Whereas in *Powell and Rainer v. U.K.*, the Court decided that "When States' positive obligations are involved, the Court considers that the second paragraph is not applicable, since it refers to 'interference', but that regard must be had to the fair balance that has to be struck between the competing interests of the individual and of the community as a whole" (172 Eur. Ct. H.R. [ser. A], para. 41 [1990]).

[30] *Spadea and Scalabrino v. Italy* (Judgment 28 September 1995). This case is also relevant to the situation in Georgia in that it recognized the "right to additional social protection" for two senior citizens with low incomes who were living in the disputed housing: "The Commission considers that the tenants were in fact entitled to special social protection. On the other hand, the applicants [the owners] who had purchased the flats with the intention of living there, admitted that they were not in urgent need of the flats, although they were obliged to buy another flat to live in. The Commission therefore considers that, in the present case, the additional social protection afforded to the tenants was not disproportionate to the aim of social justice pursued by the relevant legislation" (para 45).

must therefore be regarded as an interference with her rights under Article 1 of Protocol No. 1.[31]

This cross-section of relevant Convention jurisprudence dealing with particular aspects of housing and property issues provide insight both into the evolving nature of the norms created by the ECHR, as well as setting the stage for a wider analysis as to the compatibility of past actions in Georgia with the ECHR and the types of positive actions which might be either obligatory or, conversely, negative duties prohibiting the development of legal measures designed to rectify the housing and property dilemmas in Georgia today. The jurisprudence just outlined reveals the importance of examining each individual situation in Georgia on a case-by-case basis. Moreover, the case law establishes important legal doctrines such as 'fair balance', 'legitimate social aim in the general interest', 'reasonableness' and 'proportionality'. These cases also show that while the ECHR allows for a *margin of appreciation* or discretion for States with respect to matters of housing law and policy, this margin is far from open-ended and must never involve acts of racial, ethnic or other forms of discrimination.

Individual refugees and IDPs who have (temporarily) lost tenancy (and/or ownership) rights to their homes have suffered *an individual and excessive burden,* not carried out in the public interest, with no fair balance having been struck and with a lack of proportionality. As a result of losing their tenancy rights – due to the entirely justified decision to flee their homes due to fear of persecution – the original inhabitants (who are now refugees or IDPs) have *prima facie* encountered and continue to encounter infringements of their rights as Georgian citizens, including, but not limited to:

a. The inability to exercise the right to return to and the restitution of their original homes and thus the very real prospect of homelessness were they to choose to return home;
b. The unjustified, unreasonable, disproportionate and arbitrary interference with the right to respect for the home and the inability to peacefully enjoy and access their possessions;
c. The unreasonable and unjustifiable deprivation of possessions, both movable and immovable;
d. The inability to have been able to exercise their rights under the housing privatization laws and to claim ownership of the original homes;
e. Treatment of a discriminatory nature based on ethnic or national origin, political belief or other grounds;
f. The inability to exercise the right to an effective remedy to be determined by a wholly fair, impartial and independent judiciary; and
g. The violation of the right to adequate housing, as well as the inability to enjoy the full realization of this right at present.

[31] *Loizidou v. Turkey* (40/1993/435/514, judgment 18 December 1996).

While the individual modalities of each particular case will invariably differ, sometimes by reasonably large degrees and just marginally so in others, this series of seven *prima facie* violations of the housing and property rights of refugees and IDPs indicate the importance of finding a clear, measured and consistent means to rectify this situation. Initially, it may be useful to examine how, in other post-conflict societies, the problems associated with the secondary occupation of housing or property have been addressed. In so doing, it will become apparent that this can be accomplished in a manner fully consistent with internationally recognized human rights standards, and in such a way that detriment to either the original inhabitant or the secondary occupant can be effectively precluded [...]

HOMELESSNESS AND LANDLESSNESS

The combination of conflict, displacement, destroyed housing, the absence of the rule of law, a dysfunctional economy, and other factors often lead to considerable levels of homelessness and landlessness within postconflict environments. Many homeless and/or landless households tend to be female- or child-headed and lacking the social patronage networks that might enable them to access land and housing. The way in which homelessness undermines the dignity, autonomy, and productive capacities of affected households in Afghanistan is described in the following excerpt.

Liz Alden Wily (August 2004) *Rural Land Relations in Conflict: A Way Forward*, Kabul: Afghanistan Research and Evaluation Unit (AREU).

Homelessness could be the bottom-line in keeping people poor: Without homes of their own, landless families are doubly disadvantaged. They are unable to negotiate favourable labour contracts and for the sake of shelter, especially during winter, may endure excessive levels of exploitation, including providing unpaid domestic and child labour to landlords and "social favours." It has been many decades since reciprocal feudal relations existed between landlords and peasants, but the war years and the constrained conditions of the present have almost entirely removed responsibility for workers. Anecdotally, while seeing no rise in their crop shares, workers are sometimes now charged rent for their accommodation at harvest or pay this through performance of extra tasks. Rural homelessness has been under-attended to in the past. NRVA [National Risk Vulnerability Assessment] 2003 shows 15 percent of households do not own homes of their own. The exact scale of the rural homeless community is unknown largely because those who are itinerant tend to be an invisible class.

INSECURE HOUSING AND LAND TENURE

In many conflict settings, within the private rental sector, the legal position of tenants can be tenuous and leave them open to harassment and threats of arbitrary eviction.

In other instances, lower-income neighborhoods, in particular informal settlements, may not possess recognized legal security of tenure rights despite having adverse possession rights based on long-term habitation. In cases where customary tenure systems are not recognized by the state, land tenure insecurity can affect vast swathes of countryside that remain vulnerable to acquisition by those able to make claims through the formal tenure system. As the following contribution clearly shows, the lack of security of tenure due to insufficiencies in both access to and control over land are fundamental in understanding the HLP dimensions of complex emergencies.

Humanitarian Policy Group (2008) *Unchartered Territory: Land, Conflict and Humanitarian Action – Meeting Report* (Contribution by Alex de Waal).

8. De Waal outlined seven ways in which land access and control is central to understanding how complex emergencies function:

- *Taking hold of the land*: Belligerents such as rebels, governments and warlords often seek to control land (or the resources that lie beneath it) by dispossessing populations that live and use the lands they want. Humanitarian responses can often lubricate this dispossession by providing insufficient rations to the displaced (as an attempt to avoid dependency) who may then seek alternative modes of survival through wage labour, often on the very land they lost.
- *Land as a reward*: Land is often seized by belligerent groups as a means to reward their proxies or allies. Land becomes a form of loot. This is the case in Darfur with state supported militias.
- *Controlling the city*: States often seek to control urban land because they see displaced or squatter groups as a burden on services, a security threat or even a source of political discontent. As a result, states may push displacement and use the land to settle other populations or for economic activities. Humanitarian response to urban displacement tends to focus on shelter rather than addressing issues related to urban housing or land rights in any systematic way. There is a real need to develop strategies that can deal with the possibilities of complex emergencies in cities.
- *Inter-communal land conflict*: Communities can often fight amongst themselves for land with the state showing little interest or capacity to resolve. Clashes can be around boundary disputes, access to pasturelands or rights of access and decision making. Humanitarian Agencies often have to intervene in these challenging contexts and such interventions require local knowledge and engagement together with effective peacemaking mechanisms.
- *Ethnic cleansing*: Forced displacement and land seizure can often form part of a project to create ethnically homogenous areas. These situations create dilemmas for humanitarian agencies because taking people to safety risks falling in line with a strategy to ethnically cleanse an area. Furthermore the human rights principle of resisting gross abuse of rights entails taking a politically partisan stance which may expose the target population or aid workers to serious risks.

- *Controlling people*: Seizing land or forcing displacement is often a means to control populations or reduce their autonomy, sometimes as part of counter insurgency strategies. International Humanitarian Law (IHL) is limited with regard to prohibiting the destruction of material items and activities needed in order to sustain life such as livestock herding, migration for work and gathering forest products.
- *Battlefields*: Land is often the battleground on which conflicts are fought; it can lie in the way of military operations, can become a minefield or even displacement camps. This can be to the detriment of groups such as farmers who live close to the battle-lines of war (i.e. Ethiopia, Eritrea). Once again IHL is ill equipped for tackling these issues.

9. De Waal also emphasised that humanitarian crises are not an aberration of normality but rather a longer-term historical process of change. They are accelerated or traumatic transitions in which the direction is not always clear, but often involves processes of 'primary accumulation' or asset stripping. These include:

- *Urbanisation*: During displacement, populations often settle in urban areas and rarely return to rural life. Rather than being short-term IDPs, they become permanent urban squatters which impacts on their livelihoods and often leads to issues related to security of tenure.
- *Rupture of previous forms of social organisation and local authority*: Forms of authority change with war, famine and forced migration and humanitarian interventions feed into these dynamics. Authority based on land, kinship and tradition are substituted with new forms of authority that emerge around the distribution of relief.
- *Commoditisation:* War and hunger are typically marked by a shrinking of the ambit of trust and a move towards an increase in monetary relations. Items that were previously free, such as access to land, can become commoditised.
- *Extension of administrative control*: Populations that were previously autonomous may fall under state systems. Humanitarian agencies can sometimes provide a means of this extension through counting, monitoring and governing affected populations. In fact, they can often create a locus of resistance by giving protection and salaries to populations seen as a threat by governments.
- *Selective nostalgia*: Humanitarian agencies frequently try to 'return to the way things were', but these ideals are often unrealistic or even undesirable after processes of change and transition. There is a need to get to grips with the reality of change and how best to promote positive outcomes [...]

DISCRIMINATION AGAINST WOMEN WITHIN THE HLP SECTOR

Perhaps no section of society is more affected by HLP issues than women and girls, because they are often discriminated against by customary or statutory property rights systems. The ability of women to access, own, control, or inherit land and property is systematically constrained in many countries around the world. In many sub-Saharan African countries, for example, wives cannot customarily inherit land upon the death of their husband, owing to pressures to retain the land within the lineage-group of the dead man. The HIV/AIDS pandemic has resulted in an increase in the eviction of widows from the land they formerly owned and used. In certain societies, widows are expected to marry a brother or other male relative of her deceased husband (the so-called wife inheritance), though this tradition is generally forbidden by national law. Those elements of custom that provided some safety nets for women – such as the allocation of community or family land to women who have been separated from their husband – have been eroded by socioeconomic changes and increasing land scarcity.

In Rwanda, for example, women could traditionally benefit from several potential safety nets, such as *urwibutso*, which involved a gift of land from a father to his daughter; *inkuri*, a gift of land from a father to his daughter when she gave birth to a child; *intekeshwa*, a "farewell" gift from a father to a daughter upon her marriage; and *ingaligali*, which was the allocation of community land by the chief in charge of land to women who were abandoned by their husbands. However, evidence suggests that these customs are now largely inoperable because of land scarcity.

Where rights to land have been adjudicated and registered, such rights are often registered only in the name of the head of the household, generally a man, leading to the loss of whatever influence women customarily have enjoyed over the use or sale of the land. In some cases, land has been sold by a male head of the household without the consent of his spouse, leaving the family landless and the proceeds from the sale under the control of the male head of the household.

This situation is slowly changing as some countries introduce registration systems that allow for joint ownership, or registration of 'interest' in land, but it remains to be seen whether husbands and male relatives will respect women's legal rights or whether they will attempt to ignore the registered rights of women. In many parts of the world, women do not have the same access to education as men, and therefore face greater difficulties in claiming the rights that they can claim under the law. Women are also likely to shoulder the bulk of domestic responsibilities, especially those related to the care of children. Women therefore have less time than men to devote to the often complex, time-consuming, and bureaucratic processes of securing HLP rights.

In conflict and postconflict situations, women are particularly vulnerable to the temporary or permanent loss of their HLP rights. Male members of the household may be absent, due to recruitment into armed groups, death, or an attempt to seek economic opportunities elsewhere. Upon the death or absence of the male head of the household, many households suffer reduced access to land, because identifying and negotiating potential lands for cultivation is traditionally a male role in many societies. Women and girls are forced to take on multiple socioeconomic roles and may not have sufficient time to invest in maintaining control over land and other forms of property.

Sometimes, the changing responsibilities and socioeconomic roles of women can be acknowledged at the family, community, and national levels, therefore leading to an improvement in women's abilities to participate in governance of land and natural resources in the postconflict context. For example, in Liberia, the Liberia Women Initiative was heavily involved in the peace process and maintained influence thereafter. In postgenocide Rwanda too, there has been much postconflict political will for women to gain important political and socioeconomic positions, partly as a realization that women shouldered a huge burden due to the number of husbands and fathers killed during the war and genocide, and the great number of male prisoners awaiting trial.

Sadly, however, a more typical story has been that of Eritrea, where the responsibilities and experience gained by women – who played a massive role in the victory of the Eritrean People's Liberation Front – have since the end of the war been denied them. Sociocultural factors relating to gender stereotypes have prevented women from continuing to play a major role in society. This demonstrates that women's rights to land and decision-making powers cannot be guaranteed merely by legal means, but only through a combination of political will, social change, awareness raising, and relentless lobbying and advocacy.

UNADMINISTERED PUBLIC/SOCIAL HOUSING UNITS

Public or social housing resources in postconflict countries are often unadministered in the aftermath of conflict, given the absence of government and official bodies holding such responsibilities. In some postconflict settings, the amount of social housing will be negligible, but in others it can be considerable and may require proper administration and management.

Scott Leckie (30 August 1999) *Housing and Property in Kosovo: Rights, Law and Justice: Proposals for a Comprehensive Plan of Action for the Promotion and Protection of Housing and Property Rights in Kosovo*, UN Habitat.

It will be necessary for UNMIK to assert authority over abandoned property and State property used as residential housing, such as 'Solidarity housing' and 'State housing'. Abandoned property refers to empty properties, and to properties which are occupied by someone other than a lawful occupant. When the interim administration (through the network of international organizations) becomes aware of property becoming vacant, they should be sealed by KFOR, pending their allocation. The housing and property body, with the assistance of KFOR and other organizations, would progressively develop a register of abandoned properties that are occupied by displaced persons. These displaced persons should be given temporary permits on use of the abandoned house or apartment, which legitimizes their presence for a limited period of time, and also obliges them to acknowledge the rights of the absent owner. This mechanism will also keep an interim record of on-going property transactions.

Where possible, in key areas, it may be necessary to develop an inventory of housing and its state of occupation. This will facilitate both the work of the housing and property body and other agencies engaged in reconstruction and humanitarian assistance. Criteria will be developed for entitlements to alternative accommodation, as well as procedures for identifying and eliminating illegal use of multiple housing units by people without legal entitlements to those units. Procedures could also be developed to requisition vacant non-residential property in order to convert it to temporary housing space for displaced people.

Recommended Actions:

Administration and Allocation of Solidarity Housing

UNMIK Regulation No. 1999/1 placed all State property in Kosovo under its administration. To date UNMIK has not been able to administer or allocate the public housing now under its administrative mandate. It is, therefore, necessary to begin to identify all housing units officially under its administration, and to begin to develop appropriate procedures for the interim management and allocation of this housing stock.

Identification and Administration of Abandoned Housing

Carry out a comprehensive survey of which housing units and properties are currently considered, under law, as abandoned properties, thus allowing the registration of current (temporary) occupants.

Issuing Temporary, Humanitarian Permits for Abandoned Housing

Temporary humanitarian housing permits should be issued facilitating the regularization of the currently chaotic and irregular housing and property situation in Kosovo.

THE LACK OF APPROPRIATE LAND ADMINISTRATION FRAMEWORKS AND POLICIES

Many countries emerging from conflict do not have effective land administration frameworks and policies in place to provide security to land users and clear regulatory arrangements that are both fair and equitable. In some cases, this problem has itself been a contributing factor in conflicts. In Eastern Democratic Republic of Congo, for example, inequalities around land and the inability of the state to effectively and fairly administer land rights have been sources of conflict in Ituri Territory and in the Kivu Provinces. Land has also been a factor in the conflict in Sudan and remains highly problematic, as the next excerpt explains.

Sara Pantuliano (December 2007) *The Land Question: Sudan's Peace Nemesis.* Overseas Development Institute. Humanitarian Policy Group Working Paper.

A number of problems require urgent attention to ensure that land issues do not seriously undermine progress towards durable peace in the country. The absence of an overall framework to deal with land issues with the necessary urgency is apparent. This framework includes a coherent land policy, adequate legislation, functioning institutions, law enforcement capacity and supporting services. Land access issues and resulting disputes require urgent action. The commercialisation of land (not expropriation) is gathering pace in both the registered and unregistered sectors. In the registered sector, poor subsistence farmers are being pushed to sell their title without full awareness of the implications of doing so. In the unregistered domain, land grabbing – by officials affiliated to the NCP or the SPLM, the military, private investors, land speculators, religious groups and urban residents – is increasing. On the eve of the CPA [Comprehensive Peace Agreement], both the former government in Khartoum and the SPLM have been issuing new long-term land leases over community lands to privileged citizens and foreigners without any local consultation and without the genuine consent of the customary landowners (De Wit, 2004: 30). The process of land alienation is symptomatic of a lack of attention to the importance of land and property problems in the context of IDPs and refugee return, both by the GNU [Government of National Unity) and the GoSS [Government of Southern Sudan]. New expropriations or the recuperation of old land leases and concessions, legally or otherwise, may cause a new wave of displacement, or may jeopardise the chances of people returning to their areas of origin [...]

Private sector pressure on the return and resettlement process is a matter of growing concern. Further displacement may also result as returning IDPs and refugees find their land occupied by other, often more influential, parties. In some cases the GNU and the GoSS have discussed the possibility of resettlement in demarcated areas for returning citizens whose land is no longer available. Previous resettlement experiences in Sudan and elsewhere have proven largely unsuccessful, especially when aimed at rural people. People are generally allocated a single plot of limited size, when they need access to a large area to sustain their livelihoods. Compensation through customary land restitution mechanisms has been discussed as a solution to disputes during the return process, but there are no mechanisms at present to make this a legitimate and legal alternative. Likewise, there is no legislative framework to regulate monetary and in-kind compensation.

The lack of functionality of the land administration both at the central and local levels is a key part of the problem. Survey departments are in shambles, important data and records have been lost and there is no reliable information on which to base new land allocations and transfers or secure tenure rights. There is a risk that cadastral and land registry data may disappear in areas where local authorities are complicit in land speculation. Customary land management still works on a localised basis, between neighbours or members of the same family, but when larger areas and groups or outsiders are involved the customary system is largely ineffective [...]

LAND GRABBING

The arbitrary acquisition of housing, land, and property through land grabbing is commonplace in postconflict environments. In some cases, those responsible are unarmed civilians taking advantage of a breakdown in land and order, but more often, politicians, military officials, or members of non-state armed groups are responsible. It can therefore be both politically and logistically difficult to address land grabbing, especially when peace is fragile. In the best-case scenario, politicians and military leaders will take a strong stand against land grabbing during the window of opportunity in the immediate aftermath of conflict. However, the situation described in the excerpt below is more common, where land grabbing and a host of related problems have resulted in high rates of landlessness.

Rhodri C. Williams (2007) *Title through Possession or Title through Position? Respect for Rights to Housing, Land and Property in the Wake of Cambodia's Transition*. Centre on Housing Rights and Evictions.

Customary law governing land rights in Cambodia provided that legitimate possession followed the occupation and use of land ... peasants were entitled to hold land they had cleared and cultivated, but lost all claims to land they had stopped using. The French, who colonized Cambodia in the mid-nineteenth century, attempted to replace such use-based rights of possession with title-based rights of ownership, but were often unsuccessful outside of Cambodia's cities. Cambodia became independent after World War II and maintained a policy of nonalignment during the early years of the Cold War ...

In 1975, Phnom Penh fell to the Khmer Rouge, which introduced a radical regime of collectivization whereby Cambodia's cities and traditional institutions were abandoned and the entire population forced to work the land. Within weeks, Cambodia's urban areas had been entirely evacuated ... All housing and land became the property of the state and property records were systematically destroyed. During the five year reign of the Khmer Rouge an estimated one to two million people – as much as a fifth of the population – were murdered or died of overwork, starvation and disease.

In 1979, Vietnam responded to a series of border clashes with the Khmer Rouge by invading Cambodia. The Khmer Rouge leadership was driven across Cambodia's western border into Thailand and replaced by a Vietnamese-backed communist regime, the Peoples' Republic of Cambodia (PRK). Although the PRK promised to allow those displaced by the Khmer Rouge to return to their homes, they did not renounce the collectivization of land and blocked return to the cities, confiscating prime urban real estate for their own high officials. In response to this and other PRK policies, many educated former-urban dwellers also fled to Thailand, forming an alliance of necessity with the remnants of the regime that had sought to exterminate them …

Beginning in the mid-1980s, the PRK undertook pragmatic reforms, including decollectivization of land and property and the grant of concessions to exploit natural resources. The administration of these tasks was delegated to local functionaries, resulting in haphazard implementation …

In 1989, the PRK began a transition from communism … The authorities also privatized housing and land, a reform carried out with the implicit intent of cutting off claims by the 360,000 Cambodians then in exile by vesting title in whoever happened to be occupying their former homes or lands at the time … privatization was often a free-for-all, with title issuance in both urban and rural contexts contingent on bribes and political influence and many smallholders dispossessed or forced into debt.

By the late 1990s, less than 15% of the estimated 4–5 million applications for registration dating from this time had been processed, in part because of widespread refusal to pay unofficial fees up to one hundred times greater than the official price of registration.

The resulting legal ambiguity left many small farmers exposed to outright land-grabbing or subject to distress sales of their property at low prices. Meanwhile, the lack of other attractive domestic investment opportunities in Cambodia encouraged land speculation, idling large agricultural plots in the midst of increasing rural landlessness. The situation was aggravated by a nearly unregulated program of "economic concessions" of land for commercial exploitation by private enterprises [which] took up over a third of Cambodia's most productive land at their height and continue to restrict access to a large proportion of the country's arable fields.

Meanwhile, the end of the Cold War brought about a political transition in Cambodia in the form of the 1991 Paris Peace Agreements.… Although the Agreement called for the repatriation of the 360,000 Cambodian refugees from camps in Thailand, no specific provision was made for the restitution of their homes, lands and properties. In fact, although repatriation was successfully carried out, attempts merely to provide returnees with available land for farming were frustrated by uncooperative local authorities and widespread mine contamination, contributing to the present problem of rural landlessness. In 1992, the SOC formalized its reallocation of property rights by passing a land law formally extinguishing all pre-1979 rights to land.

Control of HLP resources has been an important factor in the exercise of political power in post-war Cambodia. By locking in control over the ownership and allocation of land and homes before the Peace Agreement, the CPP [Cambodian People's Party] not only denied these assets to their political opponents but also rewarded the functionaries within its own patronage network.

However, the political nature of the CPP's allocation and privatization programs dictated that HLP resources were diverted away from ordinary citizens and farmers to the benefit only of the political elite. In effect, the way in which land distribution and privatization programs were implemented decreased, rather than increased, access to land, and emphasized the primacy of political connections, rather than title, in securing and defending rights to HLP resources [...]

PARALLEL HLP SYSTEMS WITHIN A SINGLE LEGAL JURISDICTION

In many countries, particularly in Africa, customary land arrangements govern much of the territory concerned, particularly rural areas, whereas statutory laws are in place in urban zones and areas under intensive commercial production. Customary and statutory HLP laws interact in complex ways, and finding a way to manage the resulting tensions, within a rights-based context, is increasingly seen as another vital ingredient in building long-term peace.

Ruth S. Meinzen-Dick and Rajendra Pradhan (2002) *Legal Pluralism and Dynamic Property Rights*. CGIAR Systemwide Program on Collective Action and Property Rights Working Paper 22, International Food Policy Research Institute.

In most domains of social life and in most social settings more than one legal system (defined broadly) becomes relevant. For many social scientists, and especially legal anthropologists, law is not limited to acts, rules, administrative orders, court decisions etc. enacted or made by the various state organs. Law is understood very broadly as cognitive and normative orders generated and maintained in a social field such as a village, an ethnic community, an association, or a state[32]. Any social field is able to generate and enforce rules or normative and cognitive repertoires. It is thus possible to have various kinds of law such as:

- state (or statutory) law as made by legislatures and enforced by the government;
- religious law, including both law based on written doctrines and accepted
- religious practice;
- customary law, which may be formal written custom or living interpretations of custom;
- project (or donor) law, including regulations associated with particular projects or
- programs, such as an irrigation project;
- organizational law, such as rules made by user groups; and
- a range of local norms, which may incorporate elements of other laws.

The coexistence and interaction of multiple legal orders within a social setting or domain of social life is called legal pluralism.... The coexistence of several laws in

[32] S.F. Sally Moore (1973) "Law and Social Change: The Semi-Autonomous Field as an Appropriate Field of Study" *Law and Society Review* 70: 719–746.

> one domain does not mean that all laws are equal, or equally powerful. In some contexts, especially in the context of state and local community relationships, state law is usually more powerful and used by state officials (e.g., in declaring and enforcing forests as state property). Statutory law can also be used by powerful outsiders to claim resources in ways that are not locally recognized as legitimate. However, laws are only as strong as the institution or collectivity that stands behind them. Legitimating institutions vary. The state, as represented by an appropriate government agency, is important, but it is not the only relevant one, and in many cases it may not be as relevant as village or ethnic communities, users groups, irrigation management committees, and so on [...]
>
> During disputes and negotiation, claims are justified by reference to legal rules. The disputants use different normative repertoires in different contexts or forums depending on which law or interpretation of law they believe is most likely to support their claims, a process known as forum shopping.[33] Which law is accepted and enforced depends on power and social relationships between the different claimants [...]
>
> While legal pluralism is applicable in almost all contexts, it is particularly important in contexts of uncertainty. Mehta et al. (2000) identify three types of uncertainty which play an important role in shaping human behavior:
>
> - ecological uncertainty due to fluctuations in weather and other biophysical phenomena;
> - livelihood uncertainties due to fluctuations in employment or other economic phenomena;
> - and knowledge uncertainties due to incomplete understanding or predictability.
>
> To this we would add a fourth category, of social or political uncertainty due to fluctuations in regimes and social power. We feel that this fourth category is as important as the other types of uncertainty, and has particular significance for property rights. Legal pluralism can provide adaptive responses to ecological or livelihood uncertainties, as well as social or political uncertainties and changes. At the same time, legal pluralism can generate or increase knowledge uncertainties [...]

International agencies and governments are increasingly willing to engage with local or traditional forms of property rights, in an acknowledgement that statutory laws are not always enforceable, especially in rural areas. However, efforts to regulate or enhance the interaction between statutory and customary systems is by no means straightforward, as the next two readings demonstrate.

[33] Keebet von Benda-Beckmann (1984) *The Broken Staircase to Consensus: Village Justice and State Courts in Manangkabau*, Dordrecht, The Netherlands: Foris.

Johan Pottier (2005) "Customary Land Tenure in Sub-Saharan Africa Today: Meanings and Contexts" in C. Huggins and J. Clover (eds.), *From the Ground Up: Land Rights, Conflict and Peace in Sub-Saharan Africa*, Nairobi/Pretoria: ACTS Press/Institute for Security Studies.

Today, what exactly do we (and others) mean by the term 'customary land tenure'? Simple though it may sound, the question stands central to any discussion on land and land rights in relation to conflict ... much of what we know about customary land tenure has come to us via 'native courts' in the colonial era; courts that were not 'equipped to deal with the perplexing array of customary land rights, and the flexibilities embedded in them'. The colonial courts simplified by removing all reference to flexibilities and ambiguities, and ignored that negotiation was part and parcel of local ways of allocating and using land. Today, crucially, contemporary policy arenas also embrace simplification, which they do by espousing *evolutionary models* of customary land law. These models miss out on the ongoing dynamic of contemporary claims and counterclaims [...]

The 'harnessing' of so-called customary systems of land tenure may sound like a fine idea, but what have anthropologists and historians learned from field research? As already mentioned, colonial authorities moulded a customary world to suit their own purposes. What they created and sustained was later passed on to post-colonial states ... The result was a perception that customary law was coherent, static and overly legal. In other words, distinct meanings in Western law were used to describe the characteristics of customary *systems*. Customary law, as it emerged as a concept, was thought to be 'a different kind of primarily legal system carrying out many of the same functions as formal [Western] law'.

It is this kind of perception that some influential policymakers and policy-making bodies are rediscovering today. They are hunting for clear principles and clear rights, but refuse to face those aspects of customary land use – the ambiguities, the negotiations – that the simplified, colonial readings of past practice chose to disregard [...]

In contrast to the simplifying, overly legalistic approach to customary land tenure in some policy circles today, anthropologists and historians acknowledge that many diverse practices exist regarding land and access to land, and appreciate their built-in plasticity and scope for negotiation ... Despite the vast impact that codification has had, and despite evidence that contemporary policy making continues in the same simplifying/standardizing manner, 'customary land tenure' is alive and well, and changing. It takes many shapes, allows for the re-writing (and even invention) of past practices, and remains open to hard bargaining. It is this dynamic quality of customary land tenure – with its implicit recognition that there is nothing static about 'custom' – which, analytically speaking, should be valued above overly facile, legalistic interpretations. An appreciation of the dynamic quality of 'customary land tenure' should include an acknowledgement that customary law as practised today – i.e. as practised through the 'small talk' and actions of millions of farmers – is not only closely entwined with statutory law, but needs to be understood in the context of recent changes in the realm of kinship and descent organization.

Daniel Fitzpatrick (2008) "'Best Practice' Options for the Legal Recognition of Customary Tenure" *Development and Change* 36, no. 3.

Clearly there is no single 'best practice' model for recognizing customary tenure. Nevertheless, it does appear possible to identify the circumstances which dictate the choice of a particular model ...

Where, for example, land access for all customary group members is relatively secure and equitable, available forms of investment are recognized and protected, local land conflicts are infrequent, environmental resources are abundant and outside encroachment does not threaten cultural survival or livelihood security, there is little need for State intervention or regulation because the policy objectives of that regulation – social justice, economic security, environmental conservation – are being satisfied by customary structures themselves.

Where internal customary structures are sufficiently strong to promote tenure security and minimize conflict, but the group itself is at risk from outsider encroachment, the appropriate form of State intervention is simply to recognize and enforce group rights, and – where possible – to demarcate and record group boundaries. No other intervention inside the 'tenurial shell' may be necessary, other than that required by any State-sponsored resource management regime. In this case also, measure may be required to protect the legitimate interests of outsiders living on the traditional lands in question.

Where the group itself wishes to enter into land dealings with outside investors, some form of regulation will commonly be required to reduce the high level of formal uncertainty associated with such dealings, and ensure that the resulting distribution of benefits does not cause undue conflict between group members. One option discussed here for such regulation is that of group incorporation. This possibility also has the advantage of allowing mandatory internal rules and procedures to seek fair distribution of benefits and to ameliorate any discrimination against women and other less powerful members of the group. Its disadvantages largely arise from the difficulties of defining group membership and boundaries in complex customary circumstances.

Finally, where a customary group is unable to provide sufficient tenure security for its own members, perhaps due to individualization tensions or the presence of multiple arbitration authorities, further State intervention inside the 'tenurial shell' may also be required. Importantly, this intervention should not take the form of premature or quick-fix attempts to impose formalized titles on fluid customary interests. Rather, there is a range of options and issues to be considered, including decentralized Land Boards and the appropriate role for recording customary titles or transactions.

As can be seen from this brief overview of the major HLP issues encountered in postconflict situations, certain sections of the population tend to be particularly vulnerable to the loss of HLP rights. Returning refugees, IDPs, orphans, and ethnic minorities can all be vulnerable, for example.

Questions and Exercises

1. In your own words, describe some of the ways in which disputes over claims to land and property have contributed to the genesis of violent conflict around the world.
2. Choose any of the key postconflict HLP issues identified in this chapter. Based on your own experience and research, provide a short case study (300–600 words) of a country where these have been important issues (do not use the cases discussed in this book). Describe the evolution of the problem over time. Did the situation improve or deteriorate? Why?
3. What policy measures, in your opinion, could UN and other humanitarian agencies take to improve international responses to housing, land, and property rights challenges arising from conflict? Which agencies should be entrusted to oversee such responses and why?
4. Land use and access arrangements based on customary law are commonplace in a variety of countries engaged or emerging from conflict. How can customary law practices and principles assist or inhibit the broader enjoyment of HLP rights in postconflict societies?
5. Because gender issues are of major importance across the world and affect so many women and girls, they are often analyzed as a separate category deserving special attention. Alternatively, gender issues may be seen as a cross-cutting issue, to be addressed within broader sectoral discussions. Do you think that the issue of women's HLP rights in postconflict situations should be understood as a subset of postconflict HLP rights, or as a separate issue? Why?

Additional Resources

Christine Bell (2000) "Undoing the Past: Refugees, Land and Possession," in Christine Bell (ed.), *Peace Agreements and Human Rights*, Oxford University Press.

FAO (2005) *Access to Rural Land and Land Administration after Violent Conflicts*, FAO Land Tenure Studies.

Gutman and Rieff (eds.) (1999) *Crimes of War – What the Public Should Know*, New York: W.W. Norton and Company.

Arthur Helton (2002) *The Price of Indifference – Refugees and Humanitarian Action in the New Century*, Oxford University Press.

Arthur C. Helton and Natalia Voronina (2000) *Forced Displacement and Human Security in the Former Soviet Union: Law and Policy*, Ardsley, NY: Transnational Publishers Inc.

Huggins and Clover (eds.) (2005) *From the Ground Up – Land Rights, Conflict and Peace in Sub-Saharan Africa*, Institute for Security Studies, South Africa.

Inter-Agency Standing Committee (2002) *Growing the Sheltering Tree – Protecting Rights Through Humanitarian Action*, UNICEF.

International Council on Human Rights Policy (2006) "Repairing the Past? Refugees, Displaced Persons, Land and Property," in *Negotiating Justice? Human Rights and Peace Agreements*, International Council on Human Rights Policy.

ICISS (2001) *The Responsibility to Protect* (Report of the International Commission on Intervention and State Sovereignty), IDRC.

Scott Leckie (2005) "Housing, Land and Property Rights in Post-Conflict Societies: Proposals for a New United Nations Institutional and Policy Framework," in *Legal and Protection Policy Research Series*, United Nations High Commissioner for Refugees, Department of International Protection, PPLA/2005/01.

Daniel Lewis (2004) "Challenges to Sustainable Peace: Land Disputes Following Conflict," in *Symposium on Land Administration in Post Conflict Areas*, UN-Habitat.

2

The International HLP Rights Normative Framework

As Chapter 1 outlined, conflict and abuses of housing, land, and property (HLP) rights are virtually synonymous with one another. Every conflict, no matter how small, short-lived, or isolated will invariably involve violations of HLP rights. Before examining how such rights might best be enforced and protected in later chapters of this book, this chapter looks closely at the numerous international legal sources of HLP rights, their content and origins.

THE RIGHT TO HOUSING UNDER INTERNATIONAL LAW

The recognition of housing, land, and property rights by the United Nations began immediately following the creation of the organization itself, in the 1948 Universal Declaration of Human Rights, which included the right to housing[1] and the right to property.[2] Since then, HLP rights have been recognized in a series of international human rights treaties,[3] declarations, and other documents.[4]

[1] Article 25(1) of the Universal Declaration of Human Rights provides: "Everyone has the right to a standard of living adequate for the health and well-being of himself and of his family, including … housing …"

[2] Article 17 of the Universal Declaration of Human Rights provides: "(1) Everyone has the right to own property alone as well as in association with others. (2) No one shall be arbitrarily deprived of his property."

[3] Key HLP provisions occur in Article 11(1) of the International Covenant on Economic, Social and Cultural Rights (ICESCR); Article 5(e)(iii) of the International Convention on the Elimination of All Forms of Racial Discrimination (ICERD); Article 27(3) of the Convention on the Rights of the Child (CRC) and Article 14(2) of the Convention on the Elimination of All Forms of Discrimination against Women (CEDAW).

[4] Other HLP provisions are contained in the International Covenant on Civil and Political Rights (1966); International Convention Relating to the Status of Refugees (1951); International Labour Organization (ILO) Convention No. 169 Concerning Indigenous and Tribal Peoples; International Labour Organization (ILO) Convention No. 161 Concerning Occupational Health Services (1985); International Labour Organization (ILO) Convention No. 117 Concerning Social Policy (Basic Aims and Standards) (1962); International Labour Organization (ILO) Convention No. 110 Concerning

Of the various manifestations of HLP rights recognized under international human rights law, the International Convention on Economic, Social and Cultural Rights contains the most comprehensive and significant international legal source of the right to housing. Article 11(1) provides:

> The States Parties to the present Covenant recognize the right of everyone to an adequate standard of living for himself and his family, including adequate … housing, and to the continuous improvement of living conditions. The States Parties will take appropriate steps to ensure the realisation of this right, recognising to this effect the essential importance of international cooperation based on free consent.

Beyond the contents of the relevant treaties, declarations, and other documents, interpretive standards such as the *General Comments* of the UN Committee on Economic, Social and Cultural Rights,[5] The *Guiding Principles on the Rights of Internally Displaced Persons* (1998),[6] The *Principles on Housing and Property Restitution for Refugees and Displaced Persons* (2005) (the "Pinheiro Principles"),[7] and many others combine to create a very considerable body of international human rights laws and standards relevant to housing rights.

The right to adequate housing has been the most comprehensively legally clarified of all HLP-related rights. In 1991, the Committee on Economic, Social and Cultural Rights issued *General Comment 4: The Right to Adequate Housing*, in which the Committee stated that the right to housing "should not be interpreted in a narrow or restrictive sense which equates it with, for example, the shelter provided merely by having a roof over one's head or views shelter exclusively as a commodity. Rather

Plantations (1958); International Labour Organization (ILO) Convention No. 82 Concerning Social Policy (Non-Metropolitan Territories) (1947); Declaration on the Right to Development (1986); Fourth Geneva Convention Relative to the Protection of Civilian Persons in Time of War, 1977; Geneva Protocol I Additional the Geneva Conventions of 12 August 1949, and Relating to the Protection of Victims of International Armed Conflicts, 1977; Geneva Protocol II Additional to the Geneva Conventions of 12 August 1949, and Concerning Non-International Armed Conflicts (1977); Statute of the International Tribunal for Former Yugoslavia; Statute of the International Tribunal for Rwanda; Rome Statute for the Establishment of a Permanent International Criminal Court; Declaration on Social Progress and Development; The Vancouver Declaration on Human Settlements (1976); and the International Labour Organisation Recommendation Concerning Workers' Housing (1961).

5 See *General Comment No. 4: The Right to Adequate Housing (Art. 11 (1) of the Covenant)*, 13 December 1991, UN. Doc. E/1992/23; *General Comment No. 7: The right to adequate: forced evictions housing (Art. 11(1) of the Covenant)*, 20 May 1997, UN Doc. E/1998/22 and *General Comment No. 15: The Right to Water (Arts. 11 and 12 of the Covenant)*, 20 January 2003, UN Doc. E/C.12/2002/11.

6 UN Commission on Human Rights, *Report of the Representative of the Secretary-General, Mr. Francis M. Deng, Submitted Pursuant to Commission Resolution 1997/39*. Addendum: *Guiding Principles on Internal Displacement*, 11 February 1998, UN Doc. E/CN.4/1998/53/Add.2.

7 UN Sub-Commission on the Promotion and Protection of Human Rights, *Principles on Housing and Property Restitution for Refugees and Displaced Persons*, 28 June 2005, UN Doc. E/CN.4/Sub.2/2005/17.

it should be seen as the right to live somewhere in security, peace and dignity."[8] The Committee further detailed the core factors to be taken into account in determining the "adequacy" of housing: legal security of tenure; availability of services, materials, facilities, and infrastructure; affordability; habitability; accessibility; location; and cultural adequacy.[9]

Significant developments have also taken place in delineating the obligations of States toward HLP rights. In addition to the immediate obligation of nondiscrimination contained in Article 2(2) of the ICESCR,[10] States are bound by obligations to respect, protect, promote, and fulfill housing rights.[11]

States need to *respect* HLP rights by ensuring that no measures are taken that intentionally erode the legal and practical status of housing rights. Governments need to comprehensively review relevant legislation, refrain from actively violating housing rights by strictly regulating forced evictions, and ensure that the housing and related sectors are free from all forms of discrimination. States must also assess national housing conditions and accurately calculate, using statistical and other data and indicators, the true scale of nonenjoyment of these rights, as well as the precise measures required for their remedy.

States need to *protect* HLP rights by effectively preventing the denial of such rights by third parties, including landlords, property developers, social service providers, and others who are capable of restricting HLP rights.

To *promote* HLP rights, States should adopt targeted measures such as national housing strategies that specifically define the objectives for the development of the housing sector, identify the resources available to meet these goals, the most cost-effective way of using them, as well as how the responsibilities and time frame for their implementation will be applied. Such strategies should reflect extensive and genuine consultation with, and participation by, all those affected, including groups traditionally excluded from the enjoyment of HLP rights.[12]

[8] UN Committee on Economic, Social and Cultural Rights, *The Right to Adequate Housing (Art. 11(1)): CESCR General Comment 4*. UN Doc. E/1992/23 at para 7.

[9] UN Committee on Economic, Social and Cultural Rights (CESCR), *General Comment No. 4: The Right to Adequate Housing (Art. 11 (1) of the Covenant)*, 13 December 1991 U.N. Doc. E/1992/23 at para 8(a)-(g).

[10] Article 2(2) of the International Covenant on Economic, Social and Cultural Rights provides: "The States Parties to the present Covenant undertake to guarantee that the rights enunciated in the present Covenant will be exercised without discrimination of any kind as to race, colour, sex, language, religion, political or other opinion, national or social origin, property, birth or other status."

[11] See comments by the CESCR on the nature of State's obligations under Article 11(1) of the ICESCR: *General Comment No. 4: The Right to Adequate Housing (Art. 11 (1) of the Covenant)*, 13 December 1991, UN. Doc. E/1992/23 at paras 10–15.

[12] See the comments by the CESCR: "the [ICESCR] clearly requires that each State party take whatever steps are necessary for [achieving the full realization of the right to adequate housing]. This will almost invariably require the adoption of a national housing strategy.... Furthermore, steps should

Finally, the obligation to *fulfill* these rights involves issues of public expenditure, the regulation of national economies and land markets, housing subsidy programs, monitoring rent levels and other housing costs, the construction and financing of public housing, the provision of basic social services, taxation, redistributive economic measures and any other positive initiatives that are likely to result in the continually expanding enjoyment of HLP rights.

Scott Leckie (1995) "The Right to Housing," in Eide, Krause, and Rosas (eds.), *Economic, Social, and Cultural Rights: a Textbook*, Martinus Nijhoff Publishers.

The obligation to respect housing rights requires the state, and thereby all of its organs and agents, to abstain from carrying out, sponsoring or tolerating any practice, policy or legal measure violating the integrity of the individual or infringing upon his or her freedom to use those material or other resources available to them in a way they find most appropriate to satisfy individual, family, household or community housing needs.[13] Of particular importance is that the responsibility to respect housing rights requires states to eschew carrying out, advocating or condoning the practice of forced or arbitrary evictions of any persons or groups from their homes. States must also respect people's rights to build their own dwellings in a manner which most effectively suits their culture, skills, needs and wishes.[14] Honouring the right to equality of treatment, principles of non-discrimination, the right to privacy of the home and other relevant rights form constituent aspects of the duty to respect housing rights.

While the duty to respect essentially implies a series of limits of state action, the obligation to promote compels governments to recognize the multifaceted human rights dimensions of housing and to take steps to ensure that no measures are taken with the intention of deliberately eroding the legal and practical status of this right. Moreover, comprehensive legislative review should take place, with any existing legislation or policies negatively affecting the exercise of the right to housing subjected to repeal or alteration.[15] The promotion function additionally requires states

be taken to ensure coordination between ministries and regional and local authorities in order to reconcile related policies (economics, agriculture, environment, energy, etc.) with the obligations under article 11 of the Covenant," see: General Comment No. 4: The Right to Adequate Housing (Art. 11 (1) of the Covenant), 13 December 1991, UN. Doc. E/1992/23 at para 12.

13 In this context, governments should desist from restricting the right to popular participation and must accept the corresponding commitment to facilitate and create economic, social, and political conditions conducive to self-help initiatives by the beneficiaries of housing rights, as well as rights to freely organize and assemble, which are essential for the assertions of demands by dwellers or other groups.

14 In third-world cities, between 40 and 70 percent of all new housing is built by the eventual occupants themselves, most often outside legal regulations. See J. Hardoy and D. Satterthwaite (1989) *Squatter Citizen: Life in the Urban Third World*, Earthscan.

15 An extensive array of legislation will, to one degree or another, affect the scale by which the right to housing is enjoyed in any society. In addition to housing laws and tenant's rights legislation,

> to place sufficient legal and policy emphasis on the full realization of housing rights, through a series of active measures including national and/or local legislative recognition of the right, the incorporation of housing rights imperatives into housing and related policies, and the identification of discernable 'benchmarks' towards the full enjoyment of housing rights by all sectors of society […]

THE RIGHT TO LAND UNDER INTERNATIONAL LAW

Debates over how rights to land could be enshrined in international law were heavily influenced by the struggle for decolonization (especially the calls for nationalization of land used by colonial settlers) and the ideological battles of the Cold War. Many western nations conceptualized land rights primarily in terms of secure private property rights, whereas left-leaning states were unwilling to compromise on the nature of the state's right to nationalize land belonging to individuals and corporations. No agreement could be reached on how rights to land should be addressed in the International Covenant on Economic, Social and Cultural Rights, so land rights are not directly addressed in the Covenant.

The lack of attention to land rights in international agreements has led experts to claim that:

> Land tenure rights, and their administration, are largely unaffected by international law. States have, in accordance with principles of customary international law, as (re-stated in Principle 21 of the Rio Declaration), sovereignty over the natural resources within their territory in accordance with their own development policies. This includes the land within their borders. As such states are effectively free to determine both how the land within their borders is to be allocated and under what type of tenure regime.[16]

However, there are several qualifiers that should be applied to such a statement:

> First, while states are free to choose how land is allocated and how rights will be articulated and administered, they must follow a systematic legal procedure when redistributing rights to land. International law outlaws the arbitrary infringement of property rights. The Universal Declaration of Human Rights, for example, recognises every person's right to own property alone as well as in association with others and stipulates in Article 17 that '[n]o one shall be arbitrarily deprived of his property'. In addition to global treaties, to which all United Nations member states are bound, several regional treaties also limit the state's ability to dispossess

laws relating to planning, zoning regulations, building codes, land and land use laws, expropriation regulations, property laws, environmental laws, and many other legal domains can effect the realization of housing rights.

[16] Stephen Hodgson (2004) *Land and Water: The Rights Interface*, FAO.

citizens of their rights to land. The European Convention for the Protection of Human Rights and Fundamental Freedoms, for example, states that, 'every natural or legal person is entitled to peaceful enjoyment of his possessions. No one shall be deprived of his possessions except in the public interest and subject to the conditions provided for by law and by the general principles of international law.' (Protocol 1, Article 1, promulgated in 1952). The African Charter on Human and Peoples' Rights also binds states to abide by due process guarantees, outlawing arbitrary infringement of property rights. Article 14 states that, 'The right to property shall be guaranteed. It may only be encroached upon in the interest of public need or in the general interest of the community and in accordance with the provisions of appropriate laws'. A total of 53 African states have ratified the Charter. The American Convention on Human Rights stipulates in Article 21 that, 'everyone has the right to the use and enjoyment of his property ... no one shall be deprived of his property except upon payment of just compensation, for reason of public utility or social interest, and in the cases and according to the forms established by law.'

Secondly, international customary law, also places certain restrictions on the State's ability to infringe on the land rights of its citizens. While it is not legally binding, customary law evolves over time as specific principles and standards are internationally debated and discussed. Principles and standards first proposed in nonbinding documents and declarations can eventually become universally accepted as international consensus is reached on their importance.[17] International customary law demonstrates that even historical injustices around land rights that were committed decades in the past should be redressed, for example, through restitution. Despite the general principle that law should be nonretroactive, redress should be provided for historical injustices, even if they are far beyond the national equivalent of the statute of limitations. This is because the historical injustices in question have led to continuing violations of basic rights.

Thirdly, international law does provide for specific kinds of rights to land for specific groups, such as indigenous peoples and women. A multitude of international conventions have been enacted to counter discrimination on the basis of sex and to provide women with the same rights as men, including the Universal Declaration of Human Rights, the International Covenant on Civil and Political Rights, the International Covenant on Economic, Social and Cultural Rights, and in particular the Convention on the Elimination of All Forms of Discrimination Against Women (CEDAW), adopted in 1979. State parties to these conventions are required to take action to remove obstacles to the equal enjoyment of such rights, to

[17] Darrell A. Posey and Graham Dutfield (1995) *Beyond Intellectual Property: Toward Traditional Resource Rights for Indigenous Peoples and Local Communities*, IDRC. Chapter 11.

promote the rights of women through education, and to revise domestic legislation to conform to international standards.

Committees have been established to monitor implementation of these conventions and treaties, and to interpret their provisions. These committees have further strengthened women's rights to land and property under international law. The Human Rights Committee, which monitors the implementation of Covenant on Civil and Political Rights, issued General Comment 28 that stipulates that states must ensure that laws on marriage contain equal rights and obligations for both spouses, among others with regard to the ownership or administration of property, during marriage, and upon dissolution of the marriage. This means that by law, women should have the same inheritance rights as men.[18] Several regional treaties also address sexual inequality. The Women's Rights Protocol to the African Charter on Human and Peoples' Rights (adopted in July 2003) states, in Article 14, that "States Parties shall take all appropriate measures to … provide women with access to clean drinking water, sources of domestic fuel, land, and the means of producing nutritious food." In Article 19, the Charter stipulates that, "the States Parties shall take all appropriate measures to … promote women's access to and control over productive resources such as land and guarantee their right to property."

ILO Convention 169 provides specific protection for indigenous rights, and ILO monitoring bodies have confirmed and broadened this protection in their decisions. Convention 169 protects indigenous peoples from manipulation used to appropriate their land. The optional protocol to the Convention provides for the recognition of indigenous land tenure systems.[19] The convention is only legally binding on those twenty countries that have ratified it. Almost all of the signatory nations are Latin American or European states. However, legal experts have argued that the Convention is also "meaningful as part of a larger body of developments that can be understood as giving rise to new customary international law with the same normative thrust."[20] This means that even states that have not ratified the convention are increasingly called on to abide by the standards it embodies.

International human rights law, humanitarian law, and refugee law together form the legal bases for the universal recognition of housing, land, and property rights. This chapter looks briefly at the primary legal sources for these rights, and the legal resources listed further in this chapter include international charters, covenants,

18 CCPR General Comment 28 on "Equality of Rights between Men and Women" (Article 3), 2000, CCPR/C/21/Rev.1/Add.10.

19 Optional Protocol, December 16, 1996, 999 UNTS 302; cited in J. Anaya (1996) *Indigenous Peoples in International Law*, Oxford: University Press.

20 Anaya (1996), p. 49.

conventions, declarations, and recommendations. Although the legal nature of the various instruments varies, they are all relevant legal standards to refer to in support of housing rights for everyone, everywhere.

In legal terms, the most powerful documents are the conventions, covenants, and charters. The text of these treaties is first agreed on and adopted and then enters into force upon ratification by a certain number of states. Upon ratification to a certain treaty, a state undertakes a voluntary and legally binding obligation to fulfill the particular provisions contained in that treaty.

Declarations and recommendations are also of vital importance. They are not legally binding on states, but they represent the development of international legal norms and reflect the commitment of states to move in certain directions and abide by certain principles. Further, in some instances, declarations may gain the force of binding law if the declaration in question or certain provisions in the declaration achieve the status of customary law.

INTERNATIONAL CHARTERS, COVENANTS, AND CONVENTIONS

International Covenant on Economic, Social and Cultural Rights (1966)

The International Covenant on Economic, Social and Cultural Rights (ICESCR) contains the most significant articulation of the right to adequate housing. The ICESCR was adopted by UN General Assembly (UNGA) resolution 22001(XXI) on 16 December 1966 and entered into force on 3 January 1976.

The right to adequate housing is found in article 11(1). This is the most legally significant universal provision recognizing this right and has been subject to the greatest analysis, application, and interpretation of all international legal sources of housing rights. Although the ICESCR recognizes the right to housing as a part of the larger right to an adequate standard of living, under international human rights law, the right to adequate housing is understood as an independent or free-standing right. The Committee on Economic, Social and Cultural Rights (CESCR) is responsible for monitoring State party compliance with the Covenant.

Article 11(1) provides:

> The State parties to the present Covenant recognize the right of everyone to an adequate standard of living for himself and for his family, including adequate food, clothing and housing, and to the continuous improvement of living conditions. The States Parties will take appropriate steps to ensure the realization of this right, recognizing to this effect the essential importance of international co-operation based on free consent.

INTERNATIONAL COVENANT ON CIVIL AND POLITICAL RIGHTS (1966)

The International Covenant on Civil and Political Rights (ICCPR) was adopted by UNGA resolution 2200A (XXI) of 16 December 1966 and entered into force on 23 March 1976.

The ICCPR has increasingly been used to enforce housing rights; for example, homelessness has been found to threaten violations of the right to life (Article 4), and forced evictions have been found to contravene the right to be free from arbitrary or unlawful interference with the home (Article 17). The Human Rights Committee is responsible for monitoring State party compliance with the Covenant.

Article 17 provides:

> (1) No one shall be subjected to arbitrary or unlawful interference with his [or her] privacy, family, home or correspondence, nor to unlawful attacks on his [or her] honour and reputation.
> (2) Everyone has the right to the protection of the law against such interference or attacks.

Convention on the Elimination of All Forms of Racial Discrimination (1965)

The Convention on the Elimination of All Forms of Racial Discrimination was adopted by UNGA resolution 2106A (XX) on 21 December 1965 and entered into force on 4 January 1969. The Convention expressly prohibits discrimination in the housing sector. State compliance with the Convention is monitored by the UN Committee on the Elimination of All Forms of Racial Discrimination (CERD).

Article 5 provides:

> In compliance with the fundamental obligations laid down in article 2 of this Convention, States Parties undertake to prohibit and to eliminate racial discrimination in all its forms and to guarantee the right of everyone, without distinction as to race, colour, or national or ethnic origin, to equality before the law, notably in the enjoyment of the following rights:
>
> [...]
>
> (e) Economic, social and cultural rights, in particular:
>
> [...]
>
> (iii) the right to housing.

Convention on the Elimination of All Forms of Discrimination against Women (1979)

The Convention on the Elimination of All Forms of Discrimination against Women (CEDAW) was adopted by UNGA resolution 34/180 on 18 December 1979 and entered into force on 3 September 1981. The Convention protects the rights of rural women to adequate housing. State compliance with the Convention is monitored by the UN Committee on the Elimination of All Forms of Discrimination against Women.

Article 14 provides:

> 2. States Parties shall take all appropriate measures to eliminate discrimination against women in rural areas in order to ensure, on a basis of equality of men and women, that they participate in and benefit from rural development and, in particular, shall ensure to such women the right:
>
> [...]
>
> (h) to enjoy adequate living conditions, particularly in relation to housing, sanitation, electricity and water supply, transport and communications.

Convention on the Rights of the Child (1989)

The Convention on the Rights of the Child was adopted by UNGA resolution 44/25 on 20 November 1989 and entered into force on 2 September 1990. The Convention protects the housing rights of children. Compliance with this Convention is monitored by the UN Committee on the Rights of the Child.

Article 27(3) provides:

> State Parties in accordance with national conditions and within their means shall take appropriate measure to assist parents and others responsible for the child to implement this right and shall in the case of need provide material assistance and support programmes, particularly with regards to nutrition, clothing and housing.

International Convention Relating to the Status of Refugees (1951)

The Convention Relating to the Status of Refugees was adopted by UNGA resolution 429(V) on 28 July 1951 and entered into force on 22 April 1954.

Article 21 provides:

> As regards housing, the Contracting States, in so far as the matter is regulated by laws or regulations or is subject to the control of public authorities, shall accord refugees lawfully staying in their territory treatment as favourable as possible and, in any event, not less favourable than that accorded to aliens generally in the same circumstances.

International Convention on the Suppression and Punishment of the Crime of Apartheid (1973)

The Convention on the Suppression and Punishment of the Crime of Apartheid was adopted by UNGA resolution (XXVIII) of 30 November 1973 and entered into force on 18 July 1976.

Article II provides:

> For the purpose of the present Convention, the term "the crime of apartheid", which shall include similar policies and practices of racial segregation and discrimination as practised in southern Africa, shall apply to the following inhuman acts committed for the purpose of establishing and maintaining domination by one racial group of persons over any other racial group of persons and systematically oppressing them:
>
> [...]
>
> 2. Deliberate imposition on a racial group or groups of living conditions calculated to cause its or their physical destruction in whole or in part;
>
> [...]
>
> 4. Any measures, including legislative measures, designed to divide the population along racial lines by the creation of separate reserves and ghettos for the members of a racial group or groups ... the expropriation of landed property belonging to a racial group or groups or to members thereof [...]

International Convention on the Protection of the Rights of All Migrant Workers and Members of Their Families (1990)

The Convention on the Protection of the Rights of All Migrant Workers and Members of Their Families was adopted on 18 December 1990 and entered into force on 1 July 2003.

Article 43 provides:

> (1) Migrant workers shall enjoy equality of treatment with nationals of the State of employment in relation to
>
> [...]
>
> (d) Access to housing, including social housing schemes, and protection against exploitation in respect of rents.

International Labour Organization (ILO) Convention No. 169 Concerning Indigenous and Tribal Peoples (1989)

The Convention concerning Indigenous and Tribal Peoples in Independent Countries was adopted on 27 June 1989 and entered into force on 5 September 1991.

The Convention revised the Indigenous and Tribal Populations Convention no. 107 of 1957.

Article 2 provides:

1. Governments shall have the responsibility for developing, with the participation of the peoples concerned, coordinated and systematic action to protect the rights of these peoples and to guarantee respect for their integrity.
2. Such action shall include measures for:
   (a) ensuring that members of these peoples benefit on an equal footing from the rights and opportunities which national laws and regulations grant to other members of the population;
   (b) promoting the full realisation of the social, economic and cultural rights of these peoples with respect for their social and cultural identity, their customs and traditions and their institutions.

Article 7 provides:

1. The peoples concerned shall have the right to decide their own priorities for the process of development as it affects their lives, beliefs, institutions and spiritual well-being and the lands they occupy or otherwise use, and to exercise control, to the extent possible, over their own economic, social and cultural development. In addition, they shall participate in the formulation, implementation and evaluation of plans and programmes for national and regional development which may affect them directly.

Article 14 provides:

1. The rights of ownership and possession of the peoples concerned over the lands which they traditionally occupy shall be recognised. In addition, measures shall be taken in appropriate cases to safeguard the right of the peoples concerned to use lands not exclusively occupied by them, but to which they have traditionally had access for their subsistence and traditional activities. Particular attention shall be paid to the situation of nomadic peoples and shifting cultivators in this respect.

Article 16 provides:

1. Subject to the following paragraphs of this Article, the peoples concerned shall not be removed from the lands which they occupy.

2. Where the relocation of these peoples is considered necessary as an exceptional measure, such relocation shall take place only with their free and informed consent. Where their consent cannot be obtained, such relocation shall take place only following appropriate procedures established by national laws and regulations, including public inquiries where appropriate, which provide the opportunity for effective representation of the peoples concerned.

3. Whenever possible, these peoples shall have the right to return to their traditional lands, as soon as the grounds for relocation cease to exist.

4. When such return is not possible, as determined by agreement or, in the absence of such agreement, through appropriate procedures, these peoples shall be provided in all possible cases with lands of quality and legal status at least equal to that of the lands previously occupied by them, suitable to provide for their present needs and future development. Where the peoples concerned express a preference for compensation in money or in kind, they shall be so compensated under appropriate guarantees.

5. Persons thus relocated shall be fully compensated for any resulting loss or injury.

Article 17 provides:

1. Procedures established by the peoples concerned for the transmission of land rights among members of these peoples shall be respected.

Article 20 provides:

2. Governments shall do everything possible to prevent any discrimination between workers belonging to the peoples concerned and other workers, in particular as regards:

[...]

(c) medical and social assistance, occupational safety and health, all social security benefits and any other occupationally related benefits, and housing [...]

International Labour Organization (ILO) Convention No. 161 Concerning Occupational Health Services (1985)

The Convention concerning Occupational Health Services was adopted on 25 June 1985 and entered into force on 17 February 1988.

Article 5 provides:

Without prejudice to the responsibility of each employer for the health and safety of the workers in his employment, and with due regard to the necessity for the workers to participate in matters of occupational health and safety, occupational health services shall have such of the following functions as are adequate and appropriate to the occupational risks of the undertaking:

[...]

(b) surveillance of the factors in the working environment and working practices which may affect workers; health, including sanitary installations, canteens and housing where these facilities are provided by the employer [...]

International Labour Organization (ILO) Convention No. 117 Concerning Social Policy (Basic Aims and Standards) (1962)

The Convention concerning Social Policy (Basic Aims and Standards) was adopted on 22 June 1962 and entered into force on 23 April 1964.

Article 2 provides:

> The improvement of standards of living shall be regarded as the principal objective in the planning of economic development.

Article 4 provides:

> The measures to be considered by the competent authorities for the promotion of productive capacity and the improvement of standards of living of agricultural producers shall include:
>
> [...]
>
> (d) the supervision of tenancy arrangements and of working conditions with a view to securing for tenants and labourers the highest practicable standards of living and an equitable share in any advantages which may result from improvements in productivity or in price levels [...]

Article 5 provides:

> 2. In ascertaining the minimum standards of living, account shall be taken of such essential family needs of the workers as food and its nutritive value, housing, clothing, medical care and education.

International Labour Organization (ILO) Convention No. 110 Concerning Plantations (1958)

The Convention Concerning Plantations was adopted on 24 June 1958 and came into force on 22 January 1960.

Article 88 provides:

> 1. Where housing is provided by the employer the conditions under which plantation workers are entitled to occupancy shall be not less favourable than those established by national custom or national legislation.

International Labour Organization (ILO) Convention No. 82 Concerning Social Policy (Non-Metropolitan Territories) (1947)

The Convention Concerning Social Policy (Non-Metropolitan Territories) was adopted on 11 July 1947 and entered into force on 16 June 1955.

Article 4 provides:

> All possible steps shall be taken by appropriate international, regional, national and territorial measures to promote improvement in such fields as public health, housing, nutrition, education, the welfare of children, the status of women, conditions of employment, the remuneration of wage earners and independent producers, the protection of migrant workers, social security, standards of public services and general production.

Article 9 provides:

> 2. In ascertaining the minimum standards of living, account shall be taken of such essential family needs of the workers as food and its nutritive value, housing, clothing, medical care and education.

Article 15 provides:

> 7. Where food, housing, clothing and other essential supplies and services form part of remuneration, all practicable steps shall be taken by the competent authority to ensure that they are adequate and their cash value properly assessed.

Convention on the Suppression and Punishment of the Crime of Apartheid (1973)

The Convention on the Suppression and Punishment of the Crime of Apartheid was adopted by UNGA resolution (XXVIII) of 30 November 1973 and entered into force on 18 July 1976.

Article II provides:

> For the purpose of the present Convention, the term "the crime of apartheid", which shall include similar policies and practices of racial segregation and discrimination as practised in southern Africa, shall apply to the following inhuman acts committed for the purpose of establishing and maintaining domination by one racial group of persons over any other racial group of persons and systematically oppressing them:
>
> [...]
>
> 2. Deliberate imposition on a racial group or groups of living conditions calculated to cause its or their physical destruction in whole or in part;
>
> [...]
>
> 4. Any measures, including legislative measures, designed to divide the population along racial lines by the creation of separate reserves and ghettos for the members of a racial group or groups ... the expropriation of landed property belonging to a racial group or groups or to members thereof [...]

The Convention on the Rights of Persons with Disabilities (2006)

The Convention on the Rights of Persons with Disabilities was adopted by the UNGA on 13 December 2006 and entered into force on 3 May 2008. The Convention is monitored by the Committee on the Rights of Persons with Disabilities.

Article 28 provides:

> Adequate standard of living and social protection
>
> 1. States Parties recognize the right of persons with disabilities to an adequate standard of living for themselves and their families, including adequate food, clothing and housing, and to the continuous improvement of living conditions, and shall take appropriate steps to safeguard and promote the realization of this right without discrimination on the basis of disability.
>
> 2.
>
> […]
>
> d. To ensure access by persons with disabilities to public housing programmes […]

First Geneva Convention for the Amelioration of the Condition of the Wounded and Sick in Armed Forces in the Field (1949)

Article 50 provides:

> Grave breaches … shall be those involving any of the following acts, if committed against persons or property protected by the Convention: … extensive destruction and appropriation of property, not justified by military necessity and carried out unlawfully and wantonly.

Second Geneva Convention for the Amelioration of the Condition of Wounded, Sick and Shipwrecked Members of Armed Forces at Sea (1949)

Article 51 provides:

> Grave breaches … shall be those involving any of the following acts, if committed against persons or property protected by the Convention: … extensive destruction and appropriation of property, not justified by military necessity and carried out unlawfully and wantonly.

Fourth Geneva Convention Relative to the Protection of Civilian Persons in Time of War (1949)

In the context of occupied territories, Article 49 provides:

> Individual or mass forcible transfers, as well as deportations of protected persons from occupied territory to the territory of the Occupying Power or to that of any other country, occupied or not, are prohibited, regardless of their motive. Nevertheless, the Occupying Power may undertake total or partial evacuation of a given area if the security of the population or imperative military reasons so demand. Such evacuations may not involve the displacement of protected persons outside the bounds of the occupied territory except when for material reasons it is impossible to avoid such displacement. Persons thus evacuated shall be transferred back to their homes as soon as hostilities in the area in question have ceased. The Occupying Power undertaking such transfers or evacuations shall ensure, to the greatest practicable extent, that proper accommodation is provided to receive the protected persons, that the removals are effected in satisfactory conditions of hygiene, health, safety and nutrition, and that members of the same family are not separated. [...]

Article 53 provides:

> Any destruction by the Occupying Power of real or personal property belonging individually or collectively to private persons, or to the State, or to other public authorities, or to social or cooperative organizations, is prohibited, except where such destruction is rendered absolutely necessary by military operations.

Article 134 provides:

> The High Contracting Parties shall endeavour, upon the close of hostilities or occupation, to ensure the return of all internees to their last place of residence, or to facilitate their repatriation.

Protocol Additional to the Geneva Conventions of 12 August 1949, and Relating to the Protection of Victims of International Armed Conflicts (Protocol I) (1977)

Article 69 provides:

> Basic needs in occupied territories
>
> 1. ... the Occupying Power shall, to the fullest extent of the means available to it and without any adverse distinction, also ensure the provision ... means of shelter, other supplies essential to the survival of the civilian population of the occupied territory ...

Protocol Additional to the Geneva Conventions of 12 August 1949, and Relating to the Protection of Victims of Non-International Armed Conflicts (Protocol II) (1977)

Article 17 provides:

> Prohibition of forced movement of civilians
>
> 1. The displacement of the civilian population shall not be ordered for reasons related to the conflict unless the security of the civilians involved or imperative military reasons so demand. Should such displacements have to be carried out, all possible measures shall be taken in order that the civilian population may be received under satisfactory conditions of shelter, hygiene, health, safety and nutrition.
>
> 2. Civilians shall not be compelled to leave their own territory for reasons connected with the conflict.

Statute of the International Tribunal for the Prosecution of Persons Responsible for Serious Violations of International Humanitarian Law Committed in the Territory of the Former Yugoslavia since 1991 (International Tribunal for the Former Yugoslavia)

The International Tribunal for Former Yugoslavia was established in 1993 to prosecute serious crimes committed during the wars in the former Yugoslavia. The ICTY has jurisdiction over four categories of crime: grave breaches of the 1949 Geneva Conventions, violations of the laws or customs of war, genocide, and crimes against humanity.

Article 2 provides:

> Grave breaches of the Geneva Conventions of 1949
>
> The International Tribunal shall have the power to prosecute persons committing or ordering to be committed grave breaches of the Geneva Conventions of 12 August 1949, namely the following acts against persons or property protected under the provisions of the relevant Geneva Convention:
>
> [...]
>
> (d) extensive destruction and appropriation of property, not justified by military necessity and carried out unlawfully and wantonly;
>
> [...]
>
> (g) unlawful deportation or transfer or unlawful confinement of a civilian;
>
> Article 3 provides:
>
> Violations of the laws or customs of war

The International Tribunal shall have the power to prosecute persons violating the laws or customs of war. Such violations shall include, but not be limited to:

[...]

(b) wanton destruction of cities, towns or villages, or devastation not justified by military necessity;

(c) attack, or bombardment, by whatever means, of undefended towns, villages, dwellings, or buildings;

(d) seizure of, destruction or wilful damage done to institutions dedicated to religion, charity and education, the arts and sciences, historic monuments and works of art and science;

(e) plunder of public or private property.

Article 5 provides:

Crimes against Humanity

The International Tribunal shall have the power to prosecute persons responsible for the following crimes when committed in armed conflict, whether international or internal in character, and directed against any civilian population:

[...]

(d) deportation;

[...]

(h) persecutions on political, racial and religious grounds;

(i) other inhumane acts.

Statute of the International Tribunal for the Prosecution of Persons Responsible for Genocide and Other Serious Violations of International Humanitarian Law Committed in the Territory of Rwanda and Rwandan Citizens Responsible for Genocide and Other Such Violations Committed in the Territory of Neighbouring States, between 1 January 1994 and 31 December 1994

The International Criminal Tribunal for Rwanda (ICTR) was established in 1994 to prosecute persons responsible for serious violations of international humanitarian law committed in the territory of Rwanda and Rwandan citizens responsible for such violations committed in the territory of neighboring States between 1 January 1994 and 31 December 1994.

Article 3 of the Statute of the ICTR:

Crimes against Humanity

> The International Tribunal for Rwanda shall have the power to prosecute persons responsible for the following crimes when committed as part of a widespread or systematic attack against any civilian population on national, political, ethnic, racial or religious grounds:
>
> [...]
>
> d) Deportation;
>
> h) Persecutions on political, racial and religious grounds;
>
> i) Other inhumane acts.

Article 4 provides:

> The International Tribunal for Rwanda shall have the power to prosecute persons committing or ordering to be committed serious violations of Article 3 common to the Geneva Conventions of 12 August 1949 for the Protection of War Victims, and of Additional Protocol II thereto of 8 June 1977. These violations shall include, but shall not be limited to:
>
> [...]
>
> f) Pillage;
>
> [...]
>
> h) Threats to commit any of the foregoing acts.

ROME STATUTE FOR THE ESTABLISHMENT OF A PERMANENT INTERNATIONAL CRIMINAL COURT

The International Criminal Court was established in 2002 as a permanent institution to prosecute individuals for the "most serious crimes of international concern,"[21] including, genocide, crimes against humanity, war crimes, and the crime of aggression.[22]

[21] Article 1 of the Rome statue provides: "An International Criminal Court ('the Court') is hereby established. It shall be a permanent institution and shall have the power to exercise its jurisdiction over persons for the most serious crimes of international concern, as referred to in this Statute, and shall be complementary to national criminal jurisdictions. The jurisdiction and functioning of the Court shall be governed by the provisions of this Statute."

[22] Article 5 of the Rome Statute provides: "1. The jurisdiction of the Court shall be limited to the most serious crimes of concern to the international community as a whole. The Court has jurisdiction in accordance with this Statute with respect to the following crimes: (a) The crime of genocide; (b) Crimes against humanity; (c) War crimes; (d) The crime of aggression.

2. The Court shall exercise jurisdiction over the crime of aggression once a provision is adopted in accordance with articles 121 and 123 defining the crime and setting out the conditions under which the Court shall exercise jurisdiction with respect to this crime. Such a provision shall be consistent with the relevant provisions of the Charter of the United Nations."

Article 7 provides:

Crimes against humanity

1. For the purpose of this Statute, "crime against humanity" means any of the following acts when committed as part of a widespread or systematic attack directed against any civilian population, with knowledge of the attack:

[…]

(d) Deportation or forcible transfer of population;

[…]

(h) Persecution against any identifiable group or collectivity on political, racial, national, ethnic, cultural, religious, gender as defined in paragraph 3, or other grounds that are universally recognized as impermissible under international law, in connection with any act referred to in this paragraph or any crime within the jurisdiction of the Court;

[…]

(k) Other inhumane acts of a similar character intentionally causing great suffering, or serious injury to body or to mental or physical health.

Article 8 provides:

War crimes

1. The Court shall have jurisdiction in respect of war crimes in particular when committed as part of a plan or policy or as part of a large-scale commission of such crimes.

2. For the purpose of this Statute, "war crimes" means:

(a) Grave breaches of the Geneva Conventions of 12 August 1949, namely, any of the following acts against persons or property protected under the provisions of the relevant Geneva Convention:

[…]

(iv) Extensive destruction and appropriation of property, not justified by military necessity and carried out unlawfully and wantonly;

[…]

(vii) Unlawful deportation or transfer or unlawful confinement;

(b) Other serious violations of the laws and customs applicable in international armed conflict, within the established framework of international law, namely, any of the following acts:

[…]

(ii) Intentionally directing attacks against civilian objects, that is, objects which are not military objectives;

[…]

(v) Attacking or bombarding, by whatever means, towns, villages, dwellings or buildings which are undefended and which are not military objectives;

[...]

(viii) The transfer, directly or indirectly, by the Occupying Power of parts of its own civilian population into the territory it occupies, or the deportation or transfer of all or parts of the population of the occupied territory within or outside this territory;

[...]

(xiii) Destroying or seizing the enemy's property unless such destruction or seizure be imperatively demanded by the necessities of war;

[...]

(xvi) Pillaging a town or place, even when taken by assault;

(c) In the case of an armed conflict not of an international character, serious violations of article 3 common to the four Geneva Conventions of 12 August 1949, namely, any of the following acts committed against persons taking no active part in the hostilities, including members of armed forces who have laid down their arms and those placed hors de combat by sickness, wounds, detention or any other cause:

[...]

(e) Other serious violations of the laws and customs applicable in armed conflicts not of an international character, within the established framework of international law, namely, any of the following acts:

[...]

(ii) Intentionally directing attacks against buildings, material, medical units and transport, and personnel using the distinctive emblems of the Geneva Conventions in conformity with international law;

[...]

(v) Pillaging a town or place, even when taken by assault;

[...]

(viii) Ordering the displacement of the civilian population for reasons related to the conflict, unless the security of the civilians involved or imperative military reasons so demand;

[...]

(xii) Destroying or seizing the property of an adversary unless such destruction or seizure be imperatively demanded by the necessities of the conflict;

DECLARATIONS AND RECOMMENDATIONS

The Universal Declaration of Human Rights (1948)

The Universal Declaration of Human Rights (UDHR) was the first major international agreement on human rights and forms a key part of the International Bill of Rights.

It is also the first human rights instrument to recognize housing rights. The Declaration was adopted and proclaimed by the General Assembly on 10 December 1948.

Article 25 provides:

> Everyone has the right to a standard living adequate for the health and well-being of himself and of his family, including food, clothing, housing and medical care and necessary social services, and the right to security in the event of unemployment, sickness, disability, widowhood, old age or other lack of livelihood in circumstances beyond his control.

Declaration on the Rights of the Child (1959)

The Declaration on the Rights of the Child was proclaimed by UNGA resolution 1386(XIV) on 20 November 1959.

Principle 4 provides:

> The child shall enjoy the benefits of social security. He shall be entitled to grow and develop in health; to this end, special care and protection shall be provided both to him and to his mother, including adequate pre-natal and post-natal care. The child shall have the right to adequate nutrition, housing, recreation and medical services.

International Labour Organization (ILO) Recommendation No. 115 Concerning Workers' Housing (1961)

The Recommendation Concerning Workers' Housing was adopted on 28 June 1961.

Section II (Objectives of National Housing Policy) provides:

> 2. It should be an objective of national policy to promote, within the framework of general housing policy, the construction of housing and related community facilities with a view to ensuring that adequate and decent housing accommodation and a suitable living environment are made available to all workers and their families. A degree of priority should be accorded to those whose needs are most urgent.

Section III (Responsibility of Public Authorities), provides:

> 8 …
>
> (2) The responsibilities of the central body should include –
>
> […]
>
> (b) formulating workers' housing programmes, such programmes to include measures for slum clearance and the rehousing of occupiers of slum dwellings.

Section VI (Housing Standards), provides:

> 19. As a general principle, the competent authority should, in order to ensure structural safety and reasonable levels of decency, hygiene and comfort, establish

> minimum housing standards in the light of local conditions and take appropriate measures to enforce these standards.

The section on "Suggestions Concerning Methods of Application", provides:

> 5. The competent authorities should give special attention to the particular problem of housing migrant workers and, where appropriate, their families, with a view to achieving as rapidly as possible equality of treatment between migrant workers and national workers in this respect.

Declaration on the Elimination of All Forms of Racial Discrimination (1963)

The Declaration on the Elimination of All Forms of Racial Discrimination was proclaimed by UNGA resolution 1904 (XVIII) of 20 November 1963.

Article 3 provides:

> 1. Particular efforts shall be made to prevent discrimination based on race, colour or ethnic origin, especially in the fields of civil rights, access to citizenship, education, religion, employment, occupation and housing.
>
> [...]

Declaration on Social Progress and Development (1969)

The Declaration on Social Progress and Development was proclaimed by UNGA resolution 2542 (XXIV) on 11 December 1969.

Part II (Objectives), provides:

> Social progress and development shall aim at the continuous raising of the material and spiritual standards of living of all members of society, with respect for and in compliance with human rights and fundamental freedoms, through the attainment of the following main goals:
>
> Article 10
>
> [...]
>
> (f) The provision for all, particularly persons in low income groups and large families, of adequate housing and community services.
>
> [...]

Declaration on the Rights of Disabled Persons (1975)

The Declaration on the Rights of Disabled Persons was proclaimed by UNGA resolution 3447 (XXX) of 9 December 1975.

Article 9 provides:

Disabled persons have the right to live with their families or with foster parents and to participate in all social, creative or recreational activities. No disabled person shall be subjected, as far as his or her residence is concerned, to differential treatment other than that required by his or her condition or by the improvement which he or she may derive therefrom. If the stay of a disabled person in a specialized establishment is indispensable, the environment and living conditions therein shall be as close as possible to those of the normal life of a person of his or her age.

Vancouver Declaration on Human Settlements (1976)

The Vancouver Declaration on Human Settlements was adopted by the UN Conference on Human Settlements in 1976.

Section III (Guidelines for Action) provides:

8. Adequate shelter and services are a basic human right which places an obligation on Governments to ensure their attainment by all people, beginning with direct assistance to the least advantaged through guided programmes of self-help and community action. Governments should endeavour to remove all impediments hindering attainments of these goals or special importance is the elimination of social and racial segregation, inter alia, through the creation of better balanced communities, which blend different social groups, occupation, housing and amenities.

Chapter II (A.3) provides:

The ideologies of States are reflected in their human settlement policies. These being powerful instruments for change, they must not be used to dispossess people from their homes or land or to entrench privilege and exploitation. The human settlement policies must be in conformity with the declaration of principles and the Universal Declaration of Human Rights.

Declaration on Race and Racial Prejudice (1978)

The Declaration on Race and Racial Prejudice was adopted and proclaimed by the General Conference of the United Nations Educational, Scientific and Cultural Organization (UNESCO) on 27 November 1978.

Article 9 provides:

2. Special measures must be taken to ensure equality in dignity and rights for individuals and groups wherever necessary, while ensuring that they are not such as to appear racially discriminatory. In this respect, particular attention should be paid to racial or ethnic groups which are socially or economically disadvantaged, so as to afford them, on a completely equal footing and without

discrimination or restriction, the protection of the laws and regulations and the advantages of the social measures in force, in particular in regard to housing, employment and health; to respect the authenticity of their culture and values; and to facilitate their social and occupational advancement, especially through education.

ILO Recommendation No. 162 Concerning Older Workers (1980)

The ILO Recommendation No. 162 Concerning Older Workers was adopted by the General Conference of the International Labour Organisation on 23 June 1980.

Part II (Equality of Opportunity and Treatment), provides:

> 5. Older workers should, without discrimination by reason of their age, enjoy equality of opportunity and treatment with other workers as regards, in particular –
>
> Older workers should, without discrimination by reason of their age, enjoy equality of opportunity and treatment with older workers as regards, in particular ... (g) access to housing, social services and health institutions, in particular when this access is related to occupational activity or employment.

Declaration on the Right to Development (1986)

The Declaration on the Right to Development was adopted by UNGA resolution 41/128 on 4 December 1986.

Article 8 provides:

> 1. States should undertake, at the national level, all necessary measures for the realization of the right to development and shall ensure, inter alia, equality of opportunity for all in their access to basic resources, education, health services, food, housing, employment and the fair distribution of income. Effective measures should be undertaken to ensure that women have an active role in the development process. Appropriate economic and social reforms should be carried out with a view to eradicating all social injustices.

Interpretive Standards, UN Resolutions, and Other Documents

Beyond the contents of the relevant charters, conventions, and covenants, there are also a number of interpretive standards, UN resolutions, and other international documents relevant to the question of HLP rights.

Interpretive standards, such as General Comments by the UN Committee on Economic, Social and Cultural Rights, seek to clarify and elaborate on the content of HLP rights and the obligations that these rights impose. Similarly, UN resolutions are not binding on member nations; however, they form an important framework that may be drawn upon for the interpretation and development of international and domestic laws relevant to HLP rights. This section also brings together other key international documents that relate to HLP rights, including Habitat Agenda and Agenda 21.

INTERPRETIVE STANDARDS

UN Committee on Economic, Social and Cultural Rights General Comment No. 4 on the Right to Adequate Housing (1991)

The UN Committee on Economic, Social and Cultural Rights (CESCR) adopted General Comment No. 4 on the Right to Adequate Housing at the sixth session of the CESCR on 13 December 1991.

General Comment No. 4 states that the following seven components form the core contents of the human right to adequate housing:

1. Legal security of tenure;
2. Availability of services, materials, facilities and infrastructure;
3. Location;
4. Habitability;
5. Affordability;
6. Accessibility; and
7. Cultural adequacy.

General Comment No. 4 also reiterates that the right to adequate housing should not be interpreted in a narrow or restrictive sense that equates it with the shelter provided by merely having a roof over one's head or views shelter exclusively as a commodity, but that housing rights should be seen as rights to live somewhere in security, peace, and dignity.

UN Committee on Economic, Social and Cultural Rights General Comment No. 7 on Forced Evictions (1997)

The UN Committee on Economic, Social and Cultural Rights (CESCR) adopted General Comment No. 7 on Forced Evictions on 20 May 1997.

General Comment No. 7 provides the leading legal interpretation of the right to be protected against forced eviction and represents the most far-reaching decision yet under international law on forced evictions and human rights, detailing what governments, landlords, and institutions must do to prevent forced evictions.

UN Committee on Economic, Social and Cultural Rights General Comment No. 15 on the Right to Water (2005)

The UN Committee on Economic, Social and Cultural Rights (CESCR) adopted General Comment No. 15 on the Right to Water 20 January 2003.

General Comment No.7 provides, *inter alia*:

> ... The right to water is also inextricably related to the right to the highest attainable standard of health (art. 12, para. 1)3 and the rights to adequate housing and adequate food (art. 11, para. 1).

The UN Guiding Principles on Internal Displacement (1998)

The Guiding Principles on Internal Displacement were presented to the Commission on Human Rights in 1998 by the then-Representative to the UN Secretary-General on internally displaced persons, Francis Deng.

In September 2005, the heads of state and governments assembled at the World Summit in New York recognized the Guiding Principles as "an important international framework for the protection of internally displaced persons."

The Guiding Principles are based on international humanitarian and human rights law and analogous refugee law. They are intended to serve as an international standard to guide governments, international organizations, and all other relevant actors in providing assistance and protection to IDPs.

The Principles identify the rights and guarantees relevant to the protection of the internally displaced in all phases of displacement. They provide protection against arbitrary displacement, offer a basis for protection and assistance during displacement, and set out guarantees for safe return, resettlement, and reintegration. Although they do not constitute a binding instrument, the Principles reflect and are consistent with international law.

Principle 18 provides:

> 1. All internally displaced persons have the right to an adequate standard of living.
> 2. At the minimum, regardless of the circumstances, and without discrimination, competent authorities shall provide internally displaced persons with and ensure safe access to:
>   (a) Essential food and potable water;
>   (b) Basic shelter and housing;
>   (c) Appropriate clothing; and
>   (d) Essential medical services and sanitation.
> 3. Special efforts should be made to ensure the full participation of women in the planning and distribution of these basic supplies.

The UN Principles on Housing and Property Restitution for Refugees and Displaced Persons (2005) (the "Pinheiro Principles")

The UN Sub-Commission on the Promotion and Protection of Human Rights approved the Principles on Housing and Property Restitution for Refugees and Displaced Persons (the "Pinheiro Principles") in August 2005.

The aim of the principles is to provide international standards and practical guidance to States, UN agencies, and the broader international community on how best to address the complex legal and technical issues surrounding housing, land, and property restitution. The principles augment the international normative framework in the area of housing and property restitution rights, and are grounded firmly within existing international human rights and humanitarian law.

UN Resolutions

Since 1986, a series of resolutions have been adopted by various UN human rights and other bodies on the issue of HLP rights. Each of the resolutions was adopted by consensus. These resolutions have formed the legislative and political basis for instigating a broad range of activities within the UN on all aspects of HLP rights. Some of the most important provisions of these resolutions are included chronologically in this subsection.

The UN Sub-Commission on Prevention of Discrimination and Protection of Minorities resolution 1998/26 entitled "Housing and Property Restitution in the Context of the Return of Refugees and Internally Displaced Persons" on 26 August 1998

Sub-Commission resolution 1998/26 provides in part:

> 2. Reaffirms also the universal applicability of the right to adequate housing, the right to freedom of movement, the right to privacy and respect for the home and the particular importance of these rights for returning refugees and internally displaced persons wishing to return to their homes and places of habitual residence;
>
> 3. Confirms that the adoption or application of laws by States which are designed to or result in the loss or removal of tenancy, use, ownership or other rights connected with housing or property, the active retraction of the right to reside within a particular place, or laws of abandonment employed against refugees or internally displaced persons pose serious impediments to the return and reintegration of refugees and internally displaced persons and to reconstruction and reconciliation;

4. Urges all States to ensure the free and fair exercise of the right to return to one's home and place of habitual residence by all refugees and internally displaced persons and to develop effective and expeditious legal, administrative and other procedures to ensure the free and fair exercise of this right, including fair and effective mechanisms designed to resolve outstanding housing and property problems [...]

The UN Sub-Commission on Prevention of Discrimination and Protection of Minorities resolution 1998/15 entitled "Women and the right to land, property and adequate housing," adopted on 21 August 1998

Sub-Commission resolution 1998/15 provides in part:

1. [...] that the discrimination faced by women with respect to acquiring and securing land, property and housing, as well as financing for land, property and housing, constitutes a violation of women's human rights to equality, protection against discrimination and the equal enjoyment of the right to an adequate standard of living, including adequate housing;

2. Strongly urges Governments to comply fully with all of their international and regional obligations and commitments concerning women's rights to land, property, inheritance, adequate housing, including security of tenure, and an adequate standard of living;

3. Urges Governments to take all necessary measures in order to amend and/or repeal laws and policies pertaining to land, property and housing which deny women security of tenure and equal access and rights to land, property and housing, to encourage the transformation of customs and traditions which deny women security of tenure and equal access and rights to land, property and housing, and to adopt and enforce legislation which protects and promotes women's rights to own, inherit, lease or rent land, property and housing [...]

The UN Sub-Commission on Prevention of Discrimination and Protection of Minorities resolution 1997/19 entitled "Women and the right to adequate housing and to land and property," adopted on 27 August 1997

Sub-Commission resolution 1997/19 provides in part:

1. Reaffirms the universal nature and existence of the right to adequate housing in terms of its relevance to all human rights with respect to women;

2. Encourages States to comply fully with all their international and regional obligations and commitments concerning the legally recognised rights of women to land, property, inheritance, adequate housing including security of tenure, an adequate standard of living and the continuous improvement of living and housing conditions and to create opportunities for women to acquire training, education and information in all matters related to these rights;

3. Reminds Governments of the critical importance of providing women with legal resources and human rights information and education to address the violence they experience in relation to housing, and to enact and enforce laws and policies that protect women against violence in this context;

14. Requests Governments, the organisations and bodies of the United Nations and the specialized agencies actively to support local, national and international initiatives, including the development of human rights indicators, aimed at assessing and improving the housing and living conditions of women throughout the world, in full consultation with and with the full participation of women themselves, their representatives and community-based non-governmental organisations and other relevant groups [...]

UN Commission on Human Settlements Resolution 16/7 entitled: "The realization of the human right to adequate housing," adopted on 7 May 1997

Resolution 16/7 provides in part:

Aware of the right of everyone to an adequate standard of living for themselves and their families, including adequate food, clothing, housing, water, and sanitation, and to the continuous improvement of living conditions, as stated in paragraph 11 of the Habitat Agenda ...

Reaffirming the commitment of States, as set out in paragraph 39 of the Habitat Agenda, to the full and progressive realization of the right to adequate housing as provided for in international instruments ...

4. Requests that all States within the overall context of an enabling approach, to take appropriate action in order to promote, protect and ensure the full and progressive realization of the right to adequate housing, as outlined n paragraph 61 of the Habitat Agenda [...]

The UN Sub-Commission on Prevention of Discrimination and Protection of Minorities resolution 1995/27 entitled "Promoting the realization of the human right to adequate housing," adopted on 24 August 1995

Sub-Commission resolution 1995/27 provides in part:

Reaffirming the human right of every woman, man and child to a safe and secure place to live in peace and dignity, Concerned also that Governments having the legal obligation to respect, protect and fulfil the human right to adequate housing have failed to take the necessary steps to ensure the full realization of this right for everyone entitled to it;

3. Strongly encourages all Governments faithfully to implement their existing legal obligations concerning the human right to adequate housing, including the adoption of effective legislation and policies respecting, promoting and protecting the human right to adequate housing, the removal of all obstacles to the full realization of this right and the repeal of legislation and policies which contradict housing rights standards, and to refrain from violating the human right to adequate housing.

UN Sub-Commission on Prevention of Discrimination and Protection of Minorities resolution 1994/8 entitled "Children and the right to adequate housing," adopted on 26 August 1994

Sub-Commission resolution 1994/8 provides in part:

Conscious that one of the areas where the indivisibility and interdependence of human rights and of the rights of children become most apparent is with respect to the existence of widespread poverty leading to inadequate housing and living conditions, Aware of the worsening situation around the world of the living conditions of children and of the fact that tens of millions of children are being forced to live in the streets, in slums and on pavements, and that this number is growing daily,

Concerned at the especially adverse living conditions of children belonging to vulnerable groups, including indigenous people and ethnic, racial, religious and other minorities,

Reminds Governments to comply to the maximum extent of available resources with all existing obligations concerning the legally recognised rights of children to an adequate standard of living and the continuous improvement of living and housing conditions.

UN Sub-Commission on Prevention of Discrimination and Protection of Minorities resolution 1993/36 entitled "The Right to Adequate Housing", adopted on 26 August 1993

Sub-Commission resolution 1993/36 provides in part:

3. Strongly encourages all governments to pursue effective policies and legislation aimed at creating conditions towards ensuring the full realization of the right to adequate housing of the entire population concentrating on those currently homeless or inadequately housed, and to take into account the particularly negative impact on housing and living conditions that may result from the adoption of economic adjustment and other policies based exclusively upon the dictates of the free-market.

UN Commission on Human Settlements resolution 14/6 entitled "The Human Right to Adequate Housing", adopted on 5 May 1993

Sub-Commission resolution 14/6 provides in part:

> 3. Urges all States to cease any practices which could or do result in infringements of the human right to adequate housing, in particular the practice of forced mass evictions and any form of racial or other discrimination in the housing sphere;
>
> 4. Invites all States to repeal, reform or amend any existing legislation, policies, programmes or projects which in any manner negatively affect the full realization of right to adequate housing;
>
> 5. Encourages all States to take steps according to their available resources, with a view to achieving progressively the full realization of the right to adequate housing, by appropriate means, including particularly the adoption of legislative measures;
>
> 6. Urges all States to comply with existing international agreements concerning the right to adequate housing, and to this end, to establish in accordance with the human settlements parts of international human rights law, appropriate monitoring mechanisms to provide, for national and international consideration, accurate data and indicators on the extent of homelessness, inadequate housing conditions, persons without security of tenure and other issues arising from the right to adequate housing and providing insights into policy, structural and other impediments to the efficient operation of the shelter sector.

UN Sub-Commission on Prevention of Discrimination and Protection of Minorities resolution 1992/26 entitled "Promoting the Realization of the Right to Adequate Housing", adopted on 22 August 1992

Sub-Commission resolution 1992/26 provides in part:

> 2. Encourages all States to pursue effective policies and legislation aimed at creating conditions aimed at ensuring the full realization of the right to adequate housing of the entire population, concentrating on those vulnerable groups that are homeless or inadequately housed.

UN Sub-Commission on Prevention of Discrimination and Protection of Minorities resolution 1991/26 entitled "Promoting the Realization of the Right to Adequate Housing", adopted on 29 August 1991

Sub-Commission resolution 1991/26 provides in part:

> The Sub-Commission urges all States to pursue effective policies and adopt legislation aimed at ensuring the realization of the right to adequate housing of

the entire population, concentrating on those currently homeless or inadequately housed.

UN Commission on Human Rights resolution 1988/24 entitled "The Realization of the Right to Adequate Housing", adopted on 7 March 1988

Sub-Commission resolution 1988/24 provides in part:

The Commission on Human Rights decides to keep the question of the right to adequate housing under periodic review.

UNGA resolution 42/146 entitled "The Realization of the Right to Adequate Housing," adopted on 7 December 1987

UNGA resolution 42/146 provides in part:

1. Expresses its deep concern that millions of people do not enjoy the right to adequate housing;

2. Reiterates the need to take, at the national and international levels, measures to promote the right of all persons to an adequate standard of living for themselves and their families, including adequate housing;

3. Calls upon all States and international organizations concerned to pay special attention to the realization of the right to adequate housing in carrying out measures to develop national shelter strategies and settlement improvement programmes within the framework of the global strategy for shelter to the year 2000 [...]

Economic and Social Council (ECOSOC) of the United Nations resolution 1987/62 entitled "The Realization of the Right to Adequate Housing," adopted on 29 May 1987

Economic and Social Council Resolution 1987/62 provides in part:

Expresses its deep concern that millions of people do not enjoy the right to adequate housing;

2. Reiterates the need to take appropriate measures, at the national and international levels, to promote the right of all persons to an adequate standard of living for themselves and their families, including adequate housing;

3. Calls upon all States and international organizations concerned to pay special attention to the realization of the right to adequate housing in carrying out measures for the observance of the International Year of Shelter for the Homeless, *inter alia*, by developing shelter strategies and settlement improvement programmes.

Economic and Social Council (ECOSOC) of the United Nations resolution 1987/37 entitled "The International Year of Shelter for the Homeless," adopted on 28 May 1987

Economic and Social Council Resolution 1987/37 provides in part:

> ECOSOC recalls that the objective of activities before and during the Year is to improve the shelter and neighborhoods of some of the poor and disadvantaged by the end of 1987, according to national priorities, and to demonstrate by the Year 2000 ways and means of improving the shelter and neighborhoods of the poor and disadvantaged.

UN Commission on Human Rights resolution 1987/22 entitled "The Realization of the Right to Adequate Housing," adopted on 10 March 1987

Resolution 1987/22 provides in part:

> The Commission on Human Rights reiterates the need to take appropriate measures, at the national and international levels, for promoting the right of all persons to an adequate standard of living for themselves and their families, including adequate housing.

UNGA resolution 41/146 entitled "The Realization of the Right to Adequate Housing," adopted on 4 December 1986

UNGA resolution 41/146 provides in part:

> 1. Expresses its deep concern that millions of people do not enjoy the right to adequate housing;
>
> 2. Reiterates the need to take, at the national and international levels, measures to promote the right of all persons to an adequate standard of living for themselves and their families, including adequate housing;
>
> 3. Calls upon all States and international organizations concerned to intensify their efforts to achieve the objectives and goals of the International Year of Shelter for the Homeless [...]

UN Commission on Human Rights resolution 1986/36 entitled "The Realization of the Right to Adequate Housing," adopted on 12 March 1986

Resolution 1986/36 provides in part:

> The Commission on Human Rights reiterates the right of all persons to an adequate standard of living for themselves and their families, including adequate housing.

OTHER DOCUMENTS

Habitat Agenda

The Habitat Agenda was adopted by the second United Nations Conference on Human Settlements (Habitat II) at Istanbul, Turkey, on 14 June 1996. The Habitat Agenda is the main political document that came out of the Habitat II conference in Istanbul, Turkey (3–14 June 1996). Adopted by 171 countries at what was called the City Summit, it contains more than 100 commitments and 600 recommendations on human settlements issues.

Habitat Agenda, Chapter II (Commitments) provides:

> A. Adequate shelter for all
>
> 39. We reaffirm our commitment to the full and progressive realization of the right to adequate housing, as provided for in international instruments. In this context, we recognize an obligation by Governments to enable people to obtain shelter and to protect and improve dwellings and neighbourhoods. We commit ourselves to the goal of improving living and working conditions on an equitable and sustainable basis, so that everyone will have adequate shelter that is healthy, safe, secure, accessible and affordable and that includes basic services, facilities and amenities, and will enjoy freedom from discrimination in housing and legal security of tenure. We shall implement and promote this objective in a manner fully consistent with human rights standards.
>
> 40. We further commit ourselves to the objectives of:
>
> [...]
>
> (b) Providing legal security of tenure and equal access to land to all people, including women and those living in poverty; and undertaking legislative and administrative reforms to give women full and equal access to economic resources, including the right to inheritance and to ownership of land and other property, credit, natural resources and appropriate technologies;
>
> [...]
>
> (d) Ensuring transparent, comprehensive and accessible systems in transferring land rights and legal security of tenure;
>
> [...]
>
> (j) Eradicating and ensuring legal protection from discrimination in access to shelter and basic services, without distinction of any kind, such as race, colour, sex, language, religion, political or other opinion, national or social origin, property, birth or other status; similar protection should be ensured against discrimination on the grounds of disability or age;
>
> [...]

(l) Promoting shelter and supporting basic services and facilities for education and health for the homeless, displaced persons, indigenous people, women and children who are survivors of family violence, persons with disabilities, older persons, victims of natural and man-made disasters and people belonging to vulnerable and disadvantaged groups, including temporary shelter and basic services for refugees;

[...]

We commit ourselves to the goal of gender equality in human settlements development. We further commit ourselves to:

(a) Integrating gender perspectives in human settlements related legislation, policies, programmes and projects through the application of gender-sensitive analysis;

[...]

D. Gender equality

46. We commit ourselves to the goal of gender equality in human settlements development. We further commit ourselves to:

(a) Integrating gender perspectives in human settlements related legislation, policies, programmes and projects through the application of gender-sensitive analysis [...]

AGENDA 21

Agenda 21, the Rio Declaration on Environment and Development, and the Statement of principles for the Sustainable Management of Forests were adopted by more than 178 Governments at the United Nations Conference on Environment and Development (UNCED) held in Rio de Janiero, Brazil, 3–14 June 1992. Agenda 21 is a comprehensive plan of action to be taken globally, nationally, and locally by organizations of the United Nations system, governments, and major groups in every area in which human impacts on the environment. Agenda 21 provides in part:

Chapter 7.6:

Access to safe and healthy shelter is essential to a person's physical, psychological, social and economic wellbeing and should be a fundamental part of national and international action. The right to adequate housing as a basic human right is enshrined in the Universal Declaration of Human Rights and the International Covenant on Economic, Social and Cultural Rights. Despite this, it is estimated that at the present time, at least one billion people do not have access to safe and healthy shelter and that if appropriate action is not taken, this number will increase dramatically by the end of the century and beyond.

Chapter 7.9(b):

All countries should adopt and/or strengthen national shelter strategies, with targets based, as appropriate, on the principles and recommendations contained in the Global Strategy for Shelter to the Year 2000. People should be protected by law against unfair eviction from their homes or land.

Chapter 7.9(c):

All countries should, as appropriate, support the shelter efforts of the urban and rural poor, the unemployed and the no-income group by adopting and/or adapting existing codes and regulations, to facilitate their access to land, finance and low-cost building materials and by actively promoting the regularization and upgrading of informal settlements and urban slums as an expedient measure and pragmatic solution to the urban shelter deficit.

Chapter 7.30(f):

All countries should consider developing national land-resource management plans to guide land-resource development and utilization and, to that end, should ... establish appropriate forms of land tenure that provide security of tenure for all land users, especially indigenous people, women, local communities, the low-income urban dwellers and the rural poor.

Questions and Exercises

1. The legal recognition of housing, land, and property rights throughout international human rights law is far wider than is commonly assumed. But is the international HLP legal regime comprehensive as it currently stands, or are new standards required to better protect the HLP rights of people affected by conflict? If so, which three new laws or standards would you recommend?
2. What new mechanisms are required to improve the enforcement of HLP rights, particularly with respect to victims of HLP rights abuses linked to conflict?
3. Can gross and systematic abuses of HLP rights constitute a crime against humanity or a war crime? If so, which types of abuses/violations/grave breaches of international humanitarian or criminal law classify as international crimes?
4. Can individual perpetrators of HLP rights abuses be held accountable by the International Criminal Court? If so, on what grounds? Can you identify persons now living who have committed HLP crimes on such a scale that they could arguably face prosecution by the ICC?

Additional Resources

Antonio Cassese (2003) *International Criminal Law*, Oxford University Press.

COHRE (1999) *Sources No. 3: Forced Evictions and Human Rights: A Manual for Action*, Geneva: COHRE.

FAO, IDMC, OCHA, OHCHR, UN-Habitat, and UNHCR (2007) *Handbook on Housing and Property Restitution for Refugees and Displaced Persons – Implementing the Pinheiro Principles*, Geneva.

Walter Kälin (2000) *Guiding Principles on Internal Displacement – Annotations*, American Society of International Law & The Brookings Institution, Washington DC.

Susana Lastarria-Cornhiel (2005) *Gender and Property Rights within Post-Conflict Situations*, USAID Issue Paper 12.

Scott Leckie (2007) *Housing, Land and Property Restitution Rights of Refugees and Displaced Persons: Laws, Cases and Materials*, Cambridge University Press.

Scott Leckie (ed.) (2003) *National Perspectives on Housing Rights*, Kluwer International Publishers.

Scott Leckie (2001) "The Human Right to Adequate Housing," Chapter 9 in *Economic, Social and Cultural Rights: A Textbook* (Eide, Krause, and Rosas, eds.), Martinus Nijhoff Publishers, pp. 149–168.

Scott Leckie and Ezekiel Simperingham (2011) *The Possibility of Prosecuting Grave Violations of Housing, Land and Property Rights*, Displacement Solutions.

OCHA (2003) *No Refuge – The Challenge of Internal Displacement*, United Nations.

Sphere Project (2000) *Humanitarian Charter and Minimum Standards in Disaster Response*, Sphere Project.

UN Secretary-General (1993) *Forced Evictions: Analytical Report Compiled by the Secretary-General Pursuant to Commission Resolution 1993/77*, E/CN.4/1994/20.

3

Displacement, Conflict, and HLP Rights

POPULATION DISPLACEMENT: A HISTORICAL OVERVIEW

Population displacement, especially that caused by conflict, is by no means a new phenomenon. History, including holy books such as the Bible and the Koran, are replete with examples of forced displacement during wartime. It has been argued, however, that the nineteenth century saw a massive increase in the numbers of people displaced around the world, in part because of innovations in technology: improvements in both means of transport and the machinery of war.

World War I led to the displacement and migration of some 10 million people, some 10 million Germans were expelled from Central and Eastern Europe in the years following World War II, and 15 million people moved as a result of the Partition of India in 1946.[1] According to some estimates, the total number of people internally displaced globally was relatively low during the 1960s but increased significantly during the 1970s, before rising exponentially during the 1980s. However, the data should be treated with caution, because internal displacement in particular was not comprehensively monitored or studied until relatively recently.

The increase in population displacement during the 1970s and particularly the 1980s was caused, to a degree, by the proliferation of civil conflicts related to the Cold War. The Vietnam war led to massive internal displacement during the 1970s, and the people of neighboring Cambodia also suffered major displacement. Displacement was also linked to the many so-called "proxy" conflicts fought mainly in the developing world, with the support of the United States on the one hand and the USSR on the other. Conflict in Afghanistan, for example, meant that the number of Afghan refugees increased from 600,000 in 1979 to more than 2 million by 1980, nearly 4 million in 1981, and finally more than 6 million in 1990. At that

[1] Matthew J. Gibney and Randall Hansen (2005) "Preface," in Matthew J. Gibney and Randall Hansen (eds.), *Immigration and Asylum*, ABC-CLIO.

time, refugees numbered more than one-third of the total Afghan population. The Ethiopian refugee population grew from nearly 600,000 in 1977 to almost 2 million in 1979 and had the largest IDP population in the world during the early 1980s due to the civil war. Internal conflict in Mozambique caused the refugee population to grow from nearly 200,000 in 1986 to one million in 1989 and created hundreds of thousands of IDPs.

Of course, the end of the Cold War brought neither the "end of history" nor the end of conflict, as had been predicted by some. Civil wars in Sudan and the DRC, for example, triggered massive movements of people within and across borders, and the 1994 Rwandan genocide set off a chain reaction of human misery and flight that is still evident today: whereas many of the 2 million refugees who fled Rwanda in 1994 have now gone home, others continue to live in refugee camps across Africa. From 1992 to 2005, the global refugee population steadily fell, but there has been another increase since 2005. The total number of refugees worldwide now stands at about 16 million.[2]

The early 1990s saw a historic peak in IDP numbers as a result of the conflicts following the break-up of the former Yugoslavia and the Soviet Union. IDP numbers fell until 1997, when they started to increase once more. In the Middle East, conflict in Iraq has displaced millions (in 2008, IDPs totaled 2,840,000) while the protracted situation of Palestinian refugees and IDPs remains a source of humanitarian concern and a rallying point for conflict.[3] In 2008, there were some 26 million IDPs worldwide.[4] The largest number of IDPs – 11.6 million, which represents some 45 percent of the global total – live in African countries. The Americas are home to about 4.5 million IDPs, with the highest numbers currently found in Columbia; the Middle East region has around 3.9 million and South and Southeast Asia has around 3.5 million. Europe and Central Asia has an IDP population of around 2.5 million.

Many IDPs have been displaced for more than a decade and face discrimination and even violence from the state. Official information on IDPs supplied by various governments is often at odds with research conducted by United Nations agencies or NGOs. In particular, the issue of reintegration or resettlement of IDPs is often problematic, with communities continuing to experience extreme vulnerability to socioeconomic hardships even after they have been officially removed from the IDP category and have lost eligibility for assistance from humanitarian organizations. The following excerpt provides an overview of some of the key issues facing IDPs at the global level.

2 IDMC (2009) Internal Displacement: Global Overview of Trends and Developments in 2008, IDMC.
3 Id.
4 Id.

IDMC (2009) *Internal Displacement: Global Overview of Trends and Developments in 2008*, IDMC.

Protracted displacement

Some 35 countries have a significant number of IDPs living in protracted situations, where the search for durable solutions to their plight was stalled or they continued to be marginalized as a result of their displacement. It is difficult to isolate the number of IDPs in protracted situations as protracted and new displacement can be ongoing at the same time in one country.

Governments continued to promote return as the preferred durable solution for IDPs, over local integration and settlement to another area. In half the countries monitored, return was the only solution actively supported by national authorities.

The obstacles to durable solutions which IDPs in protracted situations most frequently face include lack of access to livelihoods, inadequate housing and the inability to enjoy their homes and land. Property reinstatement and compensation mechanisms are essential for activating the durable solutions process as IDPs thereby gain the means to improve their lives. They may return to their homes and land, or use compensation or the income earned from selling or renting their homes and land to integrate locally or resettle elsewhere. In almost half the countries surveyed, there was a lack of information about whether IDPs had found durable solutions. In protracted internal displacement situations, governments and international agencies should better monitor the process of attaining durable solutions, to identify and address the obstacles to return, local integration and resettlement.

Protection concerns

IDPs in 2008 were exposed to a wide range of discrimination and human rights violations as a result of deliberate policies or simple neglect. After fleeing the effects of armed conflicts, generalised violence or human rights violations, IDPs often failed to find security and safety in the place of displacement. In 26 countries, IDPs moved to areas where they still faced attacks and violence, which in most cases specifically targeted their settlements. In 14 countries, government forces or associated armed groups were among the main perpetrators. Attacks and violence were also perpetrated against IDPs in countries where international peacekeeping operations were deployed with specific mandates to provide protection to IDPs and returnees, as in Chad and the Central African Republic (CAR), Côte d'Ivoire, DRC and Sudan.

In eight countries (Ethiopia, Indonesia (in Papua), Israel (including in OPT), Myanmar, Sudan (Darfur), Turkmenistan, Uzbekistan and Zimbabwe), the displacement of some four million IDPs was not acknowledged by the national authorities. IDPs faced particular problems in maintaining livelihoods as a result of their displacement. In almost half of the countries monitored, IDPs were deprived of access to livelihoods, and many remained dependent on assistance from host communities or humanitarian organisations. This made them particularly vulnerable in

> situations of protracted displacement where humanitarian assistance was declining and development plans had not yet been implemented. In several countries, displaced children were particularly at risk of abduction and forced recruitment into armed groups. Displaced women and children were also exposed to serious risks of sexual and gender-based violence and abuses, for which perpetrators generally enjoyed impunity. In addition, many displaced women were unable to access essential reproductive health services, due to prohibitive fees, lack of health care infrastructure or insecurity. Elderly people were among the most vulnerable IDPs and lacked support to assert their rights. Inadequate housing, insufficient access to healthcare and loss of income seriously affected their ability to achieve durable solutions in safety and with dignity.
>
> Ethnic minorities were among the main groups affected by internal displacement. In at least 36 countries, ethnic minorities were forcibly displaced, as a mechanism to eliminate them or their claims for recognition or autonomy, to access natural resources in their collective territories or because they were caught up in external conflicts.

The very large and sudden population movements caused by conflict have tended to overshadow smaller, usually less visible movements of people. Many countries that have been free of large-scale civil conflict have shockingly high levels of population displacement. There are a least 451,000 IDPs in Myanmar (Burma) today, for example, largely as a result of the authoritarian government's policies of forced resettlement. Of the many kinds of population movements that occur worldwide, we can draw particular attention to episodes of forced evictions. Forced evictions are illegal under international law when they contravene due process requirements (such as adequate notice and genuine consultation before the evictions), and hence contravene the ban on "arbitrary deprivation" and the rights to adequate housing enshrined in the Universal Declaration of Human Rights. Nonetheless, programs of forced evictions, often affecting the poorest and most vulnerable sectors of society, continue to be approved and implemented by government agencies in many countries.

THE CAUSES OF POPULATION DISPLACEMENT

Paragraph 2 of the Introduction to the Guiding Principles on Internal Displacement define internally displaced persons as:

> Persons or groups of persons who have been forced or obliged to flee or to leave their homes or places of habitual residence, in particular as a result of or in order to avoid the effects of armed conflict, situations of generalised violence, violations of human rights or natural or human-made disasters, and who have not crossed an internationally recognised State border.

Many refugees are forced to flee their homes for the same reasons. In order to quality for refugee status, individuals have to show a well-founded fear of being persecuted. Such refugees are differentiated from migrants who are primarily concerned with economic opportunities in the host country.

Most displacement-causing conflicts are internal in nature rather than interstate.[5] The causes of conflicts are multiple and often complex. The driving forces that cause and sustain violence may change over time, so that different issues become seen as prominent causes of violence, or obstacles to peace, depending on the time frame concerned. As noted by the former Secretary General of the United Nations Kofi Annan, conflicts have "political, social, cultural, economic, environmental and other structural causes that often underlie the immediate symptoms of armed conflicts."[6] Common root causes of conflict include the marginalization of specific sections of society from political and social decision-making processes, for example, on the basis of ethnic background, religious affiliation, or some other marker of identity. Extreme economic inequality is also associated with conflict. Poverty is a key issue: the poorest one-sixth of the world's population experiences four-fifths of all conflicts.[7] As mentioned in Chapter 1, control over housing, land, and property rights can be part of this process of marginalization, with certain identity groups being prevented from exercising or securing their rights to land, housing, natural resources, and other property. Unfortunately, it is difficult for war-torn countries to pull themselves fully out of cycles of violence. Research suggests that about half of all countries that experience conflict will fall back into warfare within a decade of peace being declared. The work of the first UN Special Representative on Internally Displaced Persons Francis Deng contributed greatly to an enhanced awareness of these issues at the global level. The excerpt that follows describes some of the causes and the dynamics of the global displacement crisis.

Roberta Cohen and Francis Mading Deng (1998) *Masses in Flight: The Global Crisis of Internal Displacement*, Brookings Institution.

Of the world's populations at risk, internally displaced persons tend to be the most desperate. They may be forcibly resettled on political or ethnic grounds or find themselves trapped in the midst of conflicts and in the direct path of armed attack and physical violence. On the run and without documents, they are easy targets for roundups, arbitrary detention, forced conscription, and sexual assaults. Uprooted from their homes and deprived of their resource base, many suffer from profound physical and psychological trauma.... Several factors contributed to it becoming a subject of international concern. One was the growing number of

5 In many cases, however, "civil wars" will involve the direct or indirect intervention of foreign states.

6 Secretary General of the United Nations (2003) *Interim Report of the Secretary General on the Prevention of Armed Conflict*, General Assembly of the United Nations.

7 Chris Huggins and Jenny Clover, (2005) "Introduction," in Huggins and Clover (eds.).

internally displaced persons. A first counting in 1982 found 1.2 million in eleven countries. By 1997 more than 20 million were reported in thirty-five to forty countries. The main reason for this increase was internal conflict, which became far more prevalent than interstate wars in the post-cold war era … another important factor in bringing displacement to the fore was the ending of the cold war. When the superpowers were engaged in proxy wars as in Afghanistan, Angola and El Salvador, the internal displacement produced by these struggles received little or no attention. Whatever political advantage may have existed lay in supporting refugees of these conflicts […]

It was only when these geopolitical struggles began to wane that the plight of those caught within their own borders by civil wars and other forms of internal strife came into full view and were recognized as requiring international humanitarian attention. The cold war's end facilitated access to countries no longer "protected" by one superpower or another. There also came to be growing acceptance of the idea that events taking place within a state are a legitimate subject of international concern. The international human rights movement had long championed the view that human rights violations transcend frontiers and that when governments fail to meet their obligations under the UN Charter, they should be held accountable by the international community. Humanitarian organizations also began to insist that when governments denied access to populations at risk, the international community should find ways of providing assistance … The displacement issue has become more prominent also because of the realization that peace and reconstruction in war-torn societies depend in part on the effective reintegration of displaced persons […]

Increased attention to the problem of internal displacement, however, has not made it more tractable. Unlike wars between nations, civil wars, particularly when they divide countries along racial, ethnic, linguistic, or religious lines, do not resolve themselves easily or neatly. Often they recur and may persist for long periods because they leave deep wounds within the society. Many conflicts that produce mass displacement are between governments and minorities or among different ethnic groups. Often, they are incited by political leaders seeking to gain or consolidate power. Competition for scarce economic resources, resulting in disparities among different groups and the marginalization of some, also has been a significant factor contributing to the civil strife bringing about displacement … Wars within states often reflect a crisis of national identity in a society that occurs when a state becomes monopolized by and identified with the dominant group or groups to the exclusion or marginalisation of others, who are thereby denied the protection and assistance that a state owes its citizens. The displaced are perceived as the "enemy," either through their association with an insurgent group, an opposing political or ideological tendency, or more generally with an ethnic, cultural, religious or social group considered inferior, threatening, or simply, "other." The cleavages generated between the affected population and the government or controlling authorities force the displaced into a vacuum of responsibility, which often makes international involvement necessary.... conflicts rooted in racial, ethnic or religious issues frequently make displacement a weapon and sometimes even their goal. Access to internally displaced populations may be further complicated by the different manifestations of displacement. In some countries internally displaced persons cluster in camps or settlements, which may be reachable to outside assistance. In other countries they may disperse so as to avoid identification, which makes access more difficult. Or they may merge into local communities, where gaining access to them may require the development of special community-based approaches [...]

Since the late 1980s enormous progress has been made in meeting the challenges posed by humanitarian emergencies. An array of UN agencies, humanitarian organizations, and nongovernmental organizations (NGOs) have come forward to provide protection, assistance, and development aid when governments have been unable or unwilling to meet their responsibilities ... none of these organizations, however, has a global mandate to protect and assist the internally displaced. Their action is ad hoc. As various agencies pick and choose the situations in which they wish to become involved, many internally displaced persons may thus be neglected.... Furthermore, reintegration and development support have received insufficient consideration [...]

The number of civilians affected during instances of conflict has risen dramatically as the nature of conflict has changed over the past century. In earlier conflicts, the majority of casualties tended to be military personnel, with a smaller number of civilians killed or injured. In most modern conflicts, some 90 percent of casualties are civilians. In some cases, civilians are affected due to the indiscriminate use of force; in others, they are directly targeted. Ethnic cleansing, involving the forced displacement of ethnic groups, has been a feature of conflict in many parts of the world. The targeting of civilians or their property is a war crime, and international tribunals are increasingly successful at prosecuting those responsible. The case of Iraq, described in the excerpt below, presents a particularly tragic combination of factors that has resulted in large-scale population displacement over the last several decades.

Nigel Thomson (2009) "The Development of a Property Restitution System in 'Post'-Conflict Circumstances," in Scott Leckie (ed.), *Housing, Land and Property Rights in Post-Conflict United Nations and Other Peace Operations*, Cambridge University Press.

In recent Iraqi history, human rights abuses connected to HLP issues are as complex as they are continuous. The background given here provides only an impression of that complexity. While this commentary primarily looks at responses to HLP issues from March 2003, the time of the occupation of Iraq by a coalition of foreign forces, it necessarily draws upon the deeper history of Iraq's human rights abuses.

In particular, the last four decades in Iraq have been witness to a series of events involving the death and displacement of many Iraqis and the destruction of their properties. In many cases, these abuses have been caused by Iraqi government actions against its own people. These abuses flew in the face of Iraq's obligations under international law; in particular the Universal Declaration of Human Rights.[8] But there were a number of other specific international instruments that Iraq became party to and then subsequently violated. The instruments that either directly or indirectly enshrine housing, land and property rights; include:

- International Covenant on Economic, Social and Cultural Rights
- Convention on the Elimination of All Forms of Discrimination Against Women
- Convention on the Elimination of All Forms of Racial Discrimination
- International Covenant on Civil and Political Rights
- Convention on the Rights of the Child[9]

Others have suffered too during this period; in particular, Iranians and Kuwaitis. Yet, we can see the seeds of displacement and dispossession leading back even further to the colonial 'carve-up' of the Middle East decades earlier in the wake of World War I and various colonial political agendas. But it is also true to say that problems relating to border issues in the region can be traced back centuries.

In 1979, Saddam Hussein formally became President of Iraq, with the support of the Ba'athist Party (which itself dominated Iraq from the time of a second *coup detat* in 1968). From that time until Hussein's removal by a coalition of US-led foreign forces in 2003, he led a ruthless dictatorship that made war against Iraq's neighbours Iran (from September 1980 until August 1988) and later Kuwait (during 1990). As a result of his war against Iran there may have been as many as 1 million casualties.[10] There were also many Iraqis displaced along Iraq's border with Iran, and many of those displaced remain so today; occupying areas around Karbala and other parts of the country.[11] In addition to these external conflicts, Saddam presided over attacks against his own citizens, predominantly Shi'ites in the southern half of Iraq and Kurds[12] in the north during the "Anfal" campaign from 1987 to 1989. As a result of the Anfal campaign the number of killed and displaced is hard to measure. Figures vary considerably but perhaps as many as 100,000 non-combatants[13] were killed (including death as a result of the use of chemical weapons; most notably in the Kurdish town

[8] In the context of housing, land, and property rights, for example, Article 25(1), and more generally, Article 17.

[9] Although Iraq has not acceded to the Optional Protocols for the International Covenant on Civil and Political Rights, Convention on the Elimination of All Forms of Discrimination Against Women and the Convention on the Rights of the Child.

[10] The actual number of casualties has not been definitively determined and is unlikely to be.

[11] Although their status as IDPs is now probably questionable; many apparently prefer to stay around larger cities, like Karbala in the upper south, than return, for example, to the marshes of southern Iraq.

[12] Not only Kurds were singled out in this campaign. Other minorities such as Yezidis, Assyrians, and Chaldean Christians were also targeted. See: *Genocide in Iraq*, 1993, Human Rights Watch, http://hrw.org/reports/1993/iraqanfal/ANFALINT.htm (accessed 11 May 2006).

[13] Id. HRW suggests between 50,000 and possibly 100,000.

of Halabja[14]) and the displacement or forced relocation of many more. In additional, many (perhaps almost 2,000 villages[15]) were razed. In 2001, a UN Habitat Report[16] indicated that there were approximately 805,505 internally displaced persons (IDPs) (141,234 families) in the Kurdish Autonomous Region in northern Iraq. As part of the Anfal campaign, southern Arabs were often paid to move into areas cleared of Kurds and other minorities in a process known as "Arabization."

As a result of the Iraq invasion of Kuwait, in 1990, International forces under a United Nations mandate[17] forcibly removed Iraqi forces and, in the wake of Iraqi military attacks on Shi'ites in southern Iraq and Kurds and other minorities in the north, "no fly" zones were imposed.[18] In the north, the "Kurdish" regional government was beset with political infighting between 1994 and 1997 which led to armed conflict and further dispossession within that region. As at 2001, some persons that were displaced during that period of internal conflict remain so today.

As a result of international concerns about Iraq's non-compliance with UN Security Council Resolutions relating to the possible development of chemical and other weapons, and inspection of nominated sites, a US-dominated international coalition of countries (without specific UN Security Council authorization) invaded Iraq on 20 March 2003. Saddam Hussein fled and the "Coalition" established a transitional government.[19] Although the initial invasion by Coalition forces was relatively swift, there were considerable numbers of IDPs that resulted. Some of these were as a direct result of the Coalition invasion and others, indirectly, when, for example, some communities in northern Iraq, returned to their former homes (from which they were displaced in the 1980s) and forced the 'new' secondary occupants out (often those brought in as part of the "Arabization" process). Thus, the result was a wave a secondary displaced persons.

14 Id. Not strictly part of the Anfal campaign.

15 Id. As many as 4,000 Kurdish villages may have been destroyed since 1975.

16 UN Habitat, 2001, *IDP Site and Family Survey Final Report* (UN Habitat Report) at Table 2.2. The Report indicates that at the time of the survey, 14,033 families were displaced as a result of the Kurdish in-fighting and 2,763 families remained displaced as a result of conflict with the PKK (Refer to Table 2.2 of the UN Habitat Report).

17 Iraq's failure to comply with UNSCR 678 (29 November 1990) triggered the response.

18 These "no-fly zones" were supposed to prevent the Iraqi Air Force from attacking Shi'ites in the South and Kurdish and other minorities in the north. The zones were not sanctioned by specific UN Security Council Resolution, and their legal legitimacy was disputed by Iraq and other countries. The United States and the United Kingdom, however, relied on UNSCR 688 (5 April 1991) that "2. Demands that Iraq, as a contribution to remove the threat to international peace and security in the region, immediately end this repression and express the hope in the same context that an open dialogue will take place to ensure that the human and political rights of all Iraqi citizens are respected.

19 This was recognized by the United Nations Security Council Resolution 1483 (2003), 22 May 2003, which stipulated: "*Noting* the letter of 8 May 2003 from the Permanent Representatives of the United States of America and the United Kingdom of Great Britain and Northern Ireland to the President of the Security Council (S/2003/538) and recognizing the specific authorities, responsibilities, and obligations under applicable international law of these states as occupying powers under unified command (the 'Authority')."

> Displacements continue within Iraq with Iraqi refugees and IDPs now numbering almost five million. An 'insurgency' probably composed of disparate groups with differing motivations (including some foreign fighters and purely criminal elements) has led to the development of local, sometimes sectarian militias that have embarked on a spate of attacks and killings apparently motivated by religious persuasion. These killings (or the threat of violence) have caused the further displacement of many Iraqis along sectarian lines. As a result, there is evidence of Sunni Moslems moving from largely Shi'ite Moslem areas and *vice versa*.[20] Existing refugee communities are also under pressure. Palestinian refugees, particularly in Baghdad, have become the target of evictions, intimidation and violence[21] that is forcing many to leave their homes and try to cross borders in to Jordan and Syria often without success […]

It is important to note that there is rarely only a single cause of displacement: Although decision makers often categorize events as, for example, : development-induced displacement" or "conflict- induced displacement," these terms conceal as much as they reveal. Indeed, some scholars have critiqued the familiar terminology used in policy circles because it oversimplifies a remarkably diverse reality and undermines the important issue of agency on the part of the people in question.[22] In reality, the various causes of displacement are often interlinked.[23] For example, displacement due to "environmental change" or "natural disaster" has also been caused by human-made processes, such as the socioeconomic structures that result in poor populations inhabiting marginal areas, or the failure of states and communities to put adequate safeguards in place. Climatic events and other phenomena are likely to have a much more serious impact in conflict-disasters.

The following excerpt from a report on displacement in Burma illustrates the ways in which conflict, state actions justified under a rubric of "development," and so-called economic or environmental motivations are, in fact, interrelated.

> ***Displacement and Dispossession: Forced Migration and Land Rights in Burma*, COHRE, 2007.**
>
> For many Burmese citizens, patterns of migration often involve extended periods spent as migrant workers in other countries. There are at least two million migrant workers and their dependents in Thailand, most of whom come from Burma.

[20] Meeting with Chief of Mission, IOM, and the author in Amman on 2 May 2006.

[21] See UNHCR press release of April 4, 2006 at: http://www.unhcr.org/cgi-bin/texis/vtx/news/opendoc.htm?tbl=NEWS&id=4432474b4&page=news (accessed 11 May 2006). According to UNHCR, there are about 34,000 Palestinian refugees in Iraq, with about 24,000 registered with the Agency (refer to May 2 press release at http://www.unhcr.org/cgi-bin/texis/vtx/news/opendoc.htm?tbl=NEWS&id=4457314d1c&page=news (accessed 11 May 2006).

[22] See e.g., David Turton, *Conceptualising Forced Migration*, Refugee Studies Centre Working Paper No. 12. University of Oxford. 2003.

[23] Catherine Brun. Forced Migration Online Research.

Hundreds of thousands more Burmese migrants live in Bangladesh, Malaysia and Singapore. These people often endure very poor social and working conditions. The causes and other aspects of population movements *within* Burma (internal migration) and *beyond* its borders (external migration) are closely linked – and related to serious and systematic abuses of HLP and other basic rights. People who migrate in order to seek livelihoods security are usually categorised as 'economic migrants', although their reasons for moving are often similar to those of IDPs, as defined in the Guiding Principles – or in the case of crossborder migrants, refugees. Aspects of livelihoods vulnerability-induced 'economic migration' (i.e. population movement which is primarily due to people's inability to sustain livelihoods in their original location) – within and from – Burma should therefore be considered forms of 'forced migration' – usually with the State as the primary agent of displacement, due to its failure to provide good governance and services in rural areas.

Typology of displacement

Three broad, 'ideal types' can be identified within the spectrum of forced migration in Burma. These 'types' are defined according to the root causes of population movement: armed conflict; State-society conflict (man-made disasters, including military occupation and 'development'); and livelihoods vulnerability (including natural disasters).

- **Type 1: Armed conflict-induced displacement** either as a direct consequence of fighting and counter-insurgency operations (e.g. forced relocation), or because armed conflict has directly undermined human and food security. Type 1 displacement is linked to severe human rights abuses across Karen State, in eastern Tenasserim Division, southern Mon State, southern and eastern Karenni (Kayah) State, southern Shan State, and parts of Chin State and Sagaing Division. A certain amount of quantitative data is available for Type 1 IDPs in eastern Burma.
- **Type 2: Military occupation – and 'development'- induced (state-society conflict induced) displacement**: generally caused, post-armed conflict, by land confiscation by the *Tatmadaw* or other armed groups, including in the context of natural resource extraction (e.g. logging and mining); displacement due to infrastructure construction (e.g. roads, bridges, airports); also forced migration as a product of predatory taxation, forced labour and other abuses. While this form of displacement is characterised by the use of force, it is not the result of outright armed conflict. All of the border states and divisions are affected by militarisation and/or 'development'-induced displacement. This includes Arakan (Rakhine) and Kachin States, as well as a number of urban areas, (including displacement in the context of tourism development and 'urban renewal').

Both displacement types are products of conflict: Type 1 is directly caused by armed conflict; Type 2 is caused by latent conflict, or the threat of the use of force. As such, they constitute forced migration, and cause internal displacement (as defined in the Guiding Principles).

- **Type 3: Livelihoods vulnerability-induced displacement** is the primary form of internal and external migration in and from Burma (and many other developing countries). The main causes are inappropriate government policies and practices, limited availability of productive land, and poor access to markets, resulting in food insecurity; lack of education and health services; plus stresses associated with transition to a cash economy. Type 3 population movements describe a particularly vulnerable sub-group of economic migrants, and are the product of the very limited choices available to marginal populations in rural and urban areas. As such, they constitute a form of forced migration (or 'distress migration'). Migration due to opium eradication policies is included under Type 3, because the approximate causes of movement are related to livelihoods issues – i.e. (with the important exception of some War areas), people are not ordered to move. However, opium eradication-induced migration could also be considered under Type 2 forced migration, due to the forcible nature of the opium bans, the severe shock to livelihoods involved, and the links to development activities [...]

THE RIGHT TO HOUSING FOR IDPS AT THE NATIONAL LEVEL

Brookings Institute (2008) *Protecting Internally Displaced Persons: A Manual for Law and Policymakers*, Brookings Institute – University of Bern, Project on Internal Displacement.

Checklist: Issues to be Addressed by Domestic Laws and Policies

Minimum essential elements of state regulation

At a minimum, competent authorities should do the following:

Recognise the right to basic shelter and adequate housing for IDPs.

Designate a governmental agency responsible for addressing shelter and housing needs of displaced persons.

Seek and accept support from the international community if needs cannot be sufficiently satisfied at the domestic level.

Establish procedures to identify and prioritise beneficiaries of basic shelter and adequate housing on the basis of need and particular vulnerability.

Remove legal obstacles as contained, for example, in building and similar codes, for the construction of transitional shelters or the rebuilding of houses in return or relocation areas.

Create specific guarantees to protect IDPs against forced evictions when general guarantees are insufficient.

In order to ensure that IDPs can exercise their right to basic shelter and adequate housing during displacement, domestic laws and policies should:

- recognize the right to adequate housing and designate responsibility to relevant authorities to ensure, and where necessary, provide adequate shelter and housing to the displaced;
- incorporate housing issues in national coordination mechanisms, facilitating international technical assistance and empowering local government responses;
- take into account IDPs' pre-displacement and current housing traditions, practices, and needs;
- build on consultation of IDPs on their housing needs and their participation in the design of programs and services to help them meet these needs, taking into account their pre-displacement housing practices;
- assist IDPs in the emergency stage of displacement in moving themselves and their possessions to safe areas where emergency shelter is available or provided;
- provide IDPs with transitional shelter pending reconstruction or safe access to their homes in cases where rapid return is possible. Design transitional housing in grouped settlements in consultation with IDPs so as to minimize protection risks and maximize adequacy.
- provide IDPs and local host communities with appropriate assistance, allowing them to self-settle in places of their choice under adequate housing conditions, wherever possible, in cases where rapid return is not possible
- provide grouped transitional shelter in settlements that are located in safe areas with access to humanitarian aid distribution, as well as social, educational, medical facilities, and employment and livelihood opportunities in situations in which neither return nor self-settlement with host families or host communities is possible;
- provide for allocation of abandoned housing to shelter IDPs only when demonstrably necessary as a last resort on the basis of exploration of all other possible options and on an explicitly temporary basis;
- design all housing assistance to IDPs so as not only to maximize current adequacy but also to facilitate voluntary durable solutions;
- protect IDPs against forced eviction;
- provide appropriate assistance to IDPs to allow them to find adequate and sustainable housing solutions in the context of re-integration.

Similarly, the UN Development Group has issued a Guidance Note outlining the various types of durable solutions that can be pursued to assist refugees, IDPs, and returnees to resolve their predicaments caused by forced displacement.

UN Development Group Programme Group (2004) *UNDG Guidance Note on Durable Solutions for Displaced Persons (refugees, internally displaced persons, and returnees)*, UNDG.

I. Durable Solutions for Displaced Persons

Responsibility for identifying and implementing durable solutions programmes for displaced persons lies first and foremost with national authorities. It is important, therefore, that national development strategies and plans include the necessary provisions to achieve those aims. The role of the UNCT is to assist the national authorities in meeting the national development goals and in implementing programming for displaced persons and their host communities, including in areas related to attaining the MDGs, poverty reduction, capacity building and resource mobilization.

The Millennium Declaration emphasizes protecting the vulnerable and states the goal: "[T]o strengthen international cooperation, including burden-sharing in and the coordination of humanitarian assistance to countries hosting refugees, and to help all refugees and displaced persons to return voluntarily to their homes in safety and dignity and to be smoothly reintegrated into their societies."[24] The Millennium Development Goals target the most vulnerable, a category within which displaced populations fall. To attain the MDGs at the county level for the population, it is important that displaced persons are included into the national strategies and programmes.

Efforts are underway to develop coherent UN strategies in specific areas. The UN has adopted a collaborative response toward situations of internal displacement whereby a broad range of humanitarian, human rights and development actors work together in a transparent and cooperative manner.[25] For countries emerging from conflict, the programming tool 4Rs (repatriation, reintegration, rehabilitation and reconstruction) has been developed.[26] The follow-up to the report of the UNDG/ECHA working group on transition issues foresees the development of guidance to UNCTs on a UN transition strategy, based upon a joint needs assessment and resource mobilization strategy, which includes the needs of displaced persons.[27]

24 General Assembly, *United Nations Millennium Declaration*, A/RES/55/2, 18 September 2000.

25 Inter-Agency Standing Committee, Implementing the Collaborative Response to Situations of Internal Displacement: Guidance for UN Humanitarian and Resident Coordinators and Country Teams, Draft, May 2004. IASC, Policy on the Protection of Internally Displaced Persons, December 1999. Based on the collaborative approach and in consultation with the UNCT, the RC/HC oversees the development of a *Strategic Action Plan* for responding in a comprehensive and effective manner to the assistance and protection needs of the displaced.

26 UNHCR, Framework for Durable Solutions for Refuges and Persons of Concern, Geneva, May 2003.

27 UNDG/ECHA Working Group on Transition Issues, *Report of the UNDG/ECHA Working Group on Transition Issues*, February 2004.

This Note complements the guidance offered in these strategies. However, whereas the aforementioned focus primarily upon the emergency/humanitarian and transition phases, this Note focuses on the contribution that development actors can make specifically through the CCA/UNDAF process.

Population of Concern

The guidance focuses on people forcibly displaced within (internally displaced persons) and/or outside (refugees) their country as a consequence of violent conflict, human rights violations and persecution, and on people who return to their country or community of origin following a peace agreement or settlement (returnees). In addition, there are also other displaced population groups, such as people expelled or displaced by natural disasters, who may benefit from the guidance provided in this Note.[28]

Equal attention should be given to the needs of the host communities. While the burden of hosting displaced persons is often clear, the opportunities it presents are frequently underemphasized. Therefore, the needs of the host community and displaced persons should be considered collectively, while taking into account specific issues and circumstances that displaced persons may face.

Protection

Solutions for displaced persons may only be called "durable" if they receive the full and effective protection of the State of nationality (citizens) or residence and enjoy all basic human rights and have equal access to social services and economic opportunities. Basic protection standards are contained in international humanitarian law, international and regional human rights instruments, and the Refugee Convention.[29] With regard to internally displaced persons, these international legal standards have been consolidated in the Guiding Principles on Internal Displacement.[30]

[28] In many situations, people may be displaced due to a combination of different reasons that cannot be easily distinguished. In addition, people may be expelled to their country of origin from a country to which they migrated. Although they are considered to be nationals of their country of origin, they may have similar reintegration needs to those of returning refugees and IDPs.

[29] See Annex 5 for a list of key international and regional instruments relating to displaced persons. Persons fleeing a country and seeking refugee (protection) status and/or asylum elsewhere can benefit from international protection based on the aforementioned international and regional human rights and refugee instruments. The international legal regime benefiting internally displaced persons is significantly different. Although IDPs have not crossed an international border and do not, therefore, receive protection under the Refugee Convention, they are protected by relevant domestic legislation, as well as by international human rights law and, in situations of armed conflict, international humanitarian law.

[30] Drawing on international humanitarian and human rights law, as well as refugee law by analogy, the Guiding Principles on Internal Displacement identify the rights and guarantees relevant to internally displaced persons. The Principles were presented to the UN Commission on Human Rights in 1998 and have since become the established framework for describing the rights of the internally displaced. The responsibility for assisting, protecting, and identifying durable solutions for IDPs lies with the national and regional authorities. When these authorities are unable and/or unwilling to meet their

Displaced persons may face specific protection concerns, such as the continued threat of violence and discrimination on account of their ethnicity, restricted access to social services and economic rights (e.g. health and education, land and property, and gainful employment), restrictions on their ability to vote and participate in public affairs, or recognition of citizenship (statelessness). During the emergency and transition phases, they may also have experienced serious human rights violations, (e.g. physical violence, including sexual abuse and exploitation, torture, and forced return to a situation where they may have faced persecution, etc.). These and other specific protection concerns, as well as the need to address their consequences, must be incorporated in the design and implementation of durable solution strategies.

Durable Solutions

There are three broad types of policy options/responses to facilitate the transition from displacement to integration/re-integration:

1) **Voluntary** return and re-integration of displaced persons to their country and/or community of origin. This is the most desirable option.
2) The **integration** of displaced persons into new host communities in their country of nationality (IDPs) or of asylum (refugees) is an option to be considered seriously where voluntary return is not feasible within a reasonable time frame, in order to prevent displacement situations from becoming intractable and unmanageable.
3) **Integration (resettlement) in third countries** of displaced persons. This is only feasible for a relatively small number of persons each year according to well-established criteria.[31]

II. The Common Country Assessment (CCA)

When appropriate, the CCA should include an analysis of the causes of the population displacement and its impact upon the poverty and other development challenges facing the country, especially the persistence, severity and scope of the displacement.[32] Particular attention should also be given to any negative trends as well as opportunities to integrate displaced persons into host communities

responsibility, international humanitarian organizations have the right to offer their services in support of national efforts.

31 UNHCR Resettlement Handbook, July 2002.

32 Various tools are available to UNCTs to analyze the causes and impact of population displacement. For countries emerging from conflict, the conflict-related development analysis (CDA) may be of particular relevance as it follows three major stages: First, analysis of causes of conflict (i.e. causes, interest, triggers, and chains); second, analysis of the responses to conflict; and third, comparing causes with responses and drawing strategic and program conclusions from them. UNDP, Bureau for Crisis Prevention and Recovery (BCPR), *Conflict related Development Analysis (CDA)*, Working Document, July 2003. For a review of the various methodologies see Annex 3 in GTZ, *Report: Review and Analysis: Needs Assessments in Post-Conflict Situations*, prepared for the UNDP, UNDG and World Bank, April 2004.

A multitude of causes can lead to displacement. In addition to more immediate ones, such as violent conflict, persecution, serious human rights abuses, and natural disasters, attention should be given to the root causes, such as exclusion and inequality among groups, competition for access to natural resources and discriminatory policies and practices.

Opportunities to solve displacement situations can be seized through various channels, such as:

- Negotiating peace agreements and amnesties;
- Promoting self-reliance and poverty reduction strategies;
- Increasing respect for human rights and the rule of law, including rights at work;
- Enhancing participation in the institutions and processes of governance; and
- Promoting justice, tolerance and reconciliation among divided communities.

Data collection and analysis is the first step in ensuring a coherent analysis in the context of the CCA. However, existing data collection on displaced persons and host communities is geared toward shorter-term relief-recovery activities.[33] Due attention should, therefore, be given to collecting and analyzing data relevant to implementing durable solutions strategies.[34] Among the key variables are:

- **Demographic data**: to establish a profile (including a gender and age breakdown) of the displaced population and the host community, to identify vulnerable populations (e.g. the disabled, female-headed households, and separated children), and to assess the priorities of the displaced persons and the host communities;
- **Socio-economic data**: to understand the livelihood and assess/prioritize the needs of the host community in relation to, e.g., access to land and natural resources, skills requirement, employment and income generating opportunities, the environment, housing, health and education infrastructure, and farming systems;
- **Protection data**: to identify gaps in the protection of human rights and identify specific protection issues, e.g. the legal status of displaced persons (residence permits, nationality), the presence of discriminatory regulations and practices (freedom of movement, right to return, property ownership); and continued threat of violence, restricted access to social services, economic rights, and to participate in public affairs; and

33 UNHCR publishes regular statistics and profiles of refugees and other persons of concern to its Office. The Humanitarian Information Centre, managed by OCHA, collects detailed information in emergency situations. The Norwegian Refugee Council manages a detailed information system on internally displaced persons. UNRWA publishes data on Palestinian refugees.

34 Planning for durable solutions of displaced persons is often hampered by insufficient information about when and where people will return to. The setting-up of an effective data collection system can also serve as an early warning system.

- **Institutional data**: to assess the capacity of the national and local authorities as well as civil society to implement a durable solutions strategy.

Based upon an analysis of the causes for displacement, the opportunities for a solution, and the available data, the UNCT should undertake an assessment of the impact of displaced persons and of a durable solutions strategy upon the other development challenges/priorities identified, in particular upon cross-cutting issues such as human rights, gender equality, employment and the environment. At the same time, the UNCT should ensure that the other development challenges/priorities take into account the needs of the displaced and their host communities.

III. UNDAF – Strategic Planning for Durable Solutions

When developing strategies to address displacement, several operational gaps need to be overcome. These include:

- **Institutional**: Among international agencies and government institutions different operating modalities and cultures exist.
- **Financial**: Funding is often **either** for emergency/humanitarian **or** development assistance.
- **Temporal**: Gaps can appear immediately after a crisis subsides and widen when emergency assistance declines and before long-term development activities begin.
- **Different programme formulation processes and budgeting cycles**: Whereas development partners use multi-year planning and budgeting cycles, humanitarian actors work with shorter-term perspectives and tools.

Harmonizing and simplifying the sometimes disparate interventions of humanitarian and development actors can be better achieved through joint assessments, results-based programming, and undertaking joint resource mobilization strategies as well as monitoring and evaluations.[35]

Although each situation is unique and must be analyzed and tailored according to the specific circumstances, planning and implementation strategies should be:

- **Integrated**, emphasizing the linkages among the emergency/humanitarian, transition and development phases. Isolated interventions in a single or even a few sectors or focusing on a specific group of population will not have the desired impact/outcome. It also requires that programmes focusing on displaced persons and their host communities are harmonized to avoid discrepancies and tensions, which can be achieved through a joint planning and implementation strategy among UNCT agencies.
- **Participatory**, through providing the displaced persons and their host communities with the necessary tools to make their own decisions.

[35] UNDG, Guidance Note on Joint Programming, October 2003.

- **Community-based**, ensuring that the needs of the community as a whole are addressed to reduce the stigma of the 'displaced person' label and to share responsibilities for hosting/integrating displaced populations.
- **Encouraging self-reliance**, to reduce dependency upon external assistance through developing technical, entrepreneurial and organizational skills to assist the community as a whole and to promote income-generating initiatives that enable displaced persons to contribute to the development of the host country.

A framework for durable solutions

Based upon operational experiences, three approaches have been developed to facilitate strategic planning for durable solutions.[36]

- Pending the identification and implementation of durable solutions, development programmes should promote self-reliance for displaced persons through emphasizing capacity building and empowerment. Such policies will prepare the displaced for their eventual return and integration, as well as alleviate the burden on – and, where applicable, reduce the poverty of – the host communities.
- Return is the most desirable solution, but integrated approaches are essential to link shorter-term humanitarian relief with longer-term development strategies, as well as the four different phases of repatriation, reintegration, rehabilitation, and reconstruction.[37]
- For the displaced for whom return is not an option, local integration into their host communities should be considered. Local integration of long-term displaced persons is often a very complex and sensitive issue, but one that, can be eased by applying self-reliance strategies (see bullet above). The socio-economic and political dimensions need to be carefully assessed.

Pursuing any of the three approaches requires careful assessment of the role various actors. Ownership and active engagement by the national/local Government is critical. As the timing of the CCA/UNDAF process is being aligned with the formulation of national development plans and the PRSP, concerted efforts should be made to incorporate durable solutions for displaced persons into these instruments[38]

FORCED EVICTIONS

Forced eviction occurs when people are involuntarily removed from their homes or land directly or indirectly owing to the actions of the State. The UN Committee on

36 Interagency programs have been initiated in Afghanistan, Armenia, Burundi, Eritrea, Liberia, Serbia and Montenegro, Sierra Leone, Sri Lanka, Uganda, and Zambia, among others. Similar programs will be developed in Angola, Ecuador, Somalia, Sudan, and Tanzania.

37 For a practical example of a detailed checklist of activities that a UNCT need to consider, see Annex 3: Iraq Reconstruction Needs Assessment: Checklist for Reintegration.

38 UNDG (2003) Guidance Note: UN Country Team Engagement in PRSPs, UNDG.

Economic, Social and Cultural Rights defines forced eviction as "the permanent or temporary removal against their will of individuals, families and/or communities from the homes and/or land which they occupy, without the provision of, and access to, appropriate forms of legal or other protection."[39] Forced eviction includes cases where individuals, families, or groups are resettled to other areas with state assistance. States have given various reasons for the forcible eviction of their citizens, such as the clearing or so-called "upgrading" of low-income informal housing; the flooding of inhabited areas due to the creation of dams for hydroelectric power generation or other purposes; or the protection of the environment. Whatever the reasons given, forced evictions are almost always in breach of international law. The Committee on Economic, Social and Cultural Rights has devoted considerable attention to forced evictions and has asserted that "instances of forced eviction are *prima facie* incompatible with the requirements of the [International Covenant on Economic, Social and Cultural Rights] and can only be justified in the most exceptional circumstances, and in accordance with the relevant principles of international law."[40] Even in situations where it may be necessary to impose limitations on citizen's property rights, full compliance with article 4 of the International Covenant on Economic, Social and Cultural Rights is required so that any limitations imposed must be "determined by law only insofar as this may be compatible with the nature of these [i.e. economic, social and cultural] rights and solely for the purpose of promoting the general welfare in a democratic society."

Regional human rights bodies have supported the ICESCR's ban on forced eviction. In the case of *The Social and Economic Rights Action Center/Center for Economic and Social Rights v. Nigeria*, the African Commission on Human and Peoples' Rights noted:

> At a very minimum, the right to shelter obliges the … government not to destroy the housing of its citizens and not to obstruct efforts by individuals or communities to rebuild lost homes. The State's obligation to respect housing rights requires it, and thereby all of its organs and agents, to abstain from carrying out, sponsoring or tolerating any practice, policy or legal measure violating the integrity of the individual or infringing upon his or her freedom to use those material or other resources available to them in a way they find most appropriate to satisfy individual, family, household or community housing needs […][41]

Victims of forced eviction may not always be treated as IDPs, though in reality they, like those affected by conflict, may have been victims of violence. Some

[39] UN Committee on Economic, Social and Cultural Rights, "The right to adequate housing (art.11.1): forced evictions," General Comment No. 7 (1997), UN Doc. HRI/GEN/1/Rev.7 (1997), para. 3.

[40] General Comment No. 4 (1991) on the right to adequate housing, para. 18.

[41] Cited in Human Rights Watch (2007) *"They Pushed Down the Houses": Forced Evictions and Insecure Land Tenure for Luanda's Urban Poor*, HRW.

element of force or coercion is always threatened or present during forced evictions, which can involve armed elements of the state security apparatus, such as the police or military. However, evictions are illegal if the procedure fails to include adequate safeguards, even if the eviction itself does not involve the threat of force. Victims of forced displacement may find themselves in similar socioeconomic circumstances to IDPs, lacking shelter and access to land.

Forced eviction is perpetrated all over the world, in both developed and developing countries. Massive numbers of people are often affected. The Office of the High Commissioner for Human Rights cites the example of an unnamed West African city, where in 1990, "300,000 people were deprived of their homes and possessions within a matter of hours, receiving no warning, compensation, resettlement or legal redress. They had established the neighbourhood concerned more than 30 years before the eviction took place."[42] More recently in Zimbabwe, the infamous Operation Murambatsvina displaced more than 700,000 men, woman, and children, and left more than 100,000 families homeless.[43] The following case, from Angola, illustrates the brutality that is often involved when state agents forcibly evict citizens from their homes, and the range of human rights provisions that are breached in the process.

Human Rights Watch (2007) *"They Pushed Down the Houses": Forced Evictions and Insecure Land Tenure for Luanda's Urban Poor*, Human Rights Watch.

In Luanda, Angola's capital, the government has forcibly and violently evicted thousands of people living in informal housing areas with little or no notice. In violation of Angola's own laws and its international human rights obligations, the government has destroyed houses, crops and residents' personal possessions without due process and has rarely provided compensation. The evictions have taken place in a city where the majority of the population lives in informal housing areas with lack of clarity over land possession and ownership, and consequent insecurity of land tenure. The victims are poor and vulnerable Angolans. They include women supporting families on their own, elderly persons and children. Many fled to Luanda during the country's long civil war, seeking shelter and protection from conflict zones or from agricultural areas destroyed by fighting and insecurity. The government's large scale evictions have resulted in further displacement and left many individuals homeless and destitute with no access to legal remedy.

[42] Office of the High Commissioner for Human Rights (1996) *Fact Sheet No.25, Forced Evictions and Human Rights*. United Nations.

[43] Sean Romero (2007) "Mass Forced Evictions and the Human Right to Adequate Housing in Zimbabwe" in *Northwestern Journal of International Human Rights*, Volume 5, Issue 2, Northwestern University School of Law.

... 18 mass evictions [were] carried out by the government between 2002 and 2006.... In total, more than 3,000 houses were destroyed and many small-scale cultivated land plots were seized, affecting some 20,000 people ...

Evictees from the evictions researched for this report and SOS staff members who witnessed such evictions told Human Rights Watch that uniformed police officers and local government officials used intimidation, violence, and excessive force when carrying out evictions. Police and government officials often forcibly tried to prevent residents from rescuing their personal belongings from demolition. Evictees described how police officers, sometimes accompanied by members of private security companies, used firearms to intimidate residents, shooting into the air or to the ground. Four residents, including a five-year-old child, were shot at or hit by stray bullets. Many others were beaten with batons and gun butts.

Several residents of neighborhoods where evictions occurred were arbitrarily detained by police, generally for short periods. They were held during and after evictions, sometimes for days, without being informed of the reason for their arrest or the formal charges being brought against them. Many of those arrested told Human Rights Watch that they were physically abused while in police custody. SOS Habitat staff members present during the evictions documented in this report were harassed and sometimes arbitrarily arrested while trying to obtain information about the eviction or simply attempting to explain the evictees' rights to government officials.

In most of the evictions researched by Human Rights Watch and SOS Habitat, the Angolan government provided evictees with little or no information about the purpose of their eviction and the use planned for the land they occupied. The government also failed to discuss with the affected communities possible alternative solutions to their forcible removal. The majority of evictees interviewed by Human Rights Watch did not receive formal notification of their eviction. They described how they were caught unaware by the sudden arrival of police, bulldozers, and trucks to evict them from their land and homes.

In the few situations where the government provided notice of evictions, it failed to allow residents sufficient time before their removal and did not include accurate information about the authority that issued the eviction order, its legal grounds, and the appropriate body for appealing such decisions. In most of the evictions, the Angolan government failed to ascertain whether residents held a formal title or other legal claim to the land they occupied before evicting them.

In addition, the Angolan authorities carried out these forced evictions without a proper and consistent procedure in place to determine the form or amount of compensation to individual evictees. Often compensation was offered to residents after their property and belongings had been destroyed, without the possibility to negotiate the amount in question. The Angolan Government has provided general information on relocation and resettlement sites that it has established for low income families in Luanda. But the government's information has not included precise details on the total number of evictees that received land plots or housing as compensation after evictions from the areas researched by Human Rights Watch and SOS Habitat.

Many evictees who were relocated by the government were not consulted about their removal to a particular site and were often resettled in these new sites unwillingly. The relocation areas were too distant from the evictees' original places of residence and employment. The sites were also not adequately supplied with services, such as transportation, health care, and schools when the evictees arrived. Women and children were particularly affected by the loss of income generating activities in local markets and the disruption to access to education.

To date, the Angolan government has not fully addressed the violations of Angolans' rights documented in this report. The number of evictees today in need of urgent humanitarian assistance is not alarmingly high; however, this is not a result of the Angolan government acting in accordance with the law and providing evictees with necessary assistance. Rather, failing to receive such government assistance, evictees were forced to find their own often inadequate solutions to continue their lives and rebuild shelter elsewhere.

Moreover, the government's conduct in carrying out the evictions documented in this report was in clear violation of its obligations under both international and Angolan law. Angola is a party to the International Covenant on Economic, Social and Cultural Rights (ICESCR). Article 11 of the Covenant establishes the obligation to protect the right to adequate housing, which includes protection against forced evictions. International law recognizes the right for governments to expropriate land from private citizens even without their consent or to forcibly evict residents. However, such measures can only be taken in the most exceptional circumstances, with a clearly identified public interest and with appropriate processes in place.

For a compulsory eviction to comply with international standards, governments must ensure that feasible alternatives are explored and that individuals have a right to compensation for both real estate and personal property. They must also apply minimum procedural protections that include genuine consultation with those affected; adequate and reasonable notice of the date of eviction; timely information on the proposed evictions, including, where possible, the alternative purpose for which the land is to be used; proper identification of the staff carrying out the evictions; and the availability of legal remedies for those affected.

The forced evictions documented in this report and, in many instances, the conduct of police officers and government officials implementing the evictions also involve violations of rights enshrined in the International Covenant on Civil and Political Rights (ICCPR), to which Angola is a party. Rights violated include the right not to be subjected to arbitrary or unlawful interference with one's privacy and home (Article 17), and the right to liberty and security of the person (Article 9)....

In the evictions researched by Human Rights Watch and SOS Habitat, insecure land tenure stemming from the overwhelming informality of housing and land possession, have made many poor Angolans particularly vulnerable to forced evictions. Secure land tenure gives residents clear legal rights against the government or private entities who make competing claims to the land. The UN Committee on Economic, Social and Cultural Rights has stated that irrespective of the type of tenure, all persons should possess a degree of security of tenure that guarantees legal protection against forced evictions, harassment, and other threats.

The excerpt that follows suggests that land tenure reform which may be presented as benefiting indigenous communities, may have negative effects, whether intended or not, on the livelihoods and wider territorial and natural resource rights of indigenous peoples. The concept of land tenure security, in this context, should be carefully interrogated.

Marcus Colchester (2007) *Beyond Tenure: Rights-Based Approaches to Peoples and Forests*, Forest People's Programme (footnotes as from original).

The fundamental importance of land to rural communities has long been recognized by the development community, for example in the endorsement of the FAO's 'Peasants' Charter' by 145 countries in 1979. Recognising that 'the rural poor must be given access to land and water resources', the Charter went on to insist on the need for agrarian reforms to achieve 'broad-based community control and management of land and water rights' ... and programmes 'to ensure the conservation and management of fishery and forestry resources through arrangements involving local communities' [...]

Many land titling programmes fail to take into account forest peoples' customary forms of land management and ownership. Some agrarian reforms have specifically targeted forests, clearing forests for colonists with scant regard for forest peoples' rights. Some agrarian reform programmes in effect parcel up what were customarily owned lands and reallocate them to individuals. Although intended to provide land security and promote development, all too often such individualisation of land leads to the break up of communal lands and accelerate the dispossession of the original owners who, even if they secure titles, as quickly lose them in the land markets which follow.[44] Exactly these problems ensued in the USA with the passing of the General Allotment Act (the notorious 'Dawes Act') in 1887 which led to the loss of some 36 million out of a remaining 56 million hectares of officially recognised indigenous peoples' lands and forests.[45] Most *adivasi* lands

[44] Griffiths (2004), op. cit. footnote 12; Colchester and Lohmann (1993), op. cit. footnote 13.

[45] Angie Debo (1940) *And Still the Waters Run: the Betrayal of the Five Civilized Tribes*, Princeton University Press, Princeton; K. Carter (1999) *The Dawes Commission and the Allotment of the Five Civilized Tribes, 1893–1914*, Ancestry.com, Utah; Charles Wilkinson (2005) *Blood Struggle: The Rise of Modern Indian Nations*, New York: WW Norton and Company, 43–49.

in India have likewise been titled as individual *patta* and, even though laws are meant to prevent the transfer of titles to non-tribals, land markets have led to the loss of much tribal land.[46] In Vietnam, efforts to provide rural people with long-term leaseholds on State lands, while broadly welcomed as an improvement over the stifling conditions of 'collectivisation', have created serious problems for ethnic minorities. As objects of discrimination, targets of corruption and lacking the political connections needed to get titles – as well as lacking fluency in Vietnamese and market savvy – many highlanders have lost out to incoming settlers, condemning them, according to one study, 'to a deplorable existence in more remote areas or to work as landless laborers'. Individualised tenure has not allowed for collective forms of tenure and land management and has been used to disqualify customary land-use systems like swidden agriculture which the State has a policy of eradicating.[47]

In Venezuela, under the 1960 Agrarian Reform Law, title was initially handed out to indigenous peoples as individual lots and, later, was accorded to indigenous communities as communal titles to small pieces of land. The result was to 'peasantise' indigenous peoples' land ownership, reducing their rights to small parts of their once extensive territories and making them vulnerable to land invasion by settlers.[48] In Peru, the law which provides for the titling for so-called 'native communities' likewise has been interpreted as only allowing relatively small land areas to be allotted to indigenous peoples, leading to the break-up of their territories and allowing the government to hand out logging concessions on what are in fact indigenous lands.[49] In Guyana, the government likewise accords title to only small parts of the indigenous peoples' lands, the procedure for which has been found to be in violation of the country's obligations under international human rights laws.[50] An important conclusion from these experiences is that the wrong kind of law may be

[46] Christoph von Furer-Haimendorf (1982) *Tribes of India: The Struggle for Survival*, Berkeley: University of California Press; B. D. Sharma (1990) *Report of the Commissioner for Scheduled Castes and Scheduled Tribes*, Delhi: Government of India.

[47] Claes Corlin (2004) "Hmong and the Land Question in Vietnam: National Policy and Local Concepts of the Environment," in Nicholas Tapp, Jean Michaud, Christian Culas and Gary Yia Lee (eds.), *Hmong/Miao in Asia*, Bangkok: Silkworm Book, 295–320, esp. 301.

[48] Nelly Arvelo-Jimenez (1980) "Programmes among Indigenous Peoples in Venezuela and Their Impact: A Critique," in F. Barbira-Scazzocchio (ed.), *Land, People and Planning in Contemporary Amazonia*. Cambridge: Centre for Latin American Studies, 210–221; Marcus Colchester (1995) *Venezuela: Violations of Indigenous Rights*, Chadlington: World Rainforest Movement; German Freire (2002) *The Piaroa: Environment and Society in Transition: A Study of Land Use and Social Change in the Middle Orinoco, Venezuela*, Ph. D. dissertation, University of Oxford.

[49] A. Chirif, P. García, and R. Chase-Smith (1991) *El Indígena y Su Territorio: estrategias para la defensa de los pueblos y territorios indígenas en la cuenca amazónica*, Lima: Oxfam-America-COICA; Alexandre Surralles and Pedro Garcia Hierro (eds.) (2004) *Tierra Adentro: Territorio Indigena y Percepcion del Entorno*, IWGIA: Copenhagen.

[50] CERD/C/GUY/CO/14.

worse than no law, creating a legal mechanism for the loss, invasion and takeover of forest peoples' customary lands [...]

DISTINGUISHING POSTCONFLICT AND POSTDISASTER

HLP issues do not arise exclusively within the context of conflict; they also arise invariably following natural disasters. For several years, various UN agencies have been involved in programs designed to assist those affected by disaster to enjoy the full spectrum of HLP rights in the aftermath of the disaster concerned. The following excerpt from a UN Habitat publication addresses the issues that distinguish postconflict and postdisaster issues as they relate to HLP rights.

UN-HABITAT (2009) *Scoping Report: Addressing Land Issues after Natural Disasters*, UN Habitat

"Why disaster guidelines are necessary: Distinguishing post-conflict and post-disaster land issues"

A number of agencies, including UN-HABITAT, FAO, USAID and ODI have prepared operational guidelines and analytical frameworks to address land issues after armed conflicts. The UN Guiding Principles on Internal Displacement encompass cases of natural disaster and armed conflict. While there are many similarities between land issues after conflict and disaster, there are important differences that underscore the need for a separate set of guidelines on land and natural disasters. The need for separate guidelines on post-disaster land responses, identified by the Early Recovery Cluster in 2007, is confirmed by heightened disaster risks as a result of global climate change, and increased human settlement vulnerability as result of global population growth.

Post-conflict and post-disaster land issues can be similar because both situations tend to involve displacement, death and destruction. In both cases, the land governance system can enter a state of flux as a result of new needs, actors and incentives. Within this context of system change, the following land-specific risks can arise in cases of both conflict and disaster:-

- Temporary living centres may be built on inappropriate land.
- The process of return may be marked by land grabbing, ad hoc land occupation and political score-settling.
- A residual caseload of displaced persons may not be able to return (including renters, squatters and the landless).
- Land rights may be uncertain because of a lack of records, loss or destruction of records, or damage to community-based land governance systems.
- Uncertainty of land tenure may lead to disputes and delays in reconstruction, or to reconstruction in inappropriate locations.

- A failure t identify heirs in an authoritative manner may lead to family disputes, and delays in reconstruction and recovery.
- Powerful individuals may take advantage of inheritance uncertainty to deny entitlements and access to land for vulnerable groups, including widows and orphans.
- Land may be acquired for resettlement and infrastructure in inappropriate locations, or through methods that are productive of conflict.

Although there are many potential similarities, land issues after natural disasters can differ from armed conflict in a number of important respects:-

Government Capacity and National Politics

- While natural disasters can occur in a war-torn context, disasters that occur in the absence of war tend to be associated with less politicised and conflict-ridden circumstances. As a result, there may be more government capacity and greater political space to resolve longer term land issues. At the same time, a national government may be reluctant to confront deeper land-related issues in a post disaster context, and relatively less willing to request international assistance in cases of disaster than conflict, particularly in relation to land issues, because the request may imply a lack of capacity on its part. The government may also take an unduly short term view of land responses, in order to be seen to deliver quick recovery and reconstruction results.

The Significance of Sudden Onset

- The shock to the land system tends to be shorter, but potentially sharper, in the case of sudden onset natural disasters than in the context of armed conflict.
- The deaths of land owners, and loss of land records (if any), will occur in a much more compressed period of time in the case of natural disasters.
- The generally localised or isolated impact nature of disasters can mean that surplus housing stock is available to absorb displaced persons.
- While it will be possible to identify high disaster risk areas, and engage in activities to reduce the ability to plan and prepare for particular cases of displacement.
- Sudden onset disasters can result in significant loss of land, due to landslides, flooding or other hazards that render land unsafe for habitation, livelihoods or other uses. Addressing the land needs of landowners who have lost land as a result of a disaster is often a distinctive imperative of post disaster land programming.
- The sudden onset of a disaster, and its relatively localised impact, may reduce the risk that abandoned land or housing will be occupied by persons other than the pre-displacement owner (i.e the "secondary occupier" problem).

Landowner Return to Unoccupied Land

- A relative absence of secondary occupiers should facilitate return and r-occupation of land by pre-disaster landowners, because landowners can return without the need to evict secondary occupiers. This should reduce (but not eliminate) the need for specialist judicial institutions to adjudicate claims for property restitution (e.g. a land claims commission). At the same time, specialist institutions and responses may still be required to protect victims, including women and others with weaker forms of tenure, from the risk of land grabbing by neighbours, government bodies or social elites.
- A relative absence of secondary occupiers means that residual caseloads of displaced persons unable to return are more likely to be those who are not land owners (including renters, squatters and the landless). In other words, because landowners can return without the need to evict secondary occupiers, those who are unable to return are more likely to be groups who lacked access to land, or sufficient security of tenure prior to the disaster.

The Need to engage in Future Disaster Risk Reduction

- The greater risk to land restitution for displaced victims is not secondary occupation but the need to engage in future disaster risk reduction. The need to minimise the risk of future disasters may require special planning mechanisms that restrict reconstruction in inappropriate or unsafe locations.
- The need to minimise the risk of future disasters may lead to relocation of infrastructure and government facilities.

All these issues will affect analysis and assessment of land issues after natural disasters. It is important not to approach natural disasters from a "conflict" perspective, or at least a perspective that cannot adapt to the particular circumstances of natural disasters. Large-scale disasters can traumatise a land governance system at least as much as armed conflict. But the system itself may be in a relatively better position to recover and respond to emerging land issues, either because the disaster itself is more localised in effect of because the operating environment is less degraded by civil war or ethnic conflict. In other words, while there will be pre-disaster land governance problems that are magnified by the disaster, the risk of the system *as a whole* being thrown into chaos appears relatively lower in cases of disaster than armed conflict.

This said, two potential features of natural disasters will place more pressure on the land governance system than would be the case after armed conflict.

- The need to engage in disaster risk reduction demands a relatively high degree of capacity and coordination among land planning institutions. It also places stress on the institutions involved in relocation and re-settlement, including those charged with ensuring consultation and participation by affected groups.

- The concentration of renters, squatters and the landless in residual caseloads of persons unable to return to their pre-disaster lands will highlight the social and legal conditions that restrict access to land and its ownership in the affected country. As a result, there may be a degree of governmental caution or paralysis because addressing the land needs of renters, squatters and the landless may open a Pandora's Box of claims outside the disaster zone.

Questions and Exercises

1. Choose any country that you are familiar with from personal experience or the media, and that has a large population of IDPs. Based on your own research, describe how population displacement occurred in that country, and how the total number of displaced people has fluctuated over the past decade.
2. Is the right of an individual to own land guaranteed under international law? Is security of tenure the same as ownership? Explain your answers.
3. Do any specific kinds of communities have rights to land that differ from those of other citizens? If so, what are these different rights to land?
4. Are governments affected by conventions, treaties, and other legal documents that they have not signed or ratified? Justify your answer.

Additional Resources

Daniel Fitzpatrick (2007) *Addressing Land Issues after Natural Disasters*, UN-HABITAT.

Daniel Lewis (2004) "Challenges to Sustainable Peace: Land Disputes Following Conflict," *Symposium on Land Administration in Post Conflict Areas*, UN-Habitat.

Courtland Robinson (2003) *Risks and Rights: The Causes, Consequences, and Challenges of Development-Induced Displacement*, Brookings Institution.

Sahel and West Africa Club (2007) *Land, Agricultural Change and Conflict in West Africa: Regional Issues from Sierra Leone, Liberia and Cote D'Ivoire.*

Ashley South (2007) *Displacement and Dispossession: Forced Migration and Land Rights in Burma*, COHRE.

UN Habitat (2007) *Handbook on Land Administration and Post Conflict Peacebuilding: From Emergency to Reconstruction*, UN Habitat.

USAID (2004) *Land & Conflict – A Toolkit for Intervention*, USAID Office of Conflict Management and Mitigation.

4

HLP Restitution Rights

Theory, Law, and Concepts

[T]he basic principle that wrongfully expropriated property should be restituted (or compensation paid) applies to them all, and their implementation of this principle is a measure of the extent to which they have successfully adopted democratic institutions, the rule of law with respect to property rights, and market economy practices. As these governments seek to join western economic and political organizations, and to integrate their economies more closely with ours, we do expect them to adopt the highest international standards in their treatment of property....[1]

[R]efugees wishing to return to their homes and live at peace with their neighbours should be permitted to do so at the earliest practicable date, and that compensation should be paid for the property of those choosing not to return and for loss of or damage to property which, under principles of international law or in equity, should be made good by the Governments or authorities responsible.[2]

A principled argument in favour of restitution is that no matter how long ago the injustice occurred, its legitimisation only encourages other wrongdoings.[3]

Throughout history, millions upon millions of people have been forced by circumstances beyond their control to flee their homes, lands, and properties. In previous centuries, such displacement and loss of one's habitual residence was often accepted as a tragic but nonetheless inevitable consequence of warfare, military aggression, conquest, arbitrary confiscation of lands, and related gross and systematic violations of human rights. Throughout the latter part of the past century and now into the twenty-first century, however, what was previously considered to be the permanent nature of arbitrary displacement and the concomitant human rights violations

[1] Stuart Eizenstat, Under Secretary for Economic, Business and Agricultural Affairs, Testimony before the Commission on Security and Cooperation in Europe, Washington, DC, 25 March 1999.

[2] *UN General Assembly Resolution 194 (III) of 11 December 1948.*

[3] Elazar Barkan (2000) *The Guilt of Nations: Restitution and Negotiating Historical Injustices*, WW Norton and Co., p. xxxiii.

stemming directly from that displacement have been increasingly subject to review, reconsideration, and actual reversal.

Given the seriousness of arbitrary displacement and the unlawful expropriation of lands and homes – now often also referred to as ethnic cleansing – coupled with the continually expanding legal stature of HLP rights (as well as other human rights) as outlined in Chapter 2, the international community of nations and the body of international law they have created have given increasing recognition and attention to the practice of housing, land, and property *restitution*. These rights of refugees, internally displaced persons, and other victims of arbitrary displacement and property loss, therefore, involve not simply the return of people to their countries of origin, but also the corresponding additional right to have restored to them the housing, property, or lands from which they were originally displaced (*restitutio ad integrum*).

Numerous international and national standards have been adopted, mechanisms devised and enforced, and laws approved and implemented, such that housing, land, or property once vacated due to arbitrary displacement or confiscation can now be returned to the original owners or occupants.[4] Moreover, housing, land, and property restitution has become a common feature of peace agreements, processes linked to postconflict reconstruction, postoccupation independence, post-Communist political and legal reform, and in societies recovering from genocide. This is particularly true with respect to attempts aimed at reversing acts of ethnic cleansing and other attempts at altering the demographic nature of given nations. It is such cases, where displacement or land confiscation was grounded in racial, ethnic, and other forms of discrimination, where refugees and displaced persons have the strongest and most explicit rights to housing and property restitution. Bosnia and Herzegovina, Kosovo, and South Africa are cases in point.

It is widely recognized that conferring rights to housing, land, and property restitution also protects refugees and other displaced persons from being penalized for fleeing their homes due to circumstances far beyond their control. Ultimately, restitution is increasingly seen as indispensable for the promotion of reconciliation, reconstruction, and economic development within the society concerned. As the Chairman of the U.S. Commission on Security and Cooperation in Europe has rightly observed: "How Governments deal with past injustices is usually a telling indicator of their commitment to ensure that the same injustices do not occur again."[5]

4 For a comprehensive overview of laws and pronouncements on restitution, see: Scott Leckie (ed.) (2007) *Housing, Land and Property Restitution Rights of Refugees and Internally Displaced Persons: Laws, Cases and Materials*, Cambridge University Press.

5 Hearing on "Property Restitution, Compensation and Preservation: Competing Claims in Post-Communist Europe," 18 July 1996.

Many States have enacted legislation allowing housing, property, and land restitution to take place. Where individual States have been reluctant to accept the inherent justice associated with restitution, the international community has been increasingly supportive of and involved in other restitution efforts. It is now widely recognized, however, that it is actually very much in the self-interest (as well as legally required) of States responsible for creating the conditions that led to the flight of refugees and the subsequent confiscation of homes, lands, and properties to deal effectively and fairly with restitution claims. Only by resolving such claims and bringing finality to such issues can sustainable peace and prosperity be possible. Indeed, many assert that the ultimate willingness of Germany to address restitution claims has played a major role in the economic, political, and social success of that country since the conclusion of World War II.[6] Barkan is correct, therefore, when he asserts that:

> The process of restitution negotiation leads to a reconfiguration of both sides. While the perpetrators hope to purge their own history of guilt and legitimise their current position, the victims hope to benefit from a new recognition of their suffering and to enjoy certain material gains.[7]

EXPERIENCES AND APPROACHES TO RESTITUTION: STANDARDS, LAWS, AND POLICIES

Numerous governments and institutions are currently engaged in legislative programs designed to implement and enforce housing, property, and land restitution rights for returning refugees and other victims of human rights violations who were previously displaced from their places of original or habitual residence. Whereas historically the restitution of vacated homes, lands, and properties may have been the exception to the rule, in 2010, restitution has become increasingly commonplace, widely supported by the international community, and a fundamental feature of law and relations among States. The restitution of the homes and lands from which displaced persons were forced to flee is now a widely accepted feature of postconflict historical periods and is regularly addressed within peace agreements.

National experiences with restitution, however, vary considerably. Some States have smoothly enacted restitution laws and mechanisms allowing hundreds of thousands of displaced persons to return to their original homes. Other States have

6 "The significance of restitution becomes apparent within the context of the German refusal to deal with the past.... For Adenauer and the few who determined the outcome, a precondition for Germany's normalization was that it become a country ruled by law, and that meant recognition of its obligations to its victims. Democracy and restitution must go hand in hand."; Barkan, *The Guilt of Nations*, 27.

7 Id., 321.

encountered difficulties in implementing restitution rights, owing to intransigence by neighboring States, flawed restitution procedures, and inadequate enforcement of these rights, but have nonetheless pushed forward with restitution programs. Still others have consistently resisted recognizing restitution rights. This latter group of States, however, is rapidly declining in number and is comprised almost entirely of nondemocratic nations.

Efforts to make restitution a reality are invariably subject to local circumstances and history, but all attempts at implementing restitution rights universally reveal that although restitution is often time-consuming, politically challenging, and often exceptionally complex, the physical return of property to returning refugees or displaced persons is feasible and practical if the will to make these processes succeed is apparent. Even if the political will may not be forthcoming, this can never extinguish the rights and claims of displaced persons for the return of their homes and lands. As a result, the longer restitution is delayed, the longer the wait for true peace and reconciliation will be.

Laws, mechanisms, procedures, and programs designed to provide housing, land, and property restitution are the means by which individual victims of housing, land, property, and other human rights violations that may have forced them from their homes can exercise the broader right to an effective remedy for these infringements of their basic rights. It is through the restitution process that circumstances created because of human rights violations can be reversed, and thus returned to the state of affairs present before the violation of rights took place. Restitution is now recognized as a fundamental means for displaced persons and refugees to have restored to them the homes, lands, and properties they were forced to involuntarily flee from due to circumstances beyond their control.

Equally, restitution provides a formal and legal basis for delegitimizing the arbitrary acquisition of territory, assets, movable and immovable property, and lands. Restitution allows injury incurred due to a wrongful act to be made good. The recognition of restitution rights often provides the first official pronouncement that whatever may have taken place in the past that was responsible for people being forced to vacate their homes was wrong and should not be allowed to occur again in future. It also reaffirms the basic proposition that refugees and displaced persons should never be penalized or suffer detriment due solely to the fact that they were forced to flee their homes and lands.[8] Restitution acts as the mixture of laws, procedures, and mechanisms designed to restore human rights victims (or their heirs) to the position they were in before the internationally wrongful act occurred.

[8] Such principles have been widely recognized. For instance, Article 4 of the *Convention Governing the Specific Aspects of Refugee Problems in Africa* (1969), 1001 U.N.T.S. 45 (1969), entered into force June 20, 1974, asserts that: "Refugees who voluntarily return to their country shall in no way be penalized for having left it for any of the reasons giving rise to refugee situations."

According to the *Basic Principles and Guidelines on the Right to a Remedy and Reparation for Victims of Violations of International Human Rights and Humanitarian Law*,[9] restitution constitutes one of several forms of reparation and is intended to promote justice by redressing violations of international human rights or humanitarian law.[10] *The Basic Principles and Guidelines* assert that restitution should, where possible, restore the victim to the original situation before the violations occurred, and includes the restoration of liberty, legal rights, social status, family life and citizenship, return to one's place of residence, and restoration of employment and return of property. International jurisprudence fully supports these perspectives. In the words of the Inter-American Court on Human Rights:

> [I]t is a principle of international law, which jurisprudence has considered "even a general concept of law", that every violation of an international obligation which results in harm creates a duty to make adequate reparation.... Reparation of harm brought about by the violation of an international obligation consists in full restitution (restiutio in integrum), which includes the restoration of the prior situation, the reparation of the consequences of the violation, and indemnification for patrimonial and non-patrimonial damages, including emotional harm.[11]

Restitution rights are often established in tandem with rights to compensation. When restitution is considered to be materially impossible (determined on the basis of objective tests), substitute remedies – including damages – must be provided. It is important to emphasize at the outset, however, that restitution does not preclude the payment of compensation, just as the payment of compensation does not preclude the return of housing, land, or property. As a rule, reparation provided in one form – such as restitution – does not exclude its provision in other forms. This is a vital point within any context where governments argue that restitution claims can be dealt with solely through the payment of compensation in lieu of returning the house or land to the legitimate owner or previous occupant.[12]

9 UN doc. E/CN.4/2000/62, Annex.

10 Id. Reparation should be proportional to the gravity of the violations and harm suffered (para. 15). Reparation may be made in the following forms: restitution, compensation, rehabilitation, satisfaction, and guarantees of nonrepetition (para. 21). It should be noted that whereas the term "reparation" is commonly used to describe payments between States, usually as compensation for damage caused in war, it clearly also applies to cases of individual violations of human rights law and humanitarian law. The term "Satisfaction and guarantees of nonrepetition" includes a wide range of provisions and policy measures, including verification of the fact and full and public disclosure of the truth, official declaration or judicial decision restoring dignity and reputation, acknowledgment of the facts and acceptance of responsibility, and commemorations and tributes to victims and survivors.

11 *Velasquez Rodriguez Case (Compensatory Damages)*, 1989, 7 Inter-Am.Ct.H.R. (ser. C), as quoted in Dinah Shelton (1999) *Remedies in International Human Rights Law*, Oxford, 223.

12 It is important to point out at the outset that restitution is by all means not limited to the formal owners of property. Restitutionfd rights are relevant to owners, but also to nonowners residing with the owner at the time of flight, lawful tenants, and other residents recognized at the time of flight as legal.

Indeed, it is widely recognized that the payment of compensation alone is generally not an adequate substitute for individual effective remedies for human rights violations, which may include restitution for lost property. Even when compensation is paid, it must correspond to the value of restitution in kind. To such an amount must often also be added additional compensation payments for damages and other losses not physically involving the housing, land, or property in question. Such compensatory damages can be provided for past physical and mental suffering, future physical and mental suffering, medical expenses, loss of earnings, and on other grounds.

Explicit and implicit recognition of housing, property, and land restitution has been enshrined in a variety of bodies of law, including international human rights law and jurisprudence, international law, humanitarian law, and criminal law. Various United Nations bodies including the Security Council, General Assembly, UN Charter-based human rights bodies, and the human rights treaty bodies have each repeatedly recognized the fundamental importance of restitution in numerous contexts. In addition, unequivocal recognition of restitution rights are contained in a cross-section of peace agreements ending conflicts, in the overall policies of the UN High Commissioner for Refugees, and within many voluntary repatriation agreements organizing the return of refugees to their countries and original homes.

In one of the most significant developments within the restitution field in recent years, the UN approved the Principles on Housing and Property Restitution for Refugees and Displaced Persons, also known as the "Pinheiro Principles," in 2005. The following excerpt from the 2004 report of then UN Special Rapporteur on Housing and Property Restitution, Paulo Sergio Pinheiro, provides a brief legal commentary on several of the principles that are contained within the Pinheiro Principles:

"Housing and Property Restitution in the Context of the Return of Refugees and Internally Displaced Persons," Progress Report of the Special Raporteur, Paulo Sergio Pinheiro, Appendum, Commentary on the Draft Principles on Housing and Property Restitution for Refugees and Displaced Persons, E.CN.4/ Sub.2/2004/22/Add.1, 8 June 2004

Commentary to Section IV of the Draft Principles on Ensuring the Right to Housing and Property Restitution

37. Section IV of the Draft Principles provides specific guidance regarding how best to ensure the right to housing and property restitution in practice. The principles articulated in this section are based, in part, on the findings of the preliminary report (E/CN.4/Sub.2/2003/11), which analysed some of the common obstacles to restitution programmes, including secondary occupation, property destruction, loss

By way of example, in Bosnia and Herzegovina, both owners as well as those holding what are known as "social occupancy rights" have restitution rights under Annex 7 of the Dayton Agreement.

or destruction of property, ineffectual institutions and discriminatory restitution programmes. As such, the principles articulated in this section reflect some of the best practices which have been devised at the level of policy to address these common obstacles.

38. The right to adequate consultation and representation in decision-making has been articulated by the Committee on Economic, Social and Cultural Rights within the context of forced evictions. In its general comment No. 7, the Committee observed that affected communities should have a right to "an opportunity for genuine consultation". Similarly, Principle 28, paragraph 2, of the Guiding Principles on Internal Displacement stipulates that "Special efforts should be made to ensure the full participation of internally displaced persons in the planning and management of their return or resettlement and reintegration."

39. The provisions of the Draft Principles regarding housing and property records and documentation are meant in part to facilitate, from a logistical point of view, restitution processes through the establishment of property registration systems. In certain cases, alternative mechanisms may need to be established in order to create or recreate a system for the registration of property. One effective way to do this would be by integrating housing and property restitution protections in registration procedures for refugees and displaced persons. Many States have registration systems for the provision of humanitarian aid to the displaced, and many States include, in their registration processes, a mechanism for the collection of demographic data on the displaced population. It would seem quite feasible to widen the data collection component of these registration processes to include information regarding the housing and property situation of refugees and displaced persons at the time they fled their homes – address, length of residency, estimated value, tenure status, ownership records and any other relevant personal information related to residency, ownership, possession or use and loss of property rights.

40. Because displacement often occurs in situations of armed conflict, including of ethnic cleansing, the Draft Principles stipulate that "States shall not recognize as valid any illegal property transaction, including any transfer that was made under duress, in exchange for exit permission or documents, or which was otherwise coerced or forced." Similar language was used in Security Council resolution 820 (1993) on the situation in Bosnia and Herzegovina. This provision is consistent with basic tenets of contract law which stipulate that contracts entered into under duress or physical compulsion are void. Similarly, if a party's assent to a contract is induced by a threat from another party that leaves the victim no reasonable alternative, the contract is voidable by the victim.

41. Ensuring the rights of tenants and other non-owners is very important in situations of repatriation, resettlement and restitution, as in many cases only the minority of the affected displaced population will have actually owned their housing. Tenants and other non-owners do have rights of possession, including security of tenure, which protect them from forced eviction and displacement.

The rights articulated in the Draft Principles apply equally to tenants and other non-owners as they do to persons who own their housing.

42. Ensuring the rights of secondary occupants is also a critical concern, as secondary occupation is itself a common phenomenon in situations of displacement. Secondary occupation is also a reality which often complicates the process of return for refugees and other displaced persons. Secondary occupation may at times occur when the perpetrators of human rights abuses forcibly evict residents and subsequently loot property and move into the abandoned homes themselves. Yet, most often, secondary occupiers are themselves displaced persons. Adequately addressing the phenomenon of secondary occupation has proven extremely delicate in practice. In all cases, however, secondary occupants must be protected against forced evictions and must benefit from the procedural protections outlined in general comment No. 7 of the Committee on Economic, Social and Cultural Rights. Similarly, secondary occupants have a right to adequate housing under international human rights laws and standards, and States should adopt adequate measures to ensure that secondary occupiers are protected against homelessness, unreasonable relocation and other violations of their human rights. Due process guarantees, and access to fair and impartial legal institutions, must be assured for all parties.

43. The term "compensation" refers to a legal remedy by which a person receives monetary payment for harm suffered, for example resulting from the impossibility of restoring the person's property or house. Compensation should not be seen as an alternative to restitution and should only be used when restitution is not factually possible or when the injured party knowingly and voluntarily accepts compensation in lieu of restitution. For example, an injured party should receive compensation to remedy the wrongful dispossession of housing only if that particular housing no longer exists or if the injured party knowingly and voluntarily decides it is in his or her interest not to return to his or her home. The Draft Principles do acknowledge, however, that in some cases, a combination of compensation and restitution may be the most appropriate remedy and form of restorative justice. There is flexibility in this regard. Nonetheless, in all cases it is the injured party who should be able to knowingly and voluntarily decide whether to accept restitution, compensation, or a combination thereof.

44. In its general recommendation XXIII on the rights of indigenous peoples, the Committee on the Elimination of Racial Discrimination affirmed such a formulation in the context of indigenous land and resources, calling upon States parties "to recognize and protect the rights of indigenous peoples to own, develop, control and use their communal lands, territories and resources and, where they have been deprived of their lands and territories traditionally owned or otherwise inhabited or used without their free and informed consent, to take steps to return those lands and territories. Only when this is for factual reasons not possible, the right to restitution should be substituted by the right to just, fair and prompt compensation".

45. Similarly, Principle 29, paragraph 2, of the Guiding Principles on Internal Displacement provide that "Competent authorities have the duty and responsibility to assist returned and/or resettled internally displaced persons to recover, to the extent possible, their property and possessions which they left behind or were dispossessed of upon their displacement. *When recovery of such property and possessions is not possible, competent authorities shall provide or assist these persons in obtaining appropriate compensation or another form of just reparation*" (emphasis added).

Commentary to Section V of the Draft Principles on Strengthening, Restitution Procedures, Institutions, Mechanisms and Legal Frameworks

46. The provision that procedures, institutions, mechanisms, and legal frameworks related to the right to restitution shall be fully consistent and compatible with international human rights and humanitarian law and standards is important to ensure that principles of international human rights and humanitarian law are adequately reflected at the level of national policy-making as concerns restitution. Doing so will ultimately serve to protect all persons from future violations of human rights.

47. Effective and competent national institutions are the cornerstone of successful restitution programmes. The provisions contained in Section V on restitution procedures, institutions, mechanisms and legal frameworks are meant to provide practical guidelines for the establishment and support of institutions at national level and other institutions responsible for implementing restitution policies. Whenever possible, it is important that these institutions be directly established within peace settlement and voluntary repatriation agreements, so as to ensure that restitution is seen as an integral component of post-conflict and peace-building strategies.

48. It should be noted, in the commentary, that judicial mechanisms are especially important and that the absence of effective and accessible judicial remedies severely compromises the restitution process. This is particularly the case in post-conflict situations where internal political divisions render domestic institutions incapable of effectively administering restitution programmes, either due to institutional bias, or due to a lack of capacity and resources.

49. The Draft Principles also provide for the accessibility of restitution claims procedures, with the understanding that institutions not only must be effective in their work to implement restitution policies, they must also be accessible to those constituencies which they are meant to benefit. As such, claims procedures must be physically, linguistically and financially accessible, and special measures should be taken to ensure that especially vulnerable groups or persons are able to benefit from such institutions in an equitable and just manner.

50. The legal recognition of the right to housing and property restitution for refugees and other displaced persons is indispensable to the adequate implementation of restitution programmes and policies and their adequate

> enforcement. Legal protections should be clearly articulated in an internally consistent manner, and legal protections should be consistent with international human rights and humanitarian principles. In order to establish an adequate legal regime for the protection of the rights articulated in these Draft Principles, States will need to pursue a range of legislative measures, including the adoption, amendment, reform, or repeal of relevant laws.
>
> 51. The prohibition of arbitrary and discriminatory laws builds upon the right to non-discrimination recognized in Section I of the Draft Principles. As pointed out in the preliminary report, one of the common obstacles to the successful implementation of restitution programmes has been the establishment of policies which favour certain groups while barring others from returning to their own homes, as has been the case with the application of discriminatory abandonment laws. Discriminatory restitution programmes further entrench social divisions and animosities, and are counter to post-conflict resolution, peace-building, as well as to fundamental human rights principles and international legal obligations. As such, it is essential for States to bring their national legislation into compliance with non-discrimination standards. It also deserves mention that the privatization of refugees' properties during their stay abroad can seriously complicate the exercise of property restitution rights. Efforts should be made to ensure that privatization does not result in the loss of property restitution rights of refugees.
>
> 52. The provision of legal aid and the additional provisions concerning enforcement are critical for the effective implementation of restitution policies and programmes. The provision of legal aid again increases the accessibility of restitution claims procedures, and ensures that persons are not deterred from benefiting from such procedures because of barriers associated with understanding and navigating the law. Similarly, the adequate enforcement of judgements related to restitution is essential to the effective implementation of restitution policies and programmes, and are especially important in situations where persons have been displaced due to violence [...]

Indeed, there is nothing exceptional, rare, or revolutionary about the recognition of restitution rights in law, policy, and practice, as the Pinheiro Principles clearly show. The Pinheiro Principles are grounded in and based on a broad cross-section of preexisting international law, an analysis of which follows.

INTERNATIONAL LAW, HUMANITARIAN LAW, AND CRIMINAL LAW

General international law, international humanitarian law, and recent developments in international criminal law provide considerable legal grounds supporting the right to housing, land, and property restitution for returning refugees and displaced persons. This section will briefly outline some of the most prominent statements of law in support of restitution, all of which can be used to bolster the restitution claims of those forced to flee their homes during conflict.

General International Law

General international law approaches restitution generally through the lens of infringements of international law due to wrongful acts or omissions attributable to States. This is commonly referred to as the law of State responsibility. The *Draft Articles on State Responsibility* issued by the International Law Commission in 2000 provide perhaps the clearest elaboration of the rules of State responsibility as they potentially relate restitution claims.[13] Nine articles of the Draft Articles are particularly relevant:

> Art. 3: The characterization of an act of a State as internationally wrongful is governed by international law. Such characterization in not affected by the characterization of the same act lawful by internal law.
>
> Art 14(2): The breach of an international obligation by an act of a State having a continuing character extends over the entire period during which the act continues and remains not in conformity with the international obligation.
>
> Art. 29: The legal consequences of an internationally wrongful act under the Part do not affect the continued duty of the responsible State to perform the obligation breached.
>
> Art. 30: The State responsible for the internationally wrongful act is under an obligation: (b) to offer appropriate assurances and guarantees of non-repetition, if circumstances so require.
>
> Art. 31: The responsible State may not rely on the provisions of its internal law as justification for failure to comply with its obligations.
>
> Art 35: Full reparation for the injury caused by the internationally wrongful act shall take the form of restitution, compensation and satisfaction, either singly or in combination, in accordance with the provisions of the present Chapter.
>
> Art. 36: A State responsible for an internationally wrongful act is under an obligation to make restitution, that is, to re-establish the situation which existed before the wrongful act was committed, provided and to the extent that restitution: (a) Is not materially possible; (b) Would not involve a burden out of all proportion to the benefit deriving from restitution instead of compensation.
>
> Art 37: 1. The State responsible for an internationally wrongful act is under an obligation to compensate for the damage caused thereby, insofar as such damage is not made good by restitution. 2. The compensation shall cover any financially assessable damage including loss of profits insofar as it is established.

[13] UN Doc A/55/10 (2000): Draft Articles Provisionally Adopted by the Drafting Committee on Second Reading, Art. 36 in Report of the International Law Commission on the Work of Its Fifty-Second Session, UN GAOR, 55th Sess., Supp. No. 10, at 124, 133.

> Art 38: 1. The State responsible for an internationally wrongful act is under an obligation to give satisfaction for the injury caused by that act insofar as it cannot be made good by restitution or compensation. 2. Satisfaction may consist in an acknowledgement of the breach, an expression of regret, a formal apology or another appropriate modality. 3. Satisfaction shall not be out of proportion to the injury and may not take a form humiliating to the responsible State.

Even though the Articles are still technically in draft form, they are widely considered to constitute principles of international customary law, and are thus binding on all States. The views taken in the Articles are a clear reflection of other views on state responsibility. A legal opinion of the Inter-American Juridical Committee has asserted that restitution is required for any violation of an international obligation:

> Pursuant to the rules governing state responsibility in international law, any state that violates an international obligation must make reparations for the consequences of the violation. The reparation has the purpose of returning, to the extent possible, the situation to the way it was before the transgression occurred. Only to the extent that this would prove impossible, or that the aggrieved party would so agree, could there by room for any substitute reparation.[14]

These and similar principles have been repeatedly reaffirmed, including by the government of the United States. In *the Restatement of Foreign Relations Law of the United States*, it is clearly stipulated that for a breach of international law, "[o]rdinarily, emphasis is on forms of redress that will undo the effect of the violation, such as restoration of the status quo ante, restitution, or specific performance of an undertaking."[15] Thus, for any violation of international law – which includes the violation of a range of individual human rights norms – redress that will "undo the effect of the violation" is required. Although restitution can take various forms (even in the context of housing), in cases of illegally occupied territory, restitution in kind, that is, the return of the territory, is the only "legal" remedy, and thus all other potential remedies may not be appropriate in such cases.[16]

In terms of jurisprudence supporting the position that restitution constitutes the *primary* remedy for violations of international law, the Permanent Court of International Justice, as far back as 1928, ruled in the well-known *Chorzów Factory (Indemnity) Case* that restitution was the preferred remedy for correcting illegal governmental takings of property. The *Chorzów Factory* case sets out what are widely agreed to be the basic remedial norms for violations of international law:

14 Inter-American Juridical Committee (1992) *Legal Opinion on the Decision of the Supreme Court of the United States of America*, OAS Doc. CJI/RES.II-15/92, para. 10.

15 *Restatement (Third) of Foreign Relations Law of the United States* Sec. 432(2)(1987).

16 Ian Brownlie (1983) *Principles of Public International Law*, Oxford University Press, 210.

> The principle contained in the actual notion of an illegal act – a principle which seems to be established by international practice and in particular by the decisions of arbitral tribunals – is that reparation must, as far as possible, wipe out all the consequences of the illegal act and re-establish the situation which would, in all probability, have existed if that act had not been committed. Restitution in kind, or, if this is not possible, payment of a sum corresponding to the value which a restitution in kind would bear; the award, if need be, of damages for loss sustained which would not be covered by restitution in kind or payment in place of it – such are principles which should serve to determine the amount of compensation due for an act contrary to international law.[17]

This case was based on the specific violation of a treaty, but the Court's decision concerning the appropriate remedy did not distinguish between treaty violations and any other violations of international law. As such, a violation of customary law would presumably be subject to the same remedial norm as a violation of a treaty.[18]

These principles are self-evident in suggesting the clear preference for restitution as the primary remedy for violations of international law, in particular those violations involving the illegal confiscation of housing, land, or property. In cases involving formal expropriation of housing, land, or property – which in many cases is clearly legal under international law – illegal acts can and still do occur. According to one leading international lawyer "[i]nternational law will clearly be engaged where the expropriation is unlawful, either because of, for example, the discriminatory manner in which it is carried out or the offering of inadequate or no compensation."[19] Shaw continues, stating that "[i]n the case of an unlawful taking, full restitution in kind or its monetary equivalent was required in order to re-establish the situation which would in all probability have existed if the expropriation had not occurred, while in the case of lawful taking, the standard was the payment of the full value of the undertaking at the time of dispossession."[20] The International Court of Justice has supported this point by recognizing that in cases involving the illegal taking of property, the violating State is required to return the property to the rightful owner.[21]

[17] *Chórzow Factory (Indemnity) Case* (Germany v. Poland), 1928 PCIJ (ser. A) No. 17 (Judgment of 13 September 1928), p. 47.

[18] Frederic L. Kirgis (2001) "Restitution as a Remedy in US Courts for Violations of International Law," *American Journal of International Law* 95, no. 2: 343.

[19] Malcolm N. Shaw (1997) *International Law*, Fourth Edition, Cambridge University Press, 574. The European Energy Charter Treaty 1994 creates a principle on expropriation that it must be for a purpose that is in the public interest, not discriminatory, carried out under due process of law, and accompanied by the payment of prompt, adequate, and effective compensation (See: 34 *International Legal Materials*, 1995, 391).

[20] Shaw (1997) *International Law*, 580.

[21] *Temple of Preah-Vihear Case* (Merits)(1962) ICJ 6, at 36–37 (the International Court of Justice ruled that Cambodia must leave an illegally occupied temple compound in Thailand and restitute any religious artefacts it may have removed during the occupation).

International Humanitarian Law

The *Geneva Convention IV Relative to the Protection of Civilian Persons in Time of War (1949)* contains a variety of relevant principles:

> Art. 33 No protected person may be punished for an offence he or she has not personally committed. Collective penalties and likewise all measures of intimidation or of terrorism are prohibited. Pillage is prohibited.[22] Reprisals against protected persons and their property are prohibited.
>
> Art. 49 … Persons thus evacuated shall be transferred back to their homes as soon as hostilities in the area in question have ceased.… The Occupying Power shall not deport or transfer parts of its own civilian population into the territory it occupies.
>
> Art. 53 Any destruction by the Occupying Power of real or personal property belonging individually or collectively to private persons, or to the State, or to other public authorities, or to social or cooperative organizations, is prohibited, except where such destruction is rendered necessary by military operations.[23]
>
> Art. 147 Grave breaches … shall be those involving any of the following acts, if committed against persons or property protected by the present Convention:… extensive destruction and appropriation of property, not justified by military necessity and carried out unlawfully and wantonly. [24]

[22] Customary law and article 4 of Protocol II explicitly prohibit pillage (para. 2 (g)), a ban that protects the personal property of displaced persons (located in the camps and/or left in the homes from which they have fled) from theft and vandalism. Additional protection against the destruction of property belonging to displaced persons can be derived from article 14 of Protocol II. This article prohibits the attack, destruction, removal, or rendering useless of those objects that are considered indispensable to the survival of the civilian population, such as "foodstuffs, agricultural areas for the production of foodstuffs, crops, livestock, drinking water installations and supplies and irrigation works."

[23] Article 23 of the Hague Regulations also contains a general prohibition against the destruction or seizure of the enemy's property, unless required by military necessity. Article 25 of the Regulations prohibits the "attack or bombardment, by whatever means, of towns, villages, dwellings, or buildings which are undefended." During hostilities and/or occupation, the pillage of a town or place is prohibited by Articles 28 and 47 of the Hague Regulations. *The Hague Convention (IV) Respecting the Laws and Customs of War on Land* and the Regulations Annexed thereto contains several articles relevant to the treatment of property during warfare: Art 23 It is especially forbidden … (g) To destroy or seize the enemy's property, unless such destruction or seizure be imperatively demanded by the necessities of war; Art 25 The attack or bombardment, by whatever means, of towns, villages, dwellings, or buildings which are undefended is prohibited; Art 28 The pillage of a town or place, even when taken by assault, is prohibited.

[24] In addition to international humanitarian law, under the *Declaration on the Protection of Women and Children in Emergency and Armed Conflict* (GA Res. 3318 (XXIX) (1974)), "[a]ll forms of repression and cruel and inhuman treatment of women and children, including … destruction of dwellings and forcible eviction, committed by belligerents in the course of military operations or in occupied territories shall be considered criminal."

Protocol II Additional to the Geneva Conventions of 12 August 1949, and Relating to the Protection of Victims of Non-International Armed Conflicts (1977) further strengthens these principles:

> Art 17 (1) The displacement of the civilian population shall not be ordered for reasons related to the conflict unless the security of the civilians involved or imperative military reasons so demand. Should such displacements have to be carried out, all possible measures shall be taken in order that the civilian population may be received under satisfactory conditions of shelter, hygiene, health, safety and nutrition.
>
> 17(2) Civilians shall not be compelled to leave their own territory for reasons connected with the conflict.

Moreover, Article 46 of the Hague Regulations prohibits the confiscation of private property by the Occupying Power. Privately owned immovable property is also not subject to seizure, but can be requisitioned for the needs of the occupying force (Article 52 of the Hague Regulations).

International Criminal Law

Restitution is also a key element of the remedial measures envisaged under the rapidly growing body of international criminal law. Under the *Rome Statute of the International Criminal Court*,[25] Article 75 (Reparations to victims) specifically addresses restitution in terms of eventual Court decisions:

> 1. The Court shall establish principles relating to reparations to, or in respect of, victims, including restitution, compensation and rehabilitation. On this basis, in its decision the Court may, either upon request or on its own motion in exceptional circumstances, determine the scope and extent of any damage, loss and injury to, or in respect of, victims and will state the principles on which it is acting.
>
> 2. The Court may make an order directly against a convicted person specifying appropriate reparations to, or in respect of, victims, including restitution, compensation and rehabilitation. Where appropriate, the Court may order that the award for reparations be made through the Trust Fund provided for in article 79.
>
> 3. Before making an order under this article, the Court may invite and shall take account of representations from or on behalf of the convicted person, victims, other interested persons or interested States.

The International Criminal Tribunal for the Former Yugoslavia (ICTY) has also explicitly included restitution of property among a range of possible remedies. Article 105 of the *Rules of Procedure and Evidence of the International Tribunal for*

[25] UN Doc. A/CONF.183/9 (1998), adopted 17 July 1998.

the Prosecution of Persons Responsible for Serious Violations of Humanitarian Law Committed in the Territory of the Former Yugoslavia Since 1991 (adopted 11 February 1994) permits the Tribunal, in conjunction with a judgment of conviction, to award the restitution of property or its proceeds to victims, even property in the hands of third parties not otherwise connected with the crime of which the convicted person has been found guilty.

Statutes of Limitations and Universal Jurisdiction

Under the Geneva Conventions and related standards, there are no statutes of limitations for recognized war crimes or other grave breaches of international humanitarian or criminal law.[26] *The Convention on the Non-Applicability of Statutes of Limitations for War Crimes and Crimes against Humanity* (1968) confirms the view that war crimes are not subject to statutes of limitation but are susceptible to universal jurisdiction. Indeed, the entire concept of universal jurisdiction for grave breaches of international humanitarian law has advanced considerably in recent years. Arguably, such jurisdiction extends to grave breaches such as extensive destruction and appropriation of property not justified by military necessity and carried out unlawfully and wantonly, racial discrimination, damage to civilian property when committed wilfully, population transfer or inhuman treatment.[27]

INTERNATIONAL HUMAN RIGHTS LAW

In accordance with their domestic law and international obligations, and taking account of individual circumstances, States should provide victims of violations of international human rights and humanitarian law the following forms of reparation: restitution, compensation, rehabilitation, and satisfaction and guarantees of nonrepetition.[28]

Under international human rights law, rights to housing, land, and property restitution stem ultimately from the broader right to *an effective remedy for violations of human rights*; a right that pervades this entire body of law.[29] It is essentially on the basis of the premise that victims of wrongful acts and/or human rights

[26] This point is supported by Article 29 of the *Rome Statute of the International Criminal Court* which provides that "The crimes within the jurisdiction of the Court shall not be subject to any statute of limitations."

[27] Draft Basic Principles and Guidelines on the Right to a Remedy and Reparations for Victims of Violations of International Human Rights and Humanitarian Law (E/CN.4/2000/62) discuss the need for States to suspend any limitations until adequate remedial measures are in place.

[28] Id., Para. 21.

[29] For comprehensive coverage of such remedies, see: Dinah Shelton (1999) *Remedies in International Human Rights Law*, Oxford University Press. A right to an effective remedy for victims of violations

violations – including the arbitrary taking of homes, lands, and properties – have an enforceable right to have the act or violation remedied, repaired, and reversed.

The Right to Housing, Land, and Property Restitution

The explicit right of refugees and internally displaced persons to the restitution of housing, land, or property upon return to their places of habitual residence have been increasingly recognized as *distinct human rights* in their own right. In other words, restitution itself has been recognized as a right, above and beyond the purely remedial context just noted. For instance, UN Sub-Commission on Protection and Promotion of Human Rights resolution 1998/26 on *Housing and Property Restitution in the Context of the Return of Refugees and Internally Displaced Persons* provides a useful framework for implementing restitution rights. The resolution:

> 1. Reaffirms the right of all refugees, as defined in relevant international legal instruments, and internally displaced persons to return to their homes and places of habitual residence in their country and/or place of origin, should they so wish;
>
> 2. Reaffirms also the universal applicability of the right to adequate housing, the right to freedom of movement, the right to privacy and respect for the home and the particular importance of these rights for returning refugees and internally displaced persons wishing to return to their homes and places of habitual residence;
>
> 3. Confirms that the adoption or application of laws by States which are designed to or result in the loss or removal of tenancy, use, ownership or other rights connected with housing or property, the active retraction of the right to reside within a particular place, or laws of abandonment employed against refugees or internally displaced persons pose serious impediments to the return and reintegration of refugees and internally displaced persons and to reconstruction and reconciliation;
>
> 4. Urges all States to ensure the free and fair exercise of the right to return to one's home and place of habitual residence by all refugees and internally displaced persons and to develop effective and expeditious legal, administrative and other procedures to ensure the free and fair exercise of this right, including fair and effective mechanisms designed to resolve outstanding housing and property problems....

of international human rights and humanitarian law is found in the Universal Declaration of Human Rights (Art. 8), the International Covenant on Civil and Political Rights (Art. 2), the International Convention on the Elimination of All Forms of Racial Discrimination (Art. 6), the Convention against Torture and Other Cruel, Inhuman or Degrading Treatment or Punishment (Art. 11), the Convention on the Rights of the Child at (Art 39), the African Charter on Human and Peoples' Rights (Art. 7), the American Convention on Human Rights (Art. 25), the European Convention for the Protection of Human Rights and Fundamental Freedoms (Art. 13), and others.

Likewise, the *UN Guiding Principles on Internal Displacement*[30] also explicitly enshrine recognition of the rights of displaced persons to return to return to their homes or places of habitual residence, combined with right to recover their property and possessions they left behind or were dispossessed of upon their displacement. Section V of this important standard addresses principles relating to return, resettlement and reintegration:

> 28(1) Competent authorities have the primary duty and responsibility to establish conditions, as well as provide the means, which allow internally displaced persons to return voluntarily, in safety and with dignity, to their homes or places of habitual residence, or to resettle voluntarily in another part of the country. Such authorities shall endeavour to facilitate the reintegration of returned or resettled internally displaced persons.
>
> 28(2) Special efforts should be made to ensure the full participation of internally displaced persons in the planning and management of their return or resettlement and reintegration.
>
> 29(1) Internally displaced persons who have returned to their homes or places of habitual residence or who have resettled in another part of the country shall not be discriminated against as a result of their having been displaced. They shall have the right to participate fully and equally in public affairs at all levels and have equal access to public services.
>
> 29(2) Competent authorities have the duty and responsibility to assist returned and/or resettled internally displaced persons to recover, to the extent possible, their property and possessions which they left behind or were dispossessed of upon their displacement. When recovery of such property and possessions is not possible, competent authorities shall provide or assist these persons in obtaining appropriate compensation or another form of just reparation.
>
> 30 All authorities concerned shall grant and facilitate for international humanitarian organizations and other appropriate actors, in the exercise of their respective mandates, rapid and unimpeded access to internally displaced persons to assist in their return or resettlement and reintegration.

Similarly, the *Basic Principles and Guidelines on the Right to a Remedy and Reparation for Victims of Gross Violations of International Human Rights Law and*

[30] Principles 1 and 2 outline the scope and content of the *Guiding Principles*: 1. These Guiding Principles address the specific needs of internally displaced persons worldwide. They identify rights and guarantees relevant to the protection of persons from forced displacement and to their protection and assistance during displacement as well as during return or resettlement and reintegration. 2. For the purposes of these Principles, internally displaced persons are persons or groups of persons who have been forced or obliged to flee or to leave their homes or places of habitual residence, in particular as a result of or in order to avoid the effects of armed conflict, situations of generalized violence, violations of human rights or natural or human-made disasters, and who have not crossed an internationally recognized State border. UN Doc. E/CN.4/1998/53/Add.2 (1998).

Serious Violations of International Humanitarian Law[31] constitute one of the most comprehensive international standards pertaining to restitution. As it now stands, this text provides a detailed framework for developing a restitution program, grounded in and wholly consistent with international human rights and humanitarian law. The following provisions are particularly relevant:

> 15. Adequate, effective and prompt reparation is intended to promote justice by redressing gross violations of international human rights law or serious violations of international humanitarian law. Reparation should be proportional to the gravity of the violations and the harm suffered. In accordance with its domestic laws and international legal obligations, a State shall provide reparation to victims for acts or omissions which can be attributed to the State and constitute gross violations of international human rights law or serious violations of international humanitarian law. In cases where a person, a legal person, or other entity is found liable for reparation to a victim, such party should provide reparation to the victim or compensate the State if the State has already provided reparation to the victim.
>
> 16. States should endeavour to establish national programmes for reparation and other assistance to victims in the event that the parties liable for the harm suffered are unable or unwilling to meet their obligations.
>
> 17. States shall, with respect to claims by victims, enforce domestic judgements for reparation against individuals or entities liable for the harm suffered and endeavour to enforce valid foreign legal judgements for reparation in accordance with domestic law and international legal obligations. To that end, States should provide under their domestic laws effective mechanisms for the enforcement of reparation judgements.
>
> 18. In accordance with domestic law and international law, and taking account of individual circumstances, victims of gross violations of international human rights law and serious violations of international humanitarian law should, as appropriate and proportional to the gravity of the violation and the circumstances of each case, be provided with full and effective reparation, as laid out in principles 19 to 23, which include the following forms: restitution, compensation, rehabilitation, satisfaction and guarantees of non-repetition.
>
> 19. Restitution should, whenever possible, restore the victim to the original situation before the gross violations of international human rights law or serious violations of international humanitarian law occurred. Restitution includes, as appropriate: restoration of liberty, enjoyment of human rights, identity, family life and citizenship, return to one's place of residence, restoration of employment and return of property.

[31] Adopted and proclaimed by General Assembly resolution 60/147 of 16 December 2005.

Also of relevance, the *UN Comprehensive Human Rights Guidelines on Development-Based Displacement* (1997), recognize restitution rights for persons evicted owing to displacement due to nonconflict circumstances. [32]

The Right to Respect for the Home

Under article 17 (right to respect of the home) of the Covenant on Civil and Political Rights, "interference with one's home" can only take place "in cases envisaged by the law." It is not enough, however, that such interference is addressed in the law, but it must (particularly when involving the complete removal of ownership or tenancy rights without relocation, rehousing or compensation) "be in accordance with the provisions, aims and objectives of the Covenant and should be, in any event, reasonable in the particular circumstances."[33] The Human Rights Committee has interpreted the article 17 to mean that:

> 1. ...The obligations imposed by this article require the State to adopt legislative and other measures to give effect to the prohibition against such interferences and attacks as well as to the protection of this right....
>
> 4. The expression "arbitrary interference" is also relevant to the protection of the right provided for in article 17. In the Committee's view the expression "arbitrary interference" can also extend to interference provided for under the law. The introduction of the concept of arbitrariness is intended to guarantee that even interference provided for by a law should be in accordance with the provisions, aims and objectives of the Covenant and should be, in any event, reasonable in the particular circumstances.[34]

The pronouncement asserting that "arbitrary interference can also extend to interference provided for under the law" makes an important contribution to any efforts made by States that seek to justify their violations of international law based on the content of domestic law. Under customary law, including the *Vienna Convention on the Law of Treaties*, States are prohibited from justifying their noncompliance with international obligations due to domestic law provisions.[35]

[32] Restitution and return: Para. 25. All persons, groups and communities subjected to forced evictions have the right, but shall not be forced to return to their homes, lands or places of origin. (UN Doc. E/CN.4/Sub.2/1997/7, Annex (1997)).

[33] Human Rights Committee (1988) *General Comment No. 16 of Human Rights Committee on Article 17 of the Covenant on Civil and Political Rights (1988) (The right to respect of privacy, family, home and correspondence, and protection of honour and reputation (Article 17)).*

[34] Id.

[35] *Vienna Convention on the Law of Treaties*: Article 26 *Pacta sunt servanda*: Every treaty in force is binding upon the parties to it and must be performed by them in good faith. Article 27 *Internal law and observance of treaties*: A party may not invoke the provisions of its internal law as justification for its failure to perform a treaty. This rule is without prejudice to article 46.

At another level, the European Court on Human Rights, in the case of *Akdivar and others v. Turkey*,[36] which addressed Articles 8 and Prot 1(1) of the European Convention on Human Rights, the Court held that:

> [T]here can be no doubt that the deliberate burning of the applicants' homes and their contents constitutes at the same time a serious interference with the right to respect for their family lives and homes and with the peaceful enjoyment of possessions. No justification for these interferences being proffered by the respondent Government – which confined their response to denying involvement of the security forces in the incident – the Court must conclude that there has been a violation of both Article 8 [respect of the home] of the Convention and Article 1 of Protocol No. 1 [peaceful enjoyment of possessions].

Property Rights and the Peaceful Enjoyment of Possessions

The right to property has a long and controversial history under international human rights law. Even though the Universal Declaration recognizes property rights in Article 17,[37] the subsequent Covenants both failed to enshrine these rights, although, of course, several other rights they do enshrine are of direct relevance (housing rights, the right to respect for the home, etc.). Human rights treaties in Europe and the Americas and Africa (there is no Asian system of human rights protection, nor a regional human rights treaty) all recognize various formulations of property rights. At the same time, the jurisprudence under the European Convention of Human Rights on Article 1 of Protocol One ("the right to the peaceful enjoyment of possessions") provides a valuable source of case law on property rights anywhere. For instance, in the case of *Loizidou v. Turkey*, which involved the impossibility of return to one's property, the European Court noted that:

> ... the complaint is not limited to access to property but is much wider and concerns a factual situation: because of the continuous denial of access the applicant had effectively lost all control, as well as all possibilities to use, to sell, to bequeath, to mortgage, to develop and to enjoy her land.... The continuous denial of access must therefore be regarded as an interference with her rights under Article 1 of Protocol No. 1.[38]

The Court has also issued the following pronouncement with respect to the legitimacy of actions by the State resulting in the deprivation of property:

> In this connection, the Court recalls that not only must a measure depriving a person of his property pursue, on the facts as well as in principle, a legitimate aim 'in the

[36] Application 99/1995/605/693, Judgment 16 September 1996.

[37] Article 17(1) Everyone has the right to own property alone as well as in association with others. (2) No one shall be arbitrarily deprived of his property.

[38] *Loizidou v. Turkey* (40/1993/435/514, judgment 18 December 1996).

> public interest', but there must also be a reasonable relationship of proportionality between the aim employed and the aim sought to be realized.... The requisite balance will not be found if the person concerned has had to bear an individual and excessive burden.... Clearly, compensation terms are material to the assessment whether a fair balance has been struck between the various interests at stake and, notably, whether or not a disproportionate burden has been imposed on the person who has been deprived of his possessions.[39]

Nondiscrimination and Equality of Treatment

The principles of nondiscrimination and equality of treatment form cornerstones of human rights law and now constitute customary international law. As such, if the confiscation of housing, land or property can be argued to have been based on any discriminatory grounds, such as race, colour, sex, nationality, ethnic origin, political belief, social origin, sexual orientation, citizenship or other ground, the confiscation could lawfully be declared to be null and void, and thus subject to remedial measures including restitution. The Convention on the Elimination of Racial Discrimination, in Article 1, defines discrimination as "Any distinction, exclusion, restriction or preference based on race, colour, descent, or national or ethnic origin which has the purpose or effect of nullifying or impairing the recognition, enjoyment or exercise, on an equal footing, of human rights and fundamental freedoms in the political, economic, social, cultural or any other field of public life." At the 2001 World Conference on Racial Discrimination in South Africa, the final Durban Declaration recognises the restitution rights of refugees:

> 65. We recognise the right of refugees to return voluntarily to their homes and properties in dignity and safety, and urge all States to facilitate such return.

The Principles of Reasonableness and Proportionality

The international legal principles of *reasonableness* and *proportionality* are also important in cases dealing with housing, land, or property. If States revoked such rights in an arbitrary manner or applied the law based on racial, ethnic, or national origin or other forms of discrimination, this would necessarily be classified as both unreasonable and disproportionate, and thus a violation of international law.

The Fair Balance Doctrine

The now widely accepted *fair balance doctrine* stipulates that in determining the compatibility of a certain act by a State with regard to housing and property issues, any

[39] *Lithgow and others v. U.K* (Judgment 8 July 1986, Series A, No. 102; (1986) 8 EHRR 329, para. 120).

interference in the exercise of these rights must strike a *fair balance* between the aim sought to be achieved and the nature of the act. In determining the existence of fair balance, the European human rights bodies have noted there had been a violation of Article 1 of Protocol No. 1 (the right to the peaceful enjoyment of possessions) when no fair balance had been struck between the interest of protecting the right to property and the demands of the general interest as a result of the length of expropriation proceedings, the difficulties encountered by the applicants to obtain full payment of the compensation awarded, and the deterioration of the plots eventually returned to them.[40] In the case of *Zubani v. Italy*,[41] the Court decided that there had been a violation of Article 1 of Protocol No. 1, as no fair balance had been struck between the interest of protecting the right to property and the demands of the general interest as a result of the length of expropriation proceedings, the difficulties encountered by the applicants to obtain full payment of the compensation awarded and the deterioration of the plots eventually returned to them. On the other hand, in the case of *Papamichalopoulos and others v. Greece (14556/89)*, (9 April 1992), where applicants were unable to recover property occupied by the Greek Navy since 1976, the Court asserted that:

> In this connection, the Court recalls that not only must a measure depriving a person of his property pursue, on the facts as well as in principle, a legitimate aim 'in the public interest', but there must also be a reasonable relationship of proportionality between the aim employed and the aim sought to be realised.... The requisite balance will not be found if the person concerned has had to bear an individual and excessive burden.... Clearly, compensation terms are material to the assessment whether a fair balance has been struck between the various interests at stake and, notably, whether or not a disproportionate burden has been imposed on the person who has been deprived of his possessions.[42]

The Right to Return

The right to return is found in numerous international instruments.[43] As far back as 1946, the UN Economic and Social Council asserted that "the main task concerning displaced persons is to encourage and assist in every way possible their early

40 *Zubani v. Italy* (European Court on Human Rights, Judgment 7 August 1996).

41 European Court on Human Rights, Judgment 7 August 1996. Whereas in *Powell and Rainer v. U.K.*, the Court decided that: "When States' positive obligations are involved, the Court considers that the second paragraph is not applicable, since it refers to "interference", but that regard must be had to the fair balance that has to be struck between the competing interests of the individual and of the community as a whole" (172 Eur. Ct. H.R. (ser. A), para. 41 (1990)).

42 *Lithgow and others v. U.K* (Judgment 8 July 1986, Series A, No. 102; (1986) 8 EHRR 329, para. 120).

43 These include: UDHR (Art. 13): 1. Everyone has the right to freedom of movement and residence within the borders of each State. 2. Everyone has the right to leave any country, including his own, and to return to his country. The right to return is also addressed in: CCPR (Art. 12(4)), CERD

return to their countries of origin."[44] The UN General Assembly has repeatedly recognized rights to return of refugees, as well.[45] UNHCR's consistent position has been that: "In international human rights law, the basic principle underlying voluntary repatriation is the right to return to one's own country."[46] Legal scholar Manfred Nowak has convincingly argued that States cannot invoke the fact that refugees who have a "second home country" as a justification for preventing them from exercising rights to return.[47] Indeed, the favored and most "durable" of all solutions relating to refugee return is voluntary repatriation. Importantly, the right to return is derived from human rights law, and not exclusively from peace agreements or voluntary repatriation agreements, or other standards. As such, this right cannot be negotiated away due to its character as an individual right.

Article 12(4) of the Covenant on Civil and Political Rights provides one of the strongest codifications of the right to return. It stipulates that "No one shall be arbitrarily deprived of the right to enter his own country." In its interpretation of the meaning of this clause, the UN Human Rights Committee asserts in its General Comment No. 27 (1999) has asserted that:

> The right of a persons to enter his or her own country recognises the special relationship of a person to that country.... It includes not only the right to return after having left one's own country; it may also entitle a person to come to the country for the first time if he or she was born outside the country (for example, if that country is the person's State of nationality) (Para. 19). The scope of 'his own country' is broader than the concept of 'country of his nationality' – it is not limited to nationality in a formal sense, that is, nationality acquired at birth or be conferral; it embraces, at the very least, an individual who, because of his or her special ties to or claims in relation to a given country, cannot be considered to be

(Art. 5(d)(ii)), CRC (Art. 10(2)), ECHR (Fourth Protocol, Art. 3(2)), ACHR (Art. 22(5)), African Charter on Human and Peoples' Rights (Art. 12(2)). On the relationship between the right to return and voluntary repatriation, see: Marjoleine Zieck (1997) *UNHCR and Voluntary Repatriation of Refugees: A Legal Analysis*, Martinus Nijhoff Publishers, the Hague.

44 Resolution 8(1) of 12 February 1946.

45 For instance: General Assembly resolution 35/124 (1980), adopted 11 December 1980, provides: The General Assembly, Gravely concerned over the increasing flows of refugees in many parts of the world, Deeply disturbed by the human suffering affecting millions of men, women and children who flee or are forcibly expelled from their homelands and seek refuge in other countries, Reaffirming the right of refugees to return to their homes in their homelands....

2. Invites all Member States to convey to the Secretary-General their comments and suggestions on international co-operation to avert new flows of refugees and to facilitate the return of those refugees who with to return.

46 UNHCR (1996) *Handbook Voluntary Repatriation: International Protection*, 7.

47 He argues that "As soon as the political situation in the country of origin of refugees or displaced persons improves and these persons wish to return to their 'original home country', the establishment of a 'second home country' must not be invoked for the purpose of preventing them returning home, even if masses of people are claiming this right". Manfred Nowak (1993) *UN Covenant on Civil and Political Rights: CCPR Commentary*, Kehl, p. 220.

> a mere alien. This would be the case, for example, of nationals of a country who have there been stripped of their nationality in violation of international law, and of individuals whose country of nationality has been incorporated in or transferred to another national entity, whose nationality is being denied them (Para. 20).

The Human Rights Committee has also proclaimed that the right to return applies to descendents who have maintained a "close and enduring connection" with the area.

UNITED NATIONS BODIES

The UN Charter authorizes the establishment of various bodies including the General Assembly, the Security Council, the Economic and Social Council, and any such subsidiary bodies deemed necessary. One such subsidiary body is the Council on Human Rights. Each of these bodies has explicitly addressed and supported efforts to entrench the rights of refugees and displaced persons to housing, land, and property restitution. This section very briefly outlines how each of these bodies has done so.

UN SECURITY COUNCIL

The UN Security Council has adopted numerous resolutions regarding housing and property restitution in the context of refugee and IDP return. Most of these resolutions were adopted in reaction to specific country or regional situations. In addition to the relevant resolutions concerning Palestine, several of the countries addressed by the Security Council in this respect include: Yugoslavia (Kosovo),[48] Yugoslavia,[49] Georgia (Abkhazia),[50] Croatia,[51] Iraq (Kuwait),[52] Cyprus,[53] Namibia,[54] Cambodia,[55] Azerbaijan,[56] Tajikistan,[57] and numerous others. Other resolutions reaffirm the principle that property transactions made under duress are null and void,[58] whereas

48 Resolution 1244 (1999) (Kosovo), UN Doc. S/RES/1244 (1999), 10 June 1999.
49 SC Res. 752 (Yugoslavia), and numerous others.
50 SC Res. 876, 19 October 1993; Resolution 1036 (1996) (regarding Abkhazia and the Republic of Georgia), 12 January 1996; Resolution 971 (1995) (regarding Abkhazia and the Republic of Georgia), 12 January 1995.
51 Resolution 1009 (1995) (regarding the Republic of Croatia) (relevant provisions), adopted 10 August 1995.
52 Resolution 687 (1991) (regarding Kuwait), adopted 2 March 1991.
53 SC Res. 361, 30 August 1974: Calls on parties to "permit persons who wish to do so to return to their homes."
54 SC Res. 385, 30 January 1976.
55 SC Res. 745, 28 February 1992.
56 SC Res. 853, 29 July 1993 (and others).
57 SC Res. 999, 16 June 1995 (and others).
58 SC Res. 947, 20 September 1994.

others call on parties to lift time restrictions on repossession of property and other obstacles to restitution.[59]

UN GENERAL ASSEMBLY

Like the Security Council, the UN General Assembly has also adopted a number of country-specific resolutions regarding housing and property restitution in the context of refugee and IDP return. In addition to the annual resolutions adopted since 1948 reaffirming the right to return of Palestinian refugees to their homes and places of residence,[60] the General Assembly has routinely issued similar pronouncements in support of refugees in numerous countries.[61]

TREATY BODIES

Various United Nations Treaty Bodies – those Committees entrusted with monitoring compliance with particular human rights treaties – have explicitly addressed housing and property restitution for refugees and internally displaced persons. Several such initiatives are addressed here.

The Committee on the Elimination of All Forms of Racial Discrimination

The Committee on the Elimination of Racial Discrimination (CERD) monitors compliance with the UN Convention on the Elimination of All Forms of Racial Discrimination, the most important international treaty specifying the measures to undertake in order to eliminate racial discrimination. The Convention entered into force on 4 January 1969. CERD has adopted several explicit decisions regarding

[59] SC Res. 1019, 9 November 1995.

[60] It should also be noted that General Assembly resolutions on Palestine have increasingly addressed the specific property components of eventual return. For instance, UNGA Res A/RES/51/129 of December 1996 affirms that: "Palestinian Arab refugees are entitled to their property and to the income derived therefrom, in conformity with the principles of justice and equity". It "requests the Secretary-General to take all appropriate steps ... for the protection of Arab property, assets and property rights in Israel and to preserve and modernize the existing records."

[61] To cite but one of numerous such examples: Resolution 51/114 (1997) (on the Situation of human rights in Rwanda), adopted 12 December 1996, provides: 7. Invites all States, the organizations and bodies of the United Nations system and intergovernmental and non-governmental organizations to continue and to intensify their contributions of financial and technical support to accelerate the efforts of the Government of Rwanda to, inter alia, restore the judicial system, promote reconciliation through the recently established Commission for National Reconciliation and safely reintegrate returning refugees in conditions of safety and dignity, including addressing competing claims to housing and property.

housing and property restitution for refugees and IDPs.[62] In *General Recommendation 22 (1997) (Article 5 on refugees and displaced persons)*,[63] CERD made the following pronouncements, strongly supporting restitution rights:

> Conscious of the fact that foreign military, non-military and/or ethnic conflicts have resulted in massive flows of refugees and the displacement of persons on the basis of ethnic criteria in many parts of the world, 2. Emphasizes in this respect that: (a) All such refugees and displaced persons have the right freely to return to their homes of origin under conditions of safety; (b) States parties are obliged to ensure that the return of such refugees and displaced persons is voluntary and to observe the principle of non-refoulement and non-expulsion of refugees; (c) All such refugees and displaced persons have, after their return to their homes of origin, the right to have restored to them property of which they were deprived in the course of the conflict and to be compensated appropriately for any such property that cannot be restored to them. Any commitments or statements relating to such property made under duress are null and void; (d) All such refugees and displaced persons have, after their return to their homes of origin, the right to participate fully and equally in public affairs at all levels and to have equal access to public services and to receive rehabilitation assistance.

CERD expressed similar sentiments in *General Recommendation No. 23 (1997) (on indigenous people's)*.[64] This text outlines the rights of indigenous peoples to have any lands and territories which they were deprived from, subject to restitution. Paragraph 5 stipulates:

> The Committee especially calls upon States parties to recognize and protect the rights of indigenous peoples to own, develop, control and use their communal lands, territories and resources and, where they have been deprived of their lands and territories traditionally owned or otherwise inhabited or used without their free and informed consent, to take steps to return those lands and territories. Only when this is for factual reasons not possible, the right to restitution should be substituted by the right to just, fair and prompt compensation. Such compensation should as far as possible take the form of lands and territories.

62 CERD has also addressed the issues of restitution relating to Palestinian refugees: "The right of many Palestinians to return and possess their homes in Israel is currently denied. The State party should give high priority to remedying this situation. Those who cannot repossess their homes should be entitled to compensation." UN doc: CERD/C/304/Add.45.

63 UN Doc. A/51/18 (1997), adopted 23 August 1996.

64 The Recommendation states, *inter alia*, 3. The Committee is conscious of the fact that in many regions of the world indigenous peoples have been, and are still being, discriminated against and deprived of their human rights and fundamental freedoms and in particular that they have lost their land and resources to colonists, commercial companies and State enterprises. Consequently, the preservation of their culture and their historical identity has been and still is jeopardized. UN Doc. A/52/18, annex V (1998), adopted 18 August 1997.

The Committee on Economic, Social and Cultural Rights

The Committee on Economic, Social and Cultural Rights is entrusted with monitoring compliance with the Covenant on Economic, Social and Cultural Rights, the premier international treaty on these rights. The Committee, in addition to addressing restitution issues in the context of States reports, has also addressed these themes in two of its general comments: General Comment No. 7 (1997) (on forced evictions)[65] and General Comment No. 4 (1991) (the right to adequate housing).[66]

Human Rights Committee

As previously mentioned, the Human Rights Committee monitors compliance with the Covenant on Civil and Political Rights and has specifically addressed restitution issues within various general comments (see right to return, earlier in this chapter).

Committee against Torture

The Committee against Torture monitors State compliance with the Convention against Torture. Although this Committee has not addressed restitution, given its mandate, it has issued important decisions equating the practice of house demolitions to violations of the Convention. In one such instance, the Committee declared that:

> (j) Israeli policies on house demolitions, which may, in certain instances, amount to cruel, inhuman or degrading treatment or punishment (Article 16 of the Convention).[67]

PEACE AGREEMENTS

In addition to the various areas of law and practice, a range of peace agreements also explicitly recognize the right of refugees and other displaced persons to return to their original homes. This is a vitally important development. It is now widely agreed that restitution will stand a greater chance of success and in getting the political attention it deserves if such assurances are included explicitly within such agreements, rather than treated as a secondary afterthought once a postconflict phase begins. In recent years, restitution considerations have been included in

[65] UN Doc. E/1998/22, annex IV (1998), Adopted 20 May 1997.
[66] UN Doc. E/1992/23 (1992), Adopted 13 December 1991.
[67] CAT/C/XXVII/Concl.5, 23 November 2001.

peace agreements or other agreements concerning the ending of armed conflicts in Kosovo,[68] Bosnia and Herzegovina,[69] Guatemala,[70] Rwanda,[71] Cambodia,[72] and Mozambique.[73] Some of these agreements are discussed elsewhere in this textbook, particularly in Chapters 5 and 8.

UN HIGH COMMISSIONER FOR REFUGEES (UNHCR)

According to the UN High Commissioner for Refugees, "in accordance with international law, repatriation should be governed by the following principles: the right to return, non-discrimination, voluntariness based on informed consent, return in conditions of safety and dignity, respect for private property and freedom of abode."[74] Voluntary repatriation as a solution to refugee situations has its origins in the 1950 General Assembly resolution adopting the UNHCR Statute. Resolution 428 (V) of 14 December 1950 calls on governments to cooperate with the High Commissioner in the performance of his functions, inter alia, by "assisting the High Commissioner in his efforts to promote the voluntary repatriation of refugees." Since then, various Executive Committee Conclusions have further elaborated the role and policy perspectives of UNHCR with respect to voluntary repatriation.[75] The more recent UNHCR Handbook on Voluntary Repatriation[76] provides additional guidance on these issues.[77] The Handbook stresses, for instance, that UNHCR's mandate includes the role of promoting "the creation of conditions that are conducive to voluntary return in safety and with dignity" and to "promote the voluntary repatriation of refugees once conditions are conducive to return."

68 *UN Security Council Resolution 1244 (1999)*, 10 June 1999.

69 *General Framework Agreement for Peace in Bosnia and Herzegovina, Annex 7 Agreement on Refugees and Displaced Persons (1996).*

70 *Agreement on the Identity and Rights of Indigenous Peoples (Guatemala Peace Accords) (31 March 1995), UN Doc. A/49/882-S/1995/256.*

71 *Arusha Peace Agreement (Rwanda) (4 August 1993).*

72 *Agreements on a Comprehensive Political Settlement of the Cambodia Conflict (1991) (relevant provisions) 'Paris Agreement'.*

73 *Protocol III of the 1992 Comprehensive Peace Agreement in Mozambique* (The Rome Process: General Peace Agreement for Mozambique, 4 October 1992. Protocol III.

74 UNHCR (1995) "Note on Voluntary Repatriation of Refugees," submitted to the Regional Conference on Assistance to Refugees, Returnees and Displaced persons in the Great Lakes Region.

75 The Executive Committee of the UN Office of the High Commissioner for Refugees (EXCOM) is made up of government representatives and is the main policy body within the Office of the High Commissioner. The EXCOM expresses its views through the issuance of EXCOM Conclusions. Though not legally binding upon State Parties to the 1951 Refugee Convention or it 1967 Protocol, EXCOM Conclusions are considered persuasive interpretations of the rights protected by those treatiesed that international cooperation be aimed at achieving this solution and should be further developed.

76 UNHCR (1996) *Handbook Voluntary Repatriation: International Protection*, Geneva.

77 Current UNHCR policy on voluntary repatriation is effectively comprised of the following core elements: (1) Repatriation should be voluntary and based on informed consent; (2) UNHCR,

Consistent with the position of international law and practice on voluntary repatriation, UNHCR has been increasingly active in its support for housing, land, and property restitution for returning refugees. Indicative of the growing seriousness accorded these issues by UNHCR, for the first time, the agency issued an internal memorandum to all offices in late 2001 outlining what is effectively UNHCR policy on the recovery of refugee homes and properties.[78] The memorandum contains a range of far-reaching provisions:

> 1. Recovery of refugees' homes and property in their countries of origin needs to be addressed consistently to ensure that effective solutions to refugee displacement are found. Experience has shown that voluntary repatriation operations are unlikely to be fully successful or sustainable in the longer term if housing and property issues – being an integral part of return in safety and dignity – are left unattended.
>
> 2. Human rights law in relation to the right to adequate housing has evolved significantly over the past decade. The right of a refugee to return to her/his country[79] is now increasingly coupled with her/his right to adequate housing.[80] In this context, the right to adequate housing has developed to extend to the right not to be arbitrarily deprived of housing and property in the first place. As corollary to this, refugees have the right to return not only to their countries of origin but also to recover the homes from which they were previously evicted (restitution). If this is not possible, then the right to adequate compensation for any loss suffered comes into play.
>
> In most circumstances, conditions of safe and dignified return will not and cannot be met without adequate safeguards designed to protect the rights of returnees to housing and property restitution.
>
> If housing is to be properly treated as an issue of human rights, then all housing-related policies and practices of UNHCR need per se to be treated as issues of refugee protection.
>
> (iii) Housing issues for refugees should be addressed at an early stage in the cycle of refugee displacement and not only after refugees have returned to their countries of origin.

governments and private organizations (NGOs) have a joint (tripartite) role to play in voluntary repatriation; (3) Voluntary repatriation should be both facilitated and promoted; (4) There must have been a change in the circumstances that led to flight; and (5) Security guarantees must be in place. These elements, of course, must be applied in conjunction with other Statutaory obligations, including the principle of *non-refoulement* and the absence of any well-founded fear of persecution.

78 UNHCR Inter-Office Memorandum No. 104/2001, 28 November 2001, UNHCR Field Office Memorandum No. 101/2001, 28 November 2001.

79 Article 13(2) of the 1948 Universal Declaration of Human Rights and Article 12 of the 1966 UN Covenant on Civil and Political Rights.

80 Article 11 of the 1966 UN Covenant on Economic, Social and Cultural Rights.

The Memorandum also outlines several steps UNHCR staff should take to strengthen the prospects for successful housing, land, and property restitution for returning refugees, including the need to promote housing and property rights within peace agreements,[81] promoting housing and property rights within repatriation plans,[82] and the need for UNHCR field offices to develop plans of action on housing and property restitution.[83] The field offices, which would generally be responsible on a daily basis for ensuring that restitution actually took place, are also encouraged in the pre-return phase to begin implementing the envisaged plans of action for housing and property restitution to identify any major housing-related obstacles to return, including the extent of secondary occupation of refugee homes, whether housing abandonment laws were adopted after flight, whether inheritance laws discriminate against women or other groups, whether unjust and arbitrary applications of law occurred after flight, whether housing and property registration records were destroyed or lost after flight, and whether effective and impartial judicial remedies are in place. It also calls on UNHCR to identify all relevant national laws relevant to the housing and property rights of returnees, in particular laws relating to the right to adequate housing and property restitution, the right to property and the peaceful

[81] UNHCR should attempt to play an active role in negotiations leading to peace agreements, with a view to ensuring that the housing and property aspects of voluntary repatriation are fully taken into account. UNHCR should seek to ensure that such agreements explicitly include provisions on the housing and property rights of those choosing to repatriate, and that judicial or other mechanisms designed to ensure the implementation of such rights are established. Where refugees voluntarily settle elsewhere, it should be stipulated that this does not affect their right to property restitution or, should this not be possible, compensation or other form of reparation.

[82] Assessment missions entrusted with preparing repatriation plans should examine how housing and property restitution will be most effectively integrated in the repatriation plan.

[83] Field Offices in countries of origin/return should develop a plan of action on housing and property restitution. This plan will form the first step in developing an effective UNHCR response to these issues. The plan should be based on both the prevailing international and (where consistent with international law) national legal normative frameworks.... Plans of action on housing and property restitution should include the promotion of measures that: Approach housing and property restitution as a human rights and refugee protection issue; Rectify and provide remedies for any unjust or arbitrary applications of law relating to refugee housing or property; Protect all persons from homelessness or other housing rights violations; Ensure consistency between domestic law and relevant international law; Ensure equal access to impartial and effective judicial and procedural remedies, including any specific mechanism established to promote housing and property restitution; Ensure that the reconstruction and rehabilitation of damaged housing is seen as an indispensable element of safe and dignified return and that these two processes are seen as forming key elements in the overall restitution process; Protect housing and property registration records where these still exist and, if necessary, re-establish housing and property registration systems; Support the establishment of legal aid centres to provide expert legal assistance to returnees seeking to invoke their rights to housing and property restitution; Ensure that effective systems are created for equitable redress and/or financial or other forms of compensation for returnees unable to exercise their rights to housing and property restitution. When developing plans of action, field offices should also take into account customary (traditional) structures for resolving disputes and addressing issues related to housing, land and property issues, as and where appropriate.

enjoyment of possessions, the right to protected against forced evictions, the right to privacy and respect for the home, the right to freedom of movement and to choose one's residence, and the rights of indigenous peoples.

The Memorandum also calls on UNHCR to promote legislative analysis,[84] legislative repeal,[85] and legislative reform.[86] Finally, the Memorandum outlines a series of measures that need to be taken to ensure the actual implementation of housing and restitution laws.[87]

VOLUNTARY REPATRIATION AGREEMENTS

Finally, even though not all voluntary repatriation agreements involving the return of refugees to their countries of origin include explicit reference to issues of housing, land, and property restitution, the clear trend over time leans heavily toward the inclusion of these issues, although their content varies across the agreements. There is an equally strong trend for more recent repatriation agreements to include such references – an indication of the growing acceptance of norms recognizing that the right to return and voluntary repatriation include the right to return to one's original homes and lands from which they were originally displaced. These rights are also increasingly linked to international human rights instruments and jurisprudence.

Among the voluntary repatriation agreements that explicitly recognize the rights of returning refugees to return to their original homes and to recover housing,

[84] Legislative analysis: Collect, translate, and analyze housing and property legislation currently in force in countries of origin.

[85] Legislative repeal: Identify any housing and property legislation that is inconsistent with international human rights standards.

[86] Legislative reform: Promote the development of a domestic legal system that is consistent with international human rights standards relating to housing and property rights.

[87] "Besides a fair and efficient property restitution framework, the consideration and promotion of additional measures may be necessary to ensure the full and effective implementation of restitution laws: Running of public information campaigns to inform claimants about their rights and obligations and to ensure that they receive the necessary guidance and counselling as to the procedures to be followed, including access to fair and effective remedies; De-mining and reconstruction projects should be tailored to support the implementation of property laws (e.g. priority of shelter projects for those who are currently occupying someone else's home); Restoration of infrastructure where it is damaged or destroyed; Establishment of mechanisms to resolve property issues of those who have decided not to return (e.g. creation of a fair and equitable environment for real estate transactions to allow displaced persons and refugees who do not wish to return to integrate into communities or environments of current displacement; such initiatives, however, must not undermine the principle of return); Creation of sufficient alternative accommodation (interim accommodation) to speed up the restitution process; Creation of social housing for those who do not have a place to return to; Establish linkage between property laws and legislation dealing with displaced persons and repatriates; In case of a flawed national property restitution framework, promote, if possible and as appropriate, proceedings to invoke the right to property before treaty bodies (e.g. European Court of Human Rights; Inter-American Commission on Human Rights)."

land, and properties that were confiscated and/or occupied by secondary occupants are agreements concerning refugees from Liberia, Angola, Rwanda, Bosnia and Herzegovina, and Croatia,[88] Georgia, Abkhazia and the Russian Federation,[89] Myanmar, Mozambique and Zimbabwe, Afghanistan and Iran, Burundi, Congo, Guatemala, South Africa and Viet Nam.

Questions and Exercises

1. Is HLP restitution a distinct, self-standing right under international human rights law? If so, why and on what grounds?
2. Which restitution standard stands the greatest chance of enforcement and why?
3. When should compensation for lost HLP rights be pursued instead of or in lieu of restitution demands?
4. Should a new international Convention on the Restitution Rights of Refugees and Displaced Persons be promulgated? If so, why and which provisions would such a new treaty contain?

Additional Resources

Amnesty International (1997) *Who's Living in My House? Obstacles to the Safe Return of Refugees and Internally Displaced People*, Report No. EUR/ID, Amnesty International Publications.

Simon Bagshaw (2003) "Property Restitution for Internally Displaced Persons: Developments in the Normative Framework," in Scott Leckie (ed.), *Returning Home: Housing and Property Restitution Rights of Refugees and Displaced Persons*, New York: Transnational Publishers.

[88] *Agreement on Return of Refugees (Between the Republic of Bosnia and Herzegovina (R.BiH) and Republic of Croatia (ROC) for return of refugees temporarily staying in Croatia)* (24 March 1995): Article 3:... Both parties will protect the refugees, disregarding their race, skin-colour, sex, language, religious, political or other conviction, national or social background, in accordance with international principles of protection of human rights and freedoms.... Article 4: The return of the refugees on the territory of Federation will be carried out according to the Plan of temporary territorial placement of the displaced persons – refugees and displaced persons as well as Program of return adopted by the Government of the Federation of Bosnia and Herzegovina.... Article 9: ROC agreed to offer to the R.BiH relevant statistics on refugees from R.BiH. The statistics relevant only for the implementation of this Agreement will refer to:... – previous and present residence in and out of ROC and R.BiH, as well as the route of movement; – other data available upon the request of one of parties to this Agreement, needed for investigation of return conditions in the sense of this Agreement.

[89] *Quadripartite Agreement on Voluntary Return of Refugees and Displaced Persons between Abkhazia, Georgia and the Russian Federation* (4 April 1994): Preamble (Para 9): Noting that the parties agree that a repatriation operation will imply prior to its implementation, that the security and living conditions, in the areas of return, are guaranteed; Article 3(f): The Parties shall ensure that repatriants, upon return, will be protected from harassment, including unauthorized charges or fees and threat to life or property. Article 3(g): Returnees shall, upon return, get back movable and immovable properties they left behind and should be helped to do so, or to receive whenever possible an appropriate compensation for their lost properties if return of property appears not feasible. The Commission mentioned under paragraph 5 below will establish a mechanism for such claims. Such compensation should be worked out in the framework of the reconstruction/rehabilitation programs to be established with a financial assistance through the United Nations Voluntary Fund.

Elizar Barkan (2000) *The Guilt of Nations: History and Injustices*, New York: W.W. Norton & Co.

COHRE (2006) *The Pinheiro Principles – United Nations Principles on Housing and Property Restitution for Refugees and Displaced Persons*, COHRE.

Hans Das (2004) "Restoring Property Rights in the Aftermath of War" *International and Comparative Law Quarterly* 53: 429–444.

International Center for Transitional Justice (2007) *The Contemporary Right to Property Restitution in the Context of Transitional Justice*, ICTJ.

J. Jackson-Preece (1998) "Ethnic Cleansing as an Instrument of National-State Creation: Changing State Practices and Evolving Legal Norms" *Human Rights Quarterly* 20, no. 4: 824.

Scott Leckie (ed.) (2007) *Housing, Land and Property Restitution Rights for Refugees and Displaced Persons: Laws, Cases and Materials*, Cambridge University Press.

(2003) *Returning Home: Housing and Property Restitution Rights of Refugees and Displaced Persons*, New York: Transnational Publishers.

(2000) "Housing and Property Issues for Refugees and Internally Displaced Persons in the Context of Return: Key Considerations for UNHCR Policy and Practice" *Refugee Survey Quarterly* 19, no. 3: 5.

Norwegian Refugee Council (2004) *ICLA Handbook, Return Facilitation, Information, Counselling and Legal Assistance*, NRC.

Paulo Sergio Pinheiro (2005) "Housing and Property Restitution in the Context of the Return of Refugees and Internally Displaced Persons" in *Final Report of the Special Rapporteur on Housing and Property Restitution in the Context of the Return of Refugees and Internally Displaced Persons*, UN Doc. E/CN.4/Sub.2/2005/17 and UN Doc. E/CN.4/Sub.2/2005/17/Add.1.

(2004) "Housing and Property Restitution in the Context of the Return of Refugees and Internally Displaced Persons" in *Progress Report of the Special Rapportuer, Paulo Sergio Pinheiro. Addendum. Commentary on the Draft Principles on Housing and Property Restitution for Refugees and Displaced Persons*, UN Doc. E/CN.4/Sub.2/2004/22/Add.1.

(2003) "Housing and Property Restitution in the Context of the Return of Refugees and Internally Displaced Persons" in *Preliminary Report of the Special Rapporteur Mr. Paulo Sergio Pinheiro, submitted in accordance with the Sub-Commission Resolution 2002/7*, UN Doc. E/CN.4/Sub.2/2003/11.

(2002) "The Return of Refugees' or Displaced Persons' Property," *Working paper submitted by Mr. Paulo Sergio Pinheiro pursuant to Sub-Commission decision 2001/122*, UN Doc. E/CN.4/Sub.2/2002/17.

Rhodri C. Williams (2007) "The Contemporary Right to Property Restitution in the Context of Transitional Justice," *Occasional Paper Series*, International Center for Transitional Justice.

M. Zieck (1997) *UNHCR and Voluntary Repatriation of Refugees: A Legal Analysis*, The Hague: Martinus Nijhoff Publishers.

R.W. Zweig (1993) "Restitution of Property and Refugee Rehabilitation: Two Case Studies" *Journal of Refugee Studies* 6, no. ¼: 56–64.

5

Restitution Mechanisms and Institutional Frameworks

Many countries have engaged in processes designed to restore land, housing, and property to displaced persons, refugees, and others who were arbitrarily deprived of their homes, lands, and properties because of conflict. Other countries have dealt effectively with sometimes large-scale restitution claims procedures and have concluded – often very successfully – a comprehensive restitution process. Still others are presently considering proposals designed to allow restitution processes to proceed. Restitution processes are often complex, time-consuming exercises that address inherently controversial and politically charged issues. Care must be taken to manage the expectations of potential claimants and ensure that the restitution process is transparent and clear. The temporal and spatial boundaries of the restitution process, for example, must be clarified, justified, and explained to the population. There is no single blueprint for success, and each country must identify its own way forward while learning from international precedents and respecting national and international laws. However, if the State (generally in conjunction with international organizations) can provide the necessary combination of impartiality, political commitment, and financial support, the pay-offs can be very significant. The legitimacy of the State in the eyes of its citizens, as well as the international community, can be much enhanced, while the resolution of potentially explosive grievances over HLP rights contributes to a more stable and peaceful political and economic legacy.

This chapter will briefly outline the restitution experiences of a cross-section of diverse countries and attempt to provide an overview of the legal methodologies used to implement restitution rights, the key procedural issues involved, and the mechanisms and modalities often associated with restitution. This chapter is not comprehensive, but rather attempts to provide a cross-section of actual restitution programs and how they operate in practice.

SOUTH AFRICA

The *Land Restitution Act* (1994) acts as implementing legislation for the restitution clauses of the *Constitution of the Republic of South Africa* (Act No. 108 of 1996) that provide for restitution of property or equitable redress to a person or community dispossessed of property after 19 June 1913, as a result of past racially discriminatory laws or practices. The Act created both a Commission on Restitution of Land Rights and a Land Claims Court. The *Land Restitution Act* provides:

> 2. (1) A person shall be entitled to restitution of a right in land if- (a) he or she is a person or community dispossessed of a right in land after 19 June 1913 as a result of past racially discriminatory laws or practices or a direct descendant of such a person.... (1A) No person shall be entitled to restitution of a right in land if- (a) just and equitable compensation as contemplated in section 25(3) of the Constitution; or (b) any other consideration which is just and equitable, calculated a the time of any dispossession of such right, was received in respect of such dispossession. 3. Subject to the provisions of this Act a person shall be entitled to claim title in land if such claimant or his, her or its antecedent- (a) was prevented from obtaining or retaining title to the claimed land because of a law which would have been inconsistent with the prohibition of racial discrimination contained in section 9(3) of the Constitution had that subsection been in operation at the relevant time; and (b) proves that the registered owner of the land holds title as a result of a transaction between such registered owner or his, her or its antecedents and the claimant or his, her or its antecedents, in terms of which such registered owner or his, her or its antecedents held the land on behalf of he claimant or his, her or its antecedents.

South Africa restitution claims for lost property could, therefore, be submitted by claimants for injustices perpetrated almost a century earlier. More than 63,000 claims, involving more than 300,000 potential beneficiaries, were lodged with the Land Claims Commission by the cut-off date in 1998. More than 80 percent of the claims were urban claims. By the end of 1997, more than 150,000 hectares of land had been restored to more than 27,000 people throughout the country.[1]

During the transition to democracy in South Africa, restitution was seen by the majority population as a crucial means to counterbalance the constitutional protection of property rights that were mainly seen to benefit the white minority. Restitution was also viewed as a critical element in addressing past injustices and promoting long-term national reconciliation and social stability. It was largely agreed that to limit restitution rights to lost ownership rights would discriminate against the poor. The Act, therefore, enshrines a "right in land," meaning "any right in land whether registered or unregistered, and may include the interest of a labour tenant

[1] Dept. of Land Affairs (1997) *Annual Report.*

and sharecropper, a customary law interest, the interest of a beneficiary under a trust arrangement, and beneficial occupation for a continuous period of not less than 10 years prior to the dispossession in question." With respect to tenancies, where land is owned by the State, restitution usually also involves converting the preexisting land rights into ownership.

Despite all of the best intentions of those supporting the restitution process in South Africa, it was clear almost from the outset that – similar to all restitution efforts – the process was going to be long, arduous, and complex, but nonetheless vital for justice. This was to be the case even though strong political will existed at all levels for restitution to succeed. Geoff Budlender, who was intimately involved with the restitution process, has noted several of the key lessons of the South African restitution process, including: how to deal with successive acts of dispossession, how to deal with "current owners," how to balance judicial and administrative procedures, how to define the extent of the right to restitution, whether or not to define a limited period for exercising the right, the need for administrative discretion and flexible remedies, and the necessity of employing a rights-based approach to restitution rather than treating it as a matter of government largesse.[2]

The South African experience reveals the importance of having *flexible remedies* available for those adjudicating housing, land, and property restitution matters. Under the 1994 Act, affected persons can benefit from the *restoration* of the land that was lost or *equitable redress* that may take the form of provision of alternative land, cash compensation, or the opportunity to benefit from other government development programs. The restitution objectives of South Africa appear to have been initially bogged down by a range of legal and judicial details, many of which have been considerably decreased since the instigation of administrative (as opposed to purely judicial) procedures to deal with restitution claims. In more positive terms, the South African restitution process reveals that a country can seek to allow remedial justice for land-based human rights violations that took place almost a full century before the restitution process itself. Moreover, even though the program have faced considerable difficulties, the fact remains that the Constitution and subsequent laws clearly provided restitution rights to dispossessed persons, and hundreds of thousands of victims and heirs stand to benefit directly from restitution.

TAJIKISTAN

HLP restitution issues figured prominently during the postconflict period in Tajikistan, and the experiences of the country with restitution were remarkably

[2] Geoff Budlender (1999) "Restitution for Housing and Property Rights – Some Lessons from the South African Experience" *Refugee Survey Quarterly* 19, no. 3: 224.

successful in restoring refugee properties to them upon return. During the ethnic conflict of the early 1990s, more than 60,000 persons fled to Afghanistan and a further 500,000 moved to the capital Dushanbe or into the mountains. As a result, many of the homes of refugees and IDPs were destroyed or illegally occupied by members of opposing ethnic groups. The reconstruction of damaged housing and the illegal occupation of housing rapidly came to be seen as the largest obstacles to return once conditions of security had been established. UNHCR mediation at the government level encouraged the early introduction of legislation aimed at protecting returnee rights and discouraging the practice of illegal house occupation. UNCHR Field Officers provided mediated solutions to some of the more difficult illegal house occupations, often through informal discussions.

The Law of the Republic of Tajikistan on Forced Migrants (20 July 1994) goes into considerable detail concerning the rights of refugees and IDPs to housing and property restitution.[3] The law recognizes, for instance:

> 4. With the aim of facilitating the earliest social and economic adaptation of the refugees-citizens of the Republic of Tajikistan and forced migrants returned to the places of permanent residence, the Ministry of Internal Affairs of the Republic of Tajikistan, hukumats of oblasts, cities and rayons of the Republic of Tajikistan in common with the agencies of the Procurator's Office of the Republic of Tajikistan shall:
>
> – immediately vacate illegally occupied dwellings owned or rented by the refugees-citizens of the Republic of Tajikistan and forced migrants in houses belonging to the State or communal housing fund and pass them to their rightful owners;
>
> – in case of the destruction or loss of the State-owned dwelling, provide out of turn an available dwelling space at his whereabouts in conformity with the standards in force in the Republic. According to the wish of the victims, in return for the dwelling, allot them a land plot for the construction of a dwelling house or give them a right to join a building cooperative out of turn.

[3] The law includes: "With the aim of activating efforts on returning refugees-citizens of the Republic of Tajikistan and forced migrants to the places of permanent residence, strengthening their social and legal protection and in accordance with the statement of the government delegation of the Republic of Tajikistan on the results of the fourth round of inter-Tajik talks in Almaty, the Government of the Republic of Tajikistan resolves; 1. The ministries departments of the Republic of Tajikistan, heads of oblasts, cities and rayons of the Republic of Tajikistan shall intensify the work of the organized return of the refugees and forced migrants to the places of permanent residence and their social and legal protection. 2. With the aim of efficiently solving the questions arising in connection with the return of refugees – citizens of the Republic of Tajikistan and forced migrants to the places of permanent residence, their social and legal protection a government commission shall be set up in accordance with the supplement."

Under the same 1994 law, the relevant authorities are obliged to take measures "on returning to forced migrants the property left by them in places of their previous residence. If it is not possible to return it, then compensation shall be paid in manner and amount as determined by the Council of Ministers of the Republic of Tajikistan" (Art. 7). Article 11 obliges the government to safeguard the security of the forced migrants on their return to their places of permanent residence, as well as their rights and lawful interests. Article 12 guarantees the right to "repossess the personal property and real estate" left during the time of flight, and rights to receive a lump-sum allowance or other cash benefit, and to receive credit on preferential terms to reconstruct and build new houses and outbuildings to replace what has been destroyed. The beneficiaries of the law are also legally guaranteed freedom of movement and the right to choose one's residence, the right to rent-free accommodation in places of temporary residence, protection against forced return to the place of previous residence, and other such guarantees. In addition, the State organs are required to:

> provide a forced migrant, in the process of choosing a place of permanent residence, with accommodation from special housing resources meant for forced migrants, or enter him into the list of citizens who, according to the housing legislation of the Republic of Tajikistan, are given the right of immediately obtaining accommodation from the State housing resources as well as by purchasing housing from citizens. (Art. 6)

To cope with the large-scale secondary occupation of returnee homes, the government adopted several legislative measures, including a *Special Law on the Return of Illegally Occupied Houses* and *Resolution No. 542 of 22 August 1995 on Additional Measures Facilitating the Return of Refugees-Citizens of the Republic of Tajikistan and Forced Migrants to the Places of Permanent Residence and Their Social and Legal Protection*. These regulations stipulate that those who had illegitimately occupied the homes of refugees and IDPs were to evacuate these residences immediately.[4] Several months after the adoption of these rules, virtually all the homes concerned were in fact vacated and the original inhabitants could return to their original homes. Although most unlawful occupants eventually vacated peacefully, active eviction was required in some rare instances. Under these regulations,

[4] Resolution No. 542 states, *inter alia*: "With the aim of facilitating the earliest social and economic adaptation of the refugees-citizens of the Republic of Tajikistan and forced migrants returned to the places of permanent residence, the Ministry of Internal Affairs of the Republic of Tajikistan, hukumats of oblasts, cities and rayons of the Republic of Tajikistan in common with the agencies of the Procurator's Office of the Republic of Tajikstan shall "immediately vacate illegally occupied dwellings owned or rented by the refugees-citizens of the Republic of Tajikistan and forced migrants in houses belonging to the state or communal housing fund and pass them to their rightful owners."

criminal sanctions were applied against those who refused to vacate homes that were unlawfully occupied.[5] Laws adopted following the conflict in Tajikistan also addressed the issue of what to do about housing and property that had been damaged or destroyed during the Tajik conflict.[6] A process was developed whereby those most in need were able to receive preferential treatment in the form of prioritization in the allocation of available housing resources or the direct provision of land.

Unlike circumstances in many other countries undergoing structural political transition and where entire legal systems have been overhauled during the period in which the original inhabitants became refugees and IDPs, in Tajikistan, the legal regime remained constant throughout the flight and return process, and thus legal title did not and could not revert to anyone other than the original inhabitant. The shifting nature of legal systems and norms in other countries experiencing large-scale repatriation has tended to augment the difficulties associated with housing and property restitution.

Tajikistan's restitution laws were, for the most part, successfully enforced by the Tajik judiciary, which was strongly supported by UNHCR. Some 23,000 cases submitted by returnees from Afghanistan and elsewhere were adjudicated by the judiciary, including numerous cases concerning housing destruction and secondary occupation of refugee housing. According to one writer, "most housing and property conflicts and problems, though having been a challenge in the implementation of the repatriation programs in the post-conflict period in Tajikistan, were solved through amicable proceedings and administrative settlements. Most of the unlawful occupants eventually vacated the homes peacefully. Only in a few instances have there been reports of the need to resort to formal evictions that, in any event, occurred with procedural safeguards, including formal issuance of the court order."[7] It should also be noted that the *General Agreement on the Establishment of Peace and National Reconciliation in Tajikstan and Protocol on Refugees* (27 June 1997) reiterates that:

> The government of the Republic of Tajikistan assumes the obligation to reintegrate returning refugees and displaced persons into the social and economic life of the country, which includes the provision to them of humanitarian and financial aid, assistance in finding employment and housing and the restoration of all their rights

[5] Human Rights Watch (May 1995) *Return to Tajikistan: Continued Regional and Ethnic Tensions.*

[6] Para. 4 provides that: "[i]n case of the destruction or loss of the state-owned dwelling, provide out of turn an available dwelling space at his whereabouts in conformity with the standards in force in the Republic. According to the wish of the victims, in return for the dwelling allot them a land plot for the construction of a dwelling house or give them a right to join a building cooperative out of turn." (Unofficial translation).

[7] Louise Druke (2000) "Housing and Property Restitution for Returnees in Tajikistan in the 1990s" *Refugee Survey Quarterly* 19, no. 3: 113.

> as citizens of the Republic of Tajikstan (including the return to them of dwellings and property and guaranteed uninterrupted service ...)

MOZAMBIQUE

Although it is not widely known, section IV of Protocol III to the *General Peace Agreement* ending the lengthy civil war in Mozambique included explicit restitution rights for returning refugees. It provides:

> Mozambican refugees and displaced persons shall be guaranteed restitution of property owned by them which is still in existence and the right to take legal action to secure the return of such property from individuals in possession of it.[8]

Likewise the *Tripartite Agreement between the Government of the Republic of Mozambique, the Government of Zimbabwe and UNHCR for the Voluntary Repatriation of Mozambican Refugees from Zimbabwe* (1993) also dealt extensively with restitution and return issues:

> 1. Pursuant to the General Peace Accord, as well as other reconciliation initiatives taken by the Mozambican Government and other parties, the returnees shall have the right of return to return their former places of residence or to any other places of their choice within Mozambique. They shall not be subject to any form of legal process, persecution, discrimination or punishment for any reason whatsoever on account of their having been refugees.
>
> 2. ... the Mozambican Government shall issue, together with other relevant parties, a declaration inviting all refugees to return and guaranteeing that no one shall be punished or discriminated against on account of his religion, political affiliation or for having been in exile;
>
> ....
>
> 4. The Mozambican Government shall ensure that returnees have access to land for settlement and use, in accordance with Mozambique laws.
>
> 5. The Mozambican Government shall, in accordance with the relevant provisions of Protocol III of the General Peace Accord, assist returnees who attempt to recover their lost property. (Article 8: Treatment of Refugees)

In 1997, a Land Law was adopted, which includes provisions designed to help returnees and peasants. Under the law, the State still owns all land but grants user rights to individuals, communities, and businesses in the form of leases that can last up to 100 years. The law requires that courts recognize verbal evidence from community members regarding occupancy of land if persons do not have

8 Bina Hanchinamani (2000) "The Impact of Mozambique's Land Tenure Policy on Refugees and Internally Displaced Persons" *Human Rights Brief* 7, no. 2: 101–116.

possession of title documents, which in turn has assisted restitution even further. The law was disseminated widely through a strong civil society, Land Campaign (*Campanha Terra*), which proved important as the government came under pressure from foreign donors to change the law in order to facilitate privatization and promote land markets. Thus the land law has been the site of an intellectual struggle over the respective importance of large-scale and small-scale producers in the economic and social development of the country, as discussed by Palmer (2003).

KOSOVO

The UN Mission in Kosovo (UNMIK), in close collaboration with the UN Centre on Human Settlements (Habitat), established an independent Housing and Property Directorate (HPD) to coordinate housing law and policy, settle outstanding housing and property disputes, and promote restitution in 1999.[9] The creation of this institution took place shortly after the conclusion of the NATO air war in Kosovo, and was accomplished with such speed due to the direct involvement of the international community and its insistence on resolving housing and property disputes before these eventually became responsible for renewed conflict. As is well known, a key feature of the war was to ensure the return of all refugees to their original homes.

One of the first acts of the UNMIK authorities was to repeal several Yugoslav laws that systematically discriminated against the ethnic Albanian population in Kosovo. In trying to reverse the destructive effect of the conflict and the legacy of discrimination, it was seen as critical that a process be put in place to regularize housing and property rights based on a consistent legal framework grounded in international human rights and principles. As a result, even before the establishment of the HPD, the UNMIK issued Regulation 1999/10 "On the Repeal of Discriminatory

[9] See: *UNMIK Regulation No. 1999/23 On the Establishing of the Housing and Property Directorate and the Housing and Property Claims Commission* (15 November 1999). Section 1 of Regulation 1999/23 provides that: "1.1 The Housing and property Directorate (the "Directorate") shall provide overall direction on property rights in Kosovo until the Special Representative of the Secretary-General determines that local governmental institutions are able to carry out the functions entrusted to the Directorate. In particular, the Directorate shall: (a) Conduct an inventory of abandoned private, state and socially owned housing; (b) Supervise the utilization or rental of such abandoned property on a temporary basis for humanitarian purposes; rental monies of abandoned private and socially owned property shall be recorded in a separate account in trust for the rightful owner, subject to deduction of relevant expenses; (c) Provide guidance to UNMIK, including CIVPOL and UNHCR, as well as KFOR, on specific issues related to property rights; and (d) Conduct research leading to recommended policies and legislation concerning property rights." See also: UNCHS (Habitat) Kosovo Programme (22 September 1999) *Establishing the UNMIK Housing and Property Directorate (HPD)*.

Legislation Affecting Housing and Rights in Property." This regulation repealed two Yugoslav laws deemed to discriminate against the Albanian population in Kosovo.[10] This repeal set the tone for the intensive involvement by UNMIK in the subsequent housing and property restitution process.

The HPD functioned from 1999 to 2008. It was comprised of an Executive Secretariat, an Administrative Branch, and a Housing and Property Claims Commission (HPCC).[11] The HPCC played a role similar to that of the Commission on Real Property Claims (CRPC) in Bosnia and Herzegovina, collecting, deciding on, and resolving housing and property claims. All told, the HPCC issued more than 29,000 decisions in response to restitution claims. The HPD had a variety of functions and acted both as an overall coordinating institution for housing and property questions as well as a provider of judicial structures required to resolve housing and property disputes.[12] The HPD offered assistance to people with various housing and property problems[13] but did not deal with commercial property, claims for the return of movable property such as cars, furniture, or equipment, or the provision of compensation for the damage or destruction of housing and property.

[10] The Regulation repealed the *Law on Changes and Supplements on the Limitation of Real Estate Transactions* and the *Law on the Conditions, Ways and Procedures of Granting Farming Land to Citizens Who Wish to Work and Live in the Territory of the Autonomous Province of Kosovo and Metohija.*

[11] The HPD is based on designs included in: *Housing and Property in Kosovo: Rights, Law and Justice – Proposals for a Comprehensive Plan of Action for the Promotion and Protection of Housing and Property Rights in Kosovo* (Scott Leckie for UNCHS (Habitat), 30 August 1999).

[12] Under UNMIK Regulation 1999/23, which created the Housing and Property Directorate, the HPD: [S]hall provide overall direction on property rights in Kosovo until the Special Representative of the Secretary-General determines that local governmental institutions are able to carry out the functions entrusted to the Directorate. In particular, the Directorate shall: (a) Conduct an inventory of abandoned private, state and socially owned housing; (b) Supervise the utilization or rental of such abandoned property on a temporary basis for humanitarian purposes; rental monies of abandoned private and socially owned property shall be recorded in a separate account in trust for the rightful owner, subject to deduction of relevant expenses; (c) Provide guidance to UNMIK, including CIVPOL and UNHCR, as well as KFOR on specific issues related to property rights; and (d) Conduct research leading to recommended policies and legislation concerning property rights.

[13] The HPD offered services to people whose property problem falls into one of the following scenarios: You were an occupancy right holder, lawful possessor or owner of an apartment or house before March 24, 1989, and you lost the right because you were discriminated against; you have received notification from HPD that a claim has been lodged against your property; you entered into a property transaction between March 24, 1989 and October 13, 1999 and could not validate the transaction and register it because the law prohibited the transaction; you have received notification from HPD that a claim has been lodged against your property; you were an occupancy right holder, lawful possessor, or owner of a house or an apartment before March 24, 1999 and someone else is living in your apartment or house illegally; you have received notification from HPD that a claim has been lodged against your property. Additionally, if you are in need of temporary housing on humanitarian grounds, HPD may be able to help you under the program it is setting up with the municipalities (Source: http://www.unchs.org).

The following excerpt describes the institutional aspects of developing a property restitution mechanism.

Margaret Cordial and Knut Rosandhaug (2009) *Post-Conflict Property Restitution, the Approach in Kosovo and Lessons Learned for Future International Practice*, Vol. 1, Martinus Nijhoff Publishers.

The services of the United Nations Human Settlements Programme (UN-HABITAT) were enlisted by the SRSG in 1999 to assist in the coordination of the housing and property restitution process. UN-HABITAT facilitated, among others, an Interagency Housing and Property Task Force to conduct research and provide guidance and technical assistance on the way to tackle certain housing and property issues. Three primary areas of concern identified by UN-HABITAT as warranting urgent intervention were housing and property rights issues, the cadastre and property records and municipal government and administration …

UN-HABITAT presented an action plan for the promotion and protection of housing and property rights in Kosovo. The plan put forward comprehensive recommendations for legislative reform and the creation of a Housing and Property Directorate. It proposed the latter be entrusted with responsibility for the coordination and centralisation of UNMIK's efforts in the field of housing and property rights and it enumerated a number of tasks that were assigned to it, including the resolution of residential property disputes and the administration and allocation of abandoned residential property.

UN-HABITAT and the Civil Administration component of UNMIK (Pillar II) drafted legislation on the establishment of an independent mechanism as proposed in the Action Plan … the Housing and Property Directorate (The 'HPD') and its independent quasi judicial counterpart, the Housing and Property Claims Commission (the 'HPCC') which were mandated to achieve an "efficient and effective resolution of claims concerning residential property"… Its procedures were governed by a combination of pre-1989 domestic laws and post-1999 UNMIK laws, and it applied both domestic and international legal norms.

UNMIK also undertook other initiatives proposed by UN HABITAT to bring about reform in the property sector. In 2000 the Kosovo Cadastral Agency (the 'KCA') was established under UNMIK Administration Direction 2000/14 and was responsible for matters relating to the re-establishment of the cadastral information system in Kosovo. In 2002 legislation on a revised immovable property rights registry was promulgated and this established a Kosovo-wide system for the registration of property rights.

In June 2002, the SRSG promulgated UNMIK Regulation 2002/12 establishing an independent body, namely the Kosovo Trust Agency (the KTA) to privatise the production assets of SOEs, and administer and manage POEs. Simultaneously, the Special Chamber of the Supreme Court of Kosovo was created to adjudicate and resolve legal disputes arising from the privatisation process.

BOSNIA AND HERZEGOVINA

The Dayton Agreement ending the war in Bosnia and Herzegovina established a variety of important principles delineating rights to housing and property restitution for refugees and other displaced persons. In Annex 7 of the 1995 *General Framework Agreement for Peace in Bosnia and Herzegovina*, refugees and displaced persons were guaranteed:

1. The right freely to return to their *homes of origin*;
2. The right to have property restored which was deprived during hostilities; and
3. The right to compensation for any property *which cannot be restored* to them.[14]

Since the end of the war, almost two million people have returned to their countries and homes of origin throughout the Balkans. In 2001 alone, more refugees and IDPs (more than 110,000) were able to return home to areas controlled by opposing ethnic factions in Bosnia and Herzegovina and Croatia than at any other time since fighting ceased. Undoubtedly, the role of the international community in persuading the relevant parties to accept the contents of Annex 7, including restitution, as well as the subsequent programs such as the Property Legislation Implementation Plan (PLIP) and the Stability Pact for South Eastern Europe, have been instrumental in making the return and restitution process as extensive as it has been to date. UNHCR has instigated a number of innovative programs to encourage return, including support for local legal aid centers, large-scale shelter programs, employment creation, microcredit and community development schemes, pilot return projects, bus services, an Open Cities Initiative, and other activities seeking to make restitution a reality.[15]

UNHCR, the Office of the High Representative, and other institutions have been instrumental in promoting legislative reform involving housing and property law and in working with other institutions on these issues.[16] These agencies backed the conception, drafting, and eventual adoption of a series of laws in Bosnia and Herzegovina that overturned wartime laws on abandoned property. Among the laws adopted to repeal the abandonment laws and bring local law into conformity with

[14] *General Framework Agreement for Peace in Bosnia and Herzegovina, Annex 7 Agreement on Refugees and Displaced Persons*, Articles 1–2. Annex 7 also includes: "4. Guarantees of safety, without risk of harassment, intimidation, persecution or discrimination, particularly on account of their ethnic origin, religious belief or political opinion; 5. The obligation of the Parties to prevent activities hindering or impeding the safe and voluntary return of refugees and displaced persons; 6. Various confidence-building measures; 7. Free choice of destination; and 8. Creation of positive conditions for return."

[15] UNHCR Inspection and Evaluation Service (November 1998) *Review of the UNHCR Housing Programme in Bosnia and Herzegovina*.

[16] For comprehensive coverage of housing and property law in Bosnia, see the 1999 joint publication by UNHCR, the Office of the High Representative (OHR) and the CRPC entitled *Property and Housing Issues Affecting Repatriates and Displaced Persons in Bosnia and Herzegovina*.

international standards are the *Law on the Cessation of the Application of the Law on Abandoned Apartments* (1998) (Bosnia and Herzegovina), *Law on the Cessation of the Application of the Law on Temporary Abandoned Real Property Owned by Citizens* (3 April 1998) (Bosnia and Herzegovina), and the *Law on the Cessation of the Application of the Law on Abandoned Apartments* (2 December 1998) (Republika Srpska). These laws were approved three years after the Dayton Accords and would almost assuredly not have been adopted without the strong push by the international community to do so. Clearly, without the adoption of laws repealing both the laws and intended effects of the abandonment laws, restitution simply could not have taken place. These new laws were indispensable in creating a national legal framework in Bosnia and Herzegovina that promoted, rather than obstructed, the recovery of housing and property by returning refugees and IDPs.

RWANDA

The Arusha Agreement[17] and the accompanying Protocol on the repatriation of refugees and the resettlement of displaced persons (June 1993) provide housing and land restitution rights to Rwandan refugees. Those who had lived in exile for ten years or more, however, were excluded from these guarantees but were meant to receive alternative lands and assistance to resettle. This latter measure was ostensibly adopted "to promote social harmony and national reconciliation."[18] This measure has been widely criticized and has clearly negatively affected the rights to return of

[17] On the Arusha Agreement, see: Second Progress Report of the Secretary-General on the United Nations Assistance Mission for Rwanda (S/1994/360 (1994). See also: UNGA Res. A/Res/49/23 (1994). Article 4: provides: "With a view to promote social harmony and national reconciliation, refugees who have fled the country more than ten years ago cannot reclaim their property if it has been occupied by other individuals. To compensate them, the Government must put at their disposition land and help them to resettle." while Article 28 stipulates that "The Commission on Compensation will proceed to manage the sites of installation. The inhabitants of this site will be considered on use the model of 'village settlement types' to stimulate the creation of zones of development in a rural context and to be compatible with traditional schemes of dispersed settlements."

[18] In addition, the Regional Conference on Assistance to Refugees, Returnees and Displaced Persons in the Great Lakes Region (12–17 February 1995), recognized the following measures to be taken by both Burundi and Rwanda regarding returning refugees: Sec. C. Measures to be Taken in and/or by the Countries of Origin: Burundi.... 20. In addition, to reassure refugees and internally displaced persons, the Government should:... (e) publicly reassure refugees and internally displaced persons regarding the right to restoration of their private property, while adopting concrete measures to clarify the legal status of property left behind by refugees, including those who fled prior to October 1993, notably in 1972. Rwanda: 22.... The Conference therefore urged and encouraged the Government of Rwanda to continue with its programmes in the following areas ... (d) ensuring respect for the property rights of refugees and internally displaced persons by: i. continuing to apply concrete measures to adjudicate property disputes in a fair and expeditious manner; ii. enacting legislation to regulate the strictly temporary and provisional nature of any house occupation on an emergency basis, to be authorised and recorded by designated officials. NOTE: In regulating the manner and modalities of

refugees who fled as far back as 1959, but many of whom returned in the mid-1990s.[19] A considerable proportion of these returnees have not been able to return to their homes of origin because their houses have been destroyed, occupied by others in the intervening period and due to government relocation programs.[20] In some cases, these largely Tutsi returnees occupied Hutu homes, leading to a potentially volatile situation upon the return of many of the Hutu refugees in 1996 and 1997.[21]

A Ministerial Instruction issued in September 1996 attempted to regularize the highly volatile situation surrounding secondary occupation by entrusting "abandoned land" to the municipalities that were empowered to administer and manage these lands. Secondary occupants were allowed under the Instruction to temporarily occupy abandoned lands (e.g., where the owner is either in exile or deceased without known inheritors) as long as they made a written request to the municipal authorities, who in turn could give temporary authorization rights to reside. In all circumstances, however, the original owner maintained the right to immediate restitution should they return home. If an original inhabitant returned to find their home occupied by an unlawful secondary occupant, the occupant was given two months to vacate the premises voluntarily. If the unlawful occupant was unable to find new accommodation during the two-month period, the government (Ministry of Rehabilitation) was entrusted with finding another home or providing them with

return, UNHCR and others also urged the authorities in Rwanda and Burundi to comply with various repatriation principles, including: a) The right to return; b) Non-discrimination; c) Voluntariness based on informed consent; d) Return in conditions of safety and dignity; e) Respect for private property ("Governments must ensure re-instatement of returning refugees and IDPs in their homes and land, while finding alternative solutions when this is legally or otherwise impossible"); and f) Freedom of abode.

19 *General Assembly Resolution 51/114 (1997) on the Situation of human rights in Rwanda (A/51/619/Add.3) "reaffirms* the link between the voluntary return of refugees to their homes and the normalisation of the situation in Rwanda, and concerned that acts of intimidation and violence directed against refugees, particularly by the former Rwandan authorities, have prevented refugees from returning to their homes, [and] … 7. *Invites* all States, the organisations and bodies of the United Nations system and intergovernmental and non-governmental organisations to continue and to intensify their contributions of financial and technical support to accelerate the efforts of the Government of Rwanda to, inter alia, restore the judicial system, promote reconciliation through the recently established Commission for National Reconciliation and safely reintegrate returning refugees in conditions of safety and dignity, including addressing competing claims to housing and property."

20 The Human Rights Field Operation for Rwanda (HRFOR) has reported that property problems had been the biggest impediment to the rapid reintegration of the returnees, given that some 22 percent of the homes of returnees were destroyed, 10 percent of lands were occupied, and 8 percent of houses were occupied (E/CN.4/1997/42). In addition to these problems, return to Rwanda was further aggravated by land disputes and extreme land scarcity, and augmented by the fact effective absence of adequate property legislation. Between 1994 and 1999, UNHCR built 100,000 homes in Rwanda as a means of promoting return and stability in the nation.

21 Amnesty International (1996) *Rwanda and Burundi: The Return Home: Rumours and Realities.* Up to one million Tutsis returned to Rwanda during 1995–1996.

building materials. Such measures, however, have proven difficult to enforce. Added to this, the prohibition of property inheritance for women (only abolished in law in 1999), intimidation against lawful owners by unlawful secondary occupants, and the deliberate arrest of some returnees (thus preventing them from regaining their property) have complicated matters further. The government of Rwanda established a Ministerial Committee to deal with property and land issues, designed to restrict the illegal occupation of homes, lands, and properties, but it is unclear how effective these measures were in adequately remedying these complex problems.

The *Protocol on the Repatriation of Refugees and the Resettlement of Internally Displaced Persons* (1993) provides that the return of all refugees is an inalienable right and constitutes a factor for peace, unity, and national reconciliation. The Protocol asserts that all people who return are free "to settle down in any place of their choice" as long as "they do not encroach upon the rights of other people." It also asserts that "property is a fundamental right for all the people of Rwanda" and that "[a]ll refugees shall … have the right to repossess their property on return." However, these rights are effectively overwritten by the previously mentioned ten-year clause. The Protocol, therefore, effectively blocked the implementation of restitution rights for those who had been out of the country for more than ten years. According to one author, "[n]ot surprisingly, the 'ten-year rule' was not well received by some of the returning Tutsis and has been criticized for having no legal or moral basis but is rather a political consensus between two belligerents with the sole aim of ending the war and protecting social harmony,"[22] neither of which was achieved soon after the Accords were signed. By the time the Tutsi refugees actually returned in late 1994, the goal of creating social harmony had become an overwhelming challenge in the aftermath of the genocide.[23]

Though the ten-year rule was accepted by many on pragmatic grounds, this did not stop returning Tutsis from occupying the property of any Hutu – despite the fact that they did not systematically dispute access to their own families' former lands. Even with the ten-year rule, Article 4 of the Protocol provides that for those persons who were not able to regain their homes, the State would "compensate them by putting land at their disposal and shall help them resettle," and that "for estates which have been occupied by the Government, the returnee shall have the right for an equitable compensation by the Government". Article 2 guaranteed the right of returnees to settle freely in any place of their choice. Article 3 required the government of Rwanda to make unoccupied lands available for the establishment

[22] Quote from: Privat Rutazibwa (1995) "Esperance pour mon people et pour le monde", Ed. Centrales, Kigali, 68–69.

[23] Lisa Jones (2000) "The Evolution of Property Use in Rwanda" *Refugee Survey Quarterly* 19, no. 3: 130.

of settlement sites, including services, infrastructure, and assistance. Nevertheless, Lisa Jones quite correctly argues that "[d]espite the fact that some compensation was offered to those affected, it remains arguable that the 'ten-year rule' and villagization policy established by the Arusha Accords violated the property and housing rights of the Tutsi returnees as defined by international legal instruments and standards."[24]

In the absence of an effective property restitution mechanism, the government of Rwanda devised other means to resolve property disputes. The primary mechanism, aside from the opening-up of National Park land for residential and pastoral development, was a policy of "land sharing" – essentially a form of uncompensated expropriation. Land sharing was originally intended to avoid the eviction of secondary occupants of land belonging to another household through the division of the land in two. In some areas it was extended into a limited form of land redistribution, and land sharing continues today. Although plots were to be divided equally between the various claimants, the means by which the sharing was to be done were not fully elucidated, and the policy was not supported by law. There was considerable corruption and coercion involved in implementation of the policy. The 2005 Land Law attempts to retroactively legalize this process, though the validity of this step is questionable. There remains widespread dissatisfaction over the policy and the way it was implemented.[25]

In practice, many Tutsi returnees have been able to access land, through the land sharing policy, ad hoc land distribution by the authorities, or through purchase.[26] In some cases, Hutu involved in land disputes were falsely accused of genocide crimes.

Many returnees, as well as genocide survivors, were provided with new housing in specially constructed villages. The villagization program (outlined in Provisional Instruction 1/97) was later broadened into a nationwide settlement policy that prohibited the construction of homes in rural areas and effectively forced people to reside in villages created by the government. This has also prevented refugees from exercising their rights to restitution. UNHCR has in the past urged both the Governments of Burundi and Rwanda to:

> publicly (re)emphasise that private property rights will be fully respected, and that any occupation of land and homes will be terminated after the return of the rightful owner. In addition, national legislation, underlining this principle could regulate the strictly temporary and provisional nature of any house occupation

24 Id., 137.

25 See e.g., Chris Huggins (2009) "Land in Return, Reintegration and Recovery Processes: Some Lessons from the Great Lakes Region of Africa" in Sara Pantuliano (ed.), *Uncharted Territory: Land, Conflict and Humanitarian Action*, Practical Action.

26 See e.g., Marian Koster (2009) *Fragmented Lives: Reconstructing Rural Livelihoods in Post-Genocide Rwanda*. Ph.D. Dissertation, Wageningen University.

> on an emergency basis, to be authorised for a specified, limited period of time, and to be recorded by designated officials. Concrete measures will also need to be established to adjudicate property disputes in a fair and expeditious manner ...[27]

By 2001, international pressure and a related lack of donor funds had essentially put a stop to the villagization program, but the government restarted the program in 2007 using unpaid community labor for infrastructural development.

GUATEMALA

An agreement concluded between UNHCR and the Government of Guatemala on 13 November 1991 committed the government to ensuring "to those repatriates who were landless when they left the country, fair and legal access to land, under the same terms and conditions granted to their fellow countrymen." The agreement also includes provisions in which the government of Guatemala agreed to "undertake all possible efforts to guarantee the recovery and legalisation of such lands, or ... the compensation of such land with others of similar quality and location." UNHCR was involved in programs of documentation enabling returnees to purchase, transfer, or title land. Of the 20,000 returnees who were repatriated collectively, roughly half recovered their original lands or lands in direct compensation for lost original lands, and the other half bought new lands under a land-buying scheme. The lack of legal titles, the loss of title documents during the conflict, and the destruction of public housing, property, and land records all contributed to the difficulties of return in Guatemala. The *Agreement on Resettlement of the Population Groups Uprooted by the Armed Conflict* (Oslo, 17 June 1994) between the government of Guatemala and the Unidad Revolucionaria Nacional Guatemalteca also outlined some, but not all, issues linked to restitution and land rights.[28]

[27] UNHCR (1995) "Note on Voluntary Repatriation of Refugees", paper submitted to the Regional Conference on Assistance to Refugees, Returnees and Displaced Persons in the Great Lakes Region (12–17 February 1995, Bujumbura), p. 6, para 18.

[28] "An essential element of the resettlement process is legal security in the holding (inter alia, the use, ownership and possession) of land. In that regard, the Parties recognise the existence of a general problem which particularly affects the uprooted population. One of the principal manifestations of legal insecurity is the difficulty of producing evidence of landholding rights. This situation stems, inter alia, from: problems concerning registration; the disappearance of the files of the Instituto Nacional de Transformacion Agraria (INTA); the institutional weakness of specialized bodies and municipalities; the existence of rights based on customary systems for the holding and surveying of land; the existence of secondary occupants or the annulment of rights on the basis of the improper application of provisions concerning voluntary abandonment" (Para. 8); "In the particular case of abandonment of land as a result of armed conflict, the Government undertakes to revise and promote legal provisions to ensure that such an act is not considered to be voluntary abandonment, and to ratify the inalienable nature of landholding rights. In this context, it shall promote the return of land to the original holders and/or shall seek adequate compensatory

Cecelia Bailliet (2003) "Property Restitution in Guatemala: A Transitional Dilemma," in Scott Leckie (ed.) *Returning Home: Housing and Property Restitution Rights of Refugees and Displaced Persons*, Transnational Publishers.

Historical Background of Displacement & Dispossession

Internal displacement in Guatemala has been ongoing since the colonial epoch. The liberal reforms of the 1870's resulted in the expropriation of indigenous lands and forced eviction that has yet to cease over a century later.[29] Indigenous lands were nationalized and/or sold off to the coffee exporters. Peasants were forced to farm small parcels in the highlands (e.g. Quiche) while providing seasonal labor for the coffee plantations in the lowlands. These people formed seasonal labour needed for the expanding export crop plantations. Debt peonage evolved into a vagrancy law (1934) that required the landless to work for others at least 150 days per year. Revocation of this law occurred in 1945, and in 1952 President Arbenz enacted the Law on Agrarian Reform that distributed 10 percent of private lands and 280,000 national lands to 138,000 families. A military coup supported by the CIA and the United Fruit Company commenced a 36-year civil war that decimated the countryside. The epoch of military rule brought about a counter reform, in which peasants in the zone between Izabal and Ixcan were evicted and large tracts of land were distributed to military officials, politicians, and other elites. Scorched earth tactics resulted in the deaths of 200,000 people, destruction of 440 indigenous villages, internal displacement of 1 million persons, and external displacement of 151,000 refugees. New groups were brought in by the Army as part of a specific state policy to divide communities and break ethnic or other group identification. The Commission on Historical Clarification has characterized these actions as constituting ethnocide.

solutions" (Para. 9). The same parties also agreed under the "Indigenous Rights Accord" (Mexico City, 31 March 1995) to the following relevant restitution rights: "The rights relating to land of the indigenous peoples include both the communal or collective and the individual tenure of land, rights of ownership and possession and other real rights, and the use of natural resources for the benefit of communities without detriment to their habitat. Legislative and administrative measures must be developed to ensure recognition, the awarding of title, protection, recovery, restitution and compensation for those rights" (F1) … "*Restitution of communal lands and compensation for rights* Recognising the particularly vulnerable situation of the indigenous communities, which have historically been the victims of land plundering, the Government undertakes to institute proceedings to settle the claims to communal lands formulated by the communities and to restore or pay compensation for those lands. In particular, the Government shall adopt or promote the following measures: (a) Suspend the awarding of supplementary titles in respect of property to which the indigenous communities have claimed a right; (b) Suspend the statute of limitations in respect of any action involving the plundering of the indigenous communities; and (c) When the statute of limitations has already expired, however, establish procedures to compensate the communities which have been plundered with lands acquired for that purpose" (F7). See also: Liam Mahony (1999) *Risking Return: NGOs in the Guatemalan Refugee Repatriation*, Uppsala: Life & Peace Institute.

29 UNDP: Guatemala: La Fuerza Incluyente Del Desarollo Humano (http://www.pnud.org.gt 2000).

Displacement continues to occur as a result of multifarious causes. In the past causes were internal conflict and ethnocide; at present, forced evictions, development-based evictions, and displacement due to natural disasters constitute the root of new migration. However, the failure to provide a permanent solution for the displacement linked to the civil war reveals that this continues to be a source of continuing concern. The Inter-American Commission of Human Rights confirms that although the refugees and CPRs have been resettled, a substantial portion of internally displaced persons have not received attention.[30] Instead they remain poor, marginalized and anonymous. There has been no significant change in land distribution in the last three decades, in spite of the war and the Peace Accords.[31] Indeed, land conflicts submitted to the Presidential Office for Legal Assistance and Resolution of Land Conflicts (CONTIERRA) have increased from circa 300 in 1999 to a grand total of 1,103 in 2001.

CROATIA

The government of Croatia has also undertaken several measures in the area of housing and property restitution, although these have often been the subject of fierce criticism. The *Programme of Return and Accommodation of Expellees, Displaced Persons and Refugees* (written in cooperation with UNHCR and OSCE) was ostensibly designed to promote the return of property to persons displaced during the conflicts of the 1990s. In practice, however, the return of property was predicated on the availability and acceptability of alternative accommodation for the current secondary occupant, thus leaving former holders of occupancy rights in many instances without a restitution remedy. Although the provision of alternative housing to existing secondary occupants will always be a core component of any restitution program, care must be taken to prevent the use of such requirements as a basis for effectively halting the restitution process.

Another serious drawback to the program concerned its bias against holders of occupancy rights who were not allowed to benefit from measures of restitution. Only owners of private property are entitled to benefit from the restitution procedure,

30 Comision Interamericana de Derechos Humanos, Quinto Informe Sobre la Situacion de los Derechos Humanos en Guatemala, (OEA/Ser.L/V/II.111 Doc. 21 rev. 6 April 2001). It states that although the government promised to purchase twenty-three fincas for dispersed IDPs, it only purchased four fincas in 1999.

31 It is estimated that 65 percent of land is held by 3 percent of agro-exporters and large landowners. Small farms make up only 11 percent of the total. Instead, land fragmentation on account of demographic pressures, exhaustion of land, deforestation, and other types of environmental degradation are rising. UNDP estimates that the amount of families with direct access to land actually diminished in the past twenty years, from 61 percent to 49 percent. In the same period, the percentage of rural peasants working for others increased from 22 percent to 33 percent, the percentage of peasants renting land increased from 8 percent to 17 percent, and the landless increased from 22 percent to 33 percent.

despite the fact that many seeking restitution were classified as holding social occupancy rights, a status somewhere between outright ownership and tenancy. In addition, housing commissions, meant to be the cornerstone of the return program, have not functioned properly, and in many instances appear to have actively sought to prevent the return of property to members of non-Croatian groups.

The slow and restricted return of displaced Serbs (particularly "Krajina Serbs") to their habitual residences in Croatia has retarded the restitution process. Under the *Law on Renting Apartments in the Liberated Areas*, ethnic Croats who had left their flats during the armed conflict could successfully request that their tenancy rights be reinstated by invoking "justified reasons" for their prolonged absence (more than six months), including having fled enemy aggression. However, for ethnic Serbs in the same area, this option was not available because their flight is considered by the authorities to be "voluntary," despite UN Security Council resolutions demanding their return.[32]

The Croatian government established an Agency for Mediating Property Exchanges (AMPE) in 1997, which works to purchase real estate from owners and then rents or sells the properties only to Croatian citizens. The *Law on Compensation for Property Taken during Yugoslav Communist Rule* (1997) only permits those who were Croatian citizens to receive restitution or compensation for property taken by the Yugoslav government. As a result, courts in Croatia have refused to hear cases of Serb plaintiffs attempting to regain possession of their property. Violent forced evictions have also been common.[33]

The *Law on Temporary Take-Over of Property and Administration of Specified Property* was repealed and replaced with the *Law on Temporary Take-Over of Property and Administration* (1995). The earlier law contained a now infamous clause that stipulated that "the person whose temporary right to use the property has been annulled by a legally valid decision … cannot be deprived of the right to use the property s/he is authorised to use until s/he is given another property for possession and usage." This seemingly innocuous provision (which was subsequently declared unconstitutional) was used to justify the inability of the State to handle returning refugees, particularly ethnic Serbs. Nevertheless, the principle remains

32 A 1995 Security Council resolution "Demands that the Government of the Republic of Croatia (a) respect fully the rights of the local Serb population including their rights to remain, leave or return in safety, (b) allow access to this population by international humanitarian organisations, and (c) create conditions conducive to the return of those persons who have left their homes" (Security Council Resolution 1009 (1995) (regarding the Republic of Croatia, UN Doc. S/RES/1009 (1995), adopted 10 August 1995). The resolution also declared that the Security Council was "deeply concerned at the grave situation of persons displaced from their homes as a result of the conflict and at reports of violations of international humanitarian law …"

33 See: Centre on Housing Rights and Evictions (COHRE) (1998) *Forced Evictions: Violations of Human Rights No. 7*, Geneva, 30–32.

a key element of the Croatian Return Programme and has been heavily criticized. Under the Programme, temporary occupants may reject alternative accommodation offered by the official Housing Commission, thus endlessly prolonging the enforcement of restitution rights held by the original owners and occupants.[34] Allegations both of the working methods and lack of impartial treatment of restitution claims have persistently dogged the Housing Commission.

The restitution processes in Croatia reveal the importance of approaching property restitution with sensitivity to the specifics and history of the property rights in the country concerned, and in a manner that grounds the restitution procedures in the legal system of the State concerned, but in a manner which is wholly consistent with international legal principles regarding restitution. Once again, they also indicate the critical role that must be played by the international community in actively supporting the emergence of the rule of law, including even the construction of courts and the promotion of non-ethnically based methods of judicial decision making.[35] Without pressure from the international community, it is likely that restitution would have been resisted entirely.

INDIGENOUS PEOPLES

The rights of indigenous peoples to have restored to them land and property confiscated or expropriated by governments have been subject to increased recognition in recent years. In fact, according to Barkan, "[n]egotiating property rights – land, economic resources, and cultural property – through restitution to indigenous peoples has become the norm that defines the national conversation in many contemporary pluralistic societies.... In a growing number of cases involving indigenous groups, historical injustices have been recognised, substantial economic resources have been restituted, and even a measure of sovereignty has been recognised. Australian Aborigines, New Zealand Maoris, Native Canadians and Native Americans are all in the midst of prolonged restitution process wherein the rewriting of their identities and places in society in occurring, together with a certain redistribution of economic resources."[36]

International human rights standards are also increasingly giving recognition to the restitution rights of displaced indigenous peoples. International Labour Organisation Convention No. 169 Concerning Indigenous and Tribal Peoples (1989), for instance, Article 14 provides the following:

34 For an analysis of the drawbacks of the Croatian restitution programme, see Bayisa Wak-Woya (2000) "Property Restitution in Post-War Croatia: Problems and Perspectives. A Discussion Paper" *Refugee Survey Quarterly* 19, no. 3: 86, 98–104.

35 Id.

36 *Supra*, E. Barkan (2001) *The Guilt of Nations: Restitution and Negotiating Historical Injustices*, Baltimore: Johns Hopkins University Press, 161 and 325.

> 1. The rights of ownership and possession of the peoples concerned over the lands which they traditionally occupy shall be recognised. In addition, measures shall be taken in appropriate cases to safeguard the right of the peoples concerned to use lands not exclusively occupied by them, but to which they have traditionally had access for their subsistence and traditional activities. Particular attention shall be paid to the situation of nomadic peoples and shifting cultivators in this respect.
>
> 2. Governments shall take steps as necessary to identify the lands which the peoples concerned traditionally occupy, and to guarantee effective protection of their rights of ownership and possession.
>
> 3. Adequate procedures shall be established within the national legal system to resolve land claims by the peoples concerned.

On 23 August 1993 the United Nations Working Group on Indigenous Populations approved the Draft Declaration on the Rights of Indigenous Peoples and forwarded the Draft to the Commission on Human Rights for its approval.[37] The Declaration, U.N. document A/61/L.67, was finally adopted by the UN General Assembly on 13 September 2007. The Declaration contains a number of clauses relevant to the issue of restitution and compensation for lost lands. For example, Article 8 of the Declaration provides that:

> 1. Indigenous peoples and individuals have the right not to be subjected to forced assimilation or destruction of their culture.
> 2. States shall provide effective mechanisms for prevention of, and redress for:
>   (a) Any action which has the aim or effect of depriving them of their integrity as distinct peoples, or of their cultural values or ethnic identities;
>   (b) Any action which has the aim or effect of dispossessing them of their lands, territories or resources;
>   (c) Any form of forced population transfer which has the aim or effect of violating or undermining any of their rights …

In Article 10, the Declaration is more explicit about the procedures and mechanisms to be established when displacement of indigenous communities is being considered:

> Indigenous peoples shall not be forcibly removed from their lands or territories. No relocation shall take place without the free, prior and informed consent of the indigenous peoples concerned and after agreement on just and fair compensation and, where possible, with the option of return.

The Declaration explicitly acknowledges rights to lands, territories, and resources that indigenous peoples possess "by reason of traditional ownership or other traditional

[37] *Draft Declaration on the Rights of Indigenous Peoples*, UN Doc. E/CN.4/Sub.2/1993/29 (23 August 1993).

occupation or use, as well as those which they have otherwise acquired," and posits that "States shall give legal recognition and protection to these lands, territories and resources" (Article 26) through a process of adjudication in which indigenous people must be fully involved. Further, the Declaration recognizes rights to restitution of the lands, territories, and resources that have been confiscated without their informed consent:

> 1. Indigenous peoples have the right to redress, by means that can include restitution or, when this is not possible, just, fair and equitable compensation, for the lands, territories and resources which they have traditionally owned or otherwise occupied or used, and which have been confiscated, taken, occupied, used or damaged without their free, prior and informed consent.
>
> 2. Unless otherwise freely agreed upon by the peoples concerned, compensation shall take the form of lands, territories and resources equal in quality, size and legal status or of monetary compensation or other appropriate redress. (Article 28)

The Declaration also provides that indigenous peoples have a right to be "actively involved" in developing social and economic development programs affecting them, including housing initiatives, which should be administered through their own institutions as far as possible (Article 23).

The Declaration is nonbinding but represents a very significant contribution to the body of customary international law. Its provisions are likely to have a major impact on the actions of governments around the world. The Declaration was adopted at the UN General Assembly following a vote in which 144 states voted in favor and just four voted against: Australia, Canada, New Zealand, and the United States. All of these countries are involved in ongoing negotiations with indigenous communities over land, territory, natural resources, and related rights. Their rejection of the Declaration triggered widespread condemnation from rights activists, scholars, and indigenous people's movements.

Questions and Exercises

1. Which of the above restitution programs, in your opinion, was the most successful in protecting the HLP rights of those displaced? Why?
2. In your opinion, do internationally led restitution mechanisms such as those in Bosnia and Kosovo tend to provide more, less, or equal restitutionary justice? Explain your answer.
3. You are advising a group of 100,000 refugees on restitution strategies. The refugees have been in horrible camps for thirty years and the prospects of return to their original homes are virtually nil. At which point do your advise them to pursue compensation in lieu of restitution?
4. Class Exam Exercise – Repairing the Effects of Forced Displacement: The Case of Palestinian Refugees

Repairing the Effects of Forced Displacement: The Case of Palestinian Refugees

This is your chance to be a peacemaker. It is nearing the end of 2012, and despite the views of pessimists, realists, pragmatists, and vigorous opposition by conservative and religious groups, remarkably it appears that after sixty-four years of conflict, Israeli and Palestinian negotiators have made considerable headway toward a historic peace agreement. Well before the agreement can be signed and implemented, however, the negotiators need to find a workable, rights-based solution to the most vexing of all issues preventing peace between Israelis and Palestinians, namely, how to best repair the effects of forced displacement that have aggrieved millions of Palestinians since the creation of the State of Israel in 1948.

Today, there are some six million Palestinian refugees spread throughout the world, but concentrated in Gaza, the West Bank, Lebanon, Jordan, Syria, Iraq, within Israel itself, and in many other countries throughout the world. During the war that led to the creation of the State of Israel in 1947–1948, more than 750,000 Palestinians were forced to flee their homes and lands in search of safety and security. Today, combined with those who have subsequently faced displacement and the natural growth of Palestinian families, these millions of Palestinian refugees and internally displaced persons in need of durable solutions to their displacement. Finding viable solutions for this lengthy crisis is at the core of finding a permanent peace between the peoples of the region.

The Chief Negotiators for both sides, along with mediators from the UN, the United States, and the European Union, during the 2012 peace talks have all agreed that solutions need to be found for the Palestinian refugees and that these will have a prominent place within the eventual peace agreement. Those involved in the sensitive negotiations have each established working groups with the purpose of developing proposals that can be discussed at the highest levels and eventually be incorporated into the final peace accords.

The Palestinians have put together a team (Team Palestine), the Israelis have put together a team (Team Israel), and the international mediators (Team Mediator) will evaluate the proposals developed by each of the two teams.

The class will be divided into three equal-sized groups – Team Palestine, Team Israel, and Team Mediator. Both Team Palestine and Team Israel will develop concrete, rights-based proposals for resolving the long-standing Palestinian refugee crisis and will publicly present these to Team Mediator for consideration. Each proposal will be presented separately by the two teams to Team Mediator, which in turn will review the proposals, request clarification, and finally decide which of the two proposals (or perhaps other variations) they will recommend to be placed on the formal negotiating table for the consideration of the Chief Negotiators.

Team Palestine and Team Israel, in developing their respective plans, must create proposals that are fully consistent with *all* relevant international legal standards the address the rights of Palestinian refugees. The plan must fully protect the rights of all Palestinian refugees, their families, and heirs, and be formulated in such a way that both sides to the conflict can potentially agree with its contents.

In making your arguments, please take fully into account the following:

1. Which international legal standards most strongly and least strongly support the rights of Palestinian refugees to return to their original homes and lands? Please refer only to international laws and standards, not internal law of either Israel or the Palestinian Authority.
2. Which treaties and other norms protect the rights of Palestinian refugees?
3. If, *inter alia*, UN General Assembly Resolution 194 (1948) and UN Security Council Resolution 242 (1967) are used as the basis for developing proposals designed to remedy the forced displacement faced by Palestinian refugees, how can this best be done by both sides?
4. Which other examples of refugee return or ongoing refugee displacement can be used to strengthen (or weaken) arguments supporting the rights of Palestinian refugees to return to their original homes and lands?
5. Are the rights of Palestinian refugees different than the rights of other refugee groups? If so, how and in what manner do they differ and how can this be justified under international law?
6. New laws, procedures, and institutions will invariably be required if Palestinian refugees are to be able to exercise their rights. What new laws, procedures, and institutions will be required? How would these fit together?
7. How do rights to housing, land, and property restitution relate to rights to compensation in this case?
8. If compensation is proposed as one possible remedy to resolve the plight of Palestinian refugees, what form should this take? How would compensation arrangements be organized? Who would pay for this?

THE PROCEDURE

The entire class will be divided into three groups. One group will represent Palestine. This will be called **Team Palestine**. Another group will represent Israel. This will be called **Team Israel**. The third group will determine which side has prepared the best proposal. This will be called **Team Mediator**.

Team Palestine and Team Israel will each appoint spokespersons to make their respective presentations. All members of the two opposing teams must speak at some point during the presentations. All members of Team Tribunal will also be asked to speak.

On (date of exercise), we will hold a final presentation of the proposals developed to resolve the forced displacement of Palestinian refugees.

Team Palestine will open the proceedings with a three-minute initial statement. Team Israel will then have three minutes to introduce their positions.

Team Palestine will then make a fifteen-minute statement outlining in greater detail the precise elements of their proposed plan. This will be followed by a fifteen-minute statement by Team Israel outlining their proposed plan. As noted, both proposed plans must be fully consistent with international human rights law and all other relevant international legal standards.

This will then be followed by fifteen minutes of questioning by Team Mediator, to which members of both teams will need to respond.

Team Israel will then be given ten minutes to directly critique and question Team Palestine about their plan. In turn, Team Palestine will be given a further ten minutes to directly critique and question the plan submitted by Team Israel.

Team Mediator will then deliberate for five minutes and then issue its recommendations to the Chief Negotiators indicating which of the two plans should be discussed on the formal negotiating table. Team Mediator can also propose their own plan representing a combination of some kind of the two presented plans, or deriving from the two plans in some other way.

ORDER OF PROCEEDINGS

Opening Statement Team Palestine	3 Minutes
Opening Statement Team Israel	3 Minutes
Arguments Team Palestine	15 Minutes
Arguments Team Israel	15 Minutes
Questions by Team Mediator	15 Minutes
Critique by Team Israel	10 Minutes
Cross Examination by Team Palestine	10 Minutes
Deliberations by Team Mediator	5 Minutes
Judgment by Team Tribunal	5 Minutes

Additional Resources

Amnesty International (1996) *Report: Rwanda and Burundi, the Return Home: Rumours and Realities*, London: Amnesty International.

John Bruce (2007) *Drawing a Line under the Crisis: Reconciling Returnee Land Access and Security in Post-Conflict Rwanda*, Humanitarian Practice Network Working Paper, June 2007.

G. Budlender (2000) "Restitution for Housing and Property Rights: Some Lessons from the South-African Experience" *Refugee Survey Quarterly* 19, no. 3.

Madeline Garlick (2000) "Protection for Property Rights: A Partial Solution? The Commission for Real Property Claims of Displaced Persons and Refugees (CRPC) in Bosnia and Herzegovina" *Refugee Survey Quarterly* 19, no. 3

R. Gazmere and B. Dilip (2000) "Bhutanese Refugees: Rights to Nationality, Return and Property" *Forced Migration Review* 7.

B. Hanchinamani (2000) "The Impact of Mozambique's Land Tenure Policy on Refugees and Internally Displaced Persons" *Human Rights Brief* 7, no. 2.

Lisa Jones (2003) "Giving and Taking Away: The Difference between Theory and Practice Regarding Property in Rwanda" in Scott Leckie (ed.), *Returning Home: Housing and Property Restitution Rights of Refugees and Displaced Person*, New York: Transnational Publishers.

Domenico Nucci (2004) "Study on Arbitration, Mediation and Conciliation of Land and Property Disputes," Land and Property Study in Sudan, Project OSRO/SUD/409/HCR.

Robin Palmer (2003) "Struggling to Secure and Defend the Land Rights of the Poor in Africa" *Journal für Entwicklungspolitik* (Austrian Journal of Development Studies), XIX, no. 1: 6–21.

Permanent Court of Arbitration (2006) *Redressing Injustices Through Mass Claims Processes*, Oxford: Oxford University Press.

Rhodri Williams (2005) "Post-Conflict Property Restitution and Refugee Return in Bosnia and Herzegovina: Implications for International Standard-Setting and Practice" *NYU Journal of International Law and Politics* 37, no. 3 (Spring).

6

United Nations and Other Peace Operations and HLP Rights

INTRODUCTION

The term "peace operations" is a broad one and encompasses several kinds of interventions. We take a broad definition of peace operations as an internationally mandated, uniformed presence, either under United Nations auspices or under the authority of a regional organization like the Economic Community of West African States (ECOWAS) or the Organization of American States. The responsibilities of peace operations toward HLP rights have been increasingly recognized over the past decade. For instance, article 22(5) of the Pinheiro Principles provides that:

> International peace operations, in pursuing their overall mandate, should help to maintain a secure and stable environment wherein appropriate housing, land and property restitution policies and programs may be successfully implemented and enforced.[1]

More specifically, Article 22(6) states that:

> International peace operations, depending on the mission context, should be requested to support the protection of the right to housing, land and property restitution, including through the enforcement of restitution decisions and judgments. Member States in the Security Council should consider including this role in the mandate of peace operations.

Despite these progressive statements, however, in practice, much remains to be done to institutionalize HLP protection within peace operations. Awareness raising and training activities on HLP rights should be designed for peace operations staff, including military personnel, and would ideally be a mandatory part of pre-mission preparation. Peacekeepers may be required to protect civilian properties from

[1] UN Sub-Commission on the Promotion and Protection of Human Rights, *Principles on Housing and Property Restitution for Refugees and Displaced Persons*, 28 June 2005, UN Doc. E/CN.4/Sub.2/2005/17.

destruction or looting. More generally, they are responsible for providing military protection for civilian national and international HLP rights personnel who must work in potentially insecure postconflict situations. Humanitarians are increasingly the victims of violence in conflict-affected areas, even though deliberate attacks on humanitarian workers are prohibited by international humanitarian law and constitute war crimes.[2]

The involvement of peacekeepers – including military personnel – in human rights and humanitarian-related work raises important and difficult questions that have moral as well as political dimensions.[3] To retain local legitimacy, HLP experts and other personnel working on human rights issues must retain functional independence from military operations. There are also issues related to great differences between the institutional culture of nongovernmental organizations, for example, and the military: Analysts have observed the reluctance of many in the humanitarian and human rights communities to work with soldiers, and soldiers' similar reluctance to work with civilians in peacekeeping missions.[4] Training should therefore cover issues such as institutional cultures and coordination between military and nonmilitary actors.

PROTECTING HLP RIGHTS DURING CONFLICT

International humanitarian law demands of belligerents that they respect the principles of distinction (between combatants and noncombatants), proportionality (of violence used), and precaution (against disproportionate effects of military attacks on noncombatants) in using violent means in situations of conflict. Armed groups are clearly forbidden, under international humanitarian law, from occupying the property of civilians, destroying nonmilitary buildings and infrastructure, or displacing civilians from their places of residence, except in specific well-defined circumstances. However, in practice, the HLP rights of civilians in conflict zones have been violated repeatedly.

The Responsibility to Protect

The International Commission on Intervention and State Sovereignty (ICISS), formed in response to Kofi Annan's question of when the international community must intervene for human protection purposes, first developed the concept of the "responsibility to protect." The principle is specifically intended to ensure

2 United Nations Security Council, *Report of the Secretary-General on the Protection of Civilians in Armed Conflict*. (S/2007/643). New York: United Nations, 28 October 2007.

3 Conor Foley (2008) *The Thin Blue Line: How Humanitarianism Went to War*, Verso.

4 William G. O'Neill (2004) *A New Challenge for Peacekeepers: The Internally Displaced*. The Brookings Institution, p. 4.

that civilian populations anywhere in the world who are at risk of genocide, war crimes, ethnic cleansing, and other crimes against humanity are protected through international intervention, if necessary. HLP issues are rarely directly discussed within the responsibility to protect framework, but in practice, any international intervention launched within this framework will have responsibilities toward HLP issues, particularly through its mandate to prevent ethnic cleansing and forced displacement in general.

This concept was taken forward by the former UN Secretary General and, owing also to the initiative of a number of Global Southern states, was addressed during the 2005 World Summit of a fundamental responsibility to protect. This represents a critically important affirmation of the primary responsibility of each State to protect its citizens and persons within its jurisdiction from genocide, war crimes, ethnic cleansing, and crimes against humanity.

The United Nations Security Council has since taken important steps toward the development of a normative and operational framework for the protection of civilians through, for example, the adoption of resolution 1674 (2006). This Resolution elaborates a framework for action that provides for:

(a) Inclusion in the mandates of United Nations peacekeeping missions, where appropriate and on a case-by-case basis, of provisions for:
   (i) The protection of civilians under imminent threat of physical danger;
   (ii) Preventing and responding to sexual violence;
   (iii) Facilitating the delivery of humanitarian assistance;
   (iv) Ensuring security in and around camps for refugees and the internally displaced;
   (v) The creation of conditions conducive to their voluntary and safe return;
(b) The Council's continued collaboration with the Emergency Relief Coordinator and the latter's full association from the earliest stages of planning of United Nations peacekeeping and other relevant missions;
(c) Referral to the Council of relevant information and analysis regarding the protection of civilians.

The Security Council has increasingly provided peacekeeping operations with a stronger mandate to protect civilians, as demonstrated by the African Union–United Nations Hybrid Operation in Darfur, which is authorized to take necessary action to protect civilians (resolution 1769 (2007)). However, resolution 1769 did not refer to the Responsibility to Protect or to the Protection of Civilians Resolution, and the operation in Darfur has demonstrated limitations in its capacity to protect the most vulnerable.[5]

[5] International Coalition for the Responsibility to Protect, *Crisis in Darfur*. Accessed online on 15 July 2009, at http://www.responsibilitytoprotect.org/index.php/crises/crisis-in-darfur.

In September 2007, the UN Mission in the Central African Republic and Chad was established, with an express mandate to protect civilians with the support of the European Union operation. The Council also endorsed a policing concept aimed at ensuring the provision of law and order in refugee camps and sites with internally displaced persons in Chad (resolution 1778 (2007)). However, there have been setbacks, notably in January 2007, when the UN Security Council proposed a resolution calling for the cessation of grave violations of human rights in Burma (Myanmar). China and Russia both used their veto to block this resolution, claiming that Burma was not a threat to international peace and security, and recommending instead that the issues be taken up by the Human Rights Council.

In his 2009 report, "Implementing the responsibility to protect," Secretary-General Ban Ki Moon acknowledged that "there are substantial gaps in capacity, imagination and will across the whole spectrum of prevention and protection measures relating to the responsibility to protect. Nowhere is that gap more pronounced or more damaging than in the realm of forceful and timely response to the most flagrant crimes and violations relating to the responsibility to protect … Much more needs to be done … to internationalize such efforts and put them in the larger context of finding better ways to protect civilians."[6]

As of mid-2009, support for the responsibility to protect principle within the UN seemed strong. A General Assembly plenary debate on the Responsibility to Protect generated many statements of support from government around the world.[7]

PROTECTING CIVILIANS FROM FORCED DISPLACEMENT AND HLP DAMAGE

Those involved in peace operations have a responsibility to ensure that the HLP rights of civilians are respected. The most effective way to do this is to prevent armed groups from displacing civilians. In addition to the physical and psychological damage suffered by displaced people, the risk of damage, looting, and illegal occupation of their properties increases greatly when homes and offices are abandoned. Peacekeepers must also ensure that they, like all armed actors, respect the rules of war. In responding to aggression, peacekeeping troops must themselves respect the principles of distinction, proportionality, and precaution, and must avoid the wanton destruction of civilian housing, for example, through their actions.

[6] United Nations Security Council, *Implementing the Responsibility to Protect*. A/63/677. New York: United Nations, 12 January 2009.

[7] International Coalition for the Responsibility to Protect. (2009) *Civil Society Groups Welcome Governments' Commitment to Prevent and End Mass Atrocities*, New York: Media Release, 27 July 2009.

In some cases, HLP issues may be central to the conflict. Peacekeeping forces must make themselves aware of the struggles over land, housing, and other property in order to predict and preempt violence. In Ituri territory, Eastern Democratic Republic of Congo, long-standing land disputes are often at the root of local violence. In some cases, community leaders involved in disputes with neighboring villages made agreements with militia forces. Militia would attack and displace the neighboring villagers, helping the community control the disputed area; in return, local people would provide support for the militia in the wider ongoing conflict.[8]

If peacekeepers can gain the necessary local knowledge to identify and monitor potential flashpoints, they can potentially reduce further land-related violence.

PROTECTING HLP DOCUMENTATION

Peacekeepers should also identify and secure the cadastral offices or other facilities where housing and property records are located. In many conflicts, these records have been stolen or destroyed to undermine the property claims of document holders. In Kosovo, property records were removed by the Yugoslav authorities when they retreated in 1999.[9] The majority of the cadastre records were removed to Serbia, and property records were taken from a significant number of municipalities. Prior to independence in Timor-Leste, the central cadastral office was burned down and many other housing and land documents were stolen by Indonesian officials.

The destruction of a single cadastral building, and the records that it contains, may result in a long and complicated process of land and property registration and adjudication. The eventual cost of such a scenario is likely to be in the tens of millions of dollars, if not more. Land records should therefore be prioritized by peacekeepers as strategic assets, and sufficient resources should be allocated to ensure their protection.

UN Habitat (2008) A *Post Conflict Land Administration and Peace Building Handbook, Series 1: Countries with Land Records*, UN Habitat.

Finding the land records

Land issues are often one of the causes, if not at the heart, of violent conflict. Therefore, finding, securing and preventing the manipulation of land records are of vital importance for three main reasons: (1) a return to normality; (2) conflict

8 Thierry Vircoulon (2005) *The Ituri Paradox: When Militia Have a Land Policy and the UN Does Not.* Paper presented at the Conference on The Changing Politics of Land in Africa: Domestic Policies, Crisis Management and Regional Norms. University of the Western Cape.

9 Margaret Cordial and Knut Rosandhaug (2009) "The Response of the United Nations Interim Administration Mission in Kosovo to Address Property Rights Challenges," in Leckie (ed.), *Housing, Land and Property Rights in Post-Conflict United Nations and Other Peace Operations*, Cambridge University Press, 69.

management and dispute resolution; and (3) the prevention of discriminatory or otherwise unfair practices. Finding the current land records is very critical in the immediate aftermath of a conflict; such records include:

the land registry; cadastre; maps; possession lists; survey field records; text and graphic evidence; digital backups; paper maps

Land records can contain information that is in the interest of some parties but not of others. A dominant group losing power over an area may be prone to taking the land records with them when they withdraw, so as to have proof of the land rights situation (usually beneficial to them) that existed just before they left the area. They may also be inclined to destroy earlier information dating from before their group was the major beneficiary of the system. Furthermore, they may destroy or manipulate any up-to-date data to prevent a rapid return to normality in land issues for the incoming group.

The group taking control immediately after the withdrawal of the previously dominant one, particularly if previously the victim group, is likely to have a specific set of strategies regarding any land records that are still available. They may want to destroy details of the situation prevailing just before their arrival, particularly if these are seen as beneficial to the group previously in power. They may want to preserve older data from an earlier period, insofar as such data is beneficial to them. They may also want to alter the records they find in the land administration system in favour of their group. To formalize alterations they may turn to 'instant' tribunals, or to information emanating from previously informal and or parallel structures outside government. Returned exiles or staff with appropriate skills may quickly take over the offices and land records, and either prevent abuse of the land records as much as possible, or actually be instrumental in altering the records to suit their purposes.

Preventive action

It is possible to prevent some of these actions during an emergency post-conflict phase. However, in order to do so, the location of land records needs to be established as quickly as possible following arrival in the country. Land records are usually found in a number of different locations depending on the institutional arrangements and regulatory framework in place. The courts or separate land registries may keep some of them. In some situations, these records can overlap with the textual part of the cadastre, which may be kept by a national, regional or local cadastral authority. Such an authority may be part of general tax-related or municipal structures, or stand on its own. Cadastral authority or surveyor general's offices or lands department may keep the graphical part of the cadastre (boundaries) and the underlying survey documents. In some countries, certain private practitioners (notaries, conveyancers, surveyors) keep copies of documents prepared by them before registration, but usually this only includes certain cases within the area. This is why institutional mapping is a critical first exercise when planning the recovery of land records.

The extent to which land institutions are computerised varies greatly across different parts of the world. Increasingly, the textual part of the cadastre or the registry is computerised. This will also occasionally be the case with the graphical parts. Digital data is easier to copy and, short of specific back-up facilities, specialised companies are likely to have kept copies of such data (at least for as long as the computerised system has been in place). Although not usually up-to-date, at the very least data from these sources will reflect the situation at a certain point in time (which may not be the same across different areas). Identification of digital copies or back-ups at electronic data processing companies will depend on local intelligence or the such data being volunteered by the companies.

In some countries, registry information may be stored on microfiche, on paper, or in electronic format, or all three, depending on the nature and longevity of the information. Unless the pre-conflict system is well-documented, international experts will need assistance from their local counterparts to identify all the different locations where they can find certain subsets of the land records.

Securing the land records

Once staff have identified the whereabouts of land records and have a reasonably accurate idea of what portion of the records are not available, they should transfer the land records to a secure location as soon as possible or arrange for their protection at their current site(s).

Throughout the fluid, immediate post-conflict period, it may be wise to keep them under physical protection. Either security services can guard the premises, or the records can be physically moved to a more secure location, such as international compounds. If records are available in digital form and the necessary equipment is still operational, staff should make a back-up copy and keep it secure at an international compound. Where land records are in the hands of a group that took them away as they withdrew, every attempt must be made to recover them.

As soon as feasible, the team should prepare an inventory of the newly secured land records. Those in charge of keeping the records must then sign the inventory. Once the situation has become more stable, the inventoried land records must return to their original offices or storage facilities, unless a different or emergency institutional structure is in place. Under certain circumstances, it may be wise to make copies of the most vital land records (such as the title/land register, parcel/person indexes, cadastral register, cadastral index maps), especially where one cannot rule out the risk of data tampering. International staff should keep the copies in a secure location.

Once some form of normality has returned, the updating of the land records must resume as soon as possible, otherwise people will transfer their land outside the land administration system. For these purposes, land record offices and any agencies dealing with land dispute resolution must establish effective co-ordination and information flows between them. They must update the records automatically or regularly in batches, to show any decisions the dispute resolution agency has made. Relevant staff must put in place routine technical processes and administrative procedures as early as possible, with proper checks and balances to ensure professional handling of the records.

MONITORING CHANGES IN ACCESS TO LAND DURING CONFLICT

Though many actors may be wary of investing in contexts where peace has yet to be achieved, it makes sense for agencies to monitor the situation as a country appears to be exiting from conflict. It is vital that changes in access to land are well documented, and that warring parties are aware that they are under international scrutiny. Publishing information on violations and "naming and shaming" those responsible may dissuade the culprits from committing similar abuses in future. However, it is particularly important to ensure that publishing such information does not endanger the victims. Normally, agencies will ensure that their sources of information remain confidential.

Interviewing IDPs, who may also be victims of sexual violence or suffering from post-traumatic stress disorder, requires considerable sensitivity and an ability to cope with some of the ethical issues that may arise. This is in addition to the courage to work in risky areas and the rigor needed to double-check data and verify claims as far as possible. Often, local human rights groups will take the lead in this work, but they require the financial, technical, and political support of the international community, including peace operations, in order to function. Peacekeeping troops can also provide protection to human rights activists, public officials, and humanitarian aid workers who are documenting HLP abuses or attempting to implement restitution programmes.

In Burundi, a variety of local civil society organizations demonstrated the capacity to document and analyze the land-related challenges during the conflict, prior to the return of refugee and IDP populations. Several local organizations have also documented HLP rights abuses in Eastern DRC, despite the difficulties and dangers involved in doing so. Some best practices can be identified: UN-Habitat has led the way in its assessments of the legal framework in Somalia, which focuses on the more peaceful regions of Somaliland and Puntland. Monitoring and documentation of abuses can often be linked to awareness raising or legal aid programs, as proven by NRC in places such as Eastern Democratic Republic of Congo. Monitoring programs can also help build local and international capacity to analyze and address the land issues, and if momentum can be sustained over time, they could result in the creation of networks of experienced local, national, and international specialists ready to assist in more comprehensive interventions. Due to their experience in operating in conflict zones, humanitarian organizations have a major role to play in this regard.

HLP EXPERTISE WITHIN PEACE OPERATIONS

United Nations and other peace operations, both large and small, increasingly view HLP concerns as essential components of the peace-building process and as an indispensable prerequisite for the rule of law. The Secretary-General's August 2004 report on *The rule of law and transitional justice in conflict and post-conflict societies* explicitly recognizes this. However, all too often, specialists in rule-of-law issues, and particularly HLP rights, are absent from the design phase of peace operations. The frequent result is that the structure of peace operations do not provide for institutionalized and systematic responses to HLP challenges. When HLP-related activities are brought in at a later date, opportunities have already been lost, and HLP-related institutions are rarely fully integrated into the wider peace operation architecture.

In addition to international HLP experts, the design and implementation of peace operations depends on collaboration with local HLP specialists. Early identification of such expertise – which may be found in the human rights, law, urban planning, and agricultural sciences professions – is essential for peace operations to succeed in HLP objectives. In order to avoid peace operations removing capacity from civil society and government, a variety of collaborative mechanisms (such as secondment, short-term consultancy for individuals, and structured information exchange between institutions) should be considered in addition to direct recruitment. Some experts residing outside of their country of origin may be willing to return to their country on a temporary or permanent basis.

This is of considerable concern, especially taking into account the increasing awareness of the importance of HLP issues for postconflict stability. For example, despite the emphasis on land issues in the Arusha Peace Accords for Burundi, the UN Mission in Burundi (ONUB) did not provide support for legal or other kinds of approaches to the mass of land and shelter problems plaguing the country.[10] Despite the emphasis given to land and natural resource rights in Sudan's Comprehensive Peace Agreement (CPA), land issues were not included in UNMIS's mandate or in the UN joint strategy for Sudan and were almost entirely ignored by the UN-World Bank Joint Assessment Mission. Assessment missions for the UN Department of Peacekeeping Operations (DPKO) sometimes have as little as two weeks to compile a report for the Security Council, which includes recommendations concerning anticipated staffing needs. If more is done to develop networks or rosters of local and international country-specific expertise in land-related issues, DPKO assessments could benefit from such networks.[11] The views of the UN on questions of mandate are outlined in the following excerpt.

[10] The UN Peacebuilding Commission has since developed the Strategic Framework for Peacebuilding in Burundi, which identifies land issues as a key challenge to peace. Donors are supporting the National Commission for Land and Property, and further development of the draft land law.

[11] UN-Habitat/UNHCR (2004).

United Nations (2007) *The Rule of Law and Transitional Justice in Conflict and Post-Conflict Societies: Report of the Secretary-General.*

Identifying the role of United Nations peace operations

Not all peace operations are mandated to address transitional justice and rule of law activities. Transitional administrations in Kosovo (United Nations Interim Administration Mission in Kosovo) and Timor-Leste (United Nations Transitional Administration in East Timor/United Nations Mission of Support in East Timor), however, have had direct responsibility for the administration of judiciaries, police and prison services. Others, including those in El Salvador (United Nations Observer Mission in El Salvador) and Guatemala (United Nations Verification Mission in Guatemala), as well as more recent operations in Côte d'Ivoire (United Nations Mission in Côte d'Ivoire/United Nations Operation in Côte d'Ivoire), Liberia (United Nations Mission in Liberia) and Haiti (United Nations Stabilization Mission in Haiti), have had important rule of law and justice components, illustrating the increased attention given by the United Nations to these questions.

At the Headquarters level, support for rule of law and transitional justice aspects of peace operations includes needs assessment, mission planning, selection and deployment of specialized staff and provision of guidance and support to rule of law components of missions.

On the ground, our operations have worked, inter alia, to strengthen domestic law enforcement and justice institutions, facilitate national consultations on justice reform, coordinate international rule of law assistance, monitor and report on court proceedings, train national justice sector officials, support local judicial reform bodies and advise host country rule of law institutions. Our operations have helped national actors vet and select national police, judges and prosecutors, draft new constitutions, revise legislation, inform and educate the public, develop ombudsman institutions and human rights commissions, strengthen associations of criminal defence lawyers, establish legal aid, set up legal-training institutes and build the capacity of civil society to monitor the justice sector. Peace missions have also helped host countries to address past human rights abuses by establishing tribunals, truth and reconciliation mechanisms and victim reparation programmes.

This range of activities would be demanding in any circumstances. The challenge is compounded by the fact that the United Nations is frequently called upon to plan the rule of law components of peace operations on extremely short notice, based on short assessment visits to the host country and with minimal human and financial resources. With limited staff devoted to rule of law and transitional justice issues, the United Nations has been stretched to address rule of law planning needs for new missions, while simultaneously providing support to rule of law activities in existing operations. Matching sufficient resources in the headquarters of relevant departments with the growing demands for rule of law support to peace operations is an issue that will require early and considered attention by the Secretariat.

MOVING FROM PEACEKEEPING TO PEACEBUILDING – HLP IN PEACEBUILDING

The term "peacebuilding" was first introduced by the United Nations (UN) Secretary-General in *An Agenda for Peace* in 1992.[12] Secretary-General Boutros Boutros-Ghali emphasized the need to tackle root causes of conflict, which he termed the "underlying economic, social, cultural and humanitarian problems," through long-term interventions. He defined peacebuilding, very broadly, as "action to identify and support structures which will tend to strengthen and solidify peace in order to avoid a relapse into conflict."[13] The concept of peacebuilding has remained very broadly defined in the wider literature since this point.

However, as observers have pointed out, the list of specific issues mentioned in *An Agenda for Peace* are short-to-medium-term priorities, rather than sustained, long-term efforts to transform society.[14] The interventions mentioned included disarming combatants, restoring order, destroying weapons, repatriating refugees, training security forces, monitoring elections, advancing the protection of human rights, reforming institutions, and promoting political participation. These are all rather typical activities of peace operations; the particular value of the Secretary-General's report was to commit to a systematic approach to this issues. The UN had yet to make a commitment to working in a coordinated and coherent manner on socioeconomic issues from a peacebuilding perspective. The following excerpt outlines how HLP issues were – and were not – addressed in East Timor, the Solomon Islands, and Bougainville.

Daniel Fitzpatrick and Rebecca Monson (2009) "Balancing Rights and Norms: Property Programming in East Timor, the Solomon Islands, and Bougainville," in Leckie (ed.) *Housing, Land and Property Rights in Post-Conflict United Nations and Other Peace Operations: A Comparative Survey and Proposal for Reform*, Cambridge: Cambridge University Press.

The Nature of the Conflict

What is now known as the Autonomous Region of Bougainville (ARB) lies in the north east of the island nation of Papua New Guinea. In 1988, after years of bitterness about environmental destruction and economic neglect, some Bougainvilleans formed the Bougainville Revolutionary Army (BRA) and forced the Australian-owned Panguna mine to close. This act, coupled with Bougainvillean demands for secession, sparked a major military confrontation with Papua New Guinean forces and resulted in a wave of human rights abuses. The nine-year conflict (1989–1998) resulted in the deaths of hundreds of soldiers and rebels and

[12] United Nations, *An Agenda for Peace: Preventive Diplomacy, Peacemaking and Peacekeeping*. Report of the Secretary-General, United Nations GA and SC, A/47/277, S/24111, 17 June 1992.

[13] *An Agenda for Peace*, para 21.

[14] Henning Haugerudbraaten (1998) "Peacebuilding: Six Dimensions and Two Concepts" *African Security Review* 7, no. 6.

between 10,000–20,000 deaths of civilians, either from fighting or from disease and deprivation.[15] While the Panguna mine was not the cause of the conflict, it was associated with differing perceptions as to the legitimacy of land rights, as well as issues of access to and control over resources, and these provided a catalyst for igniting pre-existing tensions [...]

The Nature of the Intervention

Throughout the 1990s numerous initiatives unsuccessfully sought to resolve the conflict. In 1997, another peace process tentatively commenced with support from New Zealand and to a lesser extent Australia and Solomon Islands. In July 1997, senior Bougainville leaders from all factions met, and under the Burnham Declaration of 18 July 1997, committed themselves to unity and reconciliation, and to work towards a peaceful settlement through negotiations with the PNG Government. A second meeting in October 1997 involved officials representing PNG and the Bougainville factions, and the Burnham Truce was signed on 10 October. The Truce involved, among other things, agreement between the parties to respect and promote basic human rights and fundamental freedoms.[16]

In December 1997 an unarmed Truce Monitoring Group (TMG) was deployed, comprising 250 truce monitors from Australia, New Zealand, Fiji, Tonga and Vanuatu.[17] The TMG was commanded by the New Zealand Defence Force and predominantly military in composition. Even before the Truce, people began to leave care centers and return home, and once the TMG was in place the returns increased and economic activities such as copra and cocoa production resumed. The return of the population to their homes continued after the agreement to a permanent ceasefire with the Lincoln Agreement on Peace, Security and Development on Bougainville of 23 January 1998. This agreement recognized, among other things, the need for an elected 'Bougainville Reconciliation Government' (BRG) by the end of 1998 and talks on Bougainville's future political status by the end of June 1998. Clause 11 of the Lincoln Agreement addressed the need for co-operative efforts to ensure the restoration and development of Bougainville, but nowhere in the agreement were land and property issues specifically addressed. The Lincoln Agreement and the April 1998 Arawa Agreement Covering Implementation of Ceasefire also provided for the TMG and its New Zealand command to be replaced by a Peace Monitoring Group (PMG) that was commanded by Australia. At its peak the PMG comprised 235 people from Australia, New Zealand, Vanuatu and Fiji.[18] This was followed by the deployment of a UN observer mission in July 1998.

[15] See Joint Standing Committee on Foreign Affairs, DFAT. (1999). *Bougainville: The Peace Process and Beyond*. Canberra, The Parliament of the Commonwealth of Australia., 6, fn 10.

[16] Clause 1, *The Burnham Truce*, 10 October 1997.

[17] K. Claxton(1998) *Bougainville 1988–98: Five Searches for Security in the North Solomons Province of Papua New Guinea*, Canberra: Australian National University, 12–20.

[18] M. Wehner, (2001). "Introduction," in M.D. Wehner (ed.), *Without a Gun: Australians' Experiences Monitoring Peace in Bougainville*. Canberra: Pandanus Books.

1998 marked a shift in the peace process to discussion of the political issues that caused (or were likely to cause) division – disarming combatants, withdrawal of PNG security forces, policing arrangements, political structures, and Bougainville's long term political status. However, once again housing, land and property programs were not included in peace operation planning. On 30 August 2001 a final peace agreement, the Bougainville Peace Agreement was signed, which provided "for a gradual transition to autonomy and an eventual referendum on independence" for Bougainville, on the condition that the BRA disarms and the PNG Government amends the country's constitution to reflect that agreement. The referendum must take place within 10–15 years from the signing of the agreement.[19]

The PMG withdrew from Bougainville on 30 June 2003, and was replaced by the Bougainville Transition Team (BTT), which continued the peace-related activities of the PMG on a smaller scale. It withdrew on 31 December 2003, and some 12 months later the ARB came into existence when the Papua New Guinea Parliament passed constitutional amendments recognizing Bougainville as an autonomous region. Under the Constitution of the Autonomous Region of Bougainville, what lies beneath the land as well as that above is now regulated by customary law (clause 23), and the ARB must develop land policies providing for the recording of land ownership and the protection of customary owners (clause 44). The national Land Titles Commission (LTC) has not been active in Bougainville since the conflict, and will not engage in land reform or land administration unless it is requested to do so by the Bougainvillean authorities to do so.[20]

International intervention in Bougainville has been characterized by a focus on weapons disposal programs, the promotion of confidence in the peace process, and facilitating the transition towards autonomous government. Since 1997, the Australian aid program has contributed over $200 million to support Bougainville's peace process and post-conflict reconstruction,[21] but it appears that little funding has gone towards activities directed at addressing land tenure issues on Bougainville. Australia's assistance for the period 2004–2008 will continue to focus on the implementation of autonomy and the re-establishment of public administration; improvement in the delivery of essential services; and expansion of agricultural income-generating opportunities.[22] As is the case for Solomon Islands, AusAID's 'White Paper' marks an increased emphasis by Australian agencies on land tenure reform. It acknowledges the need to address land tenure issues and balance customary ownership with commercial realities. The Pacific Land Mobilisation Program will be established to provide support, when requested, for land tenure reform.

19 Clause 2, *Bougainville Peace Agreement*, signed 30 August 2001.

20 pers. comm., Joseph N. Kanawi Kiris, Chief Commissioner, Land Titles Commission.

21 AusAID (2005) *Australian Aid to Bougainville*, available at: http://www.ausaid.gov.au/country/png/bougainville.cfm, accessed on 2 June 2006

22 AusAID (2005) *Australian Aid to Bougainville*, available at: http://www.ausaid.gov.au/country/png/bougainville.cfm, accessed on 2 June 2006

Assessment and Application of International Standards

The Right to Housing

Statistical data on Bougainville is very difficult to obtain, however it is clear that many thousands of village homes were destroyed, and that more than a third of the population was displaced. While people began to leave care centres and return home even before the Burnham Truce, the extent to which they were able to return to their homes and rebuild is unclear. No provision was made for housing issues in the planning of the TMG or PMG, and under the Arawa Agreement, the role of the PMG was confined to monitoring the ceasefire, promoting confidence in the peace process, and providing assistance in the implementation of the Lincoln Agreement. Australian officials made it clear that Australia's priorities were on the restoration of law and order, and on the development of physical infrastructure in the health, education, transport and communications sectors.[23] They also emphasized that Australian could not, and should not, meet the entire development and restoration needs of the province.[24] Thus while the aid programs of Australian and New Zealand included support for NGOs engaged in peace and restoration projects, there was virtually no planned policy response to housing issues. Even more concerning is the fact that Bougainville now appears to be autonomous in more ways than one – some of the largest non-governmental aid and development agencies report that they know very little of what is occurring in Bougainville.

Restitution: The Right to Return to One's Home

Restitution and compensation were not mentioned in any of the peace agreements, and neither the TMG nor PMG developed programs for restitution or compensation to people displaced by the conflict. The focus of the TMG/PMG was very much on monitoring peace and facilitating compliance with the terms of the agreements, and any restitution or compensation that occurred seems to have been facilitated by NGOs. Further, while rights to land and access to the benefits of the mine were a key cause of the Bougainvillean conflict, in contrast to the Solomon Islands Tensions discussed above, the violence and the destruction of property was ultimately directed at indigenous Bougainvilleans as much as it was against settlers. Providing restitution in this context is highly complex. Many Bougainvilleans had been relocated from their traditional lands to other areas, and while compensation was often paid to those dislocated and the owners of the land onto which they moved, the quantum of this compensation was a key source of disputation between Bougainvilleans and CRA. In addition, as was the case in Solomon Islands, settlers from other parts of PNG had settled on Bougainville, and in many instances their rights were dubious since they had been obtained from men, despite women being the customary landowners. While clause 44 of the ARB Constitution requires that

[23] See, for instance, Joint Standing Committee on Foreign Affairs, Defence and Trade (1999) *Interim Report: Visit to Bougainville, 15–19 March 1999*; and Joint Standing Committee on Foreign Affairs.

[24] Id.

the land policies developed by the ARB comply with the right to protection from unjust deprivation of property enshrined in the national Constitution, restitution or compensation efforts aimed at reinstating the pre-conflict landholding map may serve to entrench the underlying causes of the conflict.

The Right to Security of Tenure

While the Panguna mine owners had rights to land under formal law imposed during the colonial period, the conflict on Bougainville illustrates that this is insufficient to guarantee security of tenure where there is a conflict between formal law and customary law. The major source of tenure insecurity on Bougainville was (and is) the lack of consensus as to the applicable source of law for determining land rights, and the conflict of authority between customary and central government institutions.

The ARB Constitution now recognizes customary authority over land. Clause 23 brings the formal written law into line with customary law by recognizing that what lies beneath the ARB does not have sufficient resources to record and regulate customary land tenure. Thus at present, customary institutions appear to govern Bougainville land matters in their entirety, de jure and de facto, but it is unlikely that these institutions can in themselves respond effectively to the housing, land and property problems caused by mass displacement and destruction in Bougainville.

As is the case elsewhere in Melanesia, changes occurring during colonial and post-colonial times have brought about immense changes in traditional social structures. Increased participation in the cash economy, the availability of education and increased mobility have reduced social cohesiveness, and younger people in particular are less willing to accept customary authority. These social changes, along with the commodification of land seen in Solomon Islands, have weakened traditional land management institutions. At the same time, of course, traditional institutions cannot simply be legislated away and periods of conflict can also act to undermine the state and enhance the status of traditional leaders. Thus in Bougainville communities certainly relied heavily on customary social organization and authority for general decision-making and dispute resolution. In some areas, this required more than adapting custom to modern circumstances – it required reviving it.[25] Building linkages between customary and state power is widely seen as crucial to developing sustainable state structures for Bougainville, but it remains to be seen whether customary structures are capable of resolving conflicts to the extent required to provide tenure security.

Opportunity to Access Natural Resources

The unequal distribution of benefits from natural resources was a key source of resentment against CRA. The ARB Constitution seems to have addressed the contradiction between access to minerals under customary law and those existing

[25] See A. Regan (2002) "Bougainville: Beyond Survival" *Cultural Survival Quarterly* 25, no. 3.

> under 'Western law' by recognizing that what lies beneath the ground is also regulated according to custom. Nevertheless, in June 2006, PNG media reported that the President of the ARB, Joseph Kabui, had met with an executive of a mining company while on a trip to Canada. Within days, reports emerged of a plot to assassinate Kabui, motivated by resentment about his plans to resume mining on Bougainville. Control over mining resources therefore remains a key source of conflict in Bougainville. More than customary rights to mineral resources is required. Regulations are required to ensure that those rights do not themselves lead to conflict through an even distribution and access to benefits.
>
> **Non-discrimination**
>
> Simply recognizing customary rights to land and natural resources is not sufficient to ensure stability in Bougainville. Customary authority is often an autocratic and discriminatory form of power. There is also a tension between concepts of individual rights and responsibilities, and communal rights and responsibilities. The strengthening of customary authority on Bougainville has also often been associated with discrimination against outsiders, both people from elsewhere in Bougainville and those from other parts of PNG.[26] In addition, while it is overly simplistic to state that customary land ownership is inherently and irredeemably discriminatory, it must be acknowledged that customary law does confer rights to land based on membership of a particular tribal group. As noted above, this raises questions as to how individuals can receive equal access to opportunities such as education and health care, since mining and logging royalties are provided to the customary land owners. If development on Bougainville proceeds in an uneven fashion, resentment over the unequal distribution of these benefits could lead to further conflict. Hence, again, the lesson is that land policy in peace operations must balance and respond to all aspects of international standards relating to land. In the case of Bougainville, recognizing indigenous rights to land alone is not enough. Further attention is also required to questions of non-discrimination, tenure security and equal opportunity of access to natural resources.

Indeed, it has taken many years for institutions involved in peacebuilding efforts to make commitments to addressing issues such as housing, land, and property rights. All too often, initial financial and intellectual investment in postconflict reconstruction has gradually faded as the postconflict country moves from the initial emergency phase into a transitional phase.[27] Typically, attention is focused on the high-level political aspects of the conflict, and more "local" sources of conflict are overlooked. Once a more-or-less peaceful situation of political competition has been established, and elections held, the country loses its position in the global

[26] Id.

[27] Republic of Austria (2006) *Post-Conflict Peacebuilding: Towards a Comprehensive Approach in State and Institution Building*. Background Paper presented at the 36th International Peace Academy Vienna Seminar on Peacemaking and Peacekeeping, Vienna, 28–31 May 2006.

media spotlight. As media coverage declines, so does donor commitment. There is often an awkward period during which peacekeeping operations are drawn down, and agencies more suited to "development" seek funds and slowly expand their number of personnel and their field of operations. This period of adjustment between peacekeeping and "development" activities is often perceived as a gap in concrete action on the ground, and reveals that the conceptual and practical divide between peacekeeping and development efforts has yet to be effectively bridged in practice.

Kofi Annan recognized that all too often, UN peace operations were concluded without having prepared the way for peaceful governance to take root. The Secretary-General therefore argued that the mandates given to peace operations "should include peace-building and incorporate such elements as institution-building and the promotion of good governance and the rule of law, by assisting the parties to develop legitimate and broad-based institutions."[28] Annan also argued that economic and social rehabilitation and transformation should be achieved, in addition to the more typical goal of improving the security situation in the country.

The UN took a significant step forward in December 2005, when the Peacebuilding Commission was formally established by the UN General Assembly and Security Council, alongside a Peacebuilding Fund and a Peacebuilding Support Office in the Secretariat. The Peacebuilding Commission is intended to fill the gap between the conclusion of a peace treaty and the resumption of full-fledged peacebuilding activities. The Commission supports only a small number of countries: Burundi, Sierra Leone, Liberia, and Guinea-Bissau – as well as seven additional countries that have been declared eligible by the Secretary-General or that are receiving emergency funding for urgent peacebuilding activities. The Peacebuilding Commission has identified disputes over land as one of the main causes of conflict and sociopolitical crises at the community level in both Burundi and Liberia. So far, land and natural resources issues have been largely ignored in Sierra Leone. Some observers have raised concerns about this "omission."[29] Others have noted approvingly that rather than initially tackling the full set of issues around land tenure reform – a long-term undertaking – regulations addressing restitution issues were put in place, enabling returnees to farm while the broader land reform process was undertaken.[30]

Significant funding has been committed to resolving land disputes and reforming the legal and institutional frameworks on land in Burundi. The Peacebuilding Fund

[28] United Nations Security Council (2001) *No Exit Without Strategy: Security Council Decision-Making and the Closure or Transition of United Nations Peacekeeping Operations.* Report of the Secretary General, UN S/2001/391, New York, 20 April 2001.

[29] Global Witness (2007) *Peacebuilding Ommission? A Submission on the Need to Integrate Natural Resource Management in the Peacebuilding Commission's Post-Conflict Reconstruction Strategies in Sierra Leone and Elsewhere.*

[30] UNEP, IUCN, ELI. *Meeting Report: Managing Natural Resources in Post-Conflict Societies: Lessons in Making the Transition to Peace.*

supports Burundi's National Commission for Land and other Property (known by its French acronym, CNTB) that was formally established in 2006, with a very broad three-year mandate to address land conflicts arising from repatriation, as well as illegal land transfers.[31] The Commission is composed of a twenty-three-person team recruited from various ministries.

The Peacebuilding Commission does not have the capacity to coordinate different UN agencies, and there have been some concerns that it may duplicate some strategic activities carried out elsewhere within the UN system.[32] However, it is clearly playing an important role in raising attention to countries and to issues that might otherwise be neglected by the international community.

HLP issues are important in peacebuilding from a number of perspectives. Enhancing equitable access to land, housing, and other property can help build public trust in the postconflict order. Individuals who are vulnerable to recruitment by armed groups, such as demobilized and unemployed youth, require access to land and other forms of property in order to find alternate livelihoods. When households are able to claim their HLP rights, they enjoy direct concrete benefits that represent productive assets as well as investment for the future. Secure HLP rights may allow people to use their property as collateral for loans, start small businesses, and reengage in the economy, each of which is essential for economic growth. More profoundly perhaps, improved capacity and transparency in decision making around land, housing, and other forms of property helps "ground" democratic principles in local-level institutions. When local people are involved in decision making around HLP, and when they trust the institutions responsible for distributing goods and services, they are able to see good governance in action.

PBSO (2008) *Environment: A Peacebuilding Support Office (PBSO) Briefing.* Paper Prepared in Cooperation with UNEP.

To date, the UN has not effectively integrated environment and natural resource considerations into peacebuilding. Priorities usually rest with meeting humanitarian needs, demobilization, disarmament and reintegration, supporting elections, restoring order and the rule of law, and opening the economy to attract foreign investment. The environment and natural resources are often framed as important issues to address at a later stage. This is a flawed approach, which fails to take into account the changing nature of security threats to national (and often-times regional) stability as demonstrated by the cases cited above. Integrating environment and natural resources into peacebuilding is no longer an option – it is a

[31] Under law n°1/18 of 4 May 2006, the CNTB was given several responsibilities, from providing technical and material assistance to returnees and IDPs, to updating the existing inventory of state land and reclaiming illegally occupied land.

[32] Alex J. Bellamy (2009) *Responsibility to Protect*, Polity Press, 191.

security and development imperative. This new understanding is reflected in recent high-level policy debates and statements. [...]

The following section provides some compelling reasons and supporting case studies on how environment and natural resources can contribute to peacebuilding.

- Supporting economic recovery [...]
- Supporting humanitarian needs and coping strategies: Natural resources are critical assets in humanitarian operations, providing land, water, construction materials, and renewable energy. They also support coping strategies and basic survival in the absence of sustainable livelihoods. A "do no harm" approach to environment and natural resources is therefore critical to secure and sustain humanitarian programming and prevent conflict with host communities.
- Developing sustainable livelihoods: Durable peace fundamentally depends on the development of sustainable livelihoods and on the recovery and sound management of the natural resource base. Environmental damage caused by conflicts, coping strategies, and chronic environmental problems that undermine livelihoods must, therefore, be addressed from the outset. Minimizing vulnerability to natural hazards and climate change through the management of key natural resources should also be a priority. The ability of the environment and resource base to support rural livelihoods, urban populations and economic recovery is a determining factor for lasting peace. The transparent, equitable, and legitimate definition and realization of property rights and land and resource tenure can have profound positive impacts on a country's environmental, social, and economic prospects, helping to prevent conflict and promote peace. Conversely, the lack of these rights-or the incorrect sequencing of interventions-has resulted in poor outcomes across the development spectrum.
- Contributing to dialogue, cooperation and confidence-building: Mutual need and interest to use, share or protect natural resources can be harnessed as a means to build trust, confidence and cooperation between groups, as well as within and between states (e.g. common property resources such as fisheries or forests, transboundary protected areas, and shared river basins).

SUPPORTING LOCAL DISPUTE RESOLUTION MECHANISMS

The international community is increasingly realizing the importance of supporting mechanisms to resolve housing, land, and property disputes in postconflict situations. Conflict, and related population movements and destruction of HLP resources, tends to result in an increase in the volume and complexity of land disputes, as described in Chapter 1. In some cases, land disputes may become more violent – particularly if they involve disputants who are perceived as supporting different parties in the armed conflict.[33]

[33] Land disputes may be particularly dangerous to social stability and long-term peace when they involve an "identity" dimension that was at issue in the armed conflict.

Until recently, UN agencies, bilateral donors, and multinational organizations have tended to provide support to the statutory justice system, which often would be "clogged" with complex land disputes. In many postconflict countries, HLP disputes account for three-quarters or more of all court cases.

Over the past decade, there has been a realization that in most countries, the state lacks the will or the capacity to provide unbiased, effective, and accessible means of HLP disputes. In some cases, the legitimacy of state institutions has been undermined by civil war and social conflicts; in very poor countries, and in areas where state capacity has been ravaged by protracted conflict or mass atrocity, the state is unable to afford the high financial costs of recreating and maintaining a functioning judiciary. This means that international support to the formal justice system may prove to be unsustainable.

Support of local dispute resolution systems, sometimes called "informal" systems, is therefore becoming increasingly common as part of a broader remit of restoring the rule of law. Local systems often deliver a faster, cheaper, and more culturally appropriate outcome than the statutory judicial system can provide.[34]

Transitional justice programs that support processes related to crimes committed during times of authoritarian rule or conflict can also address HLP issues. Local institutions are often called on to address property crimes committed within the context of atrocity.[35]

International support for local-level dispute resolution mechanisms often includes capacity building, monitoring, and the facilitation of improved coordination with national-level judicial processes. In some cases, international actors may facilitate the establishment of new mediation committees at the local level, but in most cases it is possible to strengthen and refine existing institutions, including customary systems.

Local and "informal" dispute resolution institutions, particularly those based on long-standing custom, have strengths and weaknesses. These are highly context-specific. However, many local institutions may have some of the following strengths: local legitimacy accessibility, public participation, flexible rules of evidence, speed restitution, reconciliation, and social pressure. The same characteristics of flexibility and cultural appropriateness that make local institutions a practical alternative to state courts can also pose significant problems: Some punishments contravene national laws or international human rights law. The practice of giving symbolic "gifts" to office bearers may become a form of corruption. Informal systems

34 C. Toulmin (2008) "Securing Land and Property Rights in Sub-Saharan Africa: The Role of Local Institutions" *Land Use Policy* 26, 10–19.

35 Chris Huggins (2009) "Linking Broad Constellations of Ideas: Transitional Justice, Land Tenure Reform, and Development," in Pablo de Greiff and Roger Duthie (eds.), *Transitional Justice and Development: Making Connections*, Social Science Research Council.

are location- or community-specific, so that they have difficulties resolving disputes with outsiders. The processes followed are not adequately regulated and violate due process criteria. Processes are not documented, making external monitoring and enforcement of decisions difficult. Systems may systematically discriminate against some members of the community, such as women or ethnic minorities.

Assumpta Naniwe-Kaburahe (2008) "The Institution of Bashingantahe in Burundi" in *Traditional Justice and Reconciliation after Violent Conflict: Learning from African Experiences*. International Institute for Democracy and Electoral Assistance.

In current usage, the term *bashingantahe* (singular *umushingantahe*) refers to men of integrity who are responsible for settling conflicts at all levels, from the top of the hill to the courts of kings …

The revival of the *bashingantahe* institution was initiated in the wake of the National Reconciliation Policy which sought to create a framework for dialogue and consultation between the different factions of the Burundian people with regard to the basic challenges facing the country. The commission charged with studying the question of national unity had recommended that the institution be adapted to the current context: 'It does not have to be mythologized but rather to be revived and given back the honour it deserves while taking into account the new state of affairs in Burundian society' (Ntahombaye and Kagabo 2003). The rehabilitation process, which was of particular interest to the *bashingantahe* who had been invested in the traditional way, began at the time of the debate on the Charter of National Unity (1991–2) and of the democratization of Burundian institutions.

From 1996 onwards the *bashingantahe* enjoyed real support as much from the government as from Burundian civil society and the international community. The latter considered the *bashingantahe* as offering a way out of the crisis and built upon the capacity of the institution's members to mobilize their fellow citizens around the ideals of peace and harmony and the positive role that they can play in the life of society. In its 'Support for the Promotion of Good Governance' project, carried out between 1999 and 2001, the United Nations Development Programme (UNDP) supported activities aimed at identifying *bashingantahe* who had been invested in the traditional way all over the country. In all, more than 34,000 households of traditionally invested and active *bashingantahe* were identified in the 17 provinces of Burundi. This operation made it possible to better understand the real situation of these *bashingantahe*, as well as their number (which would be around 64,000 if one bears in mind that most households consist of a man and a woman: normally women are invested with their husbands). In 2002, the UNDP launched a second phase of implementation of the 'Support for the Rehabilitation of the Bashingantahe Institution' project. This achieved varied results, including support to the self-structuring of the institution from the lowest level (Conseil de Colline) right up to the top (Conseil National, National Council) and through the local and provincial structures, with democratic elections held each time at different levels. This project helped not only to facilitate communication among the *bashingantahe* but also to rectify certain operational mistakes that had been fostered by years of acting in isolation, and sometimes actions dictated by the government in contradiction of the traditional philosophies of the institution.

The different organs of the institution and their respective powers and duties were entrenched in writing in the Bashingantahe Charter, adopted in April 2002 at an extraordinary congress which brought together five elected representatives from the invested *bashingantahe* in each province. The institution took the gender dimension into account by including 33 per cent of women in its management committees. The presence of women at management levels constituted a definite asset which helped to trigger positive reflection on the conditions for investiture of women in their own right – something which up until then Burundian tradition had not permitted.

Since 2002 the institution has been progressively recovering its former vitality. Investiture takes place in broad daylight, both in rural and in urban settings. According to available figures, today Burundi has nearly 100,000 *bashingantahe* (men and women) who have been invested in the traditional way ('Rapport de la Mission Indépendante' 2003: 24 ff.).

The evaluation report on the UNDP project notes the steps taken to rehabilitate the institution, and recommends that efforts be focused on activities aimed at reinforcing the capacity of the *bashingantahe* at the grass roots through training in different domains such as juridical function, general law, property law, family law, techniques for the prevention and settlement of conflicts, and basic literacy ('Rapport de la Mission Indépendante' 2003: 24). The implementation of these recommendations ought, however, to take the philosophy and ethics of the *bashingantahe* institution into account and to involve the members, some of whom have a good level of education in different areas and who should themselves be in charge of implementing the programmes of rehabilitation.

In addition, there is the issue of strengthening the technical capacities of the *bashingantahe* and their involvement in development work in order that they may learn to better apply the principles of gender equality and better manage issues related to succession and matrimonial laws, as well as support self-sufficiency in food and people's material wellbeing—important criteria for being invested as an *umushingantahe*.

Today, the institution has advantages which reinforce its legitimacy at the political and institutional level. The Arusha [Peace] Agreement [for Burundi] acknowledges that the *bashingantahe* constitute a unifying factor on the hills and that the institution is part of the judicial system. As a customary jurisdiction, the institution of *bashingantahe* has always had a place in Burundian society, which accords it a certain authority. It has some strengths but also some weaknesses, which should be rectified if it is to play its role in the establishment of the rule of law in Burundi […]

Major challenges remain, mainly involving a tendency to trivialize the institution and the development of sound collaboration between the authorities and the *bashingantahe*. Additional problems such as the integration of young people into the institution, and the investiture of women in their individual capacities, independently of their husbands, as well as the role they can play in the present context of a country recovering from crisis, also need to be resolved. These are significant challenges, but they should be tackled sensitively, without unduly disrupting an already fragile Burundian society.

***Land Conflict in Afghanistan: Building Capacity to Address Vulnerability*. AREU Issues Paper Series.**

Studies have shown that many of the incentives and imperatives for land conflict can be identified through their social, political, economic and historical context. Land conflicts are complex and often comprise an accumulation of grievances or processes occurring at multiple levels. Reflecting on the framework set out in Figure 8, it can be envisaged how change in any of the determinant factors will influence the overall nature of the conflict in question. one where land is of relatively low economic value to one or both disputants. The existence or not of strong dispute resolution structures will influence how disputes are manifested and develop. The legal context, including the type of legal basis (e.g. civil law, *Sharia*) and whether an effective framework for the implementation of decisions is in place will affect the nature of a dispute and possibilities for its resolution.

While factors influencing the emergence and dynamics of conflict are by no means restricted to those summarised in Figure 8, the key point is that minor differences in the overall context of a dispute will influence the nature of the dispute as a whole. All disputes are embedded in diverse and complex contextual realities, including historical, social, economic and political factors. The extent to which a dispute must first be studied and understood cannot be overemphasised as this is an essential first step towards determining the most suitable approach. The nature of the parties or disputants involved has an important affect on the characteristics of the conflict and resolution mechanisms that may be employed. This makes an effective stakeholder analysis an indispensable tool in dispute analysis. Stakeholder analysis, reduced to its simplest form, means identifying the parties involved in a dispute and exploring their interests and objectives in pursuing the dispute. Stakeholders to the dispute may hold either direct or indirect interests in the resource in question. Those with indirect interests will include groups affected by the broader consequences of the dispute resolution. In disputes where entitlements are complex, such as those over common property resources, there may be many legitimate stakeholders.

Power relationships between disputants will influence every stage of dispute development, manifestation and resolution. Conflict over land may be exacerbated where power asymmetries exist: the powerful may overstep their legal bounds if they fear little reprisal; the powerless may feel compelled to resort to violence or other extrajudicial actions if they are unable to otherwise protect their perceived entitlements. For example, the powerful may be able to exert an influence over the institutions and structures that would normally operate to resolve conflict, and so be encouraged to make claims to resources for which entitlements already exist.

Power imbalances between stakeholders may be a consequence of the actual power attributes (social, economic and political) of the stakeholders themselves or may be structurally imposed, for example by a policy or legal framework favouring one group over another. Consequently it is possible to distinguish between "horizontal" and "vertical" power-relationships in land conflicts. "Horizontal" are those occurring between those sharing a roughly similar power status (often members of the same social group), while vertical disputes will involve a gap between actors' socio-political influence.

The power relationship between disputants will affect how a conflict manifests itself. An imbalance will influence how actors pursue the dispute and thus how the conflict is expressed. Power imbalances are particularly significant in Afghanistan where rule of law is weak. With respect to dispute management, an effective resolution process may require special strengthening and support to the weaker actors to counterbalance the political advantages and influence held by the more powerful. For example, submissions to a provincial court by an impoverished returnee whose land has been occupied by a powerful local actor may require advocacy and scrutiny to ensure that due process is being followed.

A conflict analysis process looking at both the context of the dispute (its substance and contributory factors), and the relationship between actors involved, will inform the determination of appropriate mechanisms with which to approach the dispute. However, it is important that conflict analysis does not transgress into prejudice or determination of the rights or wrongs of the dispute.

Options for land dispute resolution

[...] Characteristics of resolution mechanisms available within each category are explored below and are summarised in Table 7. Although these are general categories of dispute resolution mechanisms, applicable in numerous non-Afghan contexts as well as Afghan contexts, they all have a degree of relevance either because they are already implemented or because they are worth exploring in the future. Resolution mechanisms that require that all parties to the conflict agree to the mechanism are termed consensual; non-consensual mechanisms are those that do not require agreement from the disputants for the mechanism to be implemented. Non-consensual approaches are usually embedded in some form of written legal framework and decisions are usually binding. The principal advantages of non-consensual dispute resolution techniques are that *if* the rules that regulate decisions are legitimate and widely known, decisions will be easy to understand. Furthermore, the decisions in most adjudicated cases are enforceable by law, with the implication that the State is the guarantor of the decision. However, where state institutions are weakened or the judicial process suspected of partiality, the legitimacy and effectiveness of the adjudication is undermined. Furthermore, non-consensual resolution mechanisms are often more time consuming and resource intensive than consensual resolution mechanisms, both during the adjudication and enforcement stages. As discussed in the LP Project's Inception Report, the GCS, which is charged with implementing non-consensual dispute resolution mechanisms, is not only ineffective but also currently overwhelmed with cases, raising the incentives to explore consensual forms of dispute resolution.

Consensual approaches to conflict management often offer a range of advantages. Evidence, such as the Typology of land conflicts, indicates that many claimants prefer to pursue resolution through a CBM – in most cases, consensual mechanisms – and are also encouraged to do so by community elders as well as officials within the GCS. Because the process is consensual, decisions are often built on compromise, which makes the process faster and decisions more easily enforceable. Indeed, consensus-based approaches to land dispute resolution are in many instances less about determining who is "right" and who is "wrong", but helping disputants to understand their respective positions and find a workable solution. Consensual mechanisms also have their drawbacks, however, such as prejudicial treatment of women, religious or ethnic minorities or where the balance of power between parties is disparate. In communities where traditional structures have broken down due to chronic displacement, consensual mechanisms may be subject to the same corrupt practices as non-consensual mechanisms.

PEACE OPERATIONS AND THE ENFORCEMENT OF POSTCONFLICT HLP POLICIES

Assessing and Responding to the Housing and Shelter Needs of the Population

In many cases, settlements will have suffered direct or indirect damage as a result of conflict. Valuable materials – such as roofing tiles and metal doors and windows – may have been stolen from homes, while public infrastructure (such as water distribution systems or generators) may have been destroyed or looted. Such damage could make it difficult for civilians to remain in their homes without succumbing to disease or suffering from extremes of weather. To minimize the risk of secondary occupation of property, peace operations should assess damage to houses and other buildings, and provide the materials necessary for their repair. An investment of materials early in a peace operation will often prove to be cheaper than attempting to evict secondary occupants or repair damage due to abandonment or multiple episodes of looting.

Preventing Secondary Occupation of Property and Enforcing Eviction Orders

Peacekeepers may be required to perform law-and-order functions, particularly in terms of preventing occupation of abandoned housing. In many countries, homes and offices may be systematically taken over by criminal gangs seeking to profit from rent payments. Rent money may then be used to purchase weapons, drugs, or carry out other illegal activities. Preventing illegal secondary occupation of vacant buildings can therefore be an important step in limiting the spread of organized crime. Prevention of illegal secondary occupation is often easier than evicting secondary occupants, which requires a legal or regulatory framework to avoid abuses associated with arbitrary decision making.

Of course, peace operations must avoid contributing to HLP abuses by indirectly supporting secondary occupation. As Article 22.7 of the UN Pinheiro Principles makes clear:

> International organizations and peace operations should avoid occupying, renting or purchasing housing, land and property over which the rights holder does not currently have access or control, and should require that their staff do the same. Similarly, international organizations and peace operations should ensure that bodies or processes under their control or supervision do not obstruct, directly or indirectly, the restitution of housing, land and property.

RAISING AWARENESS OF LAWS AND POLICIES

In many countries affected by conflict, the concept of the rule of law has never been fully established. Lawmaking institutions have lacked legitimacy among the general public or the capacity to disseminate information about laws, rights, and responsibilities. Agencies involved in peace operations can help inform the public about HLP laws and policies and help engender respect for the rule of law. A coordinated and culturally appropriate public information campaign, tailored to particular areas and local languages, and emphasizing a "respect for rights" approach can assist in defusing tensions around HLP issues. For example, a campaign on restitution policies could improve the willingness of secondary occupants to voluntarily vacate disputed properties.[36]

IMPROVING ACCESS TO LAND FOR DEMOBILIZED EX-COMBATANTS

Programs for the disarmament, demobilization, and reintegration (DDR) of former combatants are an important aspect of peace operations. If DDR is not

[36] UNHCR/UN-Habitat. *Housing, Land and Property Rights in Post-Conflict Societies: Proposals for their Integration into UN Policy and Operational Frameworks*. Paper presented at Expert Meeting, 10 and 11 November 2004 – Geneva.

systematically and effectively carried out, former combatants remain a danger to peace, either as potential soldiers in a resurgence of armed hostilities or as armed criminals engaged in robbery, extortion, and other crimes. It is important that former combatants are able to earn their livelihood through legal and sustainable means, so that they are not vulnerable to remobilization during times of political or ethnic tension. However, in practice, most of the donor funding for DDR to date appears to have been allocated to disarmament and demobilization rather than reintegration.[37]

Reintegration has both psychosocial and economic aspects. Counseling may be provided to assist the former soldiers to adjust to civilian life, and the communities that they are expected to rejoin are also consulted on their feelings. On an economic level, ex-combatants typically receive a "reintegration package" that includes such items as a small amount of cash, clothing, household goods, tools, and agricultural implements.

In many cases, ex-combatants may have become used to an urban lifestyle during the conflict, or may feel that their former status as a soldier precludes them from returning to a rural life. These individuals may have access to vocational training to help them make a living in the town of their choice.

However, others will choose to return to a rural setting. In practice, however, it may be difficult for ex-combatants to access land. In areas under customary tenure, local communities may block access to land for ex-combatants, especially those who are suspected of participation in atrocities. Where conflict has resulted in changes to settlement patterns or destruction of documents, ex-soldiers may have to make a claim to land belonging to themselves or their wider family, through local or state-run dispute resolution mechanisms, including the courts. Female ex-combatants may find it especially difficult to access land because they can be doubly discriminated against – as women, they have fewer rights to land than men, and as former soldiers, they may be marginalized in their communities. In such cases, ex-combatants will often need external assistance to obtain clear title or secure rights to the land, either individually or as part of a resettlement program.

Until relatively recently, the design of most DDR programs was based on the assumption that ex-combatants were male adults. The social, psychological, and economic difficulties faced by female ex-combatants and child soldiers were exacerbated by programs that ignored their particular needs. Thankfully this is starting to change. DDR programs should look at the obstacles to access to land for female or child ex-combatants.

[37] Tom Body (2005) *Reintegration of Ex-Combatants through Micro-Enterprise: An Operational Framework*, Ottawa: Canadian Peacekeeping Press.

Leontine Specker (2008) *The R-Phase of DDR Processes: An Overview of Key Lessons Learnt and Practical Experiences*, Netherlands Institute of International Relations, "Clingendael."

Reviews point out that rural reintegration programmes are often more successful than urban reintegration programmes. They commonly indicate that access to arable land and supportive social capital are the main determinants of successful reintegration.[38] Any strategy for rural reintegration should ideally identify suitable areas for resettlement and ensure that ex-combatants have a clear title and secure rights to land, either individually or as part of a resettlement programme.[39]

Reviews indicate that an important factor is the commonly observed discrepancy between expectations of ex-combatants (often influenced by government promises) and the realities of an opportunity-constrained environment.[40] There seems to be a risk of unrealistic promises of land and unemployment in order to achieve short-term security aims, which cannot be fulfilled and may lead to instability later.[41] It should also not be forgotten that next to ex-combatants, there are often also large numbers of refugees and IDPs returning home, potentially contributing to political and security tensions. Even though this challenge is well beyond the means and time frame of a DDR programme, land reform and access to land require attention in parallel and subsequent economic reconstruction programmes in support of reintegration efforts.[42]

Reviews thus emphasize the need for context analysis and the socio-economic profiling of ex-combatants in advance of programme appraisal, in order to improve the relevance and design of programme interventions. An ex ante analysis of the relationship between former combatants an the availability of arable land allows time to inform local officials of the pertinent problems and seek early solutions by identifying alternative sources of land or employment.[43]

The majority of ex-combatants in Uganda, for instance, were expected to and eventually did return to rural areas and start farming activities. With a large number of ex-combatants settling with families in established communities, access to land was potentially a major issue notwithstanding the fact that most ex-combatants returned to the district of their origin, where many had rights to land in one form or another. The potential constraint to economic and social integration was acknowledged from

[38] Colletta, Kostner and Wiederhofer (1997) *The Transition from War to Peace in Sub-Saharan Africa*. World Bank Discussion Paper No. 81, p. 277.

[39] Id.

[40] Id., p. 13 and p. 87.

[41] B. Hoffman and C. Gleichmann (2000) *Programmes for Demobilization and Reintegration of Ex-Combatants: Changing Perspectives in Development and Security*, p. 33.

[42] P. Douma and B. Klem, with G. Frerks, G. Gompelman, and S. Van Laar (2008) *The Struggle after Combat: The Role of NGOs in DDR Processes, a Synthesis Study*. Cordaid.

[43] Colletta, Kostner, and Wiederhofer, 1996, p. 333.

the outset. The programme attempted to quantify this constraint on the basis of the population density on cultivable land, percentage of cultivable land used and the number of ex-combatants settling in any particular district. A settlement index was made on the basis of: 1) land tenure arrangements, 2) socially acceptable use of land; and 3) soil quality, thus taking into account the differences between the districts.

Ernest Harsch (2005) "Reintegration of Ex-combatants" *Africa Renewal* 19, no. 3.

For those ex-fighters who manage to complete their schooling or vocational training, the future is not necessarily assured. Will there be jobs or other income opportunities? Most post-war economies remain exceptionally weak. Employment is limited, and few people can afford the services of the newly trained carpenters, auto mechanics or plumbers. As one demobilized Mozambican soldier put it, they were "reintegrated back into basic poverty."

Sierra Leone's experience provides some grounds for hope – along with a note of caution. A large number of ex-combatants there were able to acquire some form of livelihood, however limited. There is some indication that those who went into farming may have done better than graduates of vocational training programmes. According to Mr. Ibrahim Sarpee, a programme officer with the non-governmental Friends of Africa Relief and Development Agency, the group helped register about 100 ex-RUF fighters in Kailahun, on Sierra Leone's eastern border. Seventy-three of them went into tree-crop farming, and "they're doing well," Mr. Sarpee reports. The rest received training in soap making, tailoring and other occupations. "They're now skilled, but there's no employment."

In Liberia, the 500 ex-combatants at the Duport Road project and the more than 1,000 in the LOIC's six rural centres reflect some interest in farming. "Liberia is an agricultural nation," stresses Mr. Kpawulu. "We have vast lands, underutilized. We are unable to feed ourselves. So it is better to conscientize the young people to learn to farm."

At Duport Road, the young ex-fighters raised concerns about access to land once they return to their home areas. Project officials assured them that local village chiefs had already identified land for their use.

Whatever has been arranged for these particular ex-fighters, the issue of land is not a simple one, in either Liberia or Sierra Leone. In both countries, young people and women have traditionally been bypassed when village elders allocate community-owned lands. Such lack of access to land was one of the grievances that impelled many young people to join the armed groups in the first place.

In Liberia's Nimba and Lofa counties, there already have been renewed land tensions between members of local ethnic groups and Mandingos, who are viewed as "outsiders" and therefore not entitled to land. Since many Mandingos supported the Liberians United for Reconciliation and Democracy (LURD), the strongest of the former rebel groups, such conflicts could ultimately jeopardize the overall peace process.

Into the communities

Because of their specific mandates, most DDR programmes concentrate on ex-combatants, and less on the communities to which they will return. This has elicited some criticism that current reintegration efforts are too narrow and should do more to help broader community recovery.

Ms. Béatrice Pouligny, a senior researcher at the Centre d'études et de recherches internationales (CERI) in France, argues that an "approach which focuses on 'individual' incentives may miss the broader 'collective' dimension." Ex-combatants "cannot be considered without taking their families and social ties into account." She recommends "the broadening of the DDR framework" to include such factors. She and others have stressed the benefits of a community approach: less resentment that demobilized soldiers may be receiving "privileges" denied to others, joint projects that can help rebuild trust and greater social controls over the behaviour of former combatants.

Most DDR experts and practitioners agree that war-ravaged communities require more support, both for their own sake and to help ensure that ex-fighters are able to successfully reintegrate over the long term. As Mr. David Munyurangabo of Rwanda's DDR commission acknowledged at the Freetown conference, "Civilians should also benefit," a view echoed by many other participants. Some DDR programmes have incorporated community aspects. In the Central African Republic, for example, the UNDP and World Bank have provided $3.3 mn for a reintegration project that includes rehabilitating community infrastructure and creating income-generating activities.

Mr. Steven Ursino, UNDP's Liberia country director, told Africa Renewal that the reintegration of ex-combatants there is taking place "in a wider context" that includes the return of thousands of refugees and displaced people and the rehabilitation of communities destroyed by 14 years of war. At the Duport Road reintegration site, about 100 local farmers joined the 500 ex-combatants. They did not receive the same cash payments, but they were able to learn new farming techniques and skills.

ENFORCING LEGAL DECISIONS ON DISPUTED PROPERTY

Local responses often emerge rapidly to the array of HLP disputes found in the aftermath of conflict. In many cases, these will be relatively independent of the state. They may be based on existing custom. In other cases, they may be informal institutions created by the community to respond to a gap in state service provision. Given the challenges of reestablishing national-level institutions, state dispute resolution systems are usually slower to react following conflict.

Peacekeepers may be called on to help enforce decisions on HLP rights made by local or national justice systems, particularly when one or more of the parties involved in the dispute is armed. This may raise complicated issues around local and national legitimacy of emerging institutions and related questions of state sovereignty over the entire state territory.

Peace operations should provide support to dispute resolution systems, or national-level justice systems, in systematic ways, rather than on the basis of ad hoc decision making that can easily be misinterpreted as biased toward one or other of the parties in a dispute. In many cases, a dedicated program will be developed and implemented to monitor and support local or national institutions adjudicating in land and property disputes. Peacekeeping forces, which generally comprise police units in addition to military personnel, may then enjoy greater legitimacy in assisting with the enforcement of decisions made by these institutions.

In Kosovo, where a Housing and Property Directorate was established by the UN Mission in Kosovo (UNMIK) to process housing and land claims, evictions were carried out by officers of the Housing and Property Directorate with the support of the law enforcement authorities. Initially support was provided by international police officers (UNMIK Police) and the NATO-led military presence, KFOR, but this responsibility was gradually transferred to the local Kosovo Police Service under the direction of UNMIK police.[44]

Questions and Exercises

1. What are some of the reasons why peace operations should try to protect cadastral buildings and other institution's housing land ownership documents?
2. Imagine that you work for a local organization in a conflict-affected area, and you are documenting forced displacement and property destruction. What are some of the obstacles that you would face in your work? Are there any particular skills you would need to overcome these obstacles? How might international agencies be able to assist your institution? How might they unwittingly hinder your work?
3. Identify some local-level HLP activities that might contribute to the consolidation of peace in a postconflict society that has suffered population displacement and destruction of housing. Now identify some national-level policy interventions. What indicators could be used for monitoring, to show whether these interventions are contributing to social stability and peace?
4. Explain some of the strengths and weaknesses of local and "informal" dispute resolution systems. How might some of these weaknesses be addressed through external support, without undermining some of the strengths?
5. Imagine that you are a male ex-combatant retuning to your rural home area after the conflict is over. You were orphaned at an early age. You were raised in exile and do not know exactly where your ancestral property is located. What are some of the steps you

[44] Margaret Cordial and Knut Rosandhaug (2009) "The Response of the United Nations Interim Administration Mission in Kosovo to Address Property Rights Challenges," in Leckie (ed.), *Housing, Land and Property Rights in Post-Conflict United Nations and Other Peace Operations*. Cambridge University Press, 90.

would take to try to claim access to land in your home area? What kind of external support might help you?

6. Now imagine that you are a female ex-combatant in a similar situation to that described in Exercise 5. Would you be able to follow the same process to claim family land as your male counterpart? What extra obstacles might lie in your way? What kind of external support might help you?

Additional Resources

C. Bell (2000) *Peace Agreements and Human Rights*, Oxford University Press.

Brahimi Report – Comprehensive Review of the Whole Question of Peacekeeping Operations in All Their Aspects (A/55/305 – S/2000/809) 21 August 2000.

Brookings-Bern Project on Internal Displacement (2007) *Addressing Internal Displacement in Peace Processes, Peace Agreements and Peace-Building.*

Center for Humanitarian Dialogue and Norwegian Ministry of Foreign Affairs (2007) *Osloforum07 – Dialogue in a Divided World: Power, Potential and Pitfalls*, Geneva.

FAO (2005) *Access to Rural Land and Land Administration after Violent Conflicts*, FAO Land Tenure Studies.

ICISS (2001) *The Responsibility to Protect* (Report of the International Commission on Intervention and State Sovereignty), IDRC.

International Council on Human Rights Policy (2006) *Negotiating Justice? Human Rights and Peace Agreements*, ICHRP.

Harriet Martin (2006) *Kings of Peace, Pawns of War – The Untold Story of Peace-Making*, Continuum.

UN Habitat and UNHCR (2004) *Housing, Land and Property Rights in Post-Conflict Societies: Proposals for Their Integration into UN Policy and Operational Frameworks – Expert Meeting Report*, 10–11 November 2004, Geneva.

UN Secretary General (2004) *The Rule of Law and Transitional Justice in Conflict and Post-Conflict Societies*, UN Security Council, S/2004/616.

7

Protracted Displacement and Political Obstacles to the Protection of HLP Rights

The previous six chapters have provided a broad overview of the many complex interrelationships between conflict and HLP rights. The book has outlined both the theoretical and legal basis for the new emphasis on HLP issues by the international human rights and humanitarian communities. In many instances, this gradual strengthening in the understanding of how HLP issues are intricately linked to the cause, consequence, and cure for conflict has led to real improvements in the enjoyment of HLP rights by those affected by conflict.

The slow but consistent merging of international human rights and humanitarian perspectives on the centrality of HLP issues has meant that although HLP abuses continue on far too large a scale, the laws, systems, and institutions now in place have significantly solidified the global appreciation of the need to prevent HLP abuses and to remedy them whenever possible. The HLP progress witnessed during the past two decades in Bosnia, Kosovo, Tajikistan, South Africa, and elsewhere, even if far from perfect or comprehensive, is indicative of the fact that the international community in many ways now finds itself on the cusp of a new era, where HLP rights are treated with the seriousness and urgency that the laws recognizing them have always intended.

The next decades will need to build on the significant progress that has been made since the early 1990s and will be presented with HLP challenges that will require far greater attention, political will, and resources than have often been given to these concerns in conflicts of the recent past. In early 2010, quite literally millions of people displaced by conflict remain displaced and unable to return to their original homes, lands, or properties. In all of these instances, from Saharawis from Western Sahara and ethnic Nepalis from Bhutan to Tamil IDPs in Sri Lanka and Iraqi IDPs, people wishing to return to their original homes are actively prevented from doing so by regimes uninterested in allowing them to exercise these rights. It is these and all others affected by conflict who have yet to be able to enjoy their legitimate HLP rights as recognized under a vast array of legal standards.

To provide a deeper understanding of several particularly noteworthy cases of protracted displacement, in this chapter we include excerpts from several excellent publications addressing three major unresolved cases of displacement: Palestinian refugees, those displaced during the Cyprus conflict in the 1970s, and finally the tragic case of the Chagos Islanders.

Ilan Pappe (2006) *The Ethnic Cleansing of Palestine*, Oneworld, (Footnotes omitted)

On a cold Wednesday afternoon, 10 March 1948, a group of eleven men, veteran Zionist leaders together with young military Jewish officers, put the final touches to a plan for the ethnic cleansing of Palestine. The same evening, military orders were dispatched to the units on the ground to prepare for the systematic expulsion of the Palestinians from vast areas of the country. The orders came with a detailed description of the methods to be employed to forcibly evict the people: large-scale intimidation; laying siege to and bombarding villages and population centres; setting fire to homes, properties and goods; expulsion; demolition' and, finally, planting mines among the rubble to prevent any of the expelled inhabitants from returning. Each unit was issued with its own list of villages and neighbourhoods as the targets of this master plan. Codenamed Plan D (*Dalet* in Hebrew), this was the fourth and final version of less substantial plans that outlined the fate the Zionists had in store for Palestine and consequently for its native population. The previous three schemes had articulated only obscurely how the Zionist leadership contemplated dealing with the presence of so many Palestinians living in the land the Jewish national movement coveted as its own. This fourth and last blue-print spelled it out clearly and unambiguously: the Palestinians had to go. [...] This plan was both the inevitable product of the Zionist ideological impulse to have an exclusively Jewish presence in Palestine, and a response to developments on the ground once the British cabinet had decided to end the mandate. Clashes with local Palestinian militias provided the perfect context and pretext to implementing the ideological vision of an ethnically cleansed Palestine. The Zionist policy was first based on retaliation against Palestinian attacks in February 1947, and it transformed into an initiative to ethnically cleanse the country as a whole in March 1948.

Once the decision was taken, it took six months to complete the mission. When it was over, more than half of Palestine's native population, close to 800,000 people, had been uprooted, 531 villages had been destroyed, and eleven urban neighbour-hoods emptied of their inhabitants. The plan decided upon on 10 March 1948, and above all its systematic implementation in the following months, was a clear-cut case of an ethnic cleansing operation, regarded under international law today as a crime against humanity.

Benny Morris (2004) *The Birth of the Palestinian Refugee Problem Revisited*, Cambridge University Press.

Blocking a return

In the course of 1948 and the first half of 1949, a number of processes definitely changed the physical and demographic face of Palestine. Taken collectively, they steadily rendered the possibility of a mass refugee return more and more remote until, by mid-1949, it became virtually inconceivable. These processes were the gradual destruction of the abandoned Arab villages, the cultivation or destruction of Arab fields and the share-outs of the Arab lands to Jewish settlements, the establishment of new settlements, on abandoned lands and sites and the settlement of Jewish immigrants in empty Arab housing in the countryside and in urban neighbourhoods. Taken together, they assured that the refugees would have nowhere, and nothing, to return to.

These processes occurred under the protective carapace of the Haganah/IDF's periodically reiterated policy of preventing the return of refugees across the lines, including by fire, and of the repeated bouts of warfare between the Israeli and Arab armies, which effectively curtailed the movement of civilians near the often fluid front lines. At the same time, these processes were natural and integral, major elements in the overall consolidation of the State of Israel. They were not, at least initially, geared or primarily geared to blocking the return of the refugees. They began in order to meet certain basic needs of the new State. Some of the processes, such as the destruction of the villages and the establishment of new settlements along the borders, were dictated in large part by immediate military needs. Others were due to basic economic requirements – the kibbutzim's need for more land, the Yishuv's growing need for more agricultural produce, the new immigrants' need for housing. But, taken together, these processes substantially contributed, and were understood by the Yishuv's leaders to contribute, to definitively preventing a refugee return.

Michael Fischbaum (2003) *Records of Dispossession – Palestinian Refugee Property and the Arab-Israeli Conflict*, Columbia University Press.

The Legal Basis for Israeli Expropriation: The Custodian of Absentee Property

We can learn details of how Palestinian property was managed in the early days after the refugee exodus through a U.S. diplomatic document highlighting a June 1948 meeting between an official from the American consulate in Haifa and the Supervisor of Arab Property in the Northern District (Heb.: ha-Mefakeah 'al ha-Rekhush ha-'Aravi be-Mahoz ha-Tsafon), Naftali Lifshits.... The American interviewer came away with the opinion that the Supervisor's office was very well organized. Lifshits had divided Arab property in Haifa into three categories: Palestinian refugee property, property of Palestinians still living in the city, and property of non-Palestinian Arabs. Lifshits' office was concerned with the first and second categories only. Property in the third category was taken over by the state as "enemy" property.

Lifshits divided Palestinian property, both refugee and resident, into three types. The first was arms and ammunition, which the state confiscated from all persons (refugees, resident Palestinians, as well as Jews). Lifshits reported that he had not uncovered sizeable quantities of such war materiel. The second type of property was that which could serve the Israeli war effort, such as cloth, large amounts of foodstuffs, and petroleum products. These also were confiscated and inventoried. If this property were sold, the amounts realized were duly recorded. The Supervisor deducted three percent of the value of the sale as commission for the sale. Resident Palestinians could receive some of this money generated by the Supervisor from the sale immediately, but not all of it. Israeli authorities were worried that they might smuggle the money out of Israel whereupon it could be used to finance the Arab war effort.

Finally, the third type of property was personal and household goods. Refugee household goods were sold, destroyed if in poor shape, or used to furnish abandoned residences for new Jewish tenants. Lifshits' office recorded all information in order to be able to credit the refugee. Resident Palestinians could get their household goods back immediately, unless they too had been sold. Since military authorities had herded those Palestinians who remained into certain areas of the city following its surrender, some were cut off from their homes and property. In cases where the Supervisor had sold residents' property, they eventually were given a receipt that noted how much money the state owed them, which they could collect "later." […]

Whereas the Palestinian refugee tragedy is by far the largest unresolved refugee crisis in the world, with some seven million Palestinian refugees still without durable solutions to their displacement, dozens of additional refugee sagas continue to play out in ways where law recognizes various elements comprising the gamut of HLP rights, but politics continues to thwart attempts to claim those rights. In the following excerpt by Swiss diplomat Didier Pfirter, the proposals under the Annan Plan for resolving the Cypriot refugee property question are presented alongside some of the political stumbling blocks that eventually led to these concrete plans being rejected.

Didier Pfirter, (former legal advisor of the Good Offices of the UN Secretary General for Cyprus), *Property, Land and Return in the Comprehensive Settlement Plan of the UN Secretary General for Cyprus* (Annan Plan), 2005 (unpublished paper)

The approach of the Annan Plan

The Annan [P]lan strives to solve the imbalances created by the 1974 events in terms of displaced people and disposed owners through a two prong approach.

In negotiating the plan, a formula was developed which established a correlation between the extent of territorial adjustment and the limits on returns and restitution of properties in the Turkish Cypriot state. As the Turkish Cypriots wanted to keep these limits as low as possible, the plan went to the limits of what seemed feasible in terms of territorial adjustment.

More than half of the displaced Greek Cypriots achieved full restitution of property and return to their former homes under Greek Cypriot administration through territorial adjustment. Such adjustment affects about a quarter of the area currently under Turkish Cypriot administration. The basic philosophy behind the territorial adjustment was that it should bring less pain to the Turkish Cypriots than gain to the Greek Cypriots. The areas considered suitable for such adjustment should thus have had an almost exclusively Greek Cypriot population prior to 1974 and should preferably have less inhabitants today than then. Furthermore such areas should be contiguous with the area currently under Greek Cypriot control so as to not create enclaves. With the territorial adjustment the imbalances created by the events of 1974 are corrected to a large extent though not entirely.

In addition, Greek Cypriots can return without limitations to four important villages in the Karpas area and obtain full restitution of properties there (including almost 10% of the coastline of Cyprus). The area will be part of the Turkish Cypriot state but enjoy some local autonomy; this special provision benefits almost 5% of the displaced Greek Cypriots.

Individual return and restitution of properties in the rest of the Turkish Cypriot state go some way in further correcting the imbalance but the fact remains that in absolute terms more Greek Cypriots will be prevented from returning to their former homes and from full restitution of their properties than Turkish Cypriots – though in relative terms the Turkish Cypriots are actually more affected by the restrictions on restitution of properties. One also needs to bear in mind that the territorial adjustment and the restitution of properties inflicts [sic] important pain on the Turkish Cypriots both individually and as a society while it affects the Greek Cypriots comparatively little or not at all (territorial adjustment is entirely at the expense of the Turkish Cypriots).

The Annan Plan clearly takes an individual rather than a global approach to both the property and the return question. Where it is necessary to impose restrictions it strives to establish criteria in order to ensure that the individuals with the strongest personal interests benefit first. This is of course not always possible as the interests of individuals from the two sides often clash e.g when a legitimate owner who was displaced in 1974 and as since rebuilt his/her life on the property of such owner and cannot be expected to return to his/her place of origin after the experiences of the past and given the agreed concept of bi-zonality. No matter how refined and careful the criteria for a distinction between clashing individual interests, individual injustices are unavoidable.

For areas not affected by territorial adjustment i.e the areas currently under Greek Cypriot control and the areas which would be part of the Turkish Cypriot state, the plan in a nutshell foresees the following regimes:

Owners who lost control of their properties due to events between 1963 and 1974 are entitled to restitution of one third of such properties in terms of value and area (cumulatively) through former inhabitants are entitled to recover their homes, even if this exceeds the quota. This right prevails against current users, except where these were themselves displaced and disposed and opt for an exchange against their (former) properties or where they have substantially improved the properties in such a way that the value of the improvement exceeds that of the property in its original state. Where this current suer privilege prevents restitution, the affected owner can opt for another, equivalent property or for compensation. Owners receive full and effective compensation at current value in guaranteed bonds and appreciation certificates for any properties that cannot be restituted. A property board with some non-Cypriot members administers the whole process and adjudicates individual claims. It also provides current users with alternative accommodation and assists their rehabilitation.

The freedom of residence, which is guaranteed by the Constitution, suffers temporary limitations during the first 19 years or until Turkey becomes an EU member, whichever is the sooner. The law allows the constituent state to limit the number of permanent residents hailing from the other constituent state. They may proclaim a five year moratorium and thereafter establish limits gradually raising from 6% to 12% of the population of a municipality to 18% of the overall population of either constituent state after the 14th year. People over 65 and former inhabitants of certain Greek Cypriot villages in the Karpas (see above) and certain Turkish Cypriot villages in Tylliria are (after 2 years) exempted from any restrictions as is the establishment of secondary residences (there is also no limitation for the length of stay allowed under this title). An unlimited safeguard clause allows the constituent states to preserve their basic Greek Cypriot or Turkish Cypriot identity by taking measures to ensure that 2/3 of their Cypriot residents speak their official language as their mother tongue.

Both issues, which affect individuals very directly and intensely and which in many ways constitute "zero-sum-games" not easily prone to win-win solutions have been highly contentious and emotionally charged and continue to be so on both sides. In the case of the property problem this is understandable given the strong attachments of Cypriots to their ancestral homes and soil. In the case of return of displaced people however, both sides' fears are likely to turn out to be unfounded and the limits established by the Annan [P]lan would probably never be reached. Given the small size of the Turkish Cypriot state, the fact that 80% of Greek Cypriots have turned to urban residences, that none of the major urban centres will entirely be within the Turkish Cypriot state and put up with nuisances such as dealing with the administration in Turkish and probably paying higher income taxes. [...]

Finally, we turn to another extremely sad saga, that of the inability of the displaced Chagos Islanders to return to their island homes in the middle of the Indian Ocean. Australian social critic John Pilger provides a poignant overview of the many decades of struggle for justice by those forced from their homes.

John Pilger (2006) "Stealing a Nation," in *Freedom Next Time*, London: Bantam Press.

What happened in the Chagos Islands was so searing, it may seem barely credible. Indeed *La Lutte*, as the Chagossians call their struggle for justice and freedom, arose from a crime that allows us to glimpse how great power works behind its respectable, democratic façade and helps us to understand how much of the world is run for the benefit of the powerful, and how governments justify their actions with lies.

During the 1960s and 1970s British governments, both Labour and Tory, tricked and expelled the entire population of the Chagos, a British colonial dependency, so that their homeland could be given to a foreign power, the United States, as the site for a military base. This 'act of mass kidnapping'(3) was carried out in high secrecy, along with the conspiracy that preceded it. For almost a decade, neither Parliament nor the US Congress knew anything about it, and no journalist revealed it. When the base had been established, a group of 'defence' correspondents were flown out by the Ministry of Defence and reported as expected, as if no-one had ever lived there; BBC newsreaders still refer to US aircraft flying out to bomb Afghanistan and Iraq from the 'uninhabited' island of Diego Garcia.

The Chagossians were treated like Australia's Aborigines in the nineteenth century: they were deemed not to exist. Not only was their homeland stolen from them, they were taken out of history. Until recently, the Foreign Office website denied their very existence. Only a handful of MPs have referred to them in parliamentary debates on Britain's remaining 'overseas territories'. Not a single politician whose policy-making had brutal consequences for the islanders has ever referred to them in his or her memoirs. I know of no work of scholarship on British foreign policy that describes what happened to them, with one admirable exception: the books of Mark Curtis, who has called them 'unpeople'. (4)

Having abandoned them, seven British governments watched their vulnerable, faraway citizens live a nightmare in shanties in the Seychelles and, mainly, Mauritius, where they had been discarded, while ministers and their officials in London mounted a campaign of deception that went all the way up to the Prime Minister. This scandal continues today – even after the High Court in London ruled in 2000 that the islanders' 'wholesale removal' was an 'abject legal failure'.

Questions and Exercises

1. How, in your opinion, will the issue of Palestinian refugees be dealt with in an eventual peace agreement between Palestine and Israel? Will the refugee population be allowed to return to their original homes or will less ideal durable solutions be found, such as compensation?
2. Many have argued that HLP issues are the primary stumbling block to securing a sustainable peace agreement in Cyprus. If you were a peace mediator, what new proposals might you put forward to break the HLP impasse that so often prevents agreement?
3. You have been requested to advise the Chagos Islander population on the most effective international legal remedy to pursue in order to achieve their aim of returning to their beloved island homes. Which remedy would you propose to them and why?

Additional Resources

Ali Abunimah (2006) *One Country: A Bold Proposal to End the Israeli-Palestinian Impasse*, New York: Metropolitan Books, Henry Holt and Company.

Badil Resource Centre for Palestinian Residency & Refugee Rights (2005) *Handbook on Protection of Palestinian Refugees – Closing Protection Gaps*, Badil.

COHRE and Badil (2005) *Ruling Palestine – A History of the Legally Sanctioned Jewish-Israeli Seizure of Land and Housing in Palestine*, COHRE.

Joel Kovel (2007) *Overcoming Zionism – Creating a Single Democratic State in Israel/Palestine*, London: Pluto Press.

Virginia Tilley (2005) *The One-State Solution – A Breakthrough for Peace in the Israeli-Palestinian Deadlock*, Ann Arbor: University of Michigan Press.

8

Emerging Conceptual Issues

PEACE AGREEMENTS AND HLP RIGHTS

In recent years, there has been greater recognition of the role of HLP issues in the genesis of violent conflict, as well as the risk of secondary disputes over HLP during the postconflict period. Accordingly, many recent peace agreements pay attention to aspects of HLP rights. In recognition of this, in his 2007 report on the protection of civilians in armed conflict, the UN Secretary-General recommended:

> Restorative actions, such as the inclusion of the right to return and restitution of housing, land or property in all future peace agreements.[1]

The HLP rights of returning refugees and IDPs are commonly addressed in peace agreements. Less often, institutional arrangements for improving land administration or resolving historical land disputes may be outlined. The trend is promising, but a review of postconflict HLP rights in a number of countries suggests that sustained commitment at both the national and international levels is necessary to translate the agreements into sustained and principled action on the ground. The nature of the several protracted conflicts around the world requiring resolution – Palestine/Israel, Darfur, Iraq, Burma, and others – all place HLP issues at the direct core of both the causes and results of these conflicts, as well as their eventual just and sustainable resolution.

Peace mediators often face a difficult choice between encouraging the parties to fully develop a comprehensive peace agreement in great detail, through lengthy discussions, and settling for a broad "framework" agreement that establishes institutions and processes through which the detailed plans will be formulated. The first option involves risks for the collapse of the deal if the parties fail to agree on certain details, but can result in a solid agreement that can be implemented soon after it is

[1] UN Secertary-General, *Report on the Protection of Civilians in Armed Conflict*, UN Security Council, S/2007/643, 28 October 2007.

signed; the second option can result in a fragile agreement that can all too easily be undermined by later misunderstandings and arguments over interpretation.

Peace mediators often find the prospect of addressing the full spectrum of HLP concerns as potentially threatening to the successful conclusion of sensitive, often lengthy, and tense negotiating sessions seeking viable recipes for peace. For many mediators, the inclusion of HLP rights into what are already perceived to be their overflowing array of responsibilities may seem overly daunting and possibly obstructive of eventual agreement. There may be feelings that addressing HLP issues may attract unwelcome international attention to private negotiation processes, or conversely because there is effectively no lead agency managing or monitoring these issues under UN auspices, they will invariably fall through the cracks and not be considered important priorities in peacebuilding.[2] Because HLP rights violators themselves are often the very people negotiating peace agreements, there can be additional walls of resistance by the parties that may need to be slowly broken down before these issues can be addressed. Local political players often have considerable vested interests in housing, land, or property unlawfully acquired during the conflict in question, and as a result, peacemakers may find themselves in an uphill battle to achieve recognition of HLP issues during these undertakings and may consequently choose paths of lesser resistance.

It will be important for mediators to maintain appropriate levels of flexibility in seeking to reach an agreement, but this cannot be at the expense of HLP rights issues that are, after all, not only human rights concerns, but also development, economic, justice, and rule-of-law issues, as well. To achieve consensus among the negotiating parties on these often complex concerns, it is preferable to address HLP issues at the outset of negotiations rather than at later, more delicate stages of the process. Given the extremely high stakes involved in addressing certain HLP themes, in particular when the restitution or property, payment of reparations, and transfer of large economic assets is involved, there will always been some hesitancy by negotiating parties to come to an immediate agreement on HLP concerns. Such circumstances may call for the approval of interim measures that can be taken during the mediation, such as preventing the illegal occupation of refugee or IDP property and signaling that the parties agree in principle to resolving questions of displacement, HLP abuse, and relevant HLP disputes and claims.

[2] Indeed, as the 2000 *Brahimi Report on UN Peace Operations* noted: "There is currently no integrated planning or support cell in the Secretariat that brings together those responsible for political analysis, military operations, civilian police, electoral assistance, human rights, development, humanitarian assistance, refugees and displaced persons, public information, logistics, finance and recruitment." The situation is even more dire for HLP rights. See *Brahimi Report – Comprehensive Review of the Whole Question of Peacekeeping Operations in All Their Aspects* (A/55/305 – S/2000/809) 21 August 2000, p. xiii.

A range of contemporary peace agreements – the Dayton Accords (Bosnia-Herzegovina),[3] the Arusha Accords (Burundi), and agreements concerning Guatemala,[4] El Salvador, Kosovo, Liberia, Mozambique,[5] Sierra Leone, Sudan, Tajikistan,[6] and others – explicitly address HLP issues and, increasingly, HLP *rights* (see box). Conversely, agreements that in hindsight definitely should have included specific HLP provisions but did not – in particular the 1991 Cambodian peace settlement – have been criticized for this serious oversight.[7]

[3] "[A]ll refugees and displaced persons have the right freely to return to their homes of origin. They shall have the right to have restored to them property of which they were deprived in the course of hostilities since 1991 and to be compensated for any property that cannot be restored to them." *General Framework Agreement for Peace in Bosnia and Herzegovina, Annex 7 Agreement on Refugees and Displaced Persons (1995)*. See also: R. Williams (2006) "Post-Conflict Property Restitution and Refugee Return in Bosnia and Herzegovina: Implications for International Standard-Setting and Practice" *NYU Journal of International Law and Politics* 37, no. 3: 441.

[4] The 1995 Guatemala *Agreement on Identity and Rights of Indigenous Peoples*, for instance, elaborated rights relating to land of the indigenous peoples in the following terms: "The rights relating to land of the indigenous peoples include both the communal or collective and the individual tenure of land, rights of ownership and possession and other real rights, and the use of natural resources for the benefit of the communities without detriment to their habitat. Legislative and administrative measures must be developed to ensure recognition, the awarding of title, protection, recovery, restitution and compensation for those rights."

[5] Section IV of Protocol III to the 1992 *General Peace Agreement* ending the lengthy civil war in Mozambique, included explicit restitution rights for returning refugees: "Mozambican refugees and displaced persons shall not forfeit any of the rights and freedoms of citizens for having left their original places of residence; Mozambican refugees and displaced persons shall be registered and included in the electoral rolls together with other citizens in their places of residence; and Mozambican refugees and displaced persons shall be guaranteed restitution of property owned by them which is still in existence and the right to take legal action to secure the return of such property from individuals in possession of it."

[6] The *General Agreement on the Establishment of Peace and National Accord in Tajikistan (1997) – Protocol on Refugee Issues* stipulates that, "The Government of the Republic of Tajikistan assumes the obligation to reintegrate returning refugees and displaced persons into the social and economic life of the country, which includes the provision to them of humanitarian and financial aid, assistance in finding employment and housing and the restoration of all their rights as citizens of the Republic of Tajikistan (including the return to them of dwellings and property and guaranteed uninterrupted service), and not to institute criminal proceedings against returning refugees or displaced persons for their participation in the political confrontation and the civil war, in accordance with the legislative acts in force in the Republic."

[7] While the *Agreement on a Comprehensive Political Settlement on the Cambodia Conflict (1991) – Part V – Refugees and Displaced Persons – Annex 4 – Repatriation of Cambodian Refugees and Displaced Persons* did address some HLP issues in the following terms: "There must be full respect for the human rights and fundamental freedoms of all Cambodians, including those of the repatriated refugees and displaced persons, in recognition of their entitlement to live in peace and security, free from intimidation and coercion of any kind. These rights would include, inter alia, freedom of movement within Cambodia, the choice of domicile and employment, and the right to property," the failure to address a wide range of additional HLP issues is often believed to have created the conditions for severe HLP abuses that have taken place in Cambodia since the 1991 agreement.

HLP concerns within selected peace agreements

	Refugee and IDP Return/ Repatriation	HLP Restitution Rights	Land Reform Measures	Secondary Occupation of HLP	Legislative Repeal and Reform	Specialized Bodies on HLP Issues
Cambodia (1991)	✓					
El Salvador (1992)	✓		✓	✓	✓	✓
Mozambique (1992)	✓	✓				
Liberia (1993)	✓	✓				
Rwanda (1993)	✓	✓				
Bosnia-Herzegovina (1995)	✓	✓		✓	✓	✓
Guatemala (1995)	✓	✓	✓	✓	✓	
Croatia (1995)	✓	✓				
Tajikistan (1997)	✓	✓				✓
Sierra Leone (1999)	✓					
Burundi (2000)	✓	✓	✓	✓	✓	✓
Liberia (2003)	✓	✓				
Sudan (2004)	✓		✓	✓	✓	✓
Great Lakes Protocol (2007)	✓	✓	✓	✓	✓	✓

Although not all recent peace agreements include explicit reference to housing, land, and property issues or treat these issues in a comprehensive manner, the clear trend over time leans toward the *inclusion* of these issues. Several HLP issues appear with relative frequency within peace agreements. These include HLP issues relating to refugee and IDP return, HLP restitution rights and the mechanisms often required to administer and process restitution claims, the reform of pertinent HLP legislation, land reform measures, land tenure issues, the rights of women to equal treatment with respect to HLP rights, customary law arrangements, and HLP issues questions of compensation.

HLP ISSUES ADDRESSED IN THE 1992 EL SALVADOR AGREEMENT

Though often overlooked, the 1992 El Salvador peace agreement is exceptionally detailed in addressing a wide range of HLP concerns that were seen by the parties as fundamental causes of the grievances that led to the emergence of the conflict years earlier. This unique agreement sought to address issues that are often excluded from such agreements, such as land reform measures, the necessity of new land legislation, land tenure concerns, and the inventory of indigenous land allocations. Three years later, the 1995 Guatemala peace accords also required the government authorities to "adopt or promote measures to regularize the legal situation with regard to the communal possession of lands by communities which do not have the title deeds to those lands, including measures to award title to municipal or national lands with a clear communal tradition. To that end, an inventory of the land tenure situation shall be drawn up in each municipality."

The 1992 Peace Agreement between the Government of El Salvador and the Frente Farabundo Martí para la Liberación Nacional (1992) addresses a very wide range of HLP concerns in section 2 (the agrarian problem) of chapter V, for instance:

> Lands in excess of the constitutional limit of 245 hectares – The Government of El Salvador shall transfer rural farmland that has not yet been transferred under articles 105 and 267 of the Constitution of the Republic. It likewise undertakes to ensure that implementation of the relevant constitutional requirements is not evaded by owners of rural holdings in excess of 245 hectares.
>
> New legislation – Since the current agrarian legislation is haphazard, contradictory and incomplete, the Parties agree that it must be harmonized and unified into an agrarian code. To this end, the Government shall submit the relevant draft legislation to the Legislative Assembly no later than 12 months after the signing of this Agreement. If it fails to do so, COPAZ shall take on the task of preparing the corresponding preliminary draft.
>
> The land-tenure system in conflict zones – In accordance with the New York Agreement, the current land-tenure situation in conflict zones shall be respected until a satisfactory legal solution for the definitive land-tenure system is arrived at. Consequently, landholders shall not be evicted pending agreement on such a solution; moreover, they shall be given financial support to increase agricultural production.
>
> In view of the irregularity of the land-tenure system in conflict zones, the Parties agree on the following: Determination as to who are the "current landholders"- "Landholders" shall mean those currently occupying and/or working the land in conflict zones.
>
> Inventory of cases covered by this part of the Agreement – Within 30 days from the signing of the Agreement, FMLN shall submit an inventory of land or buildings affected by the Agreement. Upon verification that such land or buildings are in fact subject to the provisions of this Agreement, and in accordance with the procedure set forth in the next section, the Government of El Salvador shall seek to provide a satisfactory legal solution for their final disposal through the voluntary sale of such

property by the rightful owners to the current holders, on the terms referred to in section 3 (F) of this chapter. Should a rightful owner not wish to sell his property, the Government of El Salvador shall make use of the legal mechanisms at its disposal to try to resettle the peasants or small farmers on such land as may be available for the purpose and shall, as far as possible, seek to ensure that such land is situated in the same zones.

Establishment of a Special Commission – COPAZ shall appoint a special commission whose members shall be of recognized integrity and ability. The special commission, to be formed within 20 days following the signing of this Agreement, shall be entrusted with the following tasks and duties: To verify the inventory of affected land or buildings within conflict zones. Once the inventory has been verified, the special commission shall submit copies to the Government of El Salvador and to COPAZ; Should the need arise, to facilitate the settlement of disputes between current holders and rightful owners; To take any decisions and measures it deems necessary and proper for the prompt and effective fulfilment of the agreements set forth in this chapter.

Legalization of land tenure – Except for particularly complex cases, the Government of El Salvador shall legalize the land-tenure situation in conflict zones definitively within six months from the signing of the cease-fire agreement, granting, as appropriate, individual or collective title to the land.

Payment for lands – Lands shall be purchased from their former owners at market prices. The sale to the current holders shall be subject to the same conditions as those granted to beneficiaries of the reformed sector. However, special conditions may be agreed to in the interests of the peace process.

SUDAN

In other chapters, it has been argued that sustained monitoring of HLP abuses during the conflict phase can and should be achieved, usually through the courageous work of local NGOs and the diplomatic, financial, and technical support of foreign bilateral donor agencies, international NGOs, and other organizations. Such documentation can ensure that when a peace agreement becomes a possibility, HLP issues can be integrated into the discussions from the initial stages. As the following excerpt demonstrates, HLP documentation produced during the conflict can then be built on by formal assessments that can feed directly into negotiations. In the case of Sudan, for example, the 2005 Comprehensive Peace Agreement (CPA) was arrived at only through a long process overseen by the Inter-Governmental Authority on Development (IGAD), initiated in 1997 with the support of the United Nations.[8] In late 1999, the IGAD Partner Forum established a Working Group for Peace that

[8] This paragraph is based on Paul de Wit and Jeffrey Hatcher (2009) "Sudan's Comprehensive Peace Agreement: An Opportunity for Coherently Addressing Housing, Land and Property Issues?" in Scott

commissioned several research projects on themes believed to be critical in the postconflict period, including landmines, demobilization, internally displaced people, land tenure and access to land and natural resources, food security, and information/data stocktaking. These studies formed the basis for the negotiations in Naivasha several years later. The studies on land, internally displaced people, and food security, which were conducted by FAO, ensured that these issues found their way into the Comprehensive Peace Agreement. According to those involved, "it confirms the importance of these assessments, even when there is no strong national will to proceed with such an exercise":[9]

> The CPA established a National Land Commission to resolve outstanding land disputes, to develop land reform policies, to recognize customary land rights and/or law, to assess land compensation claims and to generally advise different levels of government on how to co-ordinate policies on national projects.

However, the Sudan example demonstrates the difficulties involved in ensuring that the broad principles established in peace agreements are translated into the necessary institutional reforms and changes on the ground. The Land Commissions in the North and South of the country have experienced serious political and technical challenges, and there is a broader problem related to political will to implement the CPA. Mechanisms were established to monitor the implementation of the CPA, but these seem to lack adequate political leverage to ensure compliance.

GUATEMALA

Guatemala provides another example of the difficulties of implementation. Land rights have long been a focal point for unrest in the country, which has been characterized by systematic discrimination of indigenous communities. In 1952, President Arbenz attempted a land redistribution program to alter the semifeudal structure of the rural economy, only to be ousted in a CIA-backed *coup d'etat* in 1954.[10] An insurgency movement with a strong Mayan component began waging a guerilla war in 1960, which continued until a ceasefire was declared in 1996. In 1978, indigenous people marched in Panzos, Guatemala, to demonstrate against occupation of land claimed by the Maya. The security forces repressed the demonstration, and a number of protestors were shot. One million indigenous people were displaced at the height of the conflict in the 1980s, and paramilitary groups were responsible for the deaths of hundreds of thousands of civilians, some 83 percent of whom were Maya.

Leckie (ed.), *Housing, Land and Property Rights and UN Peace Operations – A Comparative Survey and Proposals for Reform*, Cambridge University Press.

9 Id.

10 Craig Kauffman (2005) *Transitional Justice in Guatemala: Linking the Past and Future*. Paper prepared for the ISA-South Conference, Miami.

As in the case of El Salvador, the peace negotiations were generally framed by a human rights perspective, and the thirteen Accords were comprehensive in nature, addressing the root causes of conflict and the links between human rights, peace, and development.[11] The 1995 Accord on Identity and Rights of Indigenous Peoples was intended to recognize and permit the application of indigenous customary law, recognize indigenous beliefs and practices, provide indigenous groups a greater role in local governance, and address past grievances regarding usurped lands and other resources. The structural factors that prevented women from exercising their rights, including their land rights, were cited in several accords.[12] An Agreement on the Resettlement on Population Groups Uprooted by Armed Conflict was signed. Several other accords dealt with indigenous rights. Some analysis have claimed that the participation of indigenous communities and civil society groups in the negotiations was minimal, whereas others state that international support for multistakeholder input led to indigenous groups and victim's associations being included.

Sadly, Guatemala has not undergone the radical social, economic, and political transformation that could result in a more equal, prosperous, and just society. Relatively few aspects of the peace accords have been successfully implemented. In particular, representatives of indigenous people feel that the Accords dealing with the rights of Mayan communities have not been implemented.[13] The Accords do not carry the force of law and do not confer legal rights; attempts to enshrine principles developed in the Accords in law, through reform of the Constitution, were unsuccessful.[14] In Guatemala, two kinds of IDPs can be identified – those that remained in groups and identified with specific communities – known locally as "collective" IDPs – and those who were dispersed across the country, separated from their former neighbors. Only collective IDPs have been allowed to access state programs for IDPs, with dispersed IDP households often being suspected of being economic migrants rather than true IDPs.[15]

Several institutions were mandated to work on land-related issues arising from the peace accords. The National Institute for Agrarian Transformation (INTA)

[11] Cecilia Bailliet (2002) *Between Conflict and Consensus: Conciliating Land Disputes in Guatemala*. University of Oslo.

[12] Bailey Paz y Paz (2006) "Guatemala: Gender and Reparations for Human Rights Violations," in Ruth Rubio-Marín (ed.), *Engendering Reparations: Recognizing and Compensating Women Victims of Human Rights Violations*. ICTJ/IDRC.

[13] Elena Dictaan-Bang-oa and Jack Medrana (2004) "The Guatemala Peace Agreements of 1996 – A Case Study," in C.K. Roy, V. Tauli-Corpuz, and A. Romero-Medina (eds.), *Beyond the Silencing of the Guns*, Manila: Tebtebba Foundation.

[14] Bailliet, *Between Conflict and Consensus*.

[15] Id.

was mandated to distribute state land to the landless, but it was extremely corrupt and closely connected to former military personnel and wealthy landowners. Many INTA files "disappeared," making it more difficult to process claims. INTA ceased to function in 1999. Fontierras, a land fund, was established to provide credit for purchase of land on a "willing buyer-willing seller" basis, as well as to provide technical assistance programs to promote sustainable production on newly acquired land-holdings. By 2005, little more than 4,000 hectares of land had been redistributed to 600 families by Fontierras, which has been underfunded by the government. The market-based nature of the program has proved to be an obstacle, because there are few incentives for landowners to sell at market prices. The National Reparations Program (PNR, in Spanish), was established in 2004. It was originally under civil society control but in December 2005 the government took over management of the PNR, apparently due to disputes between the civil society organizations responsible.[16] The bureaucratic systems introduced by the government significantly slowed down its operations. The PNR has an annual budget of US$39 million for thirteen years, but has managed to use only a fraction of that – less than 10 percent during 2006.[17] Reparation measures included in the Accords sought to reestablish the material situation of the victims prior to the violations or to compensate for the loss resulting from the violations, and focus particularly on land restitution, housing, and productive investment.[18] However, the PNR is largely ineffective, spends most of its limited resources on its own bureaucracy, and has no registry of victims as a basis for its work.[19] Many observers have argued that different forms of restitution would be more appropriate than cash payments, though others caution that the government lacks the capacity to implement such a system.[20]

The lack of a land policy, or a land restitution policy, has been identified as a serious impediment to the resolution of land-related issues arising from the civil conflict. In addition, lack of information-sharing protocols and other fundamental institutional and legal structures have been identified as major weaknesses. The excessively bureaucratic nature of the institutions and the lack of funding for key components, suggests that lack of political will is the major impediment to resolution of the land problem in Guatemala.

16 Angela Bunch (2007) *Life Is Priceless: The Work of the National Reparations Program in Guatemala.* MA thesis, Political Science. Stanford University.

17 Id.

18 Paz y Paz Bailey, "Guatemala: Gender and Reparations."

19 IDMC, citing Congress of Guatemala, *Carta del Diputado Victor Manuel Sales Ortiz, a La Senora Louise Arbour, Alta Comisionada de la ONU*. 25 May 2006.

20 Bunch, *Life Is Priceless*.

BURUNDI

The Arusha Agreement of August 2000 is a particularly comprehensive document that recognizes the importance of land issues. Although many felt that civil society was, as usual, excluded from the process, organizations such as the Burundi Women Refugee Network were granted observer status. This resulted in the inclusion in the Agreement of a clause on the rights to land and inheritance for women.

Protocol IV of the Arusha Accords on Reconstruction and Development is of most relevance. The term "*sinistrés*" is used in the text to refer to a range of vulnerable groups, including those who had been forcible "regrouped" into camps during the war, or those IDPs who were "dispersed" across the country. Article 8 of Protocol IV states that property rights shall be guaranteed for all men, women, and children; compensation shall be payable in case of expropriation, which shall be allowed only in the public interest; all refugees and/or *sinistrés* must be able to recover their property, especially their land; if recovery proves impossible, they must receive fair compensation and/or indemnification; and that a register of rural land, the promulgation of a law on succession, and, in the longer term, a cadastral survey of rural land shall all be implemented. The Agreement also called for a Sub-Commission on Land to be established, to examine all cases of land owned by old caseload refugees and state-owned land; and examine disputed issues and allegations of abuse in the (re)distribution of land and to rule on each case.

The Accords provided for the creation of the *Commission Nationale de Réhabilitation des Sinistrés* (CNRS) that was mandated to facilitate the return of the refugees and IDPs, and address land-related issues including allegations of abuses during the (re)distribution of land, and rule on individual cases according to specific principles.[33] The CNRS was established in February 2003. In a separate Protocol, and also of great relevance for HLP rights, the agreement refers to the importance of strengthening the *Bashingantahe*, the local dispute mediators.

Despite the prioritization of HLP issues in the Accords, some observers have argued that "the focus on mechanisms for resolving individual cases" has served to distract attention and funding away from a larger, more holistic policy debate on HLP issues involving all key stakeholders. Indeed, civil society organizations attempting to open up debate on the fundamental aspects of the existing land law are finding it difficult to make headway on key issues, with many in government pushing a business-as-usual agenda unlikely to benefit the rural poor. Critics caution that the emphasis on ethnicity in the political system – for example, through the creation of an ethnic quota system – obscures the fact that access to political power and access to land are linked, and there is a risk of perpetuation of injustice unless the wider systemic issues are addressed.

TACTICAL AND STRATEGIC CONSIDERATIONS IN ADDRESSING HLP ISSUES

Peace mediators will always face an array of both tactical and strategic questions in reaching an eventual agreement between opposing parties. Some of the more central HLP considerations are outlined here.

Building HLP Rights and Expertise into the Peacemaking and Peacebuilding Toolkits

Mediators will be likely to achieve more and thus build the basis for firmer and more sustained peace when HLP issues are understood for both their complexity and their clear links to broader concerns such as the rule of law, economic vitality, and overall security. Having HLP experts as full members of peace mediation and negotiating teams will help ensure that these issues are accorded proper treatment during peace talks, and that they are appropriately formulated within any eventual peace agreement and the terms of its implementation. This will also assist in ensuring that the manner by which HLP issues are addressed is fully consistent with international human rights, refugee and humanitarian law and related standards, as well as global best practice. The role of peace mediators themselves in highlighting HLP issues is a vital one, given the fact that there is no specialized expertise on HLP issues with the relevant section of the UN, which are often involved in peacemaking, peacekeeping, and peacebuilding efforts. Neither the Department of Peacekeeping Operations, the Department of Political Affairs, the Office of the Secretary-General, nor the new Peacebuilding Commission maintain regular staff positions with particular expertise in HLP concerns.

HLP Blueprints Can Assist but Will Require Reevaluation in Every Case

Although HLP blueprints can assist in developing the broad contours of which HLP issues need to be addressed and in generally which manner, it is unlikely that a universally applicable HLP blueprint will emerge that will be directly relevant in all cases. It is clear that in considering constructive proposals to resolve complex HLP concerns, one size does not fit all. At the same time, it is clear that certain foundational principles can be applied in all peace processes, and these would include questions of refugee/IDP return, HLP restitution, the need for specialized mechanisms for resolving HLP disputes, the need to properly register HLP claims and rights, the consideration of HLP legislative and policy reform, and the need to increase housing stock and the protection afforded by security of tenure.

HLP Remedy or Reform?

In most negotiations revolving around HLP issues, peace mediators will be forced to grapple with how best to balance efforts to remedy and/or reform the HLP sector and the rights abused in the context during the conflict. Should peace mediators focus solely on remedial questions such as refugee and IDP return and the recovery of property, or should they instead focus more on the HLP causes of the conflict concerned, and emphasize the need to reform HLP arrangements that may threaten delicate peace efforts? Is reversing ethnic cleansing a sufficient enough step to ensure a sustainable peace, or will undoing past violations undo the peace deal? Can peace agreements that recognize HLP restitution rights for those forced from their homes during the conflict but that do not recognize the rights of homeless and landless slum dwellers ever succeed in building truly peaceful and stable societies? Peace mediators need to consider these and related questions and seek to ensure that HLP questions are addressed in a way, perhaps including both remedy and reform, that stands the best chance to secure the peace and prevent future conflict.

HLP Restitution or Compensation (or Both)?

Many peace mediators have had to grapple with question of whether to favor restitution rights for returning refugees and IDPs or confer compensation rights, which might be more suitable given prevailing local conditions following a conflict. Generally within peace agreements, voluntary repatriation arrangements, and broader international norms, restitution rights and compensation rights are found in tandem. Restitution – in the words of the 2005 UN Principles on Housing and Property Restitution for Refugees and Displaced Persons[21] – is the "preferred remedy for displacement," and compensation is to be relied on only when restitution is materially impossible to achieve. Even in those comparatively rare instances where compensation programs have been put into effect to resolve displacement claims, such as in Turkey where Kurdish families displaced in the 1980s were eventually accorded compensation rights for lost properties, such programs often fail to deliver. When HLP damage assessments form part of a compensation program, for instance, these processes can be manipulated far too easily by the authorities to reduce or avoid compensation payments, by tolerating arbitrary reductions in property valuations, the deliberate underestimation of land holdings, providing insufficient compensation for

[21] See: *Final Report of the Special Rapporteur on Housing and Property Restitution in the Context of the Return of Refugees and Internally Displaced Persons* (E/CN.4/Sub.2/2005/17 and E/CN.4/Sub.2/2005/17/Add.1). This document contains the official UN text of the *Principles on Housing and Property Restitution for Refugees and Displaced Persons*, as approved by UN Sub-Commission on the Protection and Promotion of Human Rights in Resolution 2005/21 of 11 August 2005.

agricultural lands, or the false exaggeration of compensation or assistance already received. Peace mediators need to design measures that clearly give preference to restitution and ensure that if compensation initiatives are undertaken, these are fair, equitable, and subject to appropriate oversight.

Preventing Future HLP Abuses

During and in the aftermath of conflict, few sectors are as vulnerable to fraud, corruption, and illicit activity as the HLP sectors. Peace mediators have important roles to play in preventing abuses by building preventative measures directly into peace agreements and implementation arrangements. A number of measures can be envisaged, perhaps most notably placing a formal restriction on HLP sales and transactions in the immediate period following a given conflict. This simple, and obviously temporary, emergency measure can assist markedly in reducing the unlawful acquisition of land by political and military elites and assist in helping reestablish the HLP rule of law that is so vital to the economic and legislative health of all countries. Considering the utility of issuing qualified or interim titles to housing, land, or property prior to formal HLP rights determinations made by the relevant judicial or specialized restitution body can also help provide a level of HLP security in the short term.

HLP RIGHTS AND TRANSITIONAL JUSTICE

Particularly over the past two decades, the international community, and particularly the growing community of academic-practitioner human rights lawyers, have played an increasingly important role in addressing crimes against humanity. The transition out of authoritarian rule or conflict is now routinely accompanied by debates over the need for transitional justice measures. Indeed, the establishment of some form of transitional justice (TJ) process is now the rule rather than the exception. Such processes may include a number of components, including:

- Prosecution of perpetrators, either on the domestic level (through regular courts or "customary" or hybrid institutions), in a hybrid internationalized court, or in an international court, such as the International Criminal Court.
- Establishing the truth about the past through the creation of truth commissions or other national efforts.
- Establishing reparations policies that take into account the requirements of, or moral obligations to, the victims. Reparations have compensatory, restorative, or rehabilitative objectives and can include symbolic measures, such as a state apology. Compensation "should be provided for any economically assessable damage ... resulting from gross violations of international human rights

law and serious violations of international humanitarian law."[22] Restitution attempts should be made to "restore the victim to the original situation before the gross violations of international human rights law and serious violations of international humanitarian law occurred."[23]

- Remembering and honoring victims through memorials and museums of memory, and by catalyzing constructive social dialogue about the past.
- Developing reconciliation initiatives without sacrificing justice and accountability for perpetrators and victims.
- Reforming institutions that have a history of abusive behavior to guarantee nonrepetition of human rights abuses.[24]

Transitional justice practitioners have in recent years started to reflect on their experiences in order to reveal the unspoken assumptions that underpin TJ processes and their conceptual and practical limitations. Several analysts have noted the privileging of civil and political rights, and the relative "invisibility" of ESC rights within the TJ field.[25] Research into the links between TJ and economic development is at a nascent stage.[26] There have been tentative attempts to examine the existing and potential relationships between HLP issues and TJ, with most studies focusing on restitution of property as a component of reparations processes.[27] To date, several Truth Commissions have identified HLP issues, particularly discriminatory laws and practices relating to land ownership, as a factor in conflict and oppression. A limited number of local TJ "courts" have addressed HLP issues, although rarely in a systematic fashion. Few TJ processes have developed comprehensive recommendations on HLP, and of those few recommendations that have been made – for example, recommending the establishment of land commissions or restitution programs – fewer still have been fully implemented by governments.

[22] Office of the High Commissioner for Human Rights (2008) *Rule-of-Law Tools for Post-Conflict States*. New York and Geneva: United Nations.

[23] Id.

[24] Adapted from *The Encyclopedia of Genocide and Crimes against Humanity* (Macmillan Reference USA, 2004), vol. 3, pp. 1045–1047. Accessed on May 2008 at: http://www.ictj.org/static/TJApproaches/WhatisTJ/macmillan.TJ.eng.pdf.

[25] See e.g., Zinaida Miller (2008) "Effects of Invisibility: In Search of the 'Economic' in Transitional Justice" *The International Journal of Transitional Justice* 2: 266–291.

[26] See e.g., Roger Duthie (2009) "Introduction," in Pablo de Greiff and Roger Duthie (eds.), *Transitional Justice and Development: Making Connections*, New York: Social Science Research Council, and various contributions to *International Journal of Transitional Justice* 2, no. 3, December 2008.

[27] See e.g., Rhodri Williams (2007) *The Contemporary Right to Property Restitution in the Context of Transitional Justice*, ICTJ Occasional Paper; Rhodri Williams (2005) "Post-Conflict Property Restitution and Refugee Return in Bosnia and Herzegovina: Implications for International Standard-Setting and Practice" *Journal of International Law and Politics* 37, no. 3; Scott Leckie (ed.) (2003) *Returning Home: Housing and Property Restitution Rights of Refugees and Displaced Persons*, Ardsley, NY: Transnational Publishers.

The most common way in which TJ processes engage with HLP issues is in the context of reparations. Reparation for harms is a well-established component of TJ processes. Restitution may include symbolic payments by guilty governments, corporations, or individual to governments or individuals for physical and psychological harms inflicted. Such payments, even though they may be substantial, are symbolic due to the fact that they can never undo the harms inflicted; no amount of money can bring back the dead or heal trauma. Several TJ processes have involved an examination of property seized or destroyed during a clearly defined period of conflict or authoritarian rule. The excerpt below summarizes experiences in four countries, revealing some of the dilemmas involved, particularly regarding the isolation of individual human rights abuses versus the recognition of wider structural oppression and discrimination.

Rhodri C. Williams (2007) *The Contemporary Right to Property Restitution in the Context of Transitional Justice*, ICTJ Occasional Paper.

Prior to World War II, restitution came to the fore as the preferred form of reparations in disputes between states. After World War II, the proliferation of international human rights rules resulted in a new understanding, according to which states responsible for violations could be obliged to make reparations – including restitution – to individual victims of human rights abuses. However, where restitution was traditionally viewed as hierarchically superior to other types of remedies such as compensation, this is no longer clearly the case in human rights settings. Many types of human rights violations do not simply result in the loss of recoverable assets, but do grave intangible harms to their victims' mental or physical integrity and dignity. As a result, the relevance of restitution as part of an integrated reparative response to contemporary human rights violations should be assessed on a case-by-case basis.

Restitution has, however, maintained its traditional high profile in remedying one distinct category of human rights violations, those involving displacement of people from their homes and lands. Although such displacement is illegal, the right of victims to return to their homes of origin is only weakly supported in international law. As a result, restitution of rights in homes, land, and property for displaced persons has come to prominence both as a formal legal remedy for displacement and as a practical means of allowing displaced people to return to their reclaimed homes – or sell them in order to finance a new life elsewhere. In other words, where international law does not set out an unambiguous right of return to homes of origin *as such*, the established right to a remedy in the form of restitution is increasingly invoked in order to achieve return and other durable solutions.

A review of four restitution case-studies – the Czech Republic, South Africa, Bosnia, and Guatemala – reflects how these developments have played out in practice. Restitution in the Czech Republic aimed to partially reconstitute the property relations that preceded communist nationalizations. Initially, the "cut-off date" selected for restitution excluded Jewish victims of the Nazis, as well as some three million ethnic Germans expelled from the Czech lands shortly before the communist takeover. A further citizenship requirement excluded thousands of exiles who defected and had their properties confiscated during the communist period. This restrictive approach was accompanied by highly decentralized procedures, which included few guarantees that the law would be applied consistently throughout the country. Although the Czech restitution program aspired to restore a measure of justice in the wake of communist dictatorship, it did not clearly correspond to a human rights based conception of reparations.

Property restitution also played an important role in the transition from apartheid in South Africa, where discriminatory confiscations left the black majority holding less than twenty percent of the land. South Africa's restitution program is more clearly addressed toward righting individual wrongs, but its delivery has been complicated by its subordination to a broader, politically contentious land redistribution program. As a result, the decision of many restitution claimants to seek compensation rather than return to their land has been seen as undermining the post-apartheid government's commitment to increasing the overall proportion of black landownership. However, recent commitments by the government to complete the process have increased the chance that restitution – if not full redistribution of land – will be achieved in a timely manner.

Bosnian restitution was an overtly human rights based remedy for resolving displacement, but was dependent on – and complicated by – massive international intervention. Restitution was conceived of as a way to secure the return of the two million civilians displaced in Bosnia's 1992–1995 conflict, both for their own good and in order to facilitate the policies of host countries that wished to sustainably repatriate large Bosnian refugee populations. However, the practical difficulties involved in seeking to undo displacement through return led to a change of focus, with restitution coming to be seen primarily as a remedy in and of itself. This greatly expedited the restitution of 200,000 claimed homes, supporting the return of about half of those displaced by the conflict and restoring an important economic asset to those who chose not to return.

Guatemala, on the other hand, illustrates the risks inherent in raising expectations regarding restitution and return in the absence of either domestic or international resolve to guarantee full implementation. Government suppression of a largely indigenous insurgency in the early 1990s led to the displacement of between one and two million Guatemalans. However, the provisions on restitution set out in the subsequent peace accords did not create clear precedence for victims of displacement vis-à-vis those who subsequently occupied their land. As a result, many victims of the conflict had to be satisfied with government commitments to provide alternate land elsewhere, a promise that was not fully borne out due to inadequate funding as well as the ongoing neglect of those groups most marginalized by virtue of their displacement.

As suggested by the presented case studies, particularly the South African example, TJ processes are often oriented toward a clear identification of "victims" so that a manageable reparations program can be established. Although Truth Commissions and other TJ institutions often acknowledge the wider harms committed against society by repressive, kleptocratic, or "absent" governments, they are wary of confounding specific and extreme abuses (often civil and political rights, such as the right to life) with more general and widespread abuses, such as denial of the right to health, development, or housing, for example. The result is often a general recognition of abuses of ESC rights, including HLP rights, as a "background" to more acute human rights abuses. Truth Commissions will often discuss the systematic nature of HLP abuses, but they fail to address these issues in their recommendations. The result is likely to be an illusory "transition" that involves the reform of a limited number of political institutions, while the socioeconomic structures reproducing and embodying injustice are maintained intact. The credibility and sustainability of such a transition are highly questionable.

In the following excerpt, the author argues that economic issues, particularly structural injustices around land ownership, are an intimate part of the dynamics of conflict, oppression, and atrocity in various countries. By isolating and "backgrounding" these issues, TJ processes may unwittingly provide a veil of legitimacy on a transition that in fact fails to address fundamental injustices and causes of social tension and violence.

Zinaida Miller (2008) "Effects of Invisibility: In Search of the 'Economic' in Transitional Justice" *The International Journal of Transitional Justice*, 2: 266–291.

The failure to include economic concerns in transitional justice mechanisms tends to make transition into a political rather than an economic story, limiting knowledge of the economic underpinnings of conflict, narrowing the story of regime change and quelling discussion of development plans by quarantining them within the state and the executive rather than making them part of the transitional justice conversation. Since transitional justice mechanisms, particularly truth commissions, are discursive tools just as much as they are instruments of accountability or reconciliation, they may frame the conflict in one dimension without providing an alternative vocabulary. Thus, apartheid in South Africa after the TRC can become a story about racism or about specific, individual rights violations rather than about long-term, systemic abuses born of a colonial project with economic objectives. It also becomes one of physicality rather than structural violence, with the physical conceivably acting as a metaphor for the

> systemic, allowing the transitional justice institution and the state to address the former while essentially backgrounding the latter.[28] The genocide in Rwanda can become a story of historic ethnic hatred between Hutu and Tutsi rather than a narrative of decades-long resource inequity, unequal land distribution and colonial constructions. These narratives, partially constructed by the new state, are potentially echoed and reinforced by transitional justice mechanisms, which narrow the narrative of the past in a variety of ways …
>
> … In Rwanda, the government has implemented a far-reaching development plan, as well as passed a land law and implemented a land policy through its Ministry of Agriculture.[29] The land law and policy have problems of their own,[30] but for the purposes of this article, it is critical primarily to note that they have been established in a parallel and unrelated mode to the post-genocide justice system. Although the land law encompasses its own narrative of Rwandan history, including of the genocide,[31] the process of development has been kept wholly separate from that of transitional justice. The assiduous divorce of development from transitional justice, when linked to the land policy's recitation of the history of Rwanda and of the genocide, indicates the ways in which state narration of the past seeps into many arenas. By separating the two areas, the government can in a certain sense *assume* a supposedly 'reconciled' story of Rwandan history while implementing a complex set of transitional justice mechanisms.

It must be acknowledged that transitional justice institutions have financial and other constraints, and are sometimes at risk of becoming overwhelmed with the sheer scale of their responsibilities. They are unlikely to represent the only, or the main, architects of HLP reform. However, as the previous excerpt implies, it is important that transitional justice processes are not completely isolated from political and economic reforms, including reforms to land laws, housing policy, and other HLP issues. Truth commissions in particular can play a role in orienting the nature of HLP reforms, setting goals that other, more specialized institutions, can work toward. In cases where truth commissions have a limited mandate, civil society

[28] Jacobus A. du Pisani and Kwang-Su Kim (2004) "Establishing the Truth about the Apartheid Past: Historians and the South African Truth and Reconciliation Commission" *African Studies Quarterly* 8, no. 1: 83.

[29] Organic Law No. 08/2005 Determining the Use and Management of Land in Rwanda, Republic of Rwanda Ministry of Lands, Environment, Forests, Water and Mines, National Land Policy (2004) [hereinafter "Land policy"].

[30] I have addressed these issues in greater detail elsewhere. See, Zinaida Miller (2007) *Constructing Sustainable Reconciliation: Land, Power, and Transitional Justice in Post-Genocide Rwanda*, Cape Town: Institute for Justice and Reconciliation.

[31] The land policy narrates a story of precolonial Rwandan harmony radically disrupted by the influence of the racist colonial administration. While the corrosive and violent Belgian influence is unquestioned by any credible source, the way in which the state has chosen to portray land issues tends to erase the possibility of precolonial resource divisions and, in particular, precolonial Hutu/Tutsi divisions….

action may force a broadening of that mandate over time. The truth commission for Guatemala had a very limited mandate in both duration and objectives. In reaction to this, a parallel civil society project was launched. The official commission, emboldened or embarrassed by the work of the civil society institution, managed to publish a comprehensive and forthright report, despite the constraints under which it was placed.[32]

The following excerpt argues that in countries where the land tenure system is systematically dysfunctional and historical injustices predate the immediate period of authoritarian rule or conflict, a limited restitution program will be neither effective nor sufficient. Instead, the government should consider a more fundamental restructuring of laws, institutions, and land distribution.

Chris Huggins (2009) "Linking Broad Constellations of Ideas: Transitional Justice, Land Tenure Reform, and Development," in Pablo de Greiff and Roger Duthie (eds.), *Transitional Justice and Development: Making Connections*, Social Science Research Council.

Given the effects of conflict and authoritarian rule on land rights, it is always necessary to restore those property rights that have been lost through abuses. However, in many countries the history of dispossession is long and complex. Two related questions arise: How far should the government "turn back the clock"? and, How fundamental should reform be? These questions have numerous and far-reaching political, human rights, and economic implications. Timor-Leste is a case in point. The country suffered successive waves of invasion and dispossession, from Portuguese colonization through Japanese occupation to Indonesian invasion. Timorese can claim land on the basis of underlying traditional interests, titles issued during both the Portuguese and Indonesian eras, or through long-term occupation. In the transitional period, the two major political parties, *Uniao Democratica Timorense* (UDT) and *Frente Revolucionara de Timor Leste* (Fretilin), have had different interests. UDT supports restoration of pre-1975 Portuguese titles, as many of its supporters reputedly held property under the Portuguese administration, while Fretilin emphasizes land justice for customary owners and dispossessed groups, with one of its leaders reportedly indicating that bona fide Indonesian titles should be recognized.[33] Customary rights have not been respected by colonial occupiers or adequately protected by law, and alienation of land during the Portuguese and Indonesian periods often represents injustice among customary rights holders. The question of historical claims to land in Timor-Leste remains largely unresolved. A law on land ownership restitution, with plans for a land claims commission, was expected in 2006 but was delayed, leading to some suspicions that government

[32] Craig Kauffman (2005) *Transitional Justice in Guatemala: Linking the Past and Future*. Paper prepared for the ISA-South Conference, Miami.

[33] Daniel Fitzpatrick (2001) "Land Policy in Post-Conflict Circumstances: Some Lessons from East Timor" *Journal of Humanitarian Assistance*, http://jha.ac/articles/a074.htm.

insiders did not want the issues resolved. In 2006, tensions between Timorese political groups and their supporters resulted in armed violence and widespread acts of arson. There were many aspects to this violence, including differences over the question of property rights.[34]

Clearly, an attempt to turn back the clock by more than a few years can be politically, economically, and technically difficult and risky. In most cases, the strategy advocated is to restore land ownership patterns to those in existence immediately prior to the conflict, through, for example, restoring the condition and integrity of land registers and conducting only as much registration and adjudication is necessary to confirm those titles. Some actors may advocate a systematic land registration exercise, whereby all landholdings in the country will be brought under the statutory system. This is frequently justified on economic grounds, on the basis that it will increase domestic and foreign investment through reducing land tenure insecurity. However, as discussed above, the risks involved are manifold. Injustices and disputes dating from colonial times, as well as more recent abuses related to conflict or authoritarianism, should be evaluated, and if necessary addressed before registration takes place. However, in practice, some actors have been accused of insisting upon registration on ideological grounds, or in order to open rural areas to the forces of globalization, without assessing the risks to community livelihoods.[35]

Critics of the "business as usual" approach point to the fact that in many cases it was precisely these land-ownership patterns that precipitated conflict. Restoring such patterns is therefore likely to lead to an eventual resumption of violence. Instead, it is argued, transitional regimes should "set aside the paradigms of the past and its outputs in the form of nefarious 'legal documents' that hold so little legitimacy and which patently obstruct arrival at compromise and peace."[36] Instead, "fundamental structural change to property norms and political decision-making is required."[37] For those who favor a radical reevaluation of land tenure patterns, the role of the state as an arbitrator of competing claims becomes a major concern.

Can the political system maintain its integrity and overcome the kind of vested interests discussed above in the case of Timor-Leste? Is the role of external actors helpful or divisive? And, how are the interests of different categories of local stakeholders reflected in the positions of civil society organizations or traditional leaders? When questions of property rights are being fundamentally reassessed, the legitimacy of those involved in the eyes of local people is paramount. Social coherence is a vital

[34] Andrew Harrington (2006) "Ethnicity, Violence and Land and Property Disputes in Timor-Leste" *East Timor Law Journal* 2.

[35] Robin Palmer, "Oxfam and Land in Post-Conflict Situations in Africa," in ACTS (2005), "Report of the Conference on Land Tenure and Conflict in Africa, Nairobi, 9–10 December, 2004."

[36] Gabriel Dolan (2007) *No Transformation in Kenya Without Addressing the Land Question*. LL.M. dissertation, Transitional Justice Institute/The Law School University of Ulster, Jordanstown.

[37] Liz Alden Wily (2008) *It's More Than about Going Home. Land in Emergency to Development Transitions in Conflict States: Who Should Do What?* Paper presented at Humanitarian Policy Group [HPG]–Overseas Development Institute [ODI] conference. "Uncharted Territory: Land, Conflict and Humanitarian Action," London, February.

question, as is the capacity of the government to manage episodes of dissent or unrest. In cases where a negotiated end to authoritarian rule or conflict has resulted in power-sharing agreements, those accused of human rights abuses (including, for example, forced displacement, land-grabbing, and other property crimes) may be powerful members of the government.[38] In short, conflict analysis is critical, and the various centripetal and centrifugal forces acting on society must be assessed.

A second major concern, which is linked to the question of social and political integrity, is the economic situation in the country. A fundamental re-evaluation of land rights is bound to affect agricultural and industrial production.

In the case of South Africa, leasing arrangements have been utilized to ensure that even after land has been transferred through restitution processes, it remains under large-scale commercial production, at least for the short-to-medium term. The South African government has chosen to limit the extent of expropriation of land during the restitution process in order to avoid undermining perceptions of land tenure security. However, the government's commitment to a business-as-usual agrarian policy has meant that those black farmers who have claimed land and have attempted to start smallholder farm enterprises are struggling to succeed within a wider economic system geared for large-scale production. While the state has provided some support, its "developmental" interventions tend to benefit commercial farmers rather than the smallholder majority. In short, while the multifaceted land reform program was intended to "restore identity and promote reconciliation, whilst redistributing wealth and strengthening the rural economy," some observers have argued that these are competing and possibly irreconcilable objectives.[39]

Every country is unique, and the extent to which macroeconomic structures can be reshaped depends not just on internal and external political relationships but also on the nature of the transition.

NATURAL DISASTERS AND HLP RIGHTS

Inter-Agency Standing Committee – Operational Guidelines on Human Rights and Natural Disasters, Brookings-Bern Project on Internal Displacement, June 2006, pp. 8–10 and 13 (footnotes omitted)

Natural disasters, that is, the consequences of events triggered by natural hazards that overwhelm local response capacity and seriously affect the social and economic development of a region, are traditionally seen as situations creating

38 Such is the case in Liberia, for example. See Abdul Rahman Lamin (2005) "Truth, Justice and Reconciliation: Analysis of the Prospects and Challenges of the Truth and Reconciliation Commission in Liberia," in Alhaji Mohamed Ba and Festus Boahen Aboagye (eds.), *A Tortuous Road to Peace: The Dynamics of Regional, UN and International Humanitarian Interventions in Liberia*, Pretoria: Institute for Security Studies.

39 Ruth Hall (2004) "Land Restitution in South Africa: Rights, Development, and the Restrained State" *Canadian Journal of African Studies* 38, no. 3: 654–671.

challenges and problems mainly of a humanitarian nature. Less attention has been devoted to human rights protection that also needs to be provided in this particular context.

The tsunamis, hurricanes and earthquakes which hit parts of Asia and the Americas in 2004/2005 have highlighted the need to be attentive to the multiple human rights challenges that persons affected by such disasters may face. All too often their human rights are not sufficiently taken into account. The problems that are often encountered by persons affected by the consequences of natural disasters include: unequal access to assistance; discrimination in aid provision; enforced relocation; sexual and gender-based violence; loss of documentation; recruitment of children into fighting forces; unsafe or involuntary return or resettlement; and issues of property restitution. The affected populations are most often forced to leave their homes or places of residence because of the destruction of houses and shelter by volcanic eruptions, tsunamis, floods, drought, landslides, earthquakes and tornados. Thus, a high number of persons also become internally displaced as a result of such disasters or the fear of future damages.

Experience has shown that, while patterns of discrimination and disregard for economic, social and cultural rights may already emerge during the emergency phase of a disaster, the longer the displacement situation lasts, the greater the risk of human rights violations.

Normally, situations affecting the human rights of persons affected by natural disasters are not consciously planned and implemented, but result from inappropriate policies or simple neglect. The vulnerability of the people affected often is the result of inadequate planning and disaster preparedness. As stated by the Secretary General, "The risks and potential for disasters associated with natural hazards are largely shaped by the prevailing levels of vulnerability and the effectiveness of measures taken to prevent, mitigate and prepare for disasters." Once the people have been affected by a disaster, however, they often encounter further challenges to the full realization of their rights. These challenges could be avoided if the relevant human rights guarantees were taken into account, at the very outset, by national as well as international actors.

States are directly responsible for respecting, protecting and fulfilling the human rights of their citizens and other persons on their territory or under their jurisdiction. Whereas national humanitarian organizations are bound by their national laws, international humanitarian organizations, while not directly bound by international human rights treaties, accept that human rights underpin all of their actions. Therefore, they should do their utmost to ensure that these rights are protected – even beyond the strict wording of their mandates and in the interest of the people directly affected. All humanitarian organizations are under the obligation not to promote, actively participate in, or in any other manner contribute to, or endorse policies or activities, which do or can lead to human rights violations by States. The challenge often is how to apply these rules in an operational context, not least given the many humanitarian and human rights dilemmas potentially faced in situations of humanitarian disasters.

There are guidelines on humanitarian action in emergencies, including situations of natural disaster. There are also standards on protecting human rights in situations of armed conflict, internal displacement and refugee situations. Guidance is lacking, however, on how to protect the human rights of individuals affected by natural disasters.

These Operational Guidelines are addressed to intergovernmental and non-governmental humanitarian actors when they are called upon to become active just before or in the aftermath of a natural disaster. The Operational Guidelines do not list the rights of persons as enshrined in international law. Rather, they focus on what humanitarian actors should do in order to implement a rights-based approach to humanitarian action in the context of natural disasters. They call on humanitarian actors to look beyond their core mandate and to have a holistic vision of the needs of the people they have been asked to serve. While these Guidelines have been drafted with the consequences of natural disasters in mind, most of them are also relevant in preparation for or after other kinds of disasters have struck.

These Operational Guidelines are informed by and draw on relevant international human rights law, existing standards and policies pertaining to humanitarian action, and human rights guidelines on humanitarian standards in situations of natural disaster. They cover relevant civil and political as well as economic, social and cultural rights. While natural disasters may occur in situations of armed conflict, international humanitarian law per se does not regulate the effects of such disasters. However, it may complement human rights law in such situations.

Guidelines

I. Persons affected by natural disasters should enjoy the same rights and freedoms under human rights law as others in their country and not be discriminated against. Targeted measures to address assistance and protection needs of specific categories of affected populations do not constitute discrimination if, and to the extent that, they are based on differing needs.

II. States have the primary duty and responsibility to provide assistance to persons affected by natural disasters and to protect their human rights.

III. Organizations providing protection and assistance to persons affected by natural disasters accept that human rights underpin all humanitarian action. In situations of natural disaster they should therefore respect the human rights of persons affected by disasters at all times and advocate for their promotion and protection to the fullest extent. Humanitarian organizations shall not promote, actively participate in, or in any other manner contribute to, or endorse policies or activities, which do or can lead to human rights violations by States. They shall strive to enable the affected people to exercise their own rights.

IV. Organizations providing protection and assistance in situations of natural disasters shall be guided by these Operational Guidelines in all of their activities, in particular when monitoring and assessing the situation and needs of affected persons, when programming and implementing their own activities as well as when entering into a dialogue with governmental authorities on the State's duties and responsibilities under international human rights and, where applicable, international humanitarian and refugee law. In doing so, they shall remain accountable to all of their relevant stakeholders, in particular to the persons affected by the natural disaster.

V. All communities affected by the natural disaster should be entitled to easy accessible information concerning: (a) the nature and level of disaster they are facing; (b) the possible risk mitigation measures that can be taken; (c) early warning information; and (d) information on ongoing humanitarian assistance, recovery efforts and their respective entitlements. They should be meaningfully consulted and given the opportunity to take charge of their own affairs to the maximum extent possible and to participate in the planning and implementation of the various stages of the disaster response.

VI. These Operational Guidelines seek to improve the practical implementation of international instruments protecting human rights. They shall not be interpreted as restricting, modifying or impairing the provisions of international human rights or, where applicable, international humanitarian and refugee law. They should be applied together with other relevant Codes of Conduct, Guidelines and Manuals.

VII. Organizations providing protection and assistance in situations of natural disasters shall endeavor to have adequate mechanisms established to ensure that the Operational Guidelines are applied and that the human rights of the affected are protected.

DISTINGUISHING POSTCONFLICT AND POSTDISASTER

UN-HABITAT, Scoping Report: Addressing Land Issues after Natural Disasters.

Why disaster guidelines are necessary: Distinguishing post-conflict and post-disaster land issues

A number of agencies, including UN-HABITAT, FAO, USAID and ODI have prepared operational guidelines and analytical frameworks to address land issues after armed conflicts. The UN Guiding Principles on Internal Displacement encompass cases of natural disaster and armed conflict. While there are many similarities between land issues after conflict and disaster, there are important differences that underscore the need for a separate set of guidelines on land and natural disasters. The need for separate guidelines on post-disaster land responses, identified by the Early Recovery Cluster in 2007, is confirmed by heightened disaster risks as a result of global climate change, and increased human settlement vulnerability as result of global population growth.

Post-conflict and post-disaster land issues can be similar because both situations tend to involve displacement, death and destruction. In both cases, the land governance system can enter a state of flux as a result of new needs, actors and incentives. Within this context of system change, the following land-specific risks can arise in cases of both conflict and disaster:

- Temporary living centres may be built on inappropriate land.
- The process of return may be marked by land grabbing, ad hoc land occupation and political score-settling.
- A residual caseload of displaced persons may not be able to return (including renters, squatters and the landless).
- Land rights may be uncertain because of a lack of records, loss or destruction of records, or damage to community-based land governance systems.
- Uncertainty of land tenure may lead to disputes and delays in reconstruction, or to reconstruction in inappropriate locations.
- A failure t identify heirs in an authoritative manner may lead to family disputes, and delays in reconstruction and recovery.
- Powerful individuals may take advantage of inheritance uncertainty to deny entitlements and access to land for vulnerable groups, including widows and orphans.
- Land may be acquired for resettlement and infrastructure in inappropriate locations, or through methods that are productive of conflict.

Although there are many potential similarities, land issues after natural disasters can differ from armed conflict in a number of important respects:

Government Capacity and National Politics

- While natural disasters can occur in a war-torn context, disasters that occur in the absence of war tend to be associated with less politicised and conflict-ridden circumstances. As a result, there may be more government capacity and greater political space to resolve longer term land issues. At the same time, a national government may be reluctant to confront deeper land-related issues in a post disaster context, and relatively less willing to request international assistance in cases of disaster than conflict, particularly in relation to land issues, because the request may imply a lack of capacity on its part. The government may also take an unduly short term view of land responses, in order to be seen to deliver quick recovery and reconstruction results.

The Significance of Sudden Onset

- The shock to the land system tends to be shorter, but potentially sharper, in the case of sudden onset natural disasters than in the context of armed conflict.

- The deaths of land owners, and loss of land records (if any), will occur in a much more compressed period of time in the case of natural disasters.
- The generally localised or isolated impact nature of disasters can mean that surplus housing stock is available to absorb displaced persons.
- While it will be possible to identify high disaster risk areas, and engage in activities to reduce the ability to plan and prepare for particular cases of displacement.
- Sudden onset disasters can result in significant loss of land, due to landslides, flooding or other hazards that render land unsafe for habitation, livelihoods or other uses. Addressing the land needs of landowners who have lost land as a result of a disaster is often a distinctive imperative of post disaster land programming.
- The sudden onset of a disaster, and its relatively localised impact, may reuce the risk that abandoned land or housing will be occupied by persons other than the pre-displacement owner (i.e the "secondary occupier" problem).

Landowner Return to Unoccupied Land

- A relative absence of secondary occupiers should facilitate return and reoccupation of land by pre-disaster landowners, because landowners can return without the need to evict secondary occupiers. This should reduce (but not eliminate) the need for specialist judicial institutions to adjudicate claims for property restitution (e.g a land claims commission). At the same time, specialist institutions and responses may still be required to protect victims, including women and others with weaker forms of tenure, from the risk of land grabbing by neighbours, government bodies or social elites.
- A relative absence of secondary occupiers means that residual caseloads of displaced persons unable to return are more likely to be those who are not land owners (including renters, squatters and the landless). In other words, because landowners can return without the need to evict secondary occupiers, those who are unable to return are more likely to be groups who lacked access to land, or sufficient security of tenure prior to the disaster.

The Need to Engage in Future Disaster Risk Reduction

- The greater risk to land restitution for displaced victims is not secondary occupation but the need to engage in future disaster risk reduction. The need to minimise the risk of future disasters may require special planning mechanisms that restrict reconstruction in inappropriate or unsafe locations.
- The need to minimise the risk of future disasters may lead to relocation of infrastructure and government facilities.

All these issues will affect analysis and assessment of land issues after natural disasters. It is important not to approach natural disasters from a "conflict" perspective, or at least a perspective that cannot adapt to the particular circumstances of natural disasters. Large-scale disasters can traumatise a land governance system at least as much as armed conflict. But the system itself may be in a relatively better position to recover and respond to emerging land issues, either because the disaster itself is more localised in effect of because the operating environment is less degraded by civil war or ethnic conflict. In other words, while there will be pre-disaster land governance problems that are magnified by the disaster, the risk of the system *as a whole* being thrown into chaos appears relatively lower in cases of disaster than armed conflict.

This said, two potential features of natural disasters will place more pressure on the land governance system than would be the case after armed conflict.

- The need to engage in disaster risk reduction demands a relatively high degree of capacity and coordination among land planning institutions. It also places stress on the institutions involved in relocation and re-settlement, including those charged with ensuring consultation and participation by affected groups.
- The concentration of renters, squatters and the landless in residual caseloads of persons unable to return to their pre-disaster lands will highlight the social and legal conditions that restrict access to land and its ownership in the affected country. As a result, there may be a degree of governmental caution or paralysis because addressing the land needs of renters, squatters and the landless may open a Pandora's Box of claims outside the disaster zone.

Questions and Exercises

1. In your opinion, do HLP issues belong in peace agreements? If so, is it possible to develop universal language that peace mediators all over the world could rely on in their efforts to bring warring parties together?
2. Do those displaced by disaster have the same rights under international law as those displaced by conflict? If so, on what legal grounds do you make this determination?
3. To what extent should land reform and redistributive justice form part of postconflict peace agreements? How can the international community best promote such initiatives?

9

Improving International Responses to HLP Rights and Conflict

The Work of NGOs in the HLP Rights Field

HUMAN RIGHTS NGOS

Human rights NGOs working on HLP issues can broadly be divided into two categories. On the one hand are "traditional" human rights organizations that historically have focused on civil and political rights. Over approximately the past two decades, such organizations have examined economic, social, and cultural rights with increasing frequency, but their methodology largely remains based on the classic "naming and shaming" model. Examples of international NGOs in this group include Human Rights Watch (HRW) and Amnesty International. The other category of human rights NGOs is organizations intentionally established to deal with ESC rights, and their methodologies may differ from the classic human rights models. The Centre on Housing Rights and Evictions (COHRE) is an example of international NGOs in this second category. There are many local NGOs around the world that fall within both categories.

There has been an ongoing debate about the ways in which the first category of organizations, traditional human rights groups, can best address ESC rights. Violations of human rights can be committed either by omission – a failure by the state or another institution to do something required of it – or by commission – an action that robs citizens of their rights. As discussed in previous chapters, governments around the world have ratified international human rights treaties that obligate them to uphold the fundamental human rights of their citizens. Rights to housing are one example. Under international human rights law, governments are forbidden from carrying out certain actions – such as forced evictions – that violate the human right to housing. Governments are also bound to invest in housing for the poor. For example, the International Covenant on Economic, Social and Cultural Rights (ICESCR), 1966, in Article 11, states that "The States Parties to the present Covenant recognize the right of everyone to an adequate standard of living for himself and his family, including adequate food, clothing and housing, and to the continuous improvement of living conditions. *The States Parties will take appropriate steps to ensure the realization of this right,* recognizing to this effect the essential importance of international co-operation based on free consent" (emphasis added).

In practice, it has proved far simpler to monitor, identify, and criticize actions committed by states that violate HLP rights than failures to take the steps necessary to enable people to realize their rights. Developing nations argue that they face severe economic constraints and are hence unable to allocate adequate resources to low-cost housing construction or land tenure reform, for example. The question of "distributional justice" – the distribution of national public resources between sectors and groups within society – is a complex one. National economic information shows that in many countries, defense spending represents a far higher proportion of the national budget than investment in low-cost housing, land policy development, or similar sectors. However, states may be able to argue that defense spending must remain high due to national security concerns, for example. In the following excerpt, the Executive Director of HRW explains why distributional justice is more difficult to address than other issues.

Kenneth Roth (2004) "Defending Economic, Social and Cultural Rights: Practical Issues Faced by an International Human Rights Organization" *Human Rights Quarterly* 26, no. 1: 63–73.

To maximise the power of international human rights organizations like Human Rights Watch – clarity is needed around three issues: violation, violator, and remedy. We must be able to show persuasively that a particular state of affairs amounts to a violation of human rights standards, that a particular violator is principally or significantly responsible, and that a widely accepted remedy for the violation exists. If any of these three elements is missing, our capacity to shame is greatly diminished [...]

Broadly speaking, [these elements are] clearest when it is possible to identify arbitrary or discriminatory governmental conduct that causes or substantially contributes to an ESC rights violation. These three dimensions are less clear when the ESC shortcoming is largely a problem of distributive justice. If all an international human rights organization can do is argue that more money be spent to uphold an ESC right – that a fixed economic pie be divided differently – our voice is relatively weak. We can argue that money [that] should be diverted from less acute exists for a government to give our voice greater weight than domestic voices. On the other hand, if we can show that the government (or other relevant actor) is contributing to the ESC shortfall through arbitrary or discriminatory conduct, we are in a powerful position to shame; we can show a violation (the rights shortfall), the violator (the government or other actor through its arbitrary or discriminatory conduct), and the remedy (reversing that conduct) [...]

> To conclude, let me offer a hypothesis about the conduct of international human rights organizations working on ESC rights. It has been clear for many years that the movement would like to do more in the ESC realm. Yet despite repeated professions of interest, its work in this area remains limited. Part of the reason, of course, is expertise; the movement must staff itself somewhat differently to document shortfalls in such matters as health or housing than to record instances of torture or political imprisonment.

For the reasons that Roth describes, traditional human rights groups have rarely criticized government fiscal policies. There is a possibility that by concentrating on abusive state interventions, rather than on the state's failures to distribute resources equally, traditional human rights organizations tend to exhibit a systematic bias against the "big government" or "welfare state" model. Using the example of the United States, the authors of the excerpt that follows imply that there are ideological factors (associated with neoliberalism) behind an approach that ignores distributive justice.

Judith R. Blau and Alberto Moncada (2005) ***Human Rights: Beyond the Liberal Vision*****, Rowman & Littlefield, 130–131.**

> While we are far from critical of HRW [Human Rights Watch], we will use this controversy for conceptual purposes. Like the ACLU [American Civil Liberties Union] which is exclusively devoted to protecting Americans' First Amendment rights, HRW in its international work focuses on harms committed by the "strong state" rather than on the ways states can bolster societal and collective rights ... many INGOs and their representatives have taken positions defending the protection of human rights in the broad sense.... One position was that bolstering "soft rights" reduces the chances of horrific abuses committed by strong states. The predisposing conditions of despots and desperation are what human rights combat. Of course, all organizations must specialize, and HRW is an exemplary world leader in dealing with the most serious human rights abuses, such as torture, human trafficking, and abuse of prisoners. However, many participants in a worldwide online discussion (sponsored by CESR) expressed views based on an understanding that highlights distributive justice. Second-generation rights – rights to a job, rights to food security, and, for vulnerable groups, rights to protection – arise from a concept of society that is very different from the liberal, individualistic one. We make this distinction here, not because we disagree with the objectives of HRW (and the ACLU), but to clarify our view that civil and political rights, as well as humanitarian justice, are part and parcel of human rights, whereas the liberal position is that civil and political rights (and for some, humanitarian laws as well) *alone* constitute human rights. Excluding socioeconomic rights from liberal rights has created enormous societal costs in America. Compared with other industrialized countries, America has the highest rates of childhood poverty, homelessness, incarceration, infant mortality, and handgun deaths, and it has the highest percentages of people without health insurance and of workers not covered by collective bargaining. The United States has the highest-paid chief executive officers and the most per capita billionaires.

> Yet 13.1 million children in America go hungry because the households in which they live are extremely poor.... A liberal society generates vulnerabilities and, therefore, a high rate of casualties.

Other observers have criticized the emphasis of some international human rights organizations on state-related violations rather than violations by businesses and international corporations.[1] However, this has changed, to a limited extent, over the last decade, and several international NGOs have released reports targeting multinational corporations.[2] The importance of distributional justice has become increasingly accepted in recent years, and even traditional human rights NGOs have been willing to address this question when it is clear that corruption, discrimination, or political self-interest prevents investment in activities that would allow citizens to fulfil their ESC rights.[3] In the case of the right to water, COHRE has argued:

> Many of the people denied such basic necessities live in countries with sufficient water supplies and finances or where the bulk of public subsidies do not primarily benefit the poorest members of society. Thus, the argument of scant resources cannot explain away these gross inadequacies. Rather, it is clear that a combination of discrimination, the lack of political will, the exclusion of communities, and inadequate legal structures result in such conditions. Most countries lack a proper system of monitoring and accountability to ensure the equitable implementation of water policies and provide redress for violations.[4]

To some extent, human rights NGOs may be wary of engaging with HLP rights because these rights are abused on a day-to-day basis in so many countries around the world. Important messages on HLP rights may be dissipated because abuses are so widespread and the global challenge seems so overwhelming. Because of this, some traditional human rights groups have chosen to focus on the most grievous abuses of HLP rights and the most vulnerable categories of rights holders. Amnesty International, for example, has focused on forced evictions, housing demolitions, and violations of indigenous land rights.[5] The HLP rights of returning refugees in the world's poorest countries, such as Burundi, have also been a focus for Amnesty International.

1 Makua Mutua (2001) "Human Rights INGOs: A Critical Evaluation" in Claude E. Welch, Jr. (ed.), *NGOs and Human Rights: Promise and Performance*, University of Pennsylvania Press, 156.

2 See e.g., Human Rights Watch (2005) *The Curse of Gold*, New York: Human Rights Watch, as well as several reports by Global Witness, an NGO which specializes in investigating the corrupt exploitation of natural resources and international trade systems.

3 See e.g., Human Rights Watch (2007) *Chop Fine: The Human Rights Impact of Local Government Corruption and Mismanagement in Rivers State, Nigeria*. Human Rights Watch.

4 COHRE web site, accessed on 30 July 2009 at http://www.cohre.org/water.

5 Amnesty International (2009) *Amnesty International Action for Economic, Social and Cultural Rights*. Accessed on 2 August 2009 at http://www.amnesty.org/en/economic-and-social-cultural-rights/ai-action-escr.

Human Rights Watch did not investigate ESC rights abuses until the late 1990s. In 1997, HRW adopted an internal policy to investigate, document, and promote compliance with the ICESCR, but only in situations where the protection of the ICESCR right is necessary to remedy a substantial violation of an ICCPR right, and where the violation of an ICESCR right is the direct result of a substantial violation of an ICCPR right. In recent years, HRW has reported on forced evictions and demolitions in countries such as Angola, Indonesia, and Zimbabwe, where government actions have been particularly brutal.

The advocacy strategies of major international human rights organizations have changed over time. Human Rights, for example, originally relied on high-level discussions with foreign policy experts within the U.S. government. Over time, it started to urge regional organizations, such as the European Union, Organization for Security and Cooperation in Europe, and the African Union, to put pressure on their member states to cease abuses. In recent years, it has opened offices in numerous countries in order both to facilitate research in these countries and to lobby parliamentarians and decision makers within these same countries. [6]

In addition to denouncing abuses, traditional human rights organizations have also advocated for stronger international human rights legislation, such as the Optional Protocol to the ICESCR, for example. Amnesty International in particular is known for its behind-the-scenes work in proposing specific wording for international human rights treaties, and has worked more closely with UN bodies than other INGOs, such as HRW.[7] INGOs have supported the establishment of networks of local NGOs in some countries (HRW supported such a network in India, for example).[8] The following excerpt emphasizes the importance of information sharing and lesson learning between organizations working on ESC rights.

Amnesty International (2005) *Human Rights for Human Dignity: A Primer on Economic, Social and Cultural Rights*, Amnesty International.

Local, national and regional human rights organizations have been defending these rights for decades. International organizations working on these rights emerged from the 1980s onwards, including the international Food First Information and Action Network (FIAN) in 1986, the Center on Economic and Social Rights in 1993, the Centre on Housing Rights and Evictions (COHRE) in 1994, and many others. There is now a broad international network of economic, social and cultural

[6] Widney Brown (2001) "Human Rights Watch: An Overview" in Claude E. Welch, Jr. (ed.), *NGOs and Human Rights: Promise and Performance*, University of Pennsylvania Press, 79.

[7] Claude E. Welch, Jr. (2001) "Amnesty International and Human Rights Watch: A Comparison" in Claude E. Welch, Jr. (ed.), *NGOs and Human Rights: Promise and Performance*, University of Pennsylvania Press, p. 88.

[8] Id., p. 101.

rights NGOs (ESCRNET). Yet scepticism on the nature of these rights persists, particularly on how to campaign against their violation. Some people within the international human rights movement question to what extent international human rights organizations should work on these issues.[9] Key challenges for those campaigning to advance economic, social and cultural rights include identifying violations, victims, violators and remedies on which to focus campaigning. How best can human rights activists transform calls for policy reforms into concrete actions that highlight the need for change to improve the lives of individuals, groups and communities?...

...While developing indicators of progress or decline in the realization of economic, social and cultural rights is an enduring challenge to the human rights community, research into violations of these rights is in many cases similar to research into violations of civil and political rights. Campaigning strategies can be based on documenting abuses of governments' duties to respect or protect rights – such as forced eviction, poisoning water supplies, and crop destruction. They can also be built on identifying the people affected and the remedies required, such as halting the abuse and providing adequate reparation, and on identifying the range of actors responsible, such as a polluting business and the state that fails to regulate the activities of its businesses, at home and abroad. Campaigning tactics such as letter-writing and publicity can have success in such cases. Skills in documenting economic, social and cultural rights are developing. They are increasingly shared internationally, through international workshops and networks, in manuals by NGOs for NGOs,[10] and through skills sharing on techniques ranging from budgetary analysis to the use of the constitution to effect change. Links between organizations working for economic, social and cultural rights around the world have never been stronger. One of the strengths of joining national campaigns with international solidarity is the ability to highlight the international dimensions of states' obligations towards economic, social and cultural rights, and how actions abroad, whether by the state, its representatives (including multilateral development banks) or its businesses, impact on the realization of human rights. The indivisibility of all human rights often emerges when human rights organizations document patterns of human rights violations. The imprisonment of people campaigning for recognition

9 See the exchange between the Executive Directors of Human Rights Watch and of Physicians for Human Rights: K. Roth (2004) "Defending Economic, Social and Cultural Rights: Practical Issues Faced by an International Human Rights Organization" *Human Rights Quarterly* 26, no. 1: 63; and L. S. Rubenstein (2004) "How International Human Rights Organizations Can Advance Economic, Social and Cultural Rights: A Response to Kenneth Roth"; K. Roth (2004) "Response to Leonard S. Rubenstein" and L. S.Rubenstein (2004) "Response by Leonard S. Rubenstein" *Human Rights Quarterly* 26, no. 4: 845, 875, 879.

10 See the recent series of manuals on the right to health, the right to food, labor rights and the right to water, published by the Human Rights Documentation Centre (HURIDOCS) and the American Academy for the Advancement of Science (AAAS), http://shr.aaas.org/escr.html. See also Law Society of Sri Lanka and the Center for Economic and Social Rights, An Activists Manual on the ICESCR, among others.

of their land rights; the use of disproportionate force in response to protests over the impact of water privatization; the lack of judicial independence in eviction cases – all demand a holistic human rights response.

The second category of human rights organizations, those which have specialized in HLP rights, often utilize a broader range of tools. In addition to denouncing abuses (colloquially known as the naming and shaming), such organizations often engage directly with governments. COHRE, for example, conducts training sessions and other capacity-building activities for governments. National organizations like Kenya Land Alliance publish detailed reviews of draft national policies and legislation in order to influence legal reform. Such organizations may also participate directly or directly in government-run commissions, task forces, and assessment missions, if the potential benefits of such collaboration outweigh the risks of legitimizing what may be an imperfect process.

AN ACTIVISTS' TASK LIST

Human rights advocates, gathered together in the mid-1990s, identified the following tasks as key to documenting and campaigning for economic, social, and cultural rights:

- identifying the rights issues of immediate concern to the country or community;
- monitoring the state's development of the conditions necessary to ensure economic, social, and cultural rights and, in particular, its implementation of related policies, plans, and legislation;
- monitoring, documenting, and reporting on the government's actions in complying with, or violating, its obligations;
- observing the government's compliance with recommendations made by international human rights bodies. This would include first-hand collection of facts and evidence from various sources;
- ascertaining the availability of legal remedies and determining their enforceability under national laws. This would involve researching the relevant laws and analyzing court decisions related to economic, social, and cultural rights claims;
- responding to individual or community complaints of violations educating the population on their economic, social, and cultural rights; and
- mobilizing and collaborating with communities and other organizations in advocacy.[11]

[11] Based on: International Human Rights Internship Program (1997) "Ripple in Still Water: Reflections by Activists on Local and National Level Work on Economic, Social and Cultural Rights," University

DEVELOPMENT NGOS

A growing number of NGOs involved in "development" activities, from the community to the macroeconomic level, purport to follow a "rights-based approach to development." This approach is a logical "mainstreaming" of the Universal Declaration of Human Rights and other international human rights law into the design and implementation of development programs, and has also been strongly influenced by the work of Nobel Prize-winning economist Amartya Sen.[12]

Former High Commissioner for Human Rights Mary Robinson has been among those arguing for a rights-based approach.

Mary Robinson (2000) *Development and Rights: The Undeniable Nexus. Speech of the High Commissioner for Human Rights*, Geneva, 26 June.

There is an unmistakable message coming through from local communities, national movements, development experts, women's groups, indigenous peoples, and human rights activists across the globe. The path to human dignity runs not through imposed technocratic solutions, imported foreign models, or presumed trade-offs between development and rights. Health, education, housing, fair justice and free political participation are not matters for charity – but rather matters of right. This is what is meant by the "rights-based approach": a participatory, empowering, accountable, and non-discriminatory development paradigm based on universal, inalienable human rights and freedoms [...]

[...] The rights-based approach provides a better understanding of, and a better response to the continuing challenges of poverty. Most by now agree that traditional, more narrow income-based definitions have not been adequate. Many aspects of poverty, some of which are crucial to a human rights analysis, are simply not reflected in the statistical indicators. Foremost are the critical vulnerability and subjective daily assaults on human dignity that accompany poverty.

The poor are subject to daily humiliation, abuse, rejection, exclusion and harassment. The poorest feel the unrelenting agony of chronic hunger, the suffering of untreated disease, and the exposure of inadequate shelter. The fundamental importance of participation and empowerment to effective development strategies must be seen as a further indication of the necessity of a rights-based approach. The social exclusion of the poor, and their lack of power in regard to insensitive local officials, corrupt institutions, and inaccessible development decision makers, all point to the need to create new mechanisms to ensure that their voice is heard, and given authority in development.

of Minnesota Human Rights Resource Center, http://www1.umn.edu/humanrts/edumat/IHRIP/ripple/toc.html.

12 See e.g., Amartya Sen (1999) *Development as Freedom*, Oxford University Press.

> Thus, from a human rights perspective, poverty must be viewed not just as a question of low income, but as a human condition characterized by the sustained deprivation of the capabilities, choices, and power necessary for the enjoyment of fundamental civil, cultural, economic, political and social rights. A human rights approach is therefore better suited to take account of the myriad of social, cultural and political aspects of the phenomenon.

Development NGOs are most directly associated with helping poor communities fulfill their rights to development through undertaking development projects, including housing, infrastructure, and other projects associated with HLP rights. In working to *realize* ESC rights, including HLP rights, development NGOs can *promote* these rights by raising awareness among project beneficiaries, and help *protect* these rights by convincing partner organizations and other key actors such as governments, international financial institutions, and intergovernmental organizations to make their policies compliant with international treaties.[13]

Even though many development-oriented NGOs claim to have a rights-based approach, the gap between aspirations and achievements remains a significant one. Development NGOs rarely conduct rigorous and regular impact assessments of their work.[14] It is often very difficult to establish the extent to which their work results in the fulfillment of human rights, and specifically the HLP rights. There have been many calls for improved transparency in the way that large development NGOs function. Many international NGOs are funded mainly from a single government in their place of origin. Others are reliant on the major private philanthropic foundations that often have particular ideological positions. This has prompted some critics to argue that some NGOs have become the tools of particular governments or multilateral organizations. Ferguson, for example, contends that "at the same time that international organizations (through structural adjustment) are eroding the power of African states (and usurping their sovereignty) they are busy making end runs around these states by directly sponsoring their own programs or interventions [through NGOs]."[15] More broadly, some analysts, particularly those on the political left, argue that mainstream NGOs are so thoroughly embedded in the international political economy of development that they are unable to provide a truly critical perspective. Rather than challenging *structural* deficiencies at the international, regional, and national levels, most NGOs challenge only certain problematic issues. They

[13] T. Jeffrey Scott (2001) "Evaluating Development-Oriented NGOs" in Claude E. Welch, Jr. (ed.), *NGOs and Human Rights: Promise and Performance*, University of Pennsylvania Press, p. 211.

[14] Id., p. 213.

[15] J. Ferguson (2006) "Transnational Topographies of Power: Beyond 'The State' and 'Civil Society' in the Study of African Politics," in Bill Maurer and Gabriele Schwab (eds.), *Accelerating Possession: Global Futures of Property and Personhood*, New York: Columbia University Press, p. 87.

therefore serve to legitimize the status quo, merely "tinkering around the edges" rather than challenging it in a substantive and radical manner.

Development agencies implementing rights-based approaches in repressive contexts may face resistance from government agencies. Local implementing partners may face threats to their careers, or even to their physical safety. In extreme circumstances, specific NGO personnel or even the entire NGO may be expelled from the country. Such was the case in Darfur in March 2009, when thirteen major international NGOs were expelled, including Oxfam GB, CARE, and Save the Children. Those organizations that remained faced a difficult dilemma: continue to denounce human rights abuses and risk expulsion, or maintain silence and risk perpetuating and even legitimizing the violations. Risk assessment tools have been developed by some agencies to assist in evaluating, managing, and reducing such risks.[16]

More often, however, development agencies are involved in a complex set of explicit and implicit negotiations with governments over the nature of their programs. The multimillion-dollar programs implemented by major NGOs represent local jobs and influence, and the presence of NGOs can thus be politically beneficial for governments. Even repressive states may be willing to make some concessions on HLP rights if it is strategically beneficial.

HUMANITARIAN NGOS

Humanitarian NGOs, which specialize in rapid responses to emergencies, have in the past tended to see HLP issues as development concerns, unrelated to the fast-changing world of relief operations.[17] Thankfully, however, some agencies are becoming increasingly aware of the importance of HLP issues in their work. The influence of the "do no harm" concept has contributed to this increasing awareness. In addition, governments and international agencies are increasingly calling for information on the HLP rights of vulnerable populations to be collected as soon as possible following a crisis. On-the-spot collection of testimony can help reduce fraudulent claims at a later date. As mentioned in the following excerpt, many humanitarian agencies utilize a version of the "sustainable livelihoods" framework to guide their responses to crisis. Such a framework, with its emphasis on the assets of the population in question, should identify the relevant land, housing, and other property issues at stake in a time of crisis.

[16] Cecilia Luttrell and Laure-Hélène Piron with Deborah Thompson (2005) *Operationalising Norwegian People's Aid's Rights-Based Approach: A Review of Lessons from International Non-Governmental Organisations of Relevance to Norwegian People's Aid's Adoption of a Rights-Based Approach*, London: Overseas Development Institute.

[17] Sara Pantuliano (2009) "Introduction" in S. Pantuliano (ed.), *Uncharted Territory: Land, Conflict and Humanitarian Action*, Practical Action.

Alex de Waal (2009) "Why Humanitarian Organizations Need to Tackle Land Issues" in S. Pantuliano (ed.), *Uncharted Territory: Land, Conflict and Humanitarian Action*, London: Practical Action.

The neglect of land issues in humanitarian response has been both striking and unsurprising. It has been striking insofar as conflicts over land play leading roles in many humanitarian emergencies, and land access and tenure issues are also central to recovery or rehabilitation. It has been predictable insofar as humanitarianism as an organized activity has only slowly come to grips with the idea that it should be concerned, not just with the preservation of bare life, but also with the protection of ways of life. Increasingly, humanitarians have come to use livelihoods frameworks for understanding and designing their interventions and, to the extent that they are concerned with livelihoods, they must be concerned with land. To be specific, they need to know about land rights and settlement and use patterns.

Why should humanitarian organizations consider land issues? There are three sets of reasons. First, without understanding why humanitarian crises happen, and why they take the form that they do, we will be handicapped in our responses. Given that land tenure lies at the centre of many humanitarian crises, we need to know about it. Second, humanitarian responses, both during the height of crisis and during what is variously called the rehabilitation or recovery phase, have an impact on land tenure and settlement patterns, and thus on the future prospects of the people affected. These are technical reasons, to improve the proficiency of action. Last, given that humanitarianism is motivated in part by an impulse to emancipate poor and peripheral people, and given that land is fundamental to autonomous and sustainable livelihoods, we should seriously consider how we can support secure access to rural and urban land …

… Humanitarian programmes are typically unacknowledged interventions in the livelihoods, authority, politics and land access of the targeted population. Relief agencies' presence and activities invariably have important unintended consequences. Prominent among these are the implications for land rights, access and use, and the settlement patterns of the affected populations. Humanitarian agencies' policies over land – in IDP camps, among remnant rural populations, on absorption into the urban fabric and on return home – are an important determinant of whether the affected population loses, keeps or gains access to land, and whether it can establish sustainable livelihoods, either urban or rural.

Humanitarian influence on the outcomes of famines and complex emergencies is limited and is strictly secondary to the political dynamics of the conflict itself. Humanitarian responses steer outcomes only at the margin. The situation is different when humanitarian agencies, usually acting in partnership with governments, actually mount initiatives that radically change the nature of the crisis itself. A dramatic example of this concerns the international NGOs that supported resettlement in Ethiopia in the late 1980s. These resettlement schemes, which were poorly planned and set up with minimal or no consultation with

> locals, quickly became a source of controversy and conflict, with some NGOs drawn in, rhetorically, on both sides of the argument (Jansson et al., 1987; Clay et al., 1988). 'Peace villages' in Sudan's Nuba Mountains are another disturbing example (Karim et al, 1996; Pantuliano, 2005). Planned resettlement has been given a bad name by these and other examples of coercive movement of people that, in the worst cases, cost tens of thousands of lives.
>
> However, it is likely that humanitarians will need to revisit planned resettlement. Most scenarios for climate change involve well-populated parts of the planet becoming uninhabitable for a variety of reasons, particularly rising sea levels. This includes the possibility that coastal cities will become inundated. The implications of the evacuation of a city such as Lagos beggar the imagination. We will need to reconsider what this means for humanitarian action and the scale of the global IDP crisis.
>
> Emergency measures such as the creation of IDP camps and other settlements are also de facto interventions in land management and land tenure. A substantial number of IDPs in camps are set to become permanent residents, and an even larger proportion of those who live there will actually become urbanites. Humanitarians need to consider that a variable but large proportion of the recipients of assistance are people in transition from rural to urban residence and livelihoods, and reconceptualise strategies accordingly.
>
> In turn we need to think through the nature of humanitarian responses to urban emergencies. These will certainly become more common, because of rapid urbanization (especially in Africa), the likelihood of urban conflicts, and the likelihood that large cities in low-lying areas will become the locus of emergencies associated with rising sea levels and climate change. We might also want to reconceptualise humanitarian relief to IDP populations, after the first year or so of displacement, as urban assistance programmes. Doing so might alter how we respond to protracted crises of displacement. It might, for example, involve extending assistance to peri-urban populations, providing them with shelter and services.
>
> There are far-reaching policy and programmatic implications to approaching humanitarian activities through the lens of land and residence rights and settlement patterns. These implications will become clear in detail as humanitarian practitioners and researchers turn their attention to the issue. This introductory chapter has sketched out some directions that it would be useful to explore. However, the main recommendation arising is that humanitarians need to become more educated in the complexities of land issues, both insofar as land plays a role in the aetiology of crises, and insofar as humanitarian activities and policies can influence land and livelihood outcomes for affected populations, in rural and urban areas. (References omitted).

As De Waal mentions, humanitarian agencies frequently assist displaced populations. The ways in which they interact with them can have major implications for the HLP rights of the displaced community and host communities. The design of IDP camps is one obvious example. The location of IDP camps may be decided unilaterally by political authorities rather than in consultation with the IDPs themselves. A second scenario is that a spontaneous camp is created by IDPs in an inappropriate area. The result can be that IDPs do not have access to natural resources traditionally used to construct housing, or are put into a situation of conflict with the surrounding communities over such natural resources. Poorly designed camps and shelters constructed using temporary materials, such as tree branches and plastic sheeting, often remain in use for far longer than originally envisaged. Humanitarian NGOs often face a dilemma: Should they (a) continue to provide support for a badly designed camp, in which housing conditions and quality of life in general is extremely poor; or (b) assist IDPs to find new alternatives, such as homes constructed of new materials in a more suitable location? Agencies face political and financial constraints in such situations, as host communities and/or national governments may be unwilling to allow the construction of more durable communities because this will represent an acknowledgment that the IDP community is likely to be present for a significant period of time. Some actors are likely to argue that the construction of durable shelters and more "livable" camps will act as an "incentive" for IDPs to remain. The distribution of seeds and tools to vulnerable populations, especially IDPs, by humanitarian agencies is another "standard" intervention repeated across the world on an almost daily basis. Some agencies are starting to ask questions about the land tenure situation in areas where seeds and tools are being distributed. "Temporary" cultivation using seeds and tools supplied by humanitarian agencies can sometimes reinforce the claims of secondary occupants, giving them, at the minimum, a temporary reprieve from eviction until their crops can be harvested. The HLP rights of the rightful property owners may thus be undermined and restitution of their property delayed.

The return of IDPs or refugees to their countries or areas of origin is also a complex issue. Humanitarian agencies, which are often called on to assist in repatriation or resettlement programs, must fully understand the history of displacement and the opportunities and risks involved in return or resettlement. All too often, however, return or resettlement creates HLP problems that only become apparent at a later date. The return of refugees and IDPs to Dili, the capital of Timor Leste, after the 1999 crisis was a source of conflict in 2006, as described in the following excerpt.

Andrew Harrington (2007) "Ethnicity, Violence, and Land and Property Disputes in Timor-Leste" *East Timor Law Journal*, no. 2.

Violence along east-west lines in Timor-Leste is not a new phenomenon. Rather, it has been noted as early as the 1940's, yet did not receive much attention from foreign scholars present. At the time it was misinterpreted as common conflict between Timorese kingdoms, typical of the colony at the time. The distinction and conflict between *firaku* and *kaladi*, or broadly speaking between east and west, has since been widely accepted within Timor-Leste [...]

[...] Immediately following the 1999 referendum, pro-autonomy militias and the Indonesian Military (TNI) pushed or forced hundreds of thousands of Timorese out of Dili and into West Timor as refugees. After violence wound down, those who had not been forced into West Timor returned to Dili first. For a variety of reasons (e.g. time and relative distance from the city – discussed further below) the first people back were mainly *firaku*. Upon arrival, they found the scorched earth campaign had left housing particularly hard-hit; the militia had "significantly damaged" up to 30% of houses in Dili, while an estimated 80% of housing across Timor-Leste as a whole was rendered uninhabitable.[18] Housing was in short supply. Those returnees who arrived in Dili first occupied various lands and properties [...]

The situation in Dili was made worse by returning refugees from West Timor and others displaced to the rest of Timor-Leste.[19] The UNHCR [United Nations High Commission for Refugees] and IOM [International Organization for Migration] were mandated to plan and implement the return process, but neither organization took complete control over the process, perhaps due to overlapping mandates. Neither agency developed policy stating precisely where returnees would ultimately return; many were therefore returned where they requested, not to where they actually originated. Accordingly, the majority of returnees were sent to Dili, as requested.[20] Transit camps were established, but after spending some time there, returnees were then expected to find their own housing or use the shelter kits given to them (ironically brought from Indonesia).[21] As the only part of the country with economic activity, many returnees remained in Dili, opting not to return to their home districts (where intact housing may not have existed). Indirectly, IOM and UNHCR repatriation activities helped concentrate approximately 53,000 returnees in Dili.[22] Not to disparage either organization, but at the time, housing was not considered a key concern. Return and repatriation were the key aims while the situation was complicated by attacks on ex-militia

[18] Scott Leckie (2005) *Legal and Protection Policy Research Series. Housing, Land, and Property Rights in Post-Conflict Societies: Proposals for a New United Nations Institutional and Policy Framework*, PPLA/2005/01.

[19] Oxfam Australia (2006) *Land and Property: Impact on Crisis and Recovery in Timor-Leste*. Unpublished Report.

[20] This was confirmed by numerous community leaders. One Chefe de Suco stated: "This time, when returning people from the camps in Dili [2006], they should be taken back to where they came from, not where they ask to go." Chefe de Suco, Kampung Alor.

[21] Dolan *et al.* "Evaluation of UNHCR's Repatriation and Reintegration Programme in East Timor, 1999–2003." United Nations High Commissioner for Refugees Evaluation and Policy Analysis Unit EPAU/2004/02 (Feb. 2004) (Dolan et al.) http://www.unhcr.org/cgibin/texis/vtx/research/opendoc.pdf?tbl=RESEARCH&id=403f62e17 (accessed on 11 October 2006).

[22] Neven Knezevic. *Timor-Leste: Background Paper on Human Rights, Refugees and Asylum Seekers*. Commissioned by United Nations High Commissioner for Refugees, Protection Information Section (DIP) (February 2005) p. 33, citing Fitzpatrick & Leckie. (Knezvic) http://www.unhcr.org/cgi-bin/texis/vtx/publ/opendoc.pdf?tbl=RSDCOI&id=4240091d4&page=publ (accessed on 31 July 2006).

members by communities, complicated further by militia attacks resulting in the death of three UNHCR workers in Atambua, West Timor. There has since been a movement within the UNHCR to recognize housing and restitution as key issues to ensure sustainable and successful returns, enshrined in the Pinheiro Principles.[23]

The large number of returnees, acute housing shortages across the country, and the lack of economic activity outside Dili caused a population boom in Dili. Accordingly, there was an extreme shortage of housing. Squatters from various parts of the country, namely from the east (*firaku*) occupied what were then 'abandoned' lands and properties. Some occupiers were able to profit handsomely by occupying multiple houses and renting them out to locals and internationals ... This illegal rent collecting group consisted largely of easterners – including a number of civil servants and government officials – and caused significant resentment and jealousy among those forced to watch what might have been their own property (or that which they felt they had a valid claim to) rented out to foreigners for large profits.[24] Aggressive means were employed to exclude former occupants from their properties, stoking anger further. Many easterners new to Dili were unable to integrate themselves into their host communities, possibly stemming from aggressive behaviour in defence of newly 'acquired' properties and a lack of previous connections to the city [...]

[...] Land and property inequalities and disputes fuelled anger and the east-west split was the vehicle. Those enduring disputes for up to six years used the security vacuum post-disintegration of Timor's security forces to exact retribution upon those illegally occupying properties around the city – exacting revenge on easterners. Pre-existing and impromptu gangs were mobilized into efficient retribution forces, commencing a large scale effort to remove people from occupied properties [...]

[...] The overall goal behind organized destruction was to push those occupying properties and controlling the markets out of Dili and back to Districts which they came from pre-1999.[25]

23 "The Pinheiro Principles" United Nations Principles on Housing and Property Restitution for Refugees and Displaced Persons Centre on Housing Rights and Evictions (August 2005). http://www.cohre.org/downloads/principles.pdf (accessed on 24 August 2006)

24 Of all the community leaders spoken with – those in Bairros and Sucos with significant violence, with little violence, with no violence, and from both the *firaku* and *kaladi* groups – they unanimously stated this as having been the case and cited inaction on the issue due to deep government involvement in the illegal rent charging crowds. Although concrete evidence that government officials are participating is lacking, in a 2005 report on rental values in Dili, "close to a quarter of respondents indicated that *they know they are renting a government property from an irregular 'landlord'* suggest[ing] that the practice of private individuals opportunistically collecting irregular payments from other private individuals for the occupancy of government properties, is relatively widespread." 2005 Dili Rental and Valuation Report. Associates in Rural Development, Inc. (ARD) p. 10. http://pdf.usaid.gov/pdf_docs/PNADE792.pdf

25 Discussion with numerous gang members, indigenous leaders, and political activists, Dili 2006.

International agencies have rarely been able to acknowledge and respond to these kinds of challenges, owing not only to generalized misgivings about becoming involved in "long-term" questions around HLP, but also to the lack of coordination that is often identified as one of the hallmarks of NGO activities. However, concerted efforts have been made within the UN system and within the humanitarian world more broadly to address HLP issues in a more integrated manner. The following excerpt puts these questions into global context and emphasizes the need for improved "collaboration, consensus and capacity." As mentioned further in the chapter, the UN recently implemented the "clusters" approach of the Inter-Agency Standing Committee, in line with the recommendations of the 2005 *Humanitarian Response Review* paper, commissioned by the UN Emergency Relief Coordinator and Under Secretary-General for Humanitarian Affairs. Under the clusters approach, all organizations (such as international and local NGOs and UN agencies) working on a specific sector meet regularly, under the leadership of a single lead agency for that cluster. The lead agency takes primary responsibility for activities within that cluster so that humanitarian needs do not go unmet due to lack of coordination.

Shelter Centre, Annual Report 2007

Shelter and settlements are often damaged or destroyed by conflicts and disasters, impacting protection, the management of risk and the rate of recovery to sustainable livelihoods. Over the eight years between 2000 and 2007, the humanitarian community only met 29 per cent of the total financial need within the shelter and non-food items sector, compared with 83 per cent of total need met in the food sector. This need was felt by the 34.4 million people who were displaced in 2006 alone, in 305 camps and centres as well as 460 urban locations worldwide, and by the many more who were not displaced.

Mitigating damage and destruction often impacts upon the collaboration between international and government stakeholders in national reconstruction, upon the sustainability of assistance and gradual handover to developmental stakeholders, and upon the form and effectiveness of response by other humanitarian sectors and cross-cutting concerns. A decision to support host families as well as refugee camps may impact national and even regional security and protection, water availability, environmental resource management, livelihoods, and health of both the displaced and their hosts. Smoke from solid fuel, for example, presents the fourth greatest risk of death and disease in the world's poorest countries, killing more than 1.5 million people each year.

Understanding these statistics and the interdependence of response has prompted the humanitarian and development communities to reassess the emphasis placed upon the shelter sector in their structures and capacities.

This re-consideration has highlighted challenges within and between these communities. Within the humanitarian community, the Humanitarian Response

Review initiated by the United Nations Emergency Relief Coordinator resulted in the Clusters Approach of the Inter-Agency Standing Committee, an approach which continues to respond to these challenges.

The contribution offered by Shelter Centre is to the community of practice of all stakeholders in the sector, integrating Shelter Centre outputs and services in support of collaboration, consensus and capacity.

WORKING IN THE HLP RIGHTS FIELD

The Importance of Multidisciplinary, Multistakeholder Approaches

The HLP field is by its very nature multidisciplinary and includes personnel who are trained in both the "hard" and "soft" sciences. A typical multistakeholder postconflict HLP operation may include personnel with backgrounds in anthropology, architecture, agricultural engineering, economics, environmental studies, geography, human rights, law, land surveying, political science, sociology, and other disciplines. A military background or training in peace and conflict studies can also offer a useful perspective on conflict dynamics.

HLP challenges are both technical and sociopolitical in nature. Specialist expertise in specific areas is vital; interventions should be based on empirical data and sound principles. However, interventions are never going to be technically perfect, particularly in postconflict contexts where domestic financial and technical capacities may be limited and political tensions constrain the options available. In many situations, the specific training that an individual brings to an intervention is less important than his or her willingness and capacity to work with people from other disciplines, and from different cultures. Team members and collaborating partners may perceive HLP challenges in very different ways. Individuals who are team-oriented, skilled in negotiation, and able to see the "big picture" are likely to make the greatest contribution.

Professionals working on HLP rights in postconflict situations are, in essence, working for those rights holders: local communities, many of whom are among the poorest in the world. In practice, though, HLP professionals must work through and with national governments, multilateral aid agencies, and other institutions that have mixed or unclear agendas. In some cases, institutions are divided on the best way to address HLP issues, and it is not clear whether HLP laws, technologies, and other tools will be used to the benefit of local communities. HLP professionals may find themselves making difficult choices. In the following excerpt, a veteran land lawyer discusses the importance of sticking to professional principles when faced with pressure from one's employer or partner organization.

Patrick McAuslan (2009) ***Emergency Lex – and Other Improbable Tales from the Law Zone.***

What should be the stance of a consultant where either during the course of a consultancy or at its outset, there appears likely to be a conflict between fundamental principles and what the client wants? Fundamental principles would include such issues as respect for human rights, the rule of law, gender equality. I have never had to confront a stark choice on these issues but there have been occasions when I have had to examine what I was doing very carefully and question whether I should be doing it or how I could ameliorate policies which were likely to infringe fundamental principles. A few examples may be given.

It was reasonably clear that nothing was going to come out of my work on land management reform in Afghanistan as warlords and other members of the ruling circles were not going to give up land forcibly seized from peasants and the urban poor. My consultancy was a wasted effort. I have since written critically on the Afghan government's disinclination to tackle the gross inequities in land management …

… In Uganda, after the saga of the 'lost amendment' to the Land Act 1998 when an amendment to improve women's rights to land was never formally passed although generally agreed to in the last hectic hours of getting the Bill through the National Assembly by the deadline stipulated in the constitution, I worked with women's groups and the relevant Minister to put together an amendment to the Act to reinstate the lost amendment. The President then announced that any such amendment would threaten the social and economic stability of Uganda – a very unlikely scenario. This did not stop women's groups from continuing to argue for the amendment nor myself from continuing to help them.

I worked on a DFID project in Rwanda to improve land management. My role was to draft secondary legislation to provide for the implementation of the Organic Land Law [OLL]. The Law made clear that its aim was to introduce a modern system of land tenure and to eliminate customary tenure altogether. Several NGOs had pointed out that the policies of the OLL would benefit the urban elite – largely Tutsi – and disadvantage the Hutu rural majority. I was not aware of this sub-theme behind the OLL before I went to Rwanda. When I became aware of it, I tried to draft secondary laws which would continue to give some recognition to customary tenure as I was aware from experience elsewhere that the 'abolition' of customary tenure is not likely to be achieved in the foreseeable future. But the OLL has the potential to lay the groundwork for severe inter-communal tensions over land in Rwanda in the future.

Faced with a stark choice between 'good' and 'evil' – for instance a request to draft a law which enables the government to seize land whenever it wants to without paying compensation, a law similar to the Unregistered Land Act 1970 of Sudan – I would try to argue against it. If the government was obdurate, I would walk away.

> But few such choices presented to a consultant are couched in such terms so there is usually room for negotiation and manoeuvre and that I think is the preferable way forward.
>
> I cannot claim that these are the only lessons to be learned. I have not attempted this kind of overview before so I am grateful for the opportunity to try out my ideas here. On further reflection, there will be I am sure further lessons. I have been working as a consultant for over 30 years and in over 35 countries so there are many experiences which I have not touched on. My last lesson however is this and it is perhaps the most important:
>
> There is always more to be learned; never think you know it all. Wherever you work and whoever you work with, you can always learn from them as they will have had experiences you have not had and they will have an understanding of their own country and its problems that however much reading you do you will never be able to come close to. You may be a consultant but you are still and always a student.

Policy making is always a highly political process. But even interventions that are often described as purely technical take place within a complex and often contested policy context and have far-reaching political implications. They may be based on unspoken assumptions that are open to dispute. These assumptions should be brought out into the open so that HLP processes are transparent and based on sound principles. As Magel argues, land surveyors must also interact with political processes.

> **Holger Magel (2002) *Surveying and Politics – A Relationship of Mutual Benefit.* Paper presented at New Technology for a New Century International Conference. FIG Working Week 2001, Seoul, Korea 6–11 May 2001.**
>
> Every surveyor knows or should know: his services are not politically neutral or free of value judgments – his contribution e.g. to the implementation of a sustainable development in the comprehensive sense of RIO 1992 (including the theme of 'Women's Access to Land') are formative policy based on democratic values! Surveying services are naturally also susceptible to political abuse – who is not aware of that! There are enough examples of this. Surveyors must not therefore carry out their role mechanically but should advise on policy openly, responsibly and on an ethical basis, and should act in each case in the light of the actual circumstances of the task and of the country concerned. It is only through this critical dialogue between politics and surveying that a relationship of mutual benefit will emerge. This demands from the surveyor that he is not only a 'homo technicus' but is also a 'homo politicus'. The universities are called on to prepare students in this respect much more than they have done hitherto. There is no doubt about it: this political work which will be indispensable in future must be carried out at the national level with fresh energy every day by every one of us.

Given the complex nature of HLP issues, it is often difficult to ensure that all stakeholders, particularly the local communities who will be most affected, are involved in the design of policies and interventions. It is often easier and cheaper to rely on the recommendations of a few experts who can be flown in for a short-term contract than to spend time and money raising awareness and developing consensus at the local and national levels. However, the question of whether all stakeholders are able to meaningfully participate in decision making is often key to the success – or failure – of any policy or program. In the excerpt below, Liz Alden Wily provides suggestions for Afghanistan's Inter-Ministerial Land Commission, based on a bottom-up, rather than top-down, model.

Liz Alden Wily (2004) *Rural Land Relations in Conflict: A Way Forward*, Kabul: Afghanistan Research and Evaluation Unit (AREU).

Reference was made at the beginning of this brief to reformist experiences beyond Afghanistan in the rural land sector. Some lessons were articulated. However, if there is a single outstanding common lesson emergent from diverse reforms, it is simply that sound process matters. Sound process in this as in other sectors relates directly to the adoption of democratic approaches, which means adopting localised and participatory process – even in the matter of policy planning. Related, the failures of mass land programming strongly suggests that incremental, learning by doing strategies yield infinitively superior results. This is a particularly crucial requirement for local support for any change in norms and procedures to be taken up and sustained. Mass public consultation programmes on national land policies developed at the centre in other countries have been insufficient to engage the necessary level of local ownership of reform to carry it through. This is so even where conventional instruments of bureaucratic coercion are amply in place. These lessons have particular importance to the way in which the newly established land commission will operate in fulfilling its mandate to deliver useful new policy and supporting legal and administrative paradigms. It will be relatively simple for this important body, with the aid of consultants, to produce hefty tomes as to the way forward, including substantial backup with survey reports. Such reports, like so many before them, risk being placed on the shelf, the difficulties of implementation simply too onerous to contemplate, without another round of expensive and internationally-driven financing.

It will be considerably more challenging but infinitely more rewarding for the land commission to adopt from the outset an empirical approach. This means tackling priority problems in units of manageable size and practically addressing these through on the ground pilot development. It suggests evolutionary policy development, which is thoroughly rooted in practical and contextually accurate experience. It suggests evolution of new norms that will have high workability and adoptability. It suggests systems development that will more genuinely build from the bottom up, and in the process more appropriately reconstruct supporting roles of district, provincial and central administrations, and the courts. It suggests systems that will be cost-effective and replicable. It suggests genuine opportunities for more inclusive and socially just regimes of land regulation and administration.

In many cases, making an improvement to the HLP situation in any given country will demand a sustained engagement. As can be seen from the previous excerpt, HLP experts may find themselves engaging with the issues through a variety of processes, including formal or informal support for local CBOs, or critical advocacy at the international level. Alternatively, sustained engagement on a particular program or institution may be possible. Such a commitment is rewarding but also can be demanding. Individuals may become associated, rightly or wrongly, with one school of thought or another. In some instances, HLP institutions will be affected by ethnic rivalries or other sociopolitical tensions. As described in the following excerpt, it is necessary, though difficult, to avoid becoming entangled in such tensions. Those who work for years on a single issue, or with a single institution, are also vulnerable to fatigue and disillusionment.

Cherryl Walker (2008) *Landmarked: Land Claims and Land Restitution in South Africa*, Ohio University Press/Jacana Press.

In my analysis I draw heavily upon my own experience, which relates largely but not exclusively to land claims in KwaZulu-Natal … In this period I learned a great deal about bureaucracy and how disabling it can be. I also learned about the destabilising consequences of working without systematic procedures and clear and defensible policy frameworks …

[…] at the time my term came to an end, the Commission and its big sister, the DLA [Department of Land Affairs] were in the midst of difficult transitions. The extraordinary fluidity and redemptive possibilities of the Mandela era were giving way to the more ordinary, pragmatic politics of the Mbeki presidency, after the second national elections of 1999. The appointment of a new Minister for Land Affairs, with a less overtly pro-poor set of priorities of land reform, precipitated a major exodus of senior DLA staff in 1999–2000. This took place amid ideological conflicts and personality tensions, some of which became entangled in debilitating ways with more or less outspoken accusations and counter-accusations of racism in the Department: of white cabals and Africanist agendas […]

[…] thousands of unprocessed claims lay buried in mute, brown-foldered mounds on desks and registry office shelves throughout the Commission offices in Pietermaritzburg when I left. I was very conscious of them and the burden of unmet expectations that they represented […]

[…] by then I was weary of the snappy, PowerPoint synopses of strengths and weaknesses, opportunities and threats through which the Commission and the DLA had been labouring in a relentless succession of strategic planning sessions since 1998. I was equally weary of bland newspaper admonitions about the importance of 'speeding up delivery' and complacent, catch-phrase explanations for the poor performance of the programme …

International HLP experts have a particular responsibility to ensure that their work responds to real needs and empowers, rather than undermines, local actors.

It is all too easy for an international HLP specialist to arrive in an unfamiliar country (known colloquially as "parachuting in"), bringing with him or her a set of preconceived ideas or approaches that may not be entirely appropriate to the context. Local expertise can easily be overlooked. A feeling of "ownership" of the process by local institutions is often lacking, making implementation of the recommendations unlikely. Collaborative approaches involving international and local experts, CBOs, and other stakeholders are more effective in capturing and addressing local nuances than the "roving consultant" model. Similar dynamics can be found between national experts residing in large cities and dominating debates on HLP issues and knowledgeable local people residing outside of the urban centers, who are marginalized from discussions.

In the following excerpt, Ambreena Manji raises two important points based on her experiences in Africa. First, she argues that demands for land reform – which implies redistribution of land – have been transformed into interventions focused on land *law* reform. Second, she contends that this phenomenon arises in part from the "entrepreneurial" activities of legal consultants who have a vested interest in the dominance of a "land law" paradigm over a "land redistribution" argument.

Ambreena Manji (2006) *The Politics of Land Reform in Africa: From Communal Tenure to Free Markets*, London/New York: Zed Books, 79–86.

A striking feature of the last two decades, which has received surprisingly little attention from academic commentators and policy-makers, has been the part played by lawyers in the contemporary land reform process …

… decisions about how to use the law, far from being a technical intra-legal issue, are deeply connected with political and economic choices …

… if law has come to be seen as central to the resolution of Africa's land problems, this is in no small part due to the interventions and activities of lawyers, and more specifically legal consultants, themselves. This is an issue that has tended to be overlooked in discussions of land reform to date with the result that neither scholars of land reform nor those concerned with the field of law and development have adequately explained the curious translation of the issue of land reform into one of law reform … I would argue that it is precisely through the entrepreneurial activities of legal professionals that the law has come to have a central place in land reform …

… technical legal consultants who have played a key role in advocating the resolution of land problems through the use of law have done so by successfully intervening to assist in the difficult task of addressing contradictory demands in relation to land. Rural inhabitants faced with long-running problems of land-grabbing, as well as chaotic systems of land administration, called on the government to address these grievances. In their turn, international financial institutions began to perceive land reform as intricately connected to questions of good governance and the efficient operation of a market economy (and, as the last two decades of land reform amply demonstrate, the demands of the Bretton Woods institutions and foreign investors are wont to take precedence over the needs of the of the rural poor.) These two developments do not in themselves explain how it came to be that legal solutions played a prominent role in land reform. It is at this point that the role of the lawyer becomes important. As experts, the skill of land-related technical legal consultants lies in 'fostering interest groups and persuading their members that their interests were inseparable from his own.'[26] As such, the boundaries between what international financial institutions, bilateral donors, and African governments want and what technical legal consultants 'make them want' are blurred....

FIELDWORK IN POSTCONFLICT AREAS – ETHICAL AND METHODOLOGICAL QUESTIONS

Conducting fieldwork in postconflict situations can involve a number of security, logistical, and ethical challenges. Postconflict environments may remain insecure for some time after the conflict has officially stopped, owing to the availability of small arms, the potential that landmines and unexploded ordinance remain in the area, and the scarcity of legal livelihood options. Transport systems and infrastructure may have been damaged or destroyed during the conflict, making it difficult to physically access more remote areas. The sociopolitical situation is likely to be extremely fluid, complex, and difficult to discern. Local people or central government officials may be suspicious of the motives of research. Many people may be suffering from post-traumatic stress disorder or may be generally experiencing heightened emotions, such as anger, fear, or depression.

These challenges require HLP researchers to take extra steps in planning their research to avoid exposing themselves or informants to risks. Before research commences, it is important to find out whether a permit is needed to conduct the research. Talk to other organizations that have conducted research in the area about their approaches to obtaining permission from the authorities. Find out where research has already been conducted by other organizations. This will help avoid duplication, "research fatigue" in informants, and will provide some security information.

Get to know the fieldwork area before arriving: talk to people who have lived there, study maps, read books and research reports. Plan the routes that will be used to travel around and find out about local hotels and towns where the research team might lodge. Read local newspapers if possible. Pay particular attention to security issues. Identify any particular areas where security seems poor and avoid these during the research. Identify several "exit routes" in case security deteriorates in the area during the research period.

[26] B. Latour (1983) "Give Me a Laboratory and I Will Raise the World" in K.D. Knorr-Cetina and M. Mulkay (eds.), *Science Observed: Perspectives in the Social Study of Science*, Sage, 150.

It is wise to develop a "Plan B" for the research in case logistical, political, or other problems make it too difficult to implement the initial plan. Do as much research from secondary sources as possible. This will save time and avoid duplication. It also minimizes the risk of "research fatigue" in informants.

Be aware of how you will be perceived locally. If you are likely to be at risk of attack, don't do the fieldwork. If you think there is little risk, consider how you can further minimize dangers, for example, by only speaking a particular language or remaining in particular geographical areas. Dress to match the social situation. Dress simply if you're in the countryside, avoid wearing jewelry, and follow local norms regarding whether to cover up particular parts of the body (legs, arms, shoulders, etc). Talk to informants as equals. It may be necessary to use straightforward vocabulary to ensure that communication is clear, but avoid "talking down" to informants. If working with an interpreter, take care to find the best interpreter available, and specify that the interpreter should not try to summarize or change your words, but should translate directly, word for word. Even subtle changes of meaning can have major repercussions in tense situations. A great deal of self-awareness is necessary at all time to avoid biases or untested assumptions finding their way into the research process. All of these issues may have different dimensions depending on whether you are an "insider" or "outsider," as discussed in the following excerpt.

Marie Smyth (2005) "Insider-Outsider Issues in Researching Violent and Divided Societies" in Elisabeth J. Porter, Gillian Robinson, and Albrecht Schnabel (eds.), *Researching Conflict in Africa: Insights and Experiences*, United Nations University Press.

In violently divided societies, it is not merely the population that are polarized and segregated, but intellectuals, academics, and researchers reflect the divisions in the society, and bring to the job of the production of ideas their various loyalties. Ideas, too, are separating into "right" and 'wrong", making for a marked dualistic thinking which is associated with the earlier stages of intellectual development. All thinkers, when exposed to life-threatening violence, will revert to this form of thinking. It is not the exclusive domain of insiders. It is a rare researcher, whether insider or outsider, that will, when faced with a threat to his or her life, entirely retain the ability to examine the situation in which the threat occurred with any kind of scientific rigour [...]

Researchers operating in conflict zones must consider issues of their safety and that of their informants. Here, the insider researcher can be at a distinct advantage, in that they may know the terrain intimately, and have a network of contacts through which they can collect information and monitor issues such as safety. However, this is not equally true of all insiders, and some outsiders are skilled at quickly establishing networks, and finding reliable advisors on issues such as safety. Insiders, too, can accept unquestioningly local superstitions and assumptions about danger and risk, which may not be real. Furthermore, insiders may be perceived as partial, as part of conflict, identified with one or the other side, consequently the risk may be greater. However, insiders are more likely than outsiders to have at their disposal more local resources to mitigate such risk.

Outsider identify can be a mixed blessing [...] in embattled communities, outsiders can be regarded with a great deal of suspicion, and subjected to intense questioning about their intentions, making it a challenge to establish sufficient trust to carry out the research.... the major disadvantage faced by outside researchers in relation to safety and risk management is that their relative lack f knowledge of the context and relative inability to interpret cues may leave them ignorant of the actual risks they are taking [...]

[...] all researchers in violent contexts, whether insider or outsider, bring to their work their own previous identifications and experiences. These inevitably affect the extent to which a researcher identifies with one or the other competing interest in the field of study. However, the influence that these factors exert is not straightforward. Over- or under-compensation for one's identity; the emotional impact of violence and the suffering it causes; over or under-identification with one cohort; and the failure to adopt a systemic analytic framework can render researchers intellectually and analytically disabled, burnt out and emotionally overwhelmed. These unfortunate fates can befall insider and outside alike.

Security concerns should be paramount during the research process. Inform your organization, relatives, and friends about the areas you will be visiting and your schedule. Keep in regular contact with your organization and any local friends or relations by mobile phone. Establish a system for regular communication and have a backup plan to be activated if contact is not made at the agreed time. Security concerns vary with the specific conditions in the country, as described by a security expert in the following excerpt. Even though conflict may be officially declared to be over, the risk of sporadic incidences of violence may remain.

David Lloyd Roberts (2005) *Safety and Security Guidelines for Humanitarian Volunteers in Conflict Areas*. International Committee of the Red Cross (ICRC). Revised and updated edition.

In terms of international law, there are three broad categories of conflict which you might encounter. Superimposed on any of these broad categories there can be additional threats of violence posed, for example, by terrorism, extremist ideology, and insurgency.

International armed conflict

An international armed conflict arises when one State uses armed force against another State or States. The term also applies to all cases of total or partial military occupation. An international armed conflict is considered to be over once active hostilities or territorial occupation have ceased. Despite the scale of such conflicts in the main, they are relatively simple situations for humanitarians to cope with. The sides are clearly defined and they even wear different uniforms. The front lines are well known. The armed forces have a structured chain of command. It is not too difficult to find a point of contact through which to notify all sides of your locations and movements in order to arrange safe passage for relief supplies and so on. Humanitarian organizations generally adopt a high profile – we are predictable and we are visible owing to our emblems.

The parties to the conflict are generally aware of their obligations under international humanitarian law and will try to meet them, but of course, there will always be exceptions. All four Geneva Conventions and Additional Protocol I apply to this type of conflict. For humanitarians, therefore, the features of international conflicts are:

classic humanitarian tasks;

relatively low level of risk;

fewer obstacles to our work than in lower-level conflict;

security primarily based on and strengthened by factors such as reliable information and a high degree of recognition and acceptance of the organization.

Non-international armed conflict

Non-international armed conflicts, also known as internal armed conflicts, take place within the territory of a State and do not involve the armed forces of any other State. In some cases the State's armed forces are used against dissident, rebel or insurgent groups. In others, there are two or more armed groups fighting within a State, but not necessarily with the involvement of government troops …

This situation is now more difficult for the humanitarian volunteer.

The opposing sides are not so well defined; perhaps not all are wearing uniforms; points of contact on one side – say the government's – might be excellent, while on the other side – perhaps to ensure its own safety and security – those contact points might be tenuous to say the least. Arranging a relief convoy, for example, might take some time as you wait for those responsible to be contacted and to give their consent. Generally, the belligerents will have a degree of respect for humanitarian workers. However, the situation in the world today is becoming less transparent. Clearly defined front lines may not even exist, or they may change very quickly, which can be dangerous for us. Large battles may occur, but a more common feature of this type of conflict is the hit-and-run skirmish in which we can unwittingly become caught up in the crossfire. The deliberate targeting of civilians is in many cases more frequent. The full range of weapons – from aircraft to mines – may be used.

For us in such cases:

The classic humanitarian tasks remain.

There is a higher level of risk.

Events are less predictable.

Contacts may be more difficult to arrange.

Greater obstacles stand in the way of our work: more restrictions, more complicated and time-consuming negotiations, more controls and more delays.

It remains important to obtain reliable information and achieve recognition and acceptance, but all this becomes more difficult.

Internal disturbances and tensions

Lower levels of internal violence go by the legal term "internal disturbances and tensions". The military tend to refer to them as "internal security operations". They are not covered by international humanitarian law but by international human rights law and standards and by the State's own domestic law. Features of such situations are typically:

violent demonstrations and riots;

mass arrests;

large numbers of persons detained for security reasons;

administrative detention for long periods;

ill-treatment and torture of detainees and keeping them incommunicado for long periods;

repressive measures taken against relatives of persons deprived of their freedom;

suspension of fundamental judicial guarantees, either de facto or de jure (proclaiming a state of emergency); large-scale measures restricting personal freedom, such as exile, assigned residence, displacement;

allegations of forced disappearances;

increase in the number of acts of violence (such as sequestration and hostage taking) which endanger defenceless persons or spread terror among the civilian population;

harassment of journalists and lawyers representing detainees and suspects, and of others who may draw attention to repression;

allegations of unlawful killings.

Violence can come from many kinds of groups, ranging from armed gangs, bandits and militants to violent sections of the civilian population opposing government forces. The nature of the violence is difficult to predict. Militias, gangs and even individuals often work in a "freelance" manner, engaging in constantly shifting alliances. There may be no clear command structure and it may be very difficult to negotiate one's safety or to rely on any guarantees obtained. There might be little respect for humanitarian workers or for what they are trying to achieve. Indeed, we can become targets because there is a misunderstanding about who or what we represent. These groups might be eager to steal our vehicles, equipment

> and supplies. In response to the threat, humanitarians in such circumstances might adopt a low profile and be much more discreet; we might reduce our visibility (e.g. by foregoing the use of emblems and using unmarked cars); we might vary our routes and times of travel. In such situations of anarchy, with a complete breakdown of law and order, the safety and security of our people becomes an overriding concern. There is a balance to be struck in such an environment between the time and effort spent on remaining secure and what, if anything, we can achieve. It is a balance that must be constantly borne in mind by those in authority, particularly heads of office in the field.
>
> The situation of humanitarians in such an environment is characterized by the following:
>
> humanitarian work certainly needed, but extremely difficult to meet that need;
>
> very high level of risk, perhaps bordering on the unacceptable;
>
> severely restricted ability to work;
>
> security based more on technical elements such as active or passive protection than on actual acceptance by all parties.

In addition to security concerns, ethical considerations should be foremost in researchers' minds when planning fieldwork. It is important that informants know exactly who the researchers are, why they are being interviewed, and how the results will be used. Issues of confidentiality should be discussed with informants. Usually, it is best not to cite the names of informants in published research about human rights abuses.

Notes should be kept secure both during and after the fieldwork period. It might be necessary to find ways to explain to local authorities and other interested parties that research notes cannot be shared with them. Type up the research data as soon as possible. Memories can fade and gaps may need to be filled in.

It is important for researchers to monitor their emotional state, particularly if they have been exposed to disturbing, distressing research findings. Researchers who feel depressed or overwhelmed should take a break from fieldwork. Emotional stress is dangerous in numerous ways, especially because it may limit the ability to accurately assess risk. Some relaxation periods should be scheduled to allow researchers to deal with stress.

The best researchers find ways to involve informants in discussing and analyzing the research findings. This might involve a "consultative session" with key informants and/or ensuring that local community groups receive copies of the findings and details how they can respond with comments. For confidentiality reasons, it may not be possible to directly involve local informants in data analysis, but they may be able to give their opinions through local community groups.

Questions and Exercises

1. What is distributional justice? What is its importance in the fulfilment of economic, social, and cultural rights?
2. Imagine that you have been asked to design an HLP strategy for a traditional international human rights NGO. The HLP campaign will focus on a Southeast Asian country with a history of forced evictions and other abuses, and a weak legal framework. What would be the key components of your HLP strategy, and in what sequence would you implement them? What other organizations would be involved in the strategy, either as partners or targets for advocacy?
3. This chapter has identified several situations in which humanitarian NGOs might unwittingly contribute to unjust or conflictual access to housing, land, or property. There are many other examples in the literature. Based on a rapid literature survey, write a case study of another real or hypothetical example. Cite at least three references.
4. Imagine that you are assisting the government of a developing country to design its first land policy. A major donor has offered to pay for the process, but insists that an experienced international consultant be involved in the process. Local organizations are wary of being locked out of the process. What are some of the processes for developing the land policy that ensure that all important stakeholders are involved, and that the policy reflects prevailing opinions in that particular country?
5. Imagine that you are a citizen of a postconflict country and are involved in documenting HLP abuses in your home city. Before starting the research, you assess the risks – physical, social, short- and long-term, that you may incur as a result of the research. What questions would you need to consider to accurately assess the risks?

Index